T0311830

Intra-Asian Trade and the World Market

Intra-Asian trade is a major theme of recent writing on Asian economic history. From the second half of the nineteenth century, intra-Asian trade flows linked Asia into an integrated economic system, with reciprocal benefits for all participants. But although this was a network from which all gained, there was also considerable inter-Asian competition between Asian producers for these Asian markets and those of the wider world.

This collection presents captivating 'snap-shots' of trade in specific commodities, alongside chapters comprehensively covering the region. The book covers China's relative backwardness, Japanese copper exports, Japan's fur trade, Siam's luxury rice trade, Korea, Japanese shipbuilding, the silk trade, the refined sugar trade, competition in the rice trade, the Japanese cotton textile trade to Africa, multilateral settlements in Asia, the cotton textile trade to Britain and the growth of the palm oil industry in Malaysia and Indonesia. The opening of Asia, especially Japan and China, liberated the creative forces of the market within the new interactive Asian economy.

This fascinating book fills a particular gap in the literature on intra-Asian trade from the sixteenth century to the present day. It will be of particular interest to historians and economists focusing on Asia.

A.J.H. Latham retired as Senior Lecturer in International Economic History at the University of Wales, Swansea, in 2003. His recent books include *Rice: The Primary Commodity*. He co-edited (with Kawakatsu) *Asia Pacific Dynamism, 1550–2000* (both are published by Routledge).

Heita Kawakatsu is Vice-Director of the International Research Centre for Japanese Studies in Kyoto, and Professor of Economic History there. His publications in Japanese include *Japanese Civilisation and the Modern West*, and he recently edited *A History of the Asia Pacific Economy, 1500 2000*.

Routledge Studies in the Modern History of Asia

Intra-Asian Trade and the World Market

Edited by
A.J.H. Latham and
Heita Kawakatsu

Routledge
Taylor & Francis Group
LONDON AND NEW YORK

First published 2006 by Routledge

Published 2017 by Routledge
2 Park Square, Milton Park, Abingdon, Oxon OX14 4RN
711 Third Avenue, New York, NY 10017, USA

*Routledge is an imprint of the Taylor & Francis Group,
an informa business*

Typeset in Times New Roman by
Newgen Imaging Systems (P) Ltd, Chennai, India

British Library Cataloguing in Publication Data
A catalogue record for this book is available from the British Library

Library of Congress Cataloging in Publication Data
A catalog record for this book has been requested

ISBN13: 978–0–415–37207–7 (hbk)
ISBN13: 978–0–415–54692–8 (pbk)

Contents

Illustrations

Figures

Tables

Graph

Contributors

David Clayton studied history and economics at the University of Manchester, where, between 1990 and 1994, he completed a PhD under the supervision of Dr Peter Lowe. He published his doctorate as *Imperialism Revisited: Political and Economic Relations between Britain and China, 1950–54* (Macmillan: Houndmills, Basingstoke and New York, 1997). He now researches the history of institutions, focussing on how they process information and regulate behaviour. His main empirical field is the history of the British Empire, especially Britain's formal and informal empires in China; he also researches business organisation in the British cotton textile industry. He is currently a Fellow of the Leverhulme Trust, working on 'Industry and Institutions: Hong Kong', a project which examines the evolution of trade regimes and regulatory functions undertaken by the colonial state, *c.*1920–70, using government records in Britain, Hong Kong and America.

Shinsuke Kaneko was born in Tokyo in 1970. He graduated from Waseda University in 1993, received his Master of Economics from Waseda University in 1996 and his PhD in Economics from Yokohama City University in 2002. He has been docent of Hiroshima Prefectural Women's University since 2003. He studies the modern economic history of Japan and Asia, and his main research interests focus upon the history of the modern Asian silk industry and inter-Asian competition in raw silk. His main works are 'Senzen-ki no Sekai Kiito Sijyo wo Meguru Asia-kan Kyoso' ('Inter-Asian competition in raw silk for the world market, 1859–1929'), *Asiya Kenkyu* No. 48-2 (2002) and 'Kiito wo Meguru Nitthuu Tiiki-kan Kyousou to Sekai Shijou: Sumiwake to Mayu Kiito Hinshitsu tono Renkan wo Tyusin-ni' ('Competition between Japan and China in the world raw silk market)' in Heita Kawakatsu (ed.), *Asia Taiheiyou Keizai-ken-shi: 1500–2000 (A History of the Asia Pacific Economy: 1500–2000* (Tokyo: Fujiwara Shoten, 2003).

Heita Kawakatsu received his DPhil from the University of Oxford, and was Professor of Economics at Waseda University, Tokyo (1990–98). He is now Professor of Economic History and Vice-Director of the International Research Centre for Japanese Studies in Kyoto. His main publications in English are 'International competition in cotton goods in the late nineteenth century' in W. Fischer *et al.* (eds), *The Emergence of a World Economy, 1500–1914* (1986) and 'The Lancashire cotton industry and its rivals' in K. Bruland and P. O'Brien (eds), *From Family Firms to Corporate Capitalism* (1998). He was co-editor (with A.J.H. Latham) of *Japanese Industrialization and the Asian Economy* (1994) and *Asia Pacific Dynamism 1550–2000* (2000). His publications in Japanese include *Japanese Civilization and the Modern West* (1991), and he has edited *The Asian Trading Sphere and Japan's Industrialisation 1500–1900* (1991); *A New Asian Drama: Five Hundred Years' Dynamism* (1994) and *A History of the Asia Pacific Economy*, 1500–2000 (2003).

Masami Kita is Professor of Economic History at Soka University, Tokyo. He took his BA and MA at Wakayama University, and his PhD (Economics) at Osaka University. In 1975–76 and 1979–80 he was Research Fellow at Glasgow University working on Scottish economic and business history, and the influence of Scottish technology in Japan in the late nineteenth century. He has written several books on Scottish studies in Japanese. He is a representative of the Friends of Scotland in Japan, and Vice-President of the International Association of Historians in Asia 2003–04.

Katsuhiko Kitagawa is a Professor in the Faculty of Economics, Kansai University. As a historian he is interested in the economic and social history of Southern Africa, as well as Japan's trade relations with Africa between the Wars. He has published two books in Japanese, *A Study in the History of Japan's Trade with South Africa* (1997) and *A Study in the Economic and Social History of Southern Africa* (2001). Amongst his articles in English are 'On the transition to market economy and the transition of the market economy in Africa' in T. Iida and T. Kashioka (eds), *The Transition to Market Economy and the Transition of the Market Economy*, International Research Centre for Japanese Studies, 1997 and 'Japan's trade with East and South Africa in the Inter-War Period: a study of Japanese Consular Reports', *Kansai University Review of Economics*, No. 3 March 2001.

Takashi Kume is a Research Assistant at the University of Tokyo. The main subject of his research is the economic history of Japan and Asia. He received his BA (1993) from the Faculty of Political Economics, Waseda University and his MA in Economics from the University of Tokyo (1996). He started his academic career in 1998 as a co-researcher at the International Research Centre for Japanese Studies, Kyoto. In 1999–2002 he also worked as a co-researcher at the Japanese Centre for Area Studies (JCAS) in the National Museum of Ethnology. His main research interest is inter-Asian competition in the 1880s–1930s, and he is currently studying the sugar market in Japan, China and India, and the sugar industry in Asia in general. His main works in Japanese include 'Inter-Asian competition in the sugar market in China 1914–1930' in Heita Kawakatsu (ed.), *A History of the Asia Pacific Economy, 1500–2000* (Tokyo: Fujiwara Shoten, 2003) and 'The pressure of imports of gray shirtings during the Meiji restoration and *Izumi Momen*' (Nihon-kenkyo 25, *Bulletin of the International Research Centre for Japanese Studies*, 2002).

A.J.H. Latham retired as Senior Lecturer in International Economic History at the University of Wales, Swansea in 2003. He was born in 1940, and educated at Merton College, Oxford, and the University of Birmingham, where he took his PhD at the Centre of West African Studies. This work led to his book *Old Calabar 1600–1891: The Impact of the International Economy upon a Traditional Society* (1973). He is the author of *The International Economy and the Undeveloped World 1865–1914* (1978) (in Japanese 1987) and *The Depression and the Developing World, 1914–1939* (1981). More recently he published *Rice: The Primary Commodity* (1998) (in Japanese 1999). He was co-editor (with Heita Kawakatsu) of *Japanese Industrialisation and the Asian Economy* (1994) and *Asia Pacific Dynamism 1550–2000* (2000), and several other collections including *The Market in History* (1986), and has published numerous articles on both African and Asian economic history. He is working on the history of the international rice trade.

Sooyoon Lee is a guest researcher at the Institute for the History of European Expansion at the University of Leiden, the Netherlands (IGEER). She obtained an MA in the Graduate School of Economics at Waseda University, Japan. Her main works in Japanese are 'A feud between Chinese, Japanese and Korean traders in the Korean open ports in the pre Sino-Japanese War Period', *Japanese Colonial History*, 12 (2000), and 'Changes in the trade mechanism of Korea during the port-opening period: Korean brokers in the open ports and foreign merchants', *Waseda Economic Studies*, 53 (2001). She is currently preparing her PhD thesis on the open port-trade in late nineteenth century Asia.

Susan Martin developed her interest in palm oil during a childhood spent in Africa, followed by fieldwork in Nigeria in 1980–81 and ten years as a lecturer in the History of West Africa at the School of Oriental and African Studies, University of London. Her attention was first drawn to South-east Asia's palm oil success story by colleagues at the University of Cambridge and the Palm Oil Research Institute of Malaysia (now the Malaysian Palm Oil Board). The research on which her paper was based was supported financially by the School of Oriental and African Studies and the Nuffield Foundation. The author is now a Senior Lecturer in Strategic Management at the University of Hertfordshire's Business School, specialising in international business. She has recently published *The UP Saga* (Copenhagen: NIAS Press, 2003).

Peter Mathias was born in 1928, and read history as an undergraduate at Jesus College, Cambridge (1948–51) and then spent a year in Harvard reading economics. He lectured in the history faculty at Cambridge University (Queens' College) 1955–68 and was then Chichele Professor of Economic History at Oxford and a Fellow of All Souls College from 1968 to 1987. He returned to Cambridge as Master of Downing College 1987–95. His main teaching and research has covered the field of British economic and business history in the eighteenth and nineteenth centuries, with wider interests in historical processes of industrialisation. He is an Honorary President of the International Economic History Association (President 1974–77). He has been President of the Economic History Society (1989–92), Honorary Treasurer of the British Academy (1980–89 – a Fellow since 1977) and was appointed CBE in 1984. He has maintained close links with Japan. His text book *The First Industrial Nation* was translated into Japanese; he has been a visiting professor at Waseda and Osaka Gakuin Universities and was research supervisor of the present Crown Prince of Japan when in Oxford in 1983–85. He is now Chairman of the Great Britain–Sasakawa Foundation and was awarded the Order of the Rising Sun in November 2003.

Toshiyuki Miyata is Associate Professor of Thai Economic History at Tokyo University of Foreign Studies, Tokyo. His main publications in Japanese are 'The development of the Thai rice export economy and Asian rivalry in rice exports: A study of Thai rice quality problems in the 1920s', in Heita Kawakatsu (ed.) *A History of Asia Pacific Economy*, Fujiwara Shoten (2003) and 'The development of the Thai rice economy from 1850 to 1939', in Hiroyoshi Kano (ed.) *The Southeast Asian History: The Development and Fall of the Colonial Economy*, Iwanami Shoten, 2001.

Shi Zhihong is Professor and Senior Researcher at the Institute of Economics, at the Chinese Academy of Social Sciences (CASS). He was born in 1949, and graduated from Peking University (1982, MA) and the Graduate School of CASS (1988, PhD). Shi Zhihong focuses on Chinese economic history, especially the rural economy and financial problems in the Ming-Qing period. His main publications are *Qingdai Qianqi de Xiaonong Jingji* (On Peasant Economy in the Early Qing Period, Beijing: China Social Sciences Press, 1994); *Zhongguo Jingji Fazhan Shi* (History of Chinese Economic Development: Editor of the Third Volume, Beijing: 1999); 'The development and underdevelopment of agriculture during the Early Qing Period', in A. Hayami and Y. Tsubouchi (eds), *Economic and Demographic Development in Rice Producing Societies*, Leuven: Leuven University Press, 1990; 'Changes in landlord economy in the Early Qing Period of China, 1644–1840', in A.J.H. Latham and H. Kawakatsu (eds), *The Evolving Structure of the East Asian Economic System Since 1700: A Comparative Analysis*, Milan: University Bocconi, 1994 and *Qingdai Qianqi Caizheng Gaishu* (A Survey of Early Qing's Financial Policy and its Revenue and Expenditure, in *Jinian Shang Hongkui Jiaoshou Shishi Shi Zhounian Lunwenji*, Beijing: Beijing University Press, 1995).

Ryuto Shimada is a Research Fellow in economic history at Waseda University, Tokyo, Japan, and currently preparing his PhD dissertation regarding the intra-Asian trade of the Dutch East India Company in the seventeenth and eighteenth centuries, at the Research School of Asian, African and Amerindian Studies (CNWS) of Leiden University, the Netherlands. He has recently published in Japanese 'Eighteenth century intra-Asian trade in Japanese copper by the Dutch East India Company: a survey based on the archives of the bookkeeper–General at Batavia', *Bulletin of the Japan–Netherlands Institute*, 28-1, 2003.

Chikashi Takahashi was born in Tokyo in 1971 and is a graduate student in the Graduate School of Economics at Waseda University. He is a part-time lecturer in the Faculty of Economics, Daito Bunka University, and a part-time lecturer in the Faculty of Human Sciences, Musashino University. He was a Research Associate of the Institute for Research in Contemporary Political and Economic Affairs, Waseda University, 2001–03. He took his Bachelor's degree at the School of Political Science and Economics, Waseda University in 1996, where he took his Masters degree in the Graduate School of Economics in 1998. His research interests are the economic history of Japan, and the history of Japanese economic thought. He has published 'Bakufu Officials' view of the Japanese economy as seen in the policy of the Direct Rule of Ezo: 'Hensakushiben' by Hakodate Bugyo, Habuto Masayasu, *History of Japanese Economic Thought*, No. 2. Also 'Fish manure demand in the early 20th century: the persistence of fish manure use and the increase of bean cake imports', *Waseda Economic Studies*, No. 52.

Masafumi Yomoda is a Research Fellow of the Japan society for the Promotion of Science. He received his MA in economics at Waseda University in 1997 and is now a candidate for PhD. His current research is on Asian and Japanese economic history in the first half of the twentieth century. His articles include '1930 nendai ni okeru Yokohama Kobe no gaisho to sekai shijo' ('Foreign merchants in Kobe and Yokohama and their market networks during the 1930s) in *Ajia Kenkyu* (Asian Studies) 46: 3–4, 2000; 'Mozo Panama-bo wo meguru sanchi kan kyoso: senzenki Taiwan Okinawa ni okeru sanchi keitai no hikaku wo tsujite' ('Interregional competition in the production of imitation Panama hats: An institutional comparison of pre-war Taiwan and Okinawa') in *Shakai Kaizai Shigaku* (Socio-Economic History) 68: 2, 2003 and 'Takakuteki boeki kessaimo no henshitsu to Ajai kaizai' ('Changes in the multilateral trade settlement network and the Asian economy'), in H. Kawakatsu (ed.), *Ajia Taiheiyo Keizaiken-shi* (*A History of the Asia Pacific Economy, 1500–2000*, (Tokyo: Fujiwara Shoten, 2003).

Foreword

This collection of chapters is of great significance – not only for the intrinsic historical importance of the papers themselves but also in a historiographical sense. Collectively they reveal the extent to which inter-Asian research scholarship in economic and business history is now flourishing, in happy integration with the work of scholars based in western countries. The range of themes in the collection is no less impressive than the range of provenance of the authors: contributors have been drawn from almost all the regions to which they have made contributions: particularly notable is the wealth of research and publications in the field now being undertaken in China, joining the longer tradition of exact scholarship in economic and business history in Japanese universities.

An underlying coherence of the volume centres on the initiative of Heita Kawakatsu, who was principally responsible, with John Latham, for convening the conference in Kyoto at which the papers were presented in September 2002. Professor Kawakatsu, through his colleagues and pupils, has established a network of collaborators across South-east Asia. As his own work exemplifies, this gives coherence to the vast and differentiated maritime area bordering a great continental land-mass, as equivalent historical focuses on the Mediterranean, the North Sea and the Atlantic have already done for other regions of the world. This framework offers a coherent structure to the great diversity of trades covered in the volume.

The extent of inter-Asian trading relations preceding the impact of Western incursions has been widely recognised for many years, as research in Asian archives by Asian scholars (particularly those based in Japan) has progressed. The scope and range of this collection is truly international in Asian and world terms demonstrating that the impact of the West, while progressively superimposing patterns of trading between Asian countries, Europe and North America from the sixteenth century onwards – adding a new and different dynamic which made the international commercial, shipping, technological and financial relations ever more complex – still did not subvert the Asian dynamic which was also progressive. The roles of Japan and China in particular are revealed, with India, Russia, Thailand, Korea, Malaysia and Indonesia also prominent in trades based on different products. Lying at the base of much commerce lay the China market. The trades in copper, fur, rice, raw and finished silk, sugar, edible oils, cotton textiles, gold and the diffusion of maritime technology structure the various essays. Asia is seen in its widest sense, with North East Asia, for example, prominent in the fur trade, with American and British commercial incursions, as well as Russian, but with China as the principal destination. The intricacy of the international relationships between different types of product, the intensity of competition and responsiveness to price and product differentiation, the pervasive role of technical change in all the products covered is a revelation. Detailed archival research in business and state archives makes this extensive revaluation possible. Indeed, the integration of micro- and macro-data is a hallmark of the volume, revealing the true complexity of the responsiveness in changing markets at the international level. Authors and organisers deserve the thanks of the wider community of all economic and business historians concerned with inter-Asian trade and relationships – including the political and the military – with the world more generally.

Peter Mathias
Downing College, Cambridge

Preface

The chapters in this collection were for the most part presented at the international symposium 'Asia in the Age of *Pax Britannica* and *Pax Americana*', held at the International Research Centre for Japanese Studies, Kyoto, Japan, 24–28 September 2002.

This symposium was particularly interested in the concept of intra-Asian trade, seeing Asia from the late nineteenth century as an integrated economic system with mutually beneficial reciprocal trade flows and payments, rather than an assortment of independent economic units. Even in the Colonial period this was true, notably in basic items like rice and cotton goods, with extensive trade between the colonies of the various powers. Burma sold rice to India, Ceylon and the Straits Settlements. French Indo-China and Siam sold rice to Hong Kong (from where it was sent on to China) and Singapore, the Dutch East Indies and the Spanish/United States Philippines. Indian owned factories in Bombay sold cotton yarn to China for handloom weavers there. Indeed, one of the primary aims of the *Pax Britannica* was to enable this interaction to take place and a measure of free trade ensured.

Such issues have been explored in a series of conferences and symposiums over the last 25 years, publications from which are listed. The chapters here are from the latest of these meetings.

Asian economic history is presently considering many issues, and no dominant theme is apparent (Van Der Eng 2004). But the concept of intra-Asian trade, and with it the expansion of the market economy, does link with the issue of the onset of globalisation which has recently provoked vigorous debate (O'Rourke and Williamson 1999, 2002, 2004; Flynn and Giraldez 2004). The growth of intra-Asian trade was a subset within this wider process of globalisation.

References

Fischer, Wolfram, McInnis, R. Marvin and Schneider, Jurgen (1986) *The Emergence of a World Economy 1500–1914*, Wiesbaden: Franz Steiner Verlag.
Flynn, D.O. and Giraldez, A. (2004) 'Path dependence, time lags and the birth of globalisation: a critique of O'Rourke and Williamson', *European Review of Economic History* 8, 81–108.

Kawakatsu, Heita (1986) 'International competition in cotton goods in the late nineteenth century: Britain versus India and East Asia' in Fischer, McInnis and Schneider (eds), *The Emergence of a World Economy 1500–1914*, Weisbaden: Franz Steiner Verlag, 619–44.

Latham, A.J.H. (1978) *The International Economy and the Undeveloped World, 1865–1914*, London: Croom Helm; Totowa, NJ: Rowman and Littlefield. In Japanese (1987) Tokyo: Nihon-Hyoron-Sha.

Latham, A.J.H. (1986) 'The international trade in rice and wheat since 1868: a study in market integration' in Fischer, McInnis and Schneider (eds) *The Emergence of a World Economy 1500–1914*, 645–64.

Latham, A.J.H. and Neal, Larry (1983) 'The international market in rice and wheat 1968–1914', *Economic History Review* 36, 260–80.

Latham, A.J.H. and Kawakatsu, Heita (eds) (1994a) *Japanese industrialisation and the Asian Economy*, London and New York: Routledge.

Latham, A.J.H. and Kawakatsu, Heita (eds) (1994b) *The Evolving Structure of the East Asian Economic System Since 1700: A Comparative Analysis*, Milan: University Bocconi, Proceedings of the Eleventh International Economic History Congress (B6).

Latham, A.J.H. and Kawakatsu, Heita (eds) (2000) *Asia Pacific Dynamism 1550–2000*, London and New York: Routledge.

O'Rourke, Kevin, H. and Williamson, Jeffrey G. (1999) *Globalization and History*, Cambridge, MA: MIT Press.

O'Rourke, Kevin, H. and Williamson, Jeffrey G. (2002) 'When did globalisation begin?', *European Review of Economic History* 6, 23–50.

O'Rourke, Kevin, H. and Williamson, Jeffrey G. (2004) 'Once more: when did globalisation begin?', *European Review of Economic History* 8, 109–17.

Pierre Van Der Eng (2004) 'Economic history of Asia: comparative perspectives, in special issue, economic history of Asia', *Australian Economic History Review* 44 (3), 215–20.

Introduction

The growth of trade between Asia and the rest of the world has always been of interest to economic historians, but more recently the growth of intra-Asian trade, or trade within Asia, has emerged as a major focus of interest. After the opening of China and Japan in the nineteenth century there was an explosion of intra-Asian trade and its corresponding payments flows. But within this network of intra-Asian trade there was also a level of inter-Asian competition, or competition between or amongst Asian rivals, to gain control of certain markets. For example Burma, Siam and French Indo-China all featured strongly in the intra-Asian rice trade, whilst at the same time engaging in inter-Asian competition between themselves. There was similar participation and competition in the cotton and silk industries, involving Japan, China and India. Many of the chapters in this collection relate to these issues.

The rapid expansion of intra-Asian trade was a feature of the late nineteenth century. Shi Zhihong by contrast examines the internal security issues which drove China to exclude itself from external trade between 1522 and 1840. He concludes that this severing of foreign trading contacts meant that China did not receive the latest ideas and inventions and fell behind the rest of the world technologically. However, even though China and indeed Japan for the most part did not trade with each other or the rest of the world during the seventeenth and eighteenth centuries, there were certain exceptions, and Ryuto Shimada examines the exports of Japanese copper to China and other Asian countries, especially that carried by the ships of the Dutch East India Company to South East Asia. Much of this copper was used to make small denomination currency, thereby expanding monetisation in these countries and stimulating economic activity there at the lowest levels. In the last half of the eighteenth century the British East India Company continued this process when it began to supply India and South East Asia with European copper. Although this flow of copper from Japan took place at an 'official' level, other trade of an almost clandestine nature was also taking place in these years. In a fascinating paper Chikashi Takahashi discusses the trade from Japan to China in luxury sea-otter furs, which came from the Ainu people of Sakhalin and the Kuril islands. But during the course of the eighteenth century British, American and Russian traders also began to come to these islands for fur, prompting the Tokugawa government to consider how to consolidate their control over these islands.

The opening of Japan to international maritime commerce meant that Japan, and indeed Asia at large, found itself without a modern steel-hulled, steam-driven shipbuilding industry. Masami Kita here explains how Japan turned to Glasgow in the late nineteenth century, to acquire the skills and education needed to establish this industry, at the same time acquiring a new work ethic. This may have been more important for Japan's long-term development than the specific technological skills it gained. One area where Japan quickly came to dominate world trade was the silk industry. Shinsuke Kaneko shows that despite competition from China and India, Japan succeeded because the middle-quality silk it produced suited the rapidly growing mass market for silk in the United States. Its rivals only produced qualities of silk suitable for their own markets and the slower growing European market. Japan, Hong Kong and India were also great competitors within Asia for the refined sugar trade, but Takashi Kume shows how Japan came to the fore using modern machinery to refine sugar from Taiwan. Hong Kong concentrated on the China market, using modern equipment built by Jardine Matheson and Swires to refine sugar from Java. But India fell behind and continued to use traditional methods, as Indian small farmers were unable to supply the large flows of raw sugar needed for modern refining equipment. Korea supplied rice, beans, hides and gold bullion to the mesh of intra-Asian trade in the late nineteenth century, taking cotton textiles in return. Yet Korea lacked a modern monetary system and suffered from very volatile and destabilising price movements. It is often argued that Japanese merchants increasingly dominated this market leading to eventual annexation. But Sooyoon Lee argues that Koreans held their own to a great extent by re-organising their own internal trade networks. Chinese merchants were also very active in Korea.

It was from the middle of the nineteenth century that intra-Asian trade really opened up, with rice a prominent item. Toshiyuki Miyata here provides a study of the activities of Tan Kim Ching, a leading ethnic Chinese miller and trader who supplied Singapore with quality 'Garden Rice' from Siam. Tan himself was prominent among the Hokkien dialect group in Singapore, but he maintained close links with the Teochew Chinese in Bangkok who managed his mills using European engineers, and he also had close connections with Siamese Royalty. Burma also was a major participant in the intra-Asian rice trade, and A.J.H. Latham discusses the fierce inter-Asian competition in this trade during the depression of the 1920s and 1930s, using the *Rangoon Gazette* as a source. Siam and French Indo-China even began to sell in the Indian and Ceylon markets which Burma traditionally regarded as its own.

The period before the Pacific war was one of depression and severe competition all over the world. Against this background Japan sought to explore the possibilities of Africa as a market, particularly for cotton textiles. Katsuhiko Kitagawa here outlines the treaty agreements which allowed Japan to sell cotton to mine workers and cash-crop growers in the Congo Basin. Masafumi Yomoda is also concerned with these depression year and examines the impact of the depression on multilateral settlement patterns in Asia, with particular reference to Japan. Previously India had been central to the whole system of international settlements, its surpluses with Europe, the United States and the rest of Asia covering its deficit with Britain. But in the 1930s this all changed, its deficit with Britain became a small surplus, and it assumed a more passive role in international settlements. As for Japan, its trade surplus with the United States became a deficit which grew rapidly. New trade barriers all over the world worked against Japan, although it did for a while enjoy a small trade surplus with South East Asia generated by United States purchases of rubber and tin. This foreshadowed the situation from the 1950s.

In these depression years, the rise of cotton textile industries in India, China, Japan in the 1920s and early 1930s brought the British cotton textile industry to the point of collapse. Tariffs against non-Empire producers like Japan were introduced. But David Clayton shows how even into the 1960s and 1970s the British cotton industry negotiated with India, Pakistan and Hong Kong to limit their exports to Britain, to slow the pace at which the Lancashire industry declined, and restrict the social and political consequences. Also dealing with the post-war period, Susan Martin returns to the theme of intra-Asian trade and inter-Asian competition, in her case in the palm oil industry. The two great rival Asian producers were Malayasia and Indonesia, which built up a massive new business. While Indonesia tended to rely on European markets, Malaysia, the leading exporter, actively opened new markets in China, India, Pakistan, Egypt and the Gulf States.

1 China's overseas trade policy and its historical results: 1522–1840

Shi Zhihong

Introduction

From the early years of the fifteenth century, Europeans began maritime explorations to find new routes to the East, which was believed to be rich in gold, silver and spice. During the late fifteenth and the early sixteenth centuries, the great navigators discovered the sea routes from Europe to Asia and the new continent of America and accomplished a round-the-world navigation. From then on, Europeans expanded their power and influence all over the world and began a new epoch in world modern history characterized by colonial plunder.

The great voyages of discovery and the colonial expansion that followed brought about unprecedented advances in social and economic development in Western Europe and promoted the rapid growth of capitalism there. They also changed the political map of the world. Small nations like Portugal, Spain, Holland, and England on the "outskirts" of European civilization now rose one after the other to be world super-powers possessing naval supremacy and vast overseas territories. The worldwide expansion of Western capitalism became the main trend of modern history and moulded the world in its own shape. Faced with this powerful force, many ancient civilizations in Asia, Africa and America declined or even disappeared.

China found no way to stand apart from this trend. Cathaysian Civilization, one of the most ancient and splendid civilizations on earth, began to decline from the sixteenth century. It is true that China continued to develop, but it gradually began to lag behind the West in economy, politics, military affairs, science and technology and many other aspects. China was finally defeated by the West in the Opium War of 1840–42 and began a period of humiliation of more than a hundred years.

How did this happen? How could a great country decline and be defeated? This situation could be looked at from many angles: politics, economy, military affairs, thinking and culture, science and technology, inner contradictions, external relations and so on. But this chapter argues that the main reason for China's fate was the restrictive overseas policy of the Ming and early Qing dynasties. Because of this, China threw away its chance to compete with the West in the major developments of modern world history, which began with the great voyages of discovery.

Ming and early Qing overseas trade policy

Ming overseas trade policy: 1368–1644

The Ming Dynasty initiated a policy of "ban on sea-borne activity" and prohibited people from going abroad during its early and middle periods. In these years, the only legal foreign trade was "tributary trade". Only those countries which sent tribute ships to the imperial court and whose names were officially recorded in *Da Ming Huidian* (Collected Statutes of the Ming Dynasty) were allowed to trade with China. Tribute ships could come only at specific times but were permitted to carry some goods for sale other than the articles of tribute. All ships which anchored at the appointed ports were required to submit their "kanhe" – a special permit issued by the Ming government – for examination.[1] The Ming government opened three coastal ports to the outside world: Ningbo in Zhejiang Province, Quanzhou in Fujian Province and Canton in Guangdong Province. Special organizations called "Shibo Tiju Si" were set up in each of the three ports to receive the envoys from abroad and handle foreign trade there.[2] In the Capital, which was Nangjing (1368–1421) and Beijing (1421–1644), an organization called Huitong Guan with similar duties was established subject to the Ministry of Rites. All foreign business with the Chinese at coastal ports or in Huitong Guan was carried out under the surveillance of imperial officials.

The Ming government controlled tributary trade entirely and had always regarded it as part of its foreign relations, but not just for business reasons. Especially in the early Ming period, emperors of the thriving newborn dynasty gave the political considerations of this trade much more importance than its economic benefits. They were keen to receive foreign envoys to establish the fame and prestige of China as a great country, for historically, the arrival of foreign tribute ships was considered an honor to China and a sign she was flourishing. To encourage more countries to send tribute ships, the early Ming rulers always gave ships which arrived preferential treatment. They not only exchanged foreign tribute articles for more valuable presents, but also bought most of the goods brought in the ships at prices above their real value. Besides, they always gave special orders to allow the goods which were left over to be sold freely in the market exempt from taxation, although according to the statutes of the Dynasty, all goods sold by the tribute ships were required to pay tax at certain rates.

Attracted by the profitable trade established by this preferential policy, many countries in the Eastern and Southern Oceans[3] sent tribute ships to China in the early Ming. During the reign of Emperor Hongwu (1368–98), more than a dozen countries were officially recorded as paying tribute to the Ming court. After Zheng He's voyages to the Western Ocean in the reigns of Emperor Yongle (1403–24) and Emperor Xuande (1426–35), Ming foreign trade extended to the periphery of the Indian Ocean, including West Asia and the east coast of Africa. The number of countries which sent tribute ships increased to more than 30, and tributary trade reached its height.

Due to the priority given to political considerations, there was little economic benefit to the Ming Dynasty from tributary trade. In fact, the Ming government spent more on the trade than it gained from it. To receive foreign envoys and their entourages, the Ming government spent a lot of money each year on food and accommodation for them during their stay in China. Money was also spent on escorting them on their journeys between coastal ports and the Capital, and on giving presents to them and their sovereigns. After Zheng He's voyages, the frequent visits of foreign ships and the increased size of their entourages made the Ming government feel it was difficult to deal with them all, and the cost of receiving foreign missions was becoming more and more burdensome. So the size and scope of the tributary trade had to be reduced. The Ming court gradually began to issue special tributary permit ("kanhe") to individual countries and limited the visits of their ships, and the number of ships and their personnel. To make the trade easier to administer, it even specified the route which they had to take and the port of entry. For example, according to *Da Ming Huidian*, Japan was only to pay tribute every ten years, its ships were to enter Ningbo Port, and the personnel of its mission were not to exceed 300, carried in at most three ships. Ryukyu was to pay tribute every two years and enter Quanzhou Port with no more than 100 persons. Zhancheng (Champa), Zhenla (Cambodia), Siam and countries in the Western Ocean were to pay tribute every three years and enter Canton, etc. Putting limits on tribute ships indicated that the Ming government had tired of receiving foreign tribute ships.

In the middle period of the Ming Dynasty, Japanese pirates compelled China's foreign policy to be more inward looking and, in the reign of Emperor Jiajing (1522–66), this led to a complete ban on sea-borne activity. The attacks by Japanese pirates in China's coastal areas began in the middle of the fourteenth century but were not a serious problem until the late fifteenth century when the Japanese entered their period of "Warring States". Due to constant civil wars and overall disorder in Japan at that time, a large number of disgruntled warriors got away from their country to the sea and, as both merchants and pirates, frequently harassed China's southeastern coast. Conflicts between tributary missions sent by different Japanese principalities often brought disasters to China too. A heated dispute on overseas policy erupted in the Ming court after the incident of "contending for right of tribute" between two Japanese missions in 1523.[4] The result was that Emperor Jiajing dissolved Shibo Tiju Si that year in all coastal ports and declared a more severe ban on sea-borne activity.[5]

The strict ban on sea-borne activity could not prevent the activities of Japanese pirates, but it did hamper the development of China's normal foreign trade. Since there was no authorized way for foreign countries and Chinese merchants to do business, smuggling in the southeastern coastal waters became rampant. Local despots and rich merchants in the southeastern provinces, sometimes supported by local officials, played a leading role in smuggling. These powerful Chinese maritime merchants, usually armed, were also themselves pirates and often colluded with the Japanese or even passed themselves off as Japanese, to kill and loot. The Ming government declared severe restrictions at seaports of entry and exit but did little to strengthen its military defenses on the coast or at sea. During the reign of Emperor Jiajing, real and fake "Japanese pirates" ran amok on China's southeastern coastal areas, greatly hampering the development of industries and commerce there.

The ban on sea-borne activity also reduced the annual income of the Ming government. It led to more financial difficulties for Zhejiang and Fujian than other provinces since much local expenditure there came from taxation of foreign trade. There were many requests to end this policy during the reign of Emperor Jiajing, and officials from Zhejiang and Fujian argued heatedly on overseas policy at the Court. With the problem of Japanese pirates solved, the Ming government changed its policy from the start of the reign of Emperor Longqing (1567–72). After 1567, Chinese merchants were allowed to trade with countries in both the Eastern and Western Oceans with the exception of Japan, and foreign ships were welcomed to China except those from Japan.[6] In 1599, Shibo Tiju Si was re-established in Canton and Ningbo. So the ban on sea-borne activity that had existed from the early Ming was finally abandoned. But this transformation was far too late as there were only a few decades left for the Ming Dynasty.

Nevertheless, opening the seas was helpful in advancing China's foreign trade. It especially encouraged ordinary Chinese to go abroad to trade with foreign countries. They had continued to do this covertly during the Ming period even when the ban on sea-borne activity was most thorough. Private trade expanded rapidly from mid-Ming in the form of large-scale smuggling, with the development of the handicraft industry and commerce. After the ban on sea-borne activity was lifted, private trade flourished more than ever before. Yuegang, a busy commercial city in the Prefecture of Zhangzhou, Fujian Province, was the leading port of departure for ordinary Chinese leaving for foreign countries at that time. According to an author living in the late sixteenth century, the benefit to Yuegang from people going abroad was an inflow of several hundred thousands taels of silver each year.[7]

To strengthen the administration of foreign trade, the Ming government established Haicheng County at Yuegang and set up a special organization there called "Du Xiang Guan" to collect taxes. The County government stipulated that all ships going abroad were to obtain special passes ("chuan yin") by paying certain fees. There were quotas for issuing such passes each year: 88 at first and then 100 and later 210. Ships going to sea were restricted to certain sizes and were not allowed to carry weapons or contraband goods. They could only go to the destinations their owners had specified in advance and were to return within a definite time limit. In addition to pass fees, the government collected three kinds of taxes when the ships returned: "shui xiang" for ships according to size, "lu xiang" for goods imported, and "jiazeng xiang" collected only from ships returning from Luzon which normally carried Mexican silver dollars alone.[8]

Allowing people to go abroad was a positive reform of the Ming Dynasty. But it came too late to benefit China. With the development of tensions between the masses and the ruling class, the Dynasty was declining at the time and had neither the strength nor the will to pursue an aggressive overseas policy. Opening the seas did not mean the Dynasty was encouraging people to go abroad to open up overseas markets, but just that it was impossible to stop them. The development of private trade in the late Ming came spontaneously from ordinary people. All the government did was control it as far as it could and collect taxes.

In short, the foreign trade policy of the late Ming was still very conservative. The Dynasty was as always more concerned with its safety than the economic benefit that might be gained from trade. Tributary trade, the only accepted form of foreign trade in early and mid Ming was regarded as a diplomatic manoeuvre to gain prestige for the Dynasty rather than a means of securing trading income. After the restrictions were eased at the ports in late Ming, it appeared foreign ships were free to come and go, and that ordinary people could go abroad. But this was not free trade as in the West. Foreigners had to do all their business via agents appointed by the government, and direct dealing with ordinary Chinese was strictly prohibited. People were not encouraged to go abroad to open up China's overseas markets, rather they were allowed to go in recognition of the fact that it was impossible to stop them leaving. A policy of encouraging overseas trade as in the West never appeared even in the last years of the Ming Dynasty.

Early Qing overseas trade policy: 1644–1840

The opening of commercial relations with overseas countries in the late Ming did not last long. It was interrupted in the early years of the Manchu Qing Dynasty which replaced the Ming and ruled China from 1644. During the first decades of its reign, the new dynasty had to suppress various Han anti-Qing forces struggling to restore the deposed dynasty. Han forces were mainly assembled in southeastern coastal areas and were always able to escape to their strongholds in the offshore islands. So soon after it entered Beijing in 1644 the Qing Dynasty declared a ban on sea-borne activity. But the ban was not effective until a more severe order was given in 1661. That was when the Manchu army defeated Zheng Chenggong (Coxinga), the most famous anti-Qing leader in the southeastern area, and forced him to withdraw to the sea with his troops. According to the new order, all people living in coastal areas had to destroy all their property and move more than a dozen kilometers inland, leaving the anti-Qing forces at sea only a deserted shore to prey upon. The ban was carried out so thoroughly that not a single boat was allowed to go to sea and none from abroad could enter a mainland port. So China stopped all its foreign commercial relations except that to a limited scale in Macao.

The Qing government reopened the seas and permitted people to go abroad again in 1684, a year after Zheng's regime in Taiwan surrendered following a naval attack from the mainland. In 1685, four customs were set up in Canton (Guangdong Province), Xiamen (Fujian Province), Ningbo (Zhejiang Province), and Songjiang (Jiangsu Province) to deal with trade with foreign countries.[9] Thus, commercial relations with overseas countries returned to normal at last after 40 years. In the second half of the reign of Emperor Kangxi (1662–1722), foreign merchant ships were allowed to trade with China at all the ports specified, and overseas activities of Chinese merchants developed rapidly, despite certain restrictions on their going abroad. According to some historical records, Chinese merchants and emigrants could be found nearly everywhere in Southern and Eastern Ocean countries. The number of Chinese, mainly from the southeastern coastal areas, in Southeast Asia was even greater than that in the late Ming period. It was said that in Jakarta alone, there were over a hundred thousand Chinese.[10]

But this situation did not last long. From the last few years of the reign of Emperor Kangxi (1662–1722), the overseas policy of the Qing became inward looking again. This was due to deep-rooted fears that domestic anti-Manchu forces, which continued even after the Manchus unified the country, would collude with Hans overseas to destroy Qing domination. Emperor Kangxi and some of his officials thought it was a serious problem that so many Hans were going abroad to settle down and live. It was said that Emperor Kangxi had dispatched his secret agents to Luzon in his later years after hearing that descendants of the deposed Ming Emperor might still be living there. Though the investigation revealed nothing, the matter aroused the Emperor's concern. So in 1717, Emperor Kangxi ordered a ban on ships going to the Southern Ocean. At the same time, the Qing government issued a series of restrictions on ships going to sea and strengthened checks at coastal ports.[11] All those who had settled in foreign countries were ordered to return to China within three years, and those who dared to emigrate again were to be extradited and executed. Though the ban on ships going to the Southern Ocean was lifted in 1727 under pressure from the court and the masses, the prohibition on people living abroad and the restrictions on ships going to sea became stricter.[12] As a result, China's trade with the Southern Ocean which had once been prosperous declined in the eighteenth century.

Trade with foreign ships at coastal ports was also put under much stricter control. The Qing government had opened four ports for trade with foreigners after it re-opened the seas in 1684. But this policy was changed during the reign of Emperor Qianlong (1736–95) in order to control foreigners' activities in China. In addition to traditional tributary countries, the Western countries began to trade with China from the mid-Ming. The Portuguese, Spaniards, Dutch, and later the English, sailed in turn to the East from the early sixteenth to the early seventeenth centuries. The new comers were both pirates and merchants who, with well-equipped fleets, harassed China's coastal ports frequently even whilst trading with it. In the second half of the seventeenth century and the first half of the eighteenth century, though the earlier colonial countries such as Portugal, Spain and Holland had declined, England as a new entrant was becoming stronger and more ambitious. English trade with China via the East India Company began in the third decade of the reign of Emperor Kangxi and developed gradually from the 1720s. At first, English merchants traded with the Chinese only at Canton. But from 1755 to 1757, restrictions on trade at Canton and heavy import and export duties there forced the East India Company to send ships north to Ningbo where trading conditions were much better. It was also much nearer the areas which produced the commodities the English wanted, like raw silk, tea, cotton, cloth, etc. The Qing government was extremely worried about the English changing the trading port, as that would reduce the income of the Guangdong Customs. But what the Qing government most feared was that it would lead to a new foreign settlement on the coast and create another Macao. At first Emperor Qianlong (1736–95 on the throne) tried to stop English ships going north to Ningbo by increasing duties at Zhejiang Customs, but he failed. So, in the winter of 1757, the Emperor declared that from the beginning of the following year, all foreign ships must anchor only at Guangdong and none was allowed to go to Ningbo again.[13] This was an important change of foreign trade policy in the early Qing which meant that the door opened to the outside world in the reign of Emperor Kangxi was again partly closed.

At the same time, the Qing government strengthened its surveillance of foreigners doing business in China through the famous "Gong Hang" (Co-Hong) system. The Qing Dynasty continued the official agency started in late Ming at trading ports to administrate its foreign trade. According to the rules, all foreign merchants had to conduct their business through a specified number of Chinese merchants appointed by the government, and they could not trade with ordinary Chinese directly. All business, either buying or selling, had to be done through these appointed agents or brokers. Ever since opening ports in the reign of Emperor Kangxi, local governments had selected these official agents from merchants dealing in foreign goods and demanded that all foreigners were to conduct their business through these special merchants alone. In Canton, these merchants were called Hang merchants, since their guild was called "Hang" (the old spelling "Hong") or "Yanghuo Hang." The number of Hang merchants at its highest point reached 26 or more and 4 at the lowest, but they were generally called "the thirteen Hangs" in history. Hang merchants established an organization called "Gong Hang" in 1720, which was dissolved the following year but restored in 1760. After closing all ports but Canton, Hang merchants became the sole agents who had an absolute monopoly of trade with foreigners, and Gong Hang was even given the role of a semi-official organization with the responsibility of collecting duties and debts for the government, supervising foreigners' activities, and acting between the government and foreigners in all matters.

The Qing government brought in many rules and regulations to limit foreigners' activities in China after Canton became the only port open to the outside world in 1757. Foreigners had to live in appointed places during their stay and abide by rules for their activities and behavior, if they did not want to be expelled and lose their commercial contacts. In Canton, the place selected for foreigners to live was a stretch of land outside the city where, with the help of Gong Hang, Western merchants built houses called "shang guan" (the word means "factory" in its old sense of the residence or station of the "factor" or agent of the home company.)[14] These were used as their counting house, warehouse, treasury and residence. Before 1840, there were 59 "shang guan" in Canton in total, more than half of them belonging to English traders. Foreign merchants had to live in their own shang guan, and the number of their foreign staff could be no more than five. Neither women nor weapons could be brought to shang guan. Foreign merchants had to leave China or go back to Macao as soon as they finished their business, and no one was allowed to stay in Canton over winter. During their stay, foreigners were prohibited from contacting the Chinese except for the Hang merchants and their interpreters. They could not leave their shang guan unless accompanied by Hang merchants or their interpreters. They could not employ Chinese servants, or take sedan. They were not allowed to address Chinese officials directly: if they had any representation to make, it had to be done through the Hang merchants. The Hang merchants were required to supervise and take care of everything for the foreigners during their stay, from the basic necessities of life to their activities and behavior, and they were not allowed to borrow money from the foreigners. The regulations also stipulated that foreign vessels of war acting as escorts to merchant ships were not allowed to enter the Bogue. Foreign merchant ships entering or leaving the Bogue had to be under full control of Chinese river pilots and the ship's compradors who had registered with the office of the Chinese magistrate at Macao and obtained a license. If any smuggling or illegal acts occurred on a ship, the ship's comprador would be punished.[15] Although these rules and regulations were only words on paper, on many occasions they did reflect the Qing rulers' concern and vigilance about the outside world.

Surveying the overseas trade policy of the early Qing, it can be said that for most of these two hundred years, China was closed or partly closed to the outside world except for a few decades during the reign of Emperor Kangxi. Compared with the Ming Dynasty, the Qing rulers' attitude toward the outside world was more restrictive. So, describing early Qing's overseas policy as a "closed-door policy" does fit the situation.

Reasons for adopting a restrictive overseas trade policy in the Ming and early Qing dynasties

As has been pointed out above, from the Ming to the early Qing, or more precisely, from the great voyages to the Opium War, capitalism grew in Western Europe. With the spread of it, came great changes to the traditional world order. Civilization in various parts of the world, formerly separated by their geographical location were now brought into contact bringing both exchange and conflict. The world become more closely inter-related. This was a time of naval supremacy and worldwide commerce and trade. Nations leading the tide of history like Portugal, Spain, Holland, and England all followed this path to become world super-powers successively. But China, an ancient civilized country not inferior in navigational skills or sea-borne trade to Western nations at the time, went against this trend and adopted a restrictive policy of limiting and even prohibiting overseas trade. So why did this happen? The reasons include the cultural and historical traditions of China, the internal political challenges facing the two dynasties involved, China's historical economic development, and the condition of its widespread domestic economy.

Cultural and historical traditions

Cathay, the ancient Chinese civilization, was based on farming. So China had a long tradition of respecting agriculture and despising commerce. It regarded farming as the source of society's wealth, and commerce was despised and regarded as unimportant. The policy of strengthening agriculture and restricting commerce appeared as early as in the Warring States period (475–221 BC). It was continued by rulers from the Qin and Han Dynasties (221 BC–AD 220). In the late feudal period, despite the rapid development of industry and commerce, the domination of physiocracy in economic thinking and state policy did not change. Rulers of the Ming and Qing Dynasties continued to make agriculture the foundation of the national economy. In their thinking, commerce was only supplementary and always associated with exorbitant profits and luxury and extravagance. So, it continued to be thought too much commerce would harm agriculture by drawing manpower from farming and would spoil the attitudes of society. The traditional Chinese ideology of respecting agriculture and despising commerce ran contrary to the need to seek overseas trade. After the discovery of the new sea routes, mercantilism became the prevailing economic philosophy in Western Europe. All major seafaring nations there emphasized the importance of trade for the prosperity of their country. They actively supported the development of overseas trade. The colonial trade of the Portuguese and the Spanish, the "Overseas Coachman" era of the Dutch, and the establishment of the British Empire were all the results of mercantilist thinking and national policy. So the Chinese traditional ideology of despising commerce was in marked contrast with the mercantalism which prevailed in the West at that time. Obviously, there were deep rooted differences in the economic thinking between China and the Western seafaring nations. This is an important reason why China adopted a restrictive overseas trade policy in the Ming–Qing period.

The Chinese traditional notion of "Hua Yi"[16] was also an important issue. The notion is a political and cultural concept of egocentrism which maintained that Chinese civilization was superior to that of other nations. Attitudes of this kind were common to all great ancient civilizations. But because China's geographic location separated it from other great ancient civilizations, and the advantageous position Chinese civilization enjoyed in its own "world", the egocentrism of the Chinese was extremely strong. China not only had an integrated and systematic concept of "Hua Yi" but also developed a set of manners and principles for dealing with the outside world. According to the concept, China was the center of the world and the Chinese emperor, the "Son of Heaven", represented the will of heaven that he should rule the entire world. Outside China were regions inhabited by "Man Yi", barbarian nations. Although these nations were rough and savage, the emperor was willing to bestow his bounties on them and consider them as subsidiary states if they were willing to become civilized and recognize him as their sovereign by presenting tribute to the imperial court. The principal aim of an ancient Chinese emperor was to establish a world order in which he was honored as the sovereign by all the nations in the world.

But China's world view was not aggressive. It emphasized China's superiority in the world, but did not favor expansion or want to force other nations to accept a unified world under the reign of China. It stood for the submission of other nations to the morality and power of China by the example of Chinese civilization. It laid stress on defending Chinese civilization and internal order from outside nations rather than on expanding China's influence on the outside world. This is the characteristic that distinguished China from other nations. From the view of the rulers of the "Heavenly Dynasty", China's internal order was sacred and inviolable and had made China what it was since it became a civilized nation. So, it was absolutely essential to guard against the contamination of outside barbarians. Only when the outside nations observed the Chinese customs and ceremonial systems, on which China's internal order were established, could they be accepted and well treated. But if they dared to challenge these customs and systems, they would be expelled and kept beyond the door.

The notion of "Hua Yi" did not inhibit China from interacting with the outside world in its early days, especially when it was very powerful as in the Han (206 BC–AD 220) and Tang (618–907) Dynasties. At that time, the rulers of China were full of self-confidence. Through their contacts with the outside world, their sense of the superiority of the "Heavenly Dynasty" and Chinese culture was psychologically satisfied. But from the sixteenth century, and especially after the seventeenth century, Chinese civilization had to face the powerful challenge of a new, unheard-of civilization brought by Europeans with gunboats. At the material level, European civilization showed itself equal to China and in some respects surpassed it. This greatly shook the rulers' "Heavenly Dynasty" concept. So, as an instinctive reaction to the West, their attitude to the outside world became more negative. They never considered Western countries to be equal. Westerners were still considered to be semi-civilized people, and Western countries trading with China were accepted only as tributaries. But this was just to guard the dignity of the "Heavenly Dynasty". Actually, the self-confidence of the "Heavenly Dynasty" had been broken. So, rulers in the Ming–Qing period changed from being open to the outside world to defending China's civilization and the internal order from foreign contamination. This was why rulers in these years more than ever drew a line of demarcation between the Chinese and foreigners and adopted a restrictive overseas trade policy.

Political issues

The primary policy aim for any regime is to guarantee its own security. The main reason for the ban on sea-borne activity during the early and middle Ming periods was the continual attacks by Japanese pirates on southeastern coastal areas. These took place from the mid fourteenth to the mid sixteenth century. The threat of Mongolian invasion in the north during the same period also contributed to the need to introduce the policy. In the early Ming, the Yuan Dynasty withdrew into the desert north of the Great Wall after being defeated by Zhu Yuanzhang and his army, but still kept some of its military forces and never gave up hope of regaining control over the whole country. Later, although the Mongols split into several parts and the Yuan Dynasty (the North Yuan) disappeared at the beginning of the fifteenth century, the threat of Mongolian invasion was not eliminated until a peace agreement between the Mings and Tartar Khan in the reign of Emperor Longqing (1567–72). Since attention had to be paid to the threat of invasion from the north during this period, it was virtually impossible for the Ming Dynasty to adopt an active policy at sea to defend its coastal areas from Japanese harassment.

The Qing's restrictive overseas trade policy was also due to domestic politics. The reason why it banned sea-borne activity in the first years of its reign, and placed restriction on people going abroad to trade even after the ban was lifted, was to cut off connectious between anti-Qing forces on the mainland and those overseas. The Qing Dynasty was set up by a small minority among the vast number of Han people it ruled. The population of the Hans was several hundred times greater than that of the Manchus. Before the Qing Dynasty, there had been no national government established by a minority group in history except the short-lived Yuan. Always bearing this in mind, from the first day the Manchu Court established control over the country, it had to guard its reign from Han resistance. This continued throughout the whole Qing period. Qing rulers knew that there were hundreds of thousands of Hans living in Southeast Asia, beyond their control. They always considered these Hans a potential anti-Manchu force. It was for this reason, as Emperor Kangxi pointed out, that the Qing Court had to adopt strict measures to restrict people going abroad, to prevent any possible plot between domestic and overseas anti-Manchu forces.

Economic issues

During the Ming and early Qing periods, the Chinese economy as a whole was self-sufficient or semi self-sufficient, with agriculture as its main sector. It is true that commerce was progressing in an unprecedented way with the development of handicraft industries and commercial agriculture, and the seeds of capitalism had emerged. But these changes only affected some parts of the country and some sectors of the economy. The demand to open up China's overseas commercial relations came mainly from the flourishing southeastern provinces. But in most of the country, particularly the inland provinces, traditional self-sufficient or semi self-sufficient agriculture was still dominant. There was no urgent demand from them to open up overseas markets. This is why whenever a debate on overseas trade took place in court, the voice for a ban on overseas trade was always louder than that against it. The officials objecting to a ban on overseas trade were mainly those managing southeastern provinces or those who came from there. Faced with the strong opposing camp, they could hardly win. Besides, they emphasized most the benefits of overseas trade to tax income and the livelihood of people in coastal areas but not the general benefits of the opening of markets overseas for China. This reveals the limited development of the commercial economy in China at the time.

It is also important to note that China was a big country with abundant natural resources and an integrated national economic system which could produce most of the products it needed and it had little dependence on the outside world. China at that time was mainly an exporter of domestic agricultural and industrial products but not an importer of foreign goods. China exported tea, raw silk and silk fabrics, chinaware, handwoven cloth, copper–nickel alloy, sugar, paper, medicinal materials, etc. and imported mainly foreign specialties or luxuries and some Japanese copper, Siamese rice, and a small amount of Western industrial products. So, it enjoyed a favorable balance of trade and imported a great quantity of silver each year until the early nineteenth century when English merchants began to bring opium on a large scale. No matter how important foreign trade was to some areas of the country and some sectors of the economy and those involved in it, foreign trade was of little importance to most of the population and the national economy on the whole. The high degree of self-sufficiency of the national economy enabled rulers in the Ming and early Qing period to believe there was no great need for foreign trade and considered it merely a one-sided favor granted to foreign countries. This attitude was shown very clearly by Emperor Qianlong in his letter to the English King George III in 1793 when a diplomatic corps led by Lord Macartney was sent to China to ask for better commercial relations between the two countries:

> The Heavenly Dynasty can produce everything and there is nothing that must be supplied by foreign countries. But since tea, chinaware and silk produced by the Heavenly Dynasty are necessities in West Ocean countries as well as yours, in order to show our understanding and sympathy and bestow the pervading benevolence of the Heavenly Dynasty to all its people, we have set up business firms (yang hang) in Macao to meet your needs.[17]

In this famous statement of the Emperor, we can sense his arrogance and his ignorance of the outside world. But what he said was quite reasonable. Since China had little need for foreign trade, when a choice had to be made between commercial interests and the security of the country, the Ming and early Qing rulers naturally gave priority to the latter.

Historical results of Ming and early Qing overseas trade policy

When the great voyages of discovery began in the fifteenth and sixteenth centuries, followed by the colonial expansion of the West, China was still strong. With its vast territory and large population, China was probably the most powerful country of the day. But this was actually when she began to fall behind. The restrictive overseas policy of the Ming and early Qing made China lose its chance to compete with the Western nations and keep its leading position in the world.

China had had the technical ability to conduct ocean voyages long before the Westerners began their great voyages. As early as in the Song Dynasty (960–1279), China had had an advanced shipbuilding industry able to construct oceangoing ships suitable for different sea conditions. It was also the first country in the world to apply the mariner's compass to seagoing ships. In the early Ming period, from AD 1405 to AD 1433, a large Chinese fleet led by the eunuch Zheng He had sailed through the South China Sea and the Straits of Malacca to enter the Indian Ocean and venture as far as the east coast of Africa in a number of expeditions. Zheng He's voyages proved China was a strong sea power with advanced shipbuilding skills and oceangoing ability, which was still technically unmatched when more than half a century later the European navigators such as Diaz, Columbus, and Da Gama started their voyages.

China did not lack an economic motive to open overseas markets at the time the Westerners began their great voyages. The rapid growth of commercialized agriculture and private handicraft industry from the mid-1400s made China need both the domestic and overseas markets. This was particularly true of the southeastern coastal provinces like Zhejiang, Fujian, and Guangdong, where people had a long history of trading and making a living overseas. More and more people from these provinces went abroad in spite of government prohibitions, and maritime smuggling became very prosperous from the late 1400s. At that time, the Chinese could be found in nearly every corner of East and Southeast Asia.

So, long before the Europeans' voyages, China had had all the necessary preconditions for oceangoing expeditions and only needed encouragement from the government. If the Ming Dynasty had done this, maybe history would have been different. But the fact is that when Zheng He's fleet finished its last voyage in 1433, the Dynasty canceled its official oceangoing expeditions and put a strict ban on people going abroad, under the policy of "not operating far away".[18] At the same time, it restated the ban on people's sea-borne activity which had existed from Emperor Hongwu's period. As a result of this short-sighted policy China lost its chance of pre-empting the Europeans in opening overseas markets in the middle of the fifteenth century. When the Europeans set sail on their oceangoing expeditions half a century later, China could only stand and watch and not compete.

The first half of the sixteenth century was still a good time for China to develop overseas commercial relations. At this time, only Portugal among the European nations had entered the West Pacific Ocean and was a potential competitor for China. The Portuguese came around the Cape of Good Hope to the East at the end of the fifteenth century. But then for about 50 years, they established colonies and traded only in the Indian Ocean and nearby archipelagoes in the South Pacific. They did not come to East Asia until the 1540s–50s when they established commercial bases in Japan (Kyushu) and China (Macao). But China missed this chance, too. As early as the 1510s, the Portuguese started contacting the Ming Dynasty. The first occasion was in 1513 when a merchant named Jorge Alvares arrived in Tunmen, Guangdong Province, and stayed there for a short time. Then, in 1517, an official mission sent by the King D. Manuel came to establish commercial relations between the two countries. But the Ming Court did not, nor did it want to, understand the significance of the arrival of the Westerners at all. It regarded the newcomers as traditional foreign tribute bearers and traders. Being dissatisfied with the behavior of the Portuguese in China and their occupation of Malacca earlier, the Ming Court eventually deported the mission in 1522 and arrested its leader Tome Pires. Two years later, the Ming Dynasty declared a strict ban on overseas activity and closed its trading ports to foreigners because of the harassment of Japanese pirates.

When the Ming Dynasty reopened its ports in 1567, the outside world had greatly changed. From the mid-1500s to the early seventeenth century, the Portuguese had extended their trading area from the South Pacific Ocean to most of Southeast and East Asia, and the Spaniards and Dutch had come in turn to the East to challenge the Portuguese. The Spaniards entered the East via the Philippines and, not long after they occupied Luzon in 1565, they established the Pacific Ocean Silk Road between Mexico and Manila. They tried to trade with China directly and sent a diplomatic mission to Beijing in 1580, but the mission was detained at Canton and sent back to Manila. After that, the Spaniards mainly traded with the Chinese in Manila and transported Chinese goods from there to Mexico along the Pacific Ocean Silk Road. The Dutch came to Asia in the early seventeenth century. They also attempted to contact China but were obstructed by the Portuguese who had occupied Macao since 1557. The Dutch occupied the Penghu Island in 1622, but they were driven from there by Chinese troops in 1624. They then began to settle in Taiwan and occupied the whole island in 1642.

So, when the Ming Dynasty lifted its ban on sea-borne commerce and re-opened its doors, it faced a very different world. By then all the main maritime trade routes were controlled by Western nations. Even in China's traditional trading area, the West Pacific Ocean, the Chinese faced strong challenges from Western nations. These were extending their influence and seizing commercial interests by sword and cannon. But if the Ming Dynasty had decided to use its military strength to compete with the Western nations, it could still have done a great deal for China interests in Asia, as it still had a huge influence in the area. Unfortunately, it did nothing. It still did not understand the significance of the changes in the outside world, let alone adapt its policies to take account of the changing world. Yes, it abandoned the ban on sea-borne activity and began to permit people to go abroad, but this did not mean that it now wanted to encourage China's overseas trade, merely that it could not stop them leaving. On the contrary, it continued to try to prevent people from going abroad to open up overseas markets by placing all sorts of obstacles in their way. Without the support of the state, Chinese merchants could not compete with Westerners in overseas markets on an equal footing. This greatly hindered the development of China's overseas trade. Since Western nations controlled all trade routes to markets outside the West Pacific Ocean, Chinese merchants had to limit their activities to their traditional trading area. They could not even compete on equal terms with Westerners in the West Pacific Ocean even though the Westerners were really only transporting goods from one place to another. For the Westerners were not individuals as such but were backed by their state political powers and military forces. The Western nations were at that time seizing colonies in China's traditional trading area in Asia and controlled nearly all the main markets there. They were using political and military force to do this. In this situation, it was obvious that Chinese going abroad, with nothing but goods, could not compete with the Western merchants, even though they did bring back a large amount of silver each year.

During the early Qing period, China as a whole lagged behind the advanced Western nations, but there were still opportunities for it to catch up. The most favorable opportunity came in the late seventeenth century, when, of the old western colonial countries, Portugal and Spain had declined. Holland had also passed its golden age of expansion and as its main arena of colonial activity was India and the East Indies, it was no-longer the main sea force in East Asia. England as a younger colonial country had not fully developed. Being immersed in domestic affairs after the Civil Wars of the 1640s, England did not extend its influence in East Asia until the eighteenth century. In these favourable political circumstances had the Qing Dynasty planned its maritime affairs better and given strong support to overseas trade, and tried to catch up with the West in military affairs, science and technology, the fate of China might not have been what it became.

But China also missed this opportunity. During the first decade of its rule, 1644–83, the Manchu Qing Dynasty had to concentrate all its efforts on unifying the country and solving various domestic problems. So it could do nothing about overseas trade, and had in fact to ban sea-borne activities to sever the links between anti-Qing forces overseas and those on the mainland. When Zheng's anti-Qing force in Taiwan was defeated in 1683, it brought about an opportune moment to plan and operate maritime affairs more widely. However, the Qing Court had no intention of doing anything except lift the ban on sea-borne activity. Emperor Kangxi was one of the most farsighted and accomplished rulers in

Chinese history. He did much to defend China's political unity and territorial integrity as well as promote its economic development. But he never truly cast his eyes overseas and think of leading China to a new future by instigating a maritime trade war with the Western nations. He never even built a navy of genuine significance to defend China's long coastline but only sought to protect it with batteries of cannons manned by small garrisons at the seaports. Emperor Kangxi knew more about the West than any other previous Chinese ruler and recognized that the future danger to China would come from the West, but he did not adopt measures to deal with the situation. His attitude to the danger and his policy was the same as previous rulers, that is, to close the door and keep the enemies out. He never gave any support to Chinese people going abroad but instead placed all sorts of obstacles before them. People were forbidden to build large oceangoing vessels; they were not allowed to have arms even to defend themselves; they were prohibited from staying overseas, and so on. Lastly, in his later years, he banned people from going to the Southern Ocean. All this greatly hindered the development of China's overseas trade.

At the very moment that Qing overseas trade policy became more restrictive, further changes were taking place in the outside world. From the eighteenth century, Britain became the rising new sea power which replaced Portugal, Spain, and Holland in the world. Britain made its first accumulation of capital in the first half of the eighteenth century. Then, from the second half of the century to the early nineteenth century, it underwent the industrial revolution and became the "workshop of the world". The industrial revolution completely changed the comparative strength between the West and China and left China far behind the advanced Western nations.

But even at this time the Qing Dynasty continued its dream that the "Heavenly Dynasty" was the world leader. When the British diplomatic corps led by Lord Macartney arrived in 1793, it was treated as a traditional tributary mission. Emperor Qianlong would not even look at the presents brought by the mission to display British advanced science and technology and also its military force. The Emperor did not understand that the balance of power between the East and West was changing dramatically, and the golden period of time when the "Heavenly Dynasty" could close its door had passed. There was little chance now that the Dynasty could catch up with the West, or even continue to keep its door closed. The national humility of the "Opium War" and the disasters the Chinese people suffered over the next 100 years was the bitter reward for the restrictive foreign policy adopted by rulers in the Ming and Qing dynasties in ignorance of world trends.

Notes

1 Kanhe was a special document with two separate parts. The Ming government stamped the edges of the two parts with a seal and issued one of them to the tributary country as identification when its ships came.

2 The Ming system of Shibo Tiju Si for managing foreign trade at seaports was adopted from that in the Song and Yuan periods when the organization was called Shibo Si. The Ming Dynasty set up its first Shibo Tiju Si in Huangdu, a small town near the mouth of the Yangtse River in 1367, one year before its first emperor Zhu Yuanzhang ascended the throne in Nanjing. Huangdu Shibo Tiju Si only existed for three years, for the Emperor thought the port was too near the Capital. But not long after the first Shibo Tiju Si was dissolved in 1370, Zhu Yuanzhang set up similar organizations again in Ningbo, Quanzhou, and Canton separately and from that time they were not changed during the whole Ming period, though they were dissolved and reestablished several times. Guesthouses attached to the three Shibo Tiju Si were constructed in 1405 and called Anyuan in Ningbo, Laiyuan in Quanzhou, and Huaiyuan in Canton. During the Ming period, these three guesthouses were very well known to the foreign tribute envoys and merchants.

3 In the Ming period, the sea area and islands east to the South China Sea along the line of about 110° east longitude were called the "Eastern Ocean", while the sea area and islands west to that line were called the "Western Ocean". The "Southern Ocean" was a name in ancient times for the Southeast Asia area, including the Malay Archipelago, the Malay Peninsula, and Indonesia. The "Eastern Ocean" mainly referred to Japan and the "Western Ocean" referred to Europe and the American nations.

4 For the details of this incident, see Hu Zongxian: *Chou hai tu bian*, Vol. 2.

5 Zhang Tingyu, *Ming shi* (Vol. 81), p. 1981.

6 Zhang xie: *Dong xi yang kao*, Vol. 7, p. 131.

7 Ibid., preface by Zhou Qiyuan, p. 17.

8 Ibid., Vol. 7. For a more detailed introduction on Du Xiang Guan and the taxes it collected, see Wan Ming: *Zhongguo rongru shijie de bulu: Ming yu Qing qianqi haiwai zhengce bijiao yanjiu*, pp. 244–257.

9 For the locations of the four customs set up after the Qing opened the sea in 1684, see Peng Zeyi's paper: *Qing chu si queguan didian he maoyi liang de kaocha*.

10 Li Changfu, *Nanyang Huaqiao Shi* (History of Overseas Chinese in the Southern Ocean), p. 30.

11 *Qing Shengzu Shilu*, Vol. 271.

12 See *Qing Shizong shilu*, Vol. 74; *Da Qing huidian shili*, Vol. 629 and Vol. 776.

13 *Qing Gaozong shilu*, Vol. 550.

14 The word means "factory" in its old sense of the residence or station of the "factor" or agent of the home company, and operated as the counting-house, warehouse, treasury, and residence of Western merchants. Before 1840, there were 59 "shang guan" in Canton altogether and more than a half of them belonged to English traders.

15 For these rules and regulations, see *Yue haiguan zhi* (Records of Guangdong Customs), Vol. 28; Vol. 29.

16 Here the Chinese character "Hua" means "China" or "Chinese" and especially refers to the Han Nationality; "Yi" refers to all barbarian nationalities other than the Han Nationality.

17 See *Qing gaozong shilu*, Vol. 1435.

18 See *Ming xuanzong shilu*, Vol. 103.

Bibliography

Braga, J.M., 1949, *The western pioneers and their discovery of Macao*. Macao.

Cai Jiude, 1951, *Wo bian shilue*, Facsimile reproduction, Shanghai.

Chao Zhongchen, 1991, *Lun Ming dai haijin zhengce de queli jiqi yanbian*, in *Zhong wai guanxi shi luncong, Vol. 3*. Beijing: Shijie Zhishi Chubanshe.

Chen Shangsheng, 1993, *Biguan yu kaifang: Zhongguo fengjian wanqi duiwai guanxi yanjiu*. Jinan: Shandong Renmin Chubanshe.

Chen Zilong *et al.* (eds), 1962, *Huang Ming jingshi wen bian*. 1638 edn, Facsimile reproduction, Beijing: Zhonghua Shuju.

Da Ming huidian, 1587 edn, 1988, Facsimile reproduction, Beijing: Zonghua Shuju.

Da Ming lu, 1990, Reproduction, Shenyang: Liaoshen Shushe.

Da Qing huidian and *Da Qing huidian shili*. 1899 edn.

Da Qing lichao shilu, 1964, Facsimile reproduction, Taibei: Hualian and Huawen.

Da Qing lu li, 1993, Reproduction, Tianjin: Tianjin Guji Chubanshe.

Fairbank, John K., 1953, *Trade and diplomacy on the China coast*. Cambridge, MA: Harvard University Press.

Fairbank, John K., (ed.), 1968, *The Chinese world order: traditional China's foreign relations*. Cambridge, MA: Harvard University Press.

Fairbank, John K. *et al.*, 1992, *East Asia: tradition and transformation*. Chinese version translated by Li Ming and others. Tianjin: Tianjin Renmin Chubanshe.

Fang Hao, 1987, *Zhong xi jiaotong shi*. Beijing: Yuelu Shushe.

Fei Chengkang, 1988, *Aomen si bai nian*. Shanghai: Shanghai Renmin Chubanshe.

Fei Xin, 1966, *Xing cha sheng lan*. 1436 edn, Reproduction, Taibei.

Gu Yingtai, 1977, *Ming shi jishi benmo*. 1658 edn, Reproduction, Beijing: Zhonghua Shuju.

Guo Yunjing, 1994, *Qing dai shangye shi*. Shenyang: Liaoning Renmin Chubanshe.

He Changling, 1972, *Huangchao jingshi wen bian*. 1873 edn, Reproduction, Taibei: Wenhai.

He Qiaoyuan, *Min shu*. 1629 edn, 1994–95, Reproduction, Fuzhon: Fujian Renmin Chubanshe.

Higgins, Roland L., 1981, *Piracy and coastal defense in the Ming period, governmental response to coastal disturbances, 1523–1549*. Ann Arbor, MI: University Microfilms International.

Huang Zhilian, 1992, *Yazhou de hua yi zhixu: Zhongguo yu Yazhou guojia guanxi xingtai lun*. Beijing: Zhongguo Renmin Daxue Chubanshe.

Hu Zongxian, 1787 edn, *Chou hai tu bian. Si ku quan shu* edn.

Hyma, Albert, 1953, *A history of the Dutch in the Far East*. Michigan.

Jiao Hong, 1984, *Guochao xian zheng lu*. 1594–1616. Facsimile reproduction, Shanghai.

Kangxi tongyi Taiwan shiliao xuanji, 1983, Xiamen: Fujian Renmin Chubanshe.

Lach, Donald F., 1965, *Asia in the making of Europe*. Chicago, Il: University of Chicago Press.

Li Changfu, 1934, *Nanyang huaqiao shi*, Shanghai: Shangwu Yinshuguan, Commercial Press.

Li Jinming, 1990, *Ming dai haiwai maoyi shi*. Beijing: Zhongguo Shehui Kexue Chubanshe.

Liang Jiabin, 1999, *Guangdong shisanhang kao*. Shanghai: Shangwu Yinshuguan.

Lin Renchuan, 1987, *Ming mo Qing chu siren haishang maoyi*. Shanghai: Huadong Shifan Daxue Chubanshe.

Liu Weiqian, 1397 edn, 1989, *Da Ming Lu*: Facsimile reproduction, Yangzhou: Jiangsu Guangling.

Ma Huan, 1966, *Yingya sheng lan*. 1451 edn, Reproduction, Taibei.

Ming shi, 1974, 1739 edn, Reproduction, Beijing.

Ming shilu, 1961–66, Facsimile reproduction, Taibei.

Morse, H.B., 1908, *The trade and administration of the Chinese empire*. Shanghai: Kelly and Walsh Ltd.

Morse, H.B., 1910–18, *The international relations of the Chinese empire*. London, New York (etc.): Longmans, Green and Co.

Peng Xinwei, 1958, *Zhongguo huobi shi*. Shanghai: Shanghai Renmin Chubanshe.

Peng Zeyi, 1984, *Qing chu si queguan didian he maoyi liang de kaocha*, in *Shehui kexue zhanxian* (Social Science Front) no. 3.

Qingchao wenxian tongkao, 1787, 1936, Reproduction, Shanghai: Shangwu Yinshuguan.

Qing dai waijiao shiliao, Jiaqing chao, 1933, Beijing: Gugong Bowuyuan.

Shen Guangyao, 1985, *Zhongguo gudai duiwai maoyi shi*. Guangzhou: Guangdong Renmin Chubanshe.

Shi Zhihong, 1990, "The development and underdevelopment of agriculture during the early Qing period (1644–1840)," in Akira Hayami and Yoshihiro Tsubouchi (eds), *Economic and demographic development in rice producing societies: some aspects of East Asian economic history (1500–1900)*, Leuven: Leuven University Press, pp. 69–88.

Shi Zhihong, 1994, "Changes in landlord economy in the early Qing period of China, 1644–1840," in A.J.H. Latham and H. Kawakatsu (eds), *The evolving structure of the East Asian economic system since 1700: a comparative analysis*, Milan: University Bocconi, pp. 27–38.

Shi Zhihong, 1994, *Qingdai qianqi de xiao nong jingji* (On peasant economy in the early Qing period), Beijing: Zhongguo Shehui Kexue Chubanshe (China Social Sciences Press).

Shi Zhihong, 1995, "Qingdai caizheng gaishu (A brief introduction on the state financial system of the Qing Dynasty)," in Shang Hongkui jiaoshou shishi shi zhounian jinian wenji (Festschrifts of 10th anniversary death of Professor Shang Hongkui), Beijing: Beijing Daxue Chubanshe (Beijing University Press), pp. 157–167.

Sun Guangqi, 1991, *Lun Yongle shiqi de haiwai kaifang*, in *Zhongwai guanxi shi luncong, Vol. 3*. Beijing: Shijie Zhishi Chubanshe.

Tian Rukang, 1957, *17–19 shiji zhongye Zhongguo fanchuan zai dongnan Yazhou*, Shanghai: Shanghai Renmin Chubanshe.

Wan Ming, 2000, *Zhongguo rongru shijie de bulu: Ming yu Qing qianqi haiwai zhengce bijiao yanjiu*. Beijing: Shehui Kexue Chubanshe.

Wang Qi, 1991, *Xu wenxian tongkao*. 1586 edn, Reproduction, Beijing: Xiandai Chubanshe (Modern Publishing House).

Wang Zhichun, 1885, *Guochao rou yuan ji*. Shanghai: Tongwen Shuju.

Weng Huiming, 1991, *Lun Ming dai qianqi Zhongguo yu Nangyang waijiao de yanbian*, in *Zhong wai guanxi shi luncong, Vol. 3*. Beijing: Shijie Zhishi Chubanshe.

Wu Jianxiong, (ed.), 1991, *Zhongguo haiyang fazhan shi lunwenji, Vol. 4*. Taibei. Academia Sinica.

Wu Jianyong, 1989, *Qing dai qianqi duiwai zhengce de xingzhi jiqi dui jingji fazhan de yingxiang*, in *Beijing shehui kexue*, no. 1.

Xie Guozhen, 1982, *Qing chu dongnan yanhai qianjie kao, Qing chu dongnan yanhai qianjie bu kao*, in *Ming Qing zhiji dangshe yundong kao*. Beijing: Zhonghua Shuju.

Xu Mingde, 1991, *Ming Qing shiqi de biguan suoguo zhengce jiqi lishi jiaoxun*, in *Zhong wai guanxi shi luncong, Vol. 3*. p. 144–169. Beijing: Shijie Zhishi Chubanshe.

Yan Ruyu, 1838 edn, *Yang fang ji yao*, in 1838 by An Kang Zhang Peng fei Lailutang.

Yong Zheng, 1738 edn, *Zhu pi yu zhi*, this is an official compiled collection of imperial instructions by Emperor Yong Zheng (1723–1735) of the Qing Dynasty.

Zhang Tingyu *et al.*, 1974, *Ming shi*. 1739 edn, Reproduction, Beijing: Zhonghua Shuju (Zhonghua Publishing House).

Zhang Weihua, 1956, *Ming dai haiwai maoyi shi jianlun*. Shanghai: Shanghai Renming Chubanshe.

Zhang Weihua, 1987, *Ming Qing zhiji Zhong xi guanxi jianshi*. Jinan: Qilu Shushe.
Zhang Xie, 1617 edn, 1981, *Dong xi yang kao*. Reproduction, Beijing: Zhonghua Shuju.
Zhang Xinglang, 1977 edn, *Zhong xi jiaotong shiliao huibian*. Beijing: Zhonghua Shuju.
Zhao Erxun *et al.*, 1928, 1976, *Qing shi gao*. Reproduction, Beijing: Zhonghua Shuju.
Zheng Hesheng and Zheng Yijun (eds.), 1980, 1983, 1989, *Zheng He xia Xiyang ziliao huibian*, 3 vols. Jinan: Qilu Shudian.

2 The golden age of Japanese copper*

The intra-Asian copper trade of the Dutch East India Company

Ryuto Shimada

Introduction

The seventeenth and eighteenth centuries were crucial eras for the formation of the modern world economic system. While Andre Gunder Frank comes to the conclusion that the Asian decline began around 1750,[1] much recent research has provided evidence that Asia continued to enjoy considerable economic development in the eighteenth century. Akira Hayami, for example, argues the case for a Japanese labour-intensive *industrious revolution*, a revolution in the method of production, which compared with the capital-intensive industrial revolution of the West.[2] This new interpretation is seen in Japanese historical studies and Asian history in general.[3] It is clear that Asian economic history in the early modern period is important and worthy of further investigation.

Recent research has revealed economic development in various Asian countries in this period, yet several problems remain unsolved. For example, much of the new research does not distinguish the difference in the degree of economic development between individual Asian countries. What is more, despite examining 'economic development', they do not ask why a 'modern national economy' based on capitalist production did not occur. Lastly, this new research does not consider current economic problems, like the global inequality of wealth distribution.

Bearing these problems in mind, the chapter investigates the global trade in Japanese copper conducted by the Dutch East India Company (de *Verenigde Oostindische Compagnie* (VOC)). In the early modern period, Japanese copper was a leading commodity in intra-Asian trade and was used in Asia to make weapons and household utensils and, more particularly, copper coins. It was vital, as at that time copper currency was widely used by the ordinary people of many Asian countries. The supply of this copper currency was essential to enable each Asian country achieve economic development.[4] So Japanese copper is one of the most interesting commodities for comprehensive analysis in the early modern Asian economy. This current survey runs from 1650 to 1800, but the main emphasis is on the eighteenth century, when Asian countries faced a decline in the inflow of Japanese copper.

The chapter will focus on the Asian economic system in the early modern period, which was driven by the intra-Asian trade in Japanese copper. This was the golden age of Japanese copper. It will also examine inter-Asian competition between Asian countries for Japanese copper in the eighteenth century and will highlight the characteristics of the so-called *industrious revolution* in Japan in these years.

Research for the chapter involved the examination of Dutch records preserved at the National Archives of the Netherlands (*Nationaal Archief* (NA), formerly *Algemeen Rijksarchief* (ARA)), which includes the Accountant General's records at the Dutch High Government of Batavia (*Hoge Regering*) (*Het Archief van de Boekhouder-Generaal te Batavia* (BGB)).

The golden age of Japanese copper

Copper production and exports in Japan

Japanese records list the annual amounts of copper produced in early modern Japan. Production reached a peak in the late seventeenth century with 90,000 piculs in 1668 and 89,000 piculs in 1700 (1 picul = *c*.60 kg). But amounts decreased in the eighteenth century. In 1711 records show 64,000 piculs with a decline to the 40,000s during 1760s and 1770s. In 1842 the amount fell to 30,000 piculs.[5] In general, copper production increased rapidly in the latter half of the seventeenth century as new vast copper mines came into operation, like the Osarizawa Mines in 1666 and the Besshi Mines in 1691. Annual volumes reached their peak before the turn of the century and then began to decrease. During the eighteenth century, the problem for the Japanese authorities was how to satisfy domestic demand, and this led to the restriction of exports as will be discussed later.

Besides the VOC, Japanese copper was exported in Chinese junks from Nagasaki and by Japanese ships via the island of Tsushima. The ultimate market for Japanese copper was the world in general, but the aforementioned traders had particular markets to supply. The VOC reshipped Japanese copper from Batavia and Malacca mainly to South Asia and Europe, as will be examined later in more detail. But Japanese copper exported by Chinese junks went chiefly to mainland China with some to Southeast Asia. That exported through Tsushima Island went to Korea. Both China and Korea used Japanese copper to make copper currency.[6]

Japanese copper exports reflected production trends. Figure 2.1 shows annual exports by the three key participants in the Japanese copper trade during the period from 1650 to 1800.[7] Although Japan had been a copper-exporting country in East Asia for several centuries, it was not until the mid-seventeenth century that the quantities of exports became important to the world economy. In 1641, the Japanese authorities granted permission to the VOC to export Japanese copper and thus the VOC began exporting great quantities. The annual amounts rapidly increased, especially after the VOC was banned from exporting Japanese silver in 1668.[8]

The situation changed in 1715 when Japan imposed legal restrictions on the export of copper by the VOC. The number of ships was limited to two a year and exports were restricted to 15,000 piculs per year.[9] The Japanese authorities continued this policy and indeed introduced further restrictions. The annual

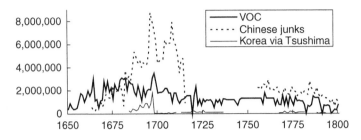

Figure 2.1 Japan's copper exports 1650–1800 (Dutch lbs).

Source: Exports to the VOC: 1650–1800: Yasuko Suzuki, 'Japanese Copper Trade by the Dutch East India Company, 1645–1805', *Bulletin of the Faculty of Letters* (Hanazono University), 32, 2000, pp. 189–91, together with BGB, NA and VOC, NA; Exports to Chinese junks: 1663–1715: Atsushi Kobata, *Nilhon Dō Kōgyō Shi no Kenkyū* (*study on the Japanes Copper Mining Industry*) Kyoto, 1993, pp. 695–7; 1755–90: Kaishu Katsu, *Suijinroku*, vol. 2, Tokyo, 1968, pp. 2–7; 1791–1800: *Nagasaki Dō Kaiwatashi Kiroku* (Arc. No. 2098–20, The Historiographical Institute, The University of Tokyo); Exports to Korea: Kazui Tashiro, '*Tsushima Han no Chōsen Yusyutsu Dō Chōtatsu ni tsuite: Bakufu no Dō Tōsei to Nissen Dō Bōeki no Suitai*' (On the Korean Exports of Copper from the Tsushima Clan), *Chōsen Gakuhō* (*Journal of the Academic Association of Koreanology in Japan*), 66, 1973, pp. 145–203.

Note
1 Dutch pound = *c.*0.494 kg.

volumes were limited to 5,000 piculs in 1742 and 6,000 piculs in 1790.[10] Actual exports differed from the amounts permitted by these restrictive acts, because employees of the VOC obtained special permission from the Japanese authorities to export more copper. The policy of restriction was the result of a decline in copper production at a time of growing domestic demand for copper cash. So while Japan was able to supply her own needs, other Asian countries faced a shortage of copper for small-denomination coinage.

Intra-Asian trade: Malacca to Batavia route

Japanese copper was usually shipped from Japan to Malacca or Batavia, after the VOC gave up the castle of Zeelandia on Taiwan in 1662. After arriving at Malacca, more than half the copper was sent to the South Asian factories of the VOC (Figure 2.2 shows the final destinations of Japanese copper through Malacca). Not much copper was unloaded and reshipped at Malacca, and most of it was carried to South Asia in the ship which brought it from Japan. Even that actually unloaded in Malacca was usually reshipped within the same book year and was rarely recorded at the end of the book year as stock.[11] But the copper from Japan to Batavia was unloaded at Batavia and then sent to Dutch factories in Asia and Europe. Therefore in the seventeenth century, the route via Malacca was much more important in terms of volumes than that of Batavia. Since most Japanese copper delivered to the VOC was sent to South Asia, it was logical to distribute it through Malacca, rather than Batavia. Moreover, it was more

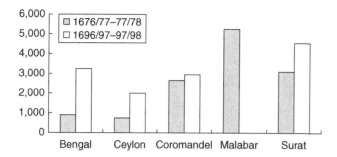

Figure 2.2 Distribution of Japanese copper via Malacca (annual average; piculs).
Source: VOC1322, VOC1330, VOC1596, VOC1580, NA.

economical to ship directly from Japan via Malacca to South Asia, avoiding unloading and reshipping.

The trade in Japanese copper from Japan to South Asia was one leg in the so-called triangular trade among Japan, India and Siam by the VOC.[12] Japanese copper was exported to India, India exported cotton textiles to Siam and Siam exported sapanwoods, deerskins and other such goods to Japan. From this triangular trade, the VOC gathered profits and used them to purchase pepper and spices in the Indonesian Archipelago for the European market.

Due to the new restriction on exports from Japan, direct trade through Malacca became difficult to carry on. Since the VOC was allowed only two ships each year from Japan under the new restrictions, they sent larger ships. The ships were sent to Batavia with Japanese copper which was reshipped at Batavia to the South Asian factories of the VOC. Ironically, because of the Japanese restriction of 1715, Batavia became a focus for the intra-Asian trade of the VOC. After 1715, almost all ships departing from Japan were destined for Batavia apart from the period 1747–52, when one of the two yearly ships from Japan sailed directly to Coromandel or Bengal in South Asia. Batavia, as a pivotal port, allocated the amount of Japanese copper to each destination and also unloaded and reshipped the Japanese copper.

Reshipments of Japanese copper to Europe were less than those to Asia. Figure 2.3 shows the quota for Europe. Japanese copper was brought to the Netherlands by the annual order of the Gentleman XVII (*Heren XVII*, the supreme board of the Company *in patria*), when the market price of copper in Amsterdam was relatively high.[13] The book year 1728/29 was the last year in which Japanese copper was reshipped to the Netherlands. According to Figure 2.3, the annual amount of Japanese copper delivered to Asian countries was roughly one million Dutch pounds in weight (1 Dutch pound = c.0.494 kg) throughout the eighteenth century. This meant that Asian countries were sharing the amount of Japanese copper in circulation and were competing with each other for it.

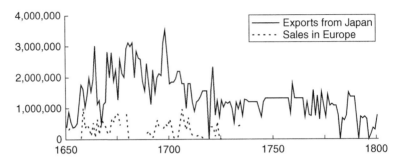

Figure 2.3 VOC trade of Japanese copper (Dutch lbs).

Source: Exports from Japan: See Figure 2.1; Sales in Europe: Kristof Glamann, 'The Dutch East India Company's Trade in Japanese Copper, 1645–1736', *Scandinavian Economic History Review*, 1953, pp. 52–3.

Note
The numbers of the sales in Europe from 1650 to 1692 indicate the imports into Europe.

The golden age of Japanese copper

The decrease in flows of Japanese silver to Asia in the mid-seventeenth century created a golden age of Japanese copper in Asia. Asian countries from Korea to the Middle East, especially China and India, imported large quantities of Japanese copper. Although some ports in Southeast Asia were not recipients like Ayutthaya in seventeenth century and Batavia in the early eighteenth century, they were, nonetheless, intermediaries in the copper trade. Japanese copper was necessary for the intra-Asian trade of the VOC, and it facilitated the international division of production among Asian countries and regions, and it stimulated Asian economic development. Thus the period from the latter half of the seventeenth century to the eighteenth century is described as the golden age of Japanese copper and its use by Asian countries may be assumed to have speeded up the transition to a monetised economy amongst ordinary people.

However, from the early eighteenth century onwards, when the Japanese authorities began to restrict the export of Japanese copper, this restriction caused a shortage in copper for small denomination currency in those Asian countries. What is more, the structure of the Japanese copper trade also began to change.

The eighteenth century

Inter-Asian competition

What was the effect of the restriction of Japanese copper exports on the Asian economy as a whole? This question will be examined through an analysis of the distribution and profit rates of the Japanese copper trade by the VOC. The effect of the restriction on the Japanese economy will be investigated also in the context of Japan's *industrious revolution*, as posed by Akira Hayami.

Distribution by the VOC

Japanese copper exported by the VOC was usually brought to factories at Bengal, Ceylon, Coromandel, Malabar and Gujarat (see Appendix). The choice of factories by the VOC was based on price or profit. The aim was to balance the profit per Dutch pound in weight at each factory with that of all the factories. Figure 2.4 shows the movement of gross profits per pound of Japanese copper at each South Asian factory. The High Government of Batavia principally sent Japanese copper to South Asia according to orders placed by the factories. But it is evident that it adjusted the amounts to maximise profits for itself, despite the efforts of stock controllers at individual factories to gain optimum profits for the factories. As a result, the profit at each South Asian factory follows similar trends, and shows similar yearly profits per weight unit.

The eighteenth century can be divided into three periods: 1700–25: in this period profits per unit decreased from the beginning of the century to around 1725. 1725–60: the profits per unit rose until around 1760. 1760–90: after 1760 profits per unit gradually diminished in all South Asian factories.

1700–25: slowdown of profits per unit. Between 1700 and 1725, profits per unit stagnated, while copper exports from Japan decreased rapidly. The main reason for this decrease was the rise in price at Nagasaki. The normal purchasing price at this port shown in Dutch records was 12.34 taels per picul in 1700, but it began to rise substantially during this period. In 1702 it was 12.84 taels, 12.80 taels in 1705, 12.85 taels in 1712, 13.25 taels in 1714 and 14.84 taels in 1716.[14]

But the impact of falling exports from Japan upon the VOC Japanese copper trade with South Asia was small. The amounts delivered at Malacca and Batavia can be seen in the Appendix. The effect of the decrease in exports from Japan was seen in the delivery of copper by the VOC to the Netherlands as imports to Europe

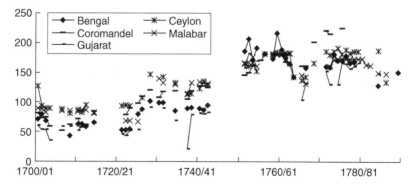

Figure 2.4 Gross profits per Dutch lbs of Japanese copper (homeland pennings).

Source: *Generaal Negotieboek*, BGB, NA.

Note
20 pennings = 1 Dutch guilder.

fell. The decline in imports to Europe reflected the decrease of exports from Japan. It also reflected the fall in the price of copper in Europe, as pointed out by Kristof Glamann.[15] So the amount delivered to South Asia remained roughly the same and fluctuated at around one million Dutch pounds per year throughout the eighteenth century and Asian countries competed for a fixed amount of Japanese copper.

At the beginning of the eighteenth century, English and Portuguese traders engaged in the copper trade from China to Indian ports. According to Dutch records at Malacca, which recorded cargoes of ships calling at Malacca, non-Dutch European traders re-exported Japanese copper from Amoy and Canton in China, Tonkin in Vietnam, and Ayutthaya in Siam, via Malacca to Madras and Surat in India. This copper was carried from Nagasaki by Chinese merchants and then sold and reshipped to English or Portuguese merchants at the home-ports of the Chinese junks. This copper amounted to over 4,000 piculs per year in the first five years of the century and caused a fall in profit for the VOC in Japanese copper sold in South Asia. Then the amount re-exported from China fell during the second five years of the century, as Japanese copper delivered to Chinese junks at Nagasaki was increasingly absorbed in mainland China.

The High Government during this period began to wonder if the Japanese trade was profitable. This was because of the decrease in copper exports from Japan, the new policy of the Japanese authorities in restricting the number of annual vessels and the rise in price at Nagasaki. Their doubts resulted in the special report in 1726 on the state of the Japan trade by Rogier Thomas van Heinigen, the Accountant General at Batavia. The report gives data on sales profits and the costs of Japanese export commodities such as copper and camphor from 1700 to 1724, as given by Kristof Glamann.[16] But profitability improved in the next period.

1725–60: large increase in profits per unit. In this period, profits per unit showed a rapid increase due to increased demand in South Asia. In fact, as shown by Figure 2.5, the copper price in South Asia increased from 250.0 in 1725 to 285.6 in 1750, given a base price in 1595 of 100.0.[17]

Figure 2.5 Copper value measured by rate of silver in east Rajasthan, 1709–50.

Source: Irfan Habib, 'Monetary System and Price', in: Tapan Raychaudhuri and Irfan Habib (eds) *The Cambridge Economic History of India*, vol. 1, Cambridge, 1982, p. 170.

Note
This is the value index when the base price is fixed at 100 in 1595.

In 1743 the Japanese authorities issued a new restriction act, ordering the annual amount exported to be limited to 5,000 piculs. Furthermore, the delivery price at Nagasaki was raised in 1750 from 12.35 to 18.00 taels.[18] This, however, did not have dire consequences on the global copper trade of the VOC. The Company wanted more Japanese copper because of the increase in South Asian demand. So long as the VOC could obtain more copper, the rise in the Japanese price did not matter. The actual copper exports from Japan had been steady at around 12,000 Dutch pounds per year, although this was only around 66.7 per cent of the amount permitted to the VOC by the Trade Act of 1715.

Another issue in this period was delivery to the Indonesian Archipelago, China and Cochin China (see Appendix). Delivery to Persia and Mocha were made only until the early eighteenth century. After the suspension of exports to the Middle East, the VOC began to deal with the Indonesian Archipelago, particularly with Semarang on the northern coast of Java Island, and also Canton and Cochin China although the volumes were not as great as subsequently.

At this time, Gustaaf Willem van Imhoff, the Governor General at Batavia, reported on the Japan trade to the Council of the Indies at the High Government. He proposed a plan of reform for the Japan trade and negotiated with the Japanese authorities to continue the copper trade from Japan. He described Japanese copper as 'the bride, around whom the Company was dancing (*dat is de bruyd, waarom wij dansen*)'.[19] The VOC was very pleased with the increase in the price of copper in South Asia and the profits from the Japanese copper trade. However, they were wary of possible competitors who might bring copper from other sources into South Asia, a concern realised in the next period.

1760–90: decrease in profits per unit. Declining profits per unit in the Japanese copper trade marked the close of the eighteenth century. Figure 2.4 shows a gradual fall in profits per unit from the South Asian trade of the VOC. This was a result of competition with the English East India Company and British private traders. As pointed out by Holden Furber, the large inflow of European copper brought by the English East India Company lowered the price of copper in South Asian markets and lessened the profit per unit of the VOC.[20] This was despite the view that Japanese copper was preferred to European copper in South Asia.[21] The success of European copper was helped by the political influence that the British achieved in India. After the battle of Plassey in 1757 British private traders engaged vigorously in the Indian coastal trade bringing European copper. But, Dutch factories in South Asia sold less Japanese copper than in the previous period as a whole.

Another point is the increase in the reshipment of Japanese copper from Batavia to China and the Indonesian Archipelago. Although the share of these reshipments from Batavia was less than 20 per cent of the VOC total, the amounts themselves increased. The VOC reshipped Japanese copper to Canton in response to the copper shortage in Cantonese market and to allow ships for the Chinese trade to have a balance in terms of cargo weight. This was why the copper trade with China did not occur on a yearly basis. On the other hand, Semarang on Java Island was the leading Dutch factory in the Indonesian Archipelago for Japanese copper sent from Batavia. Batavia also consumed copper itself during the period. (Batavia's consumption levels are excluded in Appendix.) Dutch copper coins, *duit*, were imported from the Netherlands for circulation on the island of Java even in pre-colonial days.[22] However, there were times when the High Government manufactured copper coins when facing a shortage of small denomination currency, as when they produced emergency copper coins in 1662–63.[23] These deliveries were to make profits in the Japanese copper trade rather than just to sell in South Asia alone. But for Asian countries, competition for Japanese copper was more crucial.

Japan's industrious revolution

To close, the effect of the restriction of copper exports by the Japanese authorities will be analysed with special reference to the so-called *industrious revolution* in eighteenth-century Japan.

Japan had two reasons for implementing a restrictive policy. One was a response to the decrease in copper production. The other was to secure sufficient copper for Japanese small denomination currency. Figure 2.6 shows the rice price trend at Osaka, in units of small denomination copper currency. In the early modern period, Osaka was the main distribution centre for commodities in Japan. The data for this figure are obtained by transferring the silver price data to the copper price data, and using the exchange rate at Osaka, because rice prices there were usually calculated in silver. The copper coin price increased modestly throughout the eighteenth century. This moderate upward long-term trend suggests that economic development has taken place, because the people spent money for consumption and investment, rather than hoarding it. One other point is worth noting. Previous research has indicated that the price trend in Japan was downward during the eighteenth century, but these findings were based on the silver price.[24]

Meanwhile, Akira Hayami claims a Japanese *industrious revolution*, a revolution in the method of production, took place in the eighteenth century. He argues that

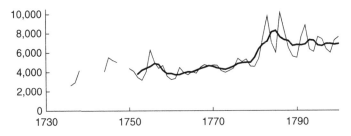

Figure 2.6 Rice price at Osaka (copper currency) 1733–1800 annual amount and five year's moving average (Kans).

Source: Silver-cash-based rice price: Masaru Iwahashi *Kinsei Nihon no Bukkashi Kenkyū* (*A Study on the Price History in Early Modern Japan*), Tokyo, 1981, pp. 274–6; Exchange rate: Hiroshi Shinbo, *Kinsei no Bukka to Keizai Hatten* (*Price and Economic Development in the Early Modern Period*), Tokyo, 1978, pp. 711–13.

Japan became an 'economic society' of small-scale family units with well-developed commerce and urban networks as early as the eighteenth century. Japan had highly developed small-scale, labour-intensive agricultural and manufacturing production units. Thus in Tokugawa society, Japan was preparing quietly for the industrialisation of the late nineteenth century. This growth-path of the Japanese economy can be called an *industrious revolution*, in contrast to the capital-intensive industrial revolution in the West.[25]

Observation of the rice price at Osaka supports the thesis of a Japanese *industrious revolution*. Japanese price trends based on copper currency were different from those based on silver currency. As copper currency began to circulate among ordinary people, they had contact with the moderate upward surge of the economy. The economy stimulated consumption and investment and facilitated economic development during the eighteenth century when the Japanese *industrious revolution* was happening. The ample supply of copper currency in eighteenth-century Japan was only possible because of the restriction on Japanese copper exports.

Conclusion

This chapter examines the Japanese copper trade of the VOC in the seventeenth and eighteenth centuries. The results can be summarised as follows:

From the mid-eighteenth century, Japan began exporting large amounts of copper. Japan was the only country in Asia that could supply such large amounts of copper at this time. Asia as a whole was the main recipient of Japanese copper. It was exported by VOC vessels and Chinese junks from Nagasaki, as well as by Japanese ships from Tsushima Island. The VOC carried Japanese copper to South Asia and Europe, while Chinese merchants delivered it to the Chinese mainland and South Asia, and Japanese ships took it to Korea by way of Tsushima. The copper was used in Asia to manufacture copper coins. This was essential, as copper currency was widely used by ordinary people across Asia, and its supply was needed for each Asian country to achieve economic development. So, early modern intra-Asian trade, strongly driven by the Japanese copper, brought economic development. Hence this period can be characterised as the golden age of Japanese copper.

The situation changed in the eighteenth century, when Japan began restricting exports of copper due to a decline in the volume of Japanese copper production, and the growing domestic demand for copper coins. Although this assisted the economic development of early modern Japan, known as the *industrious revolution*, the result was that other Asian countries faced a shortage of copper and for small denomination coins. So they had to find other materials for coins. If they failed to do so, they faced economic decline. Inter-Asian competition for Japanese copper began in the eighteenth century, but in the latter half of the eighteenth century, the English East India Company began bringing large amounts of European copper to South Asia, while competing with Japanese copper. This inflow marks the arrival of the *Pax Britannica* in Asia.

Appendix Table 2A.1 Quantities of Japanese copper reshipped from Malacca and Batavia, 1700–85

Period	Bengal	Ceylon	Coromandel	Malabar	Gujarat	Persia	Mocha	Indonesian Archipelago	Cochin-China	Canton	Sub total	Europe	Total
1700/01–1704/05 (4)	322,163	343,728	657,363	129,438	431,156	21,875	—	61	—	—	1,905,783	162,031	2,067,814
1705/06–1709/10 (3)	203,333	197,083	524,167	12,500	335,547	—	83,333	—	—	—	1,355,963	463,542	1,819,505
1710/11–1714/15 (5)	308,608	240,508	105,392	35,540	437,833	5,000	36,500	—	—	—	1,169,381	61,059	1,230,441
1715/16–1719/20 (2)	381,000	132,500	418,750	65,000	125,000	12,500	60,000	—	—	—	1,194,750	150,000	1,344,750
1720/21–1724/25 (5)	250,100	205,000	250,000	167,500	141,250	575	26,000	—	—	—	1,040,425	160,250	1,200,675
1725/26–1729/30 (5)	260,000	207,500	526,525	15,700	101,122	—	—	630	—	—	1,111,477	—	1,111,477
1730/31–1734/35 (5)	240,000	160,000	417,600	67,500	58,750	—	5,000	5,155	—	—	954,005	142,500	1,096,505
1735/36–1739/40 (4)	178,750	217,500	650,000	31,250	107,500	—	—	6,656	—	—	1,191,656	57,625	1,249,281
1740/41–1744/45 (3)	211,667	66,667	672,917	33,333	116,667	—	—	1,233	—	—	1,102,484	—	1,102,484
1745/46–1749/50 (2)	135,000	45,000	723,000	70,226	30,000	—	—	2,000	—	13,750	1,018,976	—	1,018,976
1750/51–1754/55 (3)	147,427	126,667	667,002	77,955	235,316	—	—	20,583	33,333	—	1,308,283	—	1,308,283
1755/56–1759/60 (4)	262,500	43,750	407,688	69,500	254,844	—	—	16,875	—	—	1,055,157	—	1,055,157
1760/61–1764/65 (5)	120,000	36,000	597,000	140,000	370,000	—	—	12,500	—	51,250	1,326,750	—	1,326,750
1765/66–1769/70 (5)	275,354	39,000	430,000	68,000	137,725	—	—	22,500	—	90,000	1,062,579	—	1,062,579
1770/71–1774/75 (5)	184,990	109,000	370,000	149,300	119,000	—	—	30,000	—	—	962,290	—	962,290
1775/76–1779/80 (5)	300,000	70,000	280,000	134,000	210,000	—	—	45,000	—	—	1,039,000	—	1,039,000
1780/81–1784/85 (5)	70,000	160,000	145,000	182,525	30,000	—	—	65,625	—	100,000	753,150	—	753,150

Source: BGB, NA: OBP, VOC, NA.

Note
The numbers in parentheses present the amount of available records.

Notes

* The research for this chapter was funded by the Toyota Foundation and the Daiwa Bank Foundation for Asia and Oceania together with the TANAP Project ('Towards a New Age of Partnership: A Dutch–Asian–South African Historical Research Project'), which is carried out by Dutch institutions including Leiden University and the National Archives of the Netherlands.

1 Andre Gunder Frank, *ReOrient: Global Economy in the Asian Age*, Berkeley, CA and London: University California Press, 1998.

2 Akira Hayami, 'Japan in the Eighteenth Century: Demography and Economy', in: Leonard Blussé and Femme Gaastra (eds) *On the Eighteenth Century as a Category of Asian History: Van Leur in Retrospect*, Aldershot and Brookfield: Ashgate, 1998.

3 For example, Anthony Reid (ed.) *Southeast Asia in the Early Modern Era: Trade, Power, and Belief*, Ithaca, NY and London: Cornell University Press, 1993; Blussé and Gaastra (eds) op. cit.; Frank Parlin, 'Proto-Industrialization and Pre-Colonial South Asia', *Past & Present*, 98, 1983.

4 It is important to distinguish small denomination cash such as copper coins from gold and silver currency that was used for long distance trade or for high value transactions. Examples of previous research taking this perspective are Akinobu Kuroda, *Chūka Teikoku no Kōzō to Sekai Keizai (Structure of the Chinese Empire and the World Economy)*, Nagoya: Nagoya Daigaku Shuppankai, 1994; R.J. Barendse, 'Trade and State in the Arabian Seas: A Survey from the Fifteenth to the Eighteenth Century', *Journal of World History*, 11-2, 2000.

5 Jun'nosuke Sasaki, 'Dōzan no Keiei to Gizyutsu', ('The Administration and Techniques of Copper Mines'), in: Keiji Nagahara and Keiji Yamaguchi (eds) *Kōza Nihon Gizyutsu no Shakaishi (Social History of Japanese Techniques)*, Tokyo: Nihon Hyōronsha, 1983, Vol. 5, p. 181, 1983.

6 On China, see John Hall, 'Notes on the Early Ch'ing Copper Trade with Japan', *Harvard Journal of Asiatic Studies*, 12, 1949. Regarding Korean copper coinage, see Yoohan Won, *Choseon Fugi Hwapaesa Yongu* (A Study on the Monetary History of the Latter Period of the Choson Dynasty), Seoul: Hanguk Munhwawon, 1975.

7 In Figure 2.1 the amounts of the exports to the VOC mainly relies on the work by Suzuki (Yasuko Suzuki, 'Japanese Copper Trade by the Dutch East India Company, 1646–1805', *Bulletin of the Faculty of Letters* (Hanazono University), 32, 2000). However, Suzuki's investigated only the records of the NFJ (*Het Archief van de Nederlandse Facotrij in Japan*, NA) such as journals and invoices at the Dutch factory in Japan. Thus, she could not find some years' data, which are complemented in this chapter by using the BGB as well as the OBP (*Overgekomen Brieven en Papieren*) in the VOC archives, NA.

8 Oskar Nachod, *Die Beziehungen der Niederländischen Ostindischen Kompagnie zu Japan im Siebzehnten Jahrhundert*, Leipzig: Rob. Friese Sep., 1897, pp. 316, 356.

9 Madoka Kanai, *Kinsei Nihon to Oranda (Early Modern Japan and the Netherlands)*, Tokyo: Hōsō Daigaku Kyōiku Shinkōkai, 1993, pp. 124–5.

10 Kanai, op. cit., pp. 126–9.

11 Book year in most Asian establishment of the VOC began in 1 September and ended in 31 August of the next year.

12 W.H. Moreland, *From Akbar to Aurangzeb: A Study in Indian Economic History*, London: Macmillan, 1923, pp. 62–7.

13 Kristof Glamann, 'The Dutch East India Company's Trade in Japanese Copper, 1645–1736', *Scandinavian Economic History Review*, 1, pp. 55–62, 1953.

14 Suzuki, op. cit., p. 190.

15 Glamann, op. cit., pp. 55–62.

16 VOC2039, fol. 2178r–2183r, NA; Glamann, op. cit., p. 54.

17 Irfan Habib, 'Monetary System and Price', in: Tapan Raychaudhuri and Irfan Habib (eds) *The Cambridge Economic History of India*, Vol. 1, Cambridge: Cambridge University Press, 1982, p. 170.
18 Suzuki, op. cit., p. 190.
19 J. Feenstra Kuiper, *Japan en de Buitenwereld in de 18e Eeuw,* 's-Gravenhage: Martinus Nijhoff, 1921, p. 130.
20 Holden Furber, *John Company at Work: A Study of European Expansion in India in the Late Eighteenth Century*, Cambridge, MA: Harvard University Press, 1948, p. 169; Asin Das Gupta, *Malabar in Asian Trade, 1740–1800*, Cambridge, MA: Cambridge University Press, 1967, p. 101.
21 Sinnappah Arasaratnam, *Merchants, Companies and Commerce on the Coromandel Coast, 1650–1740*, Delhi: Oxford University Press, 1986, p. 183.
22 Arent Pol, *Schepen met Geld: De Handelsmunten van de Verenigde Oostindische Compagnie, 1602–1799*, 's-Gravenhage: Sdu, 1989, pp. 42–6.
23 VOC794, pp. 175–83, NA.
24 Hiroshi Shinbo, *Kinsei Nihon no Bukkashi Kenkyū (Price and Economic Development in the Early Modern Period)*, Tokyo: Tōyō Keizai Shinpōsha, 1978, pp. 41–2.
25 Hayami, op. cit., pp. 144–5. The concept of *industrious revolution* in this paper refers to the term produced by Hayami, and was posed by him in the 1970s in Japanese (Akira Hayami, 'Keizaishakai no Seiritsu to sono Tokushitsu' (The Establishment of Economic Society and its Characteristics'), in: The Socio-Economic History Society (Japan) (ed.) *Atarashii Edo Jidaishizō wo motomete (Looking for New Perspectives of the Tokugawa Era)*, Tokyo: Tōyō Keizai Shinpōsha, 1977). His concept contrasts with the industrial revolution in the West and it is different from the concept of the industrious revolution proposed by Jan de Vries, which, in terms of De Vries, took place before the industrial revolution in the West (Jan De Vries, 'The Industrial Revolution and the Industrious Revolution', *Journal of Economic History*, 33, 1994).

3 Inter-Asian competition in the fur market in the eighteenth and nineteenth centuries

Chikashi Takahashi

Introduction

Most research about inter-Asian competition for the world market in the eighteenth and nineteenth centuries has concentrated on Japan, Korea, China and the area to the south of these countries. However, the area to the north also played a role in Asia's interaction with the world market. This chapter deals with North east Asia and the opposite shore of the Pacific in North west America, which will be referred to as the North Pacific Area. The chapter will discuss the appearance of traders from Great Britain and the United States in the North Pacific at the end of the eighteenth century and the beginning of the nineteenth century and the impact this had on Japan. Fur was the main item sought by the Westerners in this region and it was sold to China.

The fur trade in North east Asia was of ancient origin. Fur was offered as tribute to the Imperial Court of China from ethnic groups in North east Asia, and in turn Chinese silk was given as a reward. The participants in this fur trade were mainland Asians and also the people of the islands such as Sakhalin and Kuril. Furs of all kinds were sent to China, and of these sea-otter fur was the most valuable. The natural habitat of the sea-otter is the North Pacific Area, from the Kuril Islands to California.

Japan also participated in this fur trade. Some sea-otters were caught in the Kuril Islands, and furs were also carried there. Most of the furs were exported to China by way of Japan. Research into the world fur trade argues that the fur trade stimulated development in Siberia and North America.[1] But there is not much written about the Japanese fur trade, although some writers mention it as part of the trade between the Japanese and the Ainu.[2] Recently however there have been some ethnological studies which mention the fur trade. They discuss it as exchange interaction between the peoples of North east Asia, rather than trade between countries.[3] This chapter will examine the fur trade of the North Pacific Area and the fur trade of Japan.

The chapter consists of four sections. The section on the Russian fur trade deals with Russia, the section on the British and American fur trade deals with Britain and America, and the section Japanese fur trade deals with Japan. The last section on the interaction between the fur trades of major countries examines the fur trade between Japan and the others.

The Russian fur trade

In the eighteenth century, Russia expanded its activity in the North Pacific Area. After reaching Kamchatka, it advanced both to the western edge of the North American continent and south to the Kuril Islands. Trade between Russia and China took place only overland as a result of the Nerchinsk treaty of 1689 and the Kyakhta treaty of 1727.

Fur was the chief export from Russia to China during the eighteenth century. In the first half of the century, exports were mainly fur, and Russia imported in exchange silk, cotton and silver. At the middle of the century, furs still made up three-quarters of her exports, but the proportion of furs began to decline, and re-exports of foreign made woollen began to take their place. What is more, the kinds of furs changed over the century. To begin with, fox, squirrel, sable and stoat fur were exported, but later sheepskin and sea-otter fur replaced them. As for wild animal fur, sea-otter became the most important (16.7 per cent in the average from 1768 to 1785 in value).[4] From the 1720s Russia advanced her activities into the North Pacific, which was the natural habitat of the sea-otter. In consequence, sea-otter fur became part of the trade between Russia and China.

At the beginning of the nineteenth century, Russian exports of sea-otter fur to China decreased. In a document about Kyakhta in the 1820s, there is this description;

> The exports from Russia are in general furs, i.e. foxes, sables, river and sea-otters, wild cats, beavers, and millions of squirrels. The lightness, warmth, durability, and cheapness of the latter, have made them a favourite with the Chinese; and it is remarkable that the most rare and valuable furs do not fetch a good price with the Chinese, as they prefer the worst and most common. The best and most valuable are sold at Moscow and Nishney Novgorod for the use of the Russians, Turks, and Persians.[5]

So the pre-eminence of sea-otter fur in the trade between Russia and China changed because it was too expensive. Valuable furs were exported to countries other than China at the beginning of the nineteenth century. China traded with Russia only over land, but Russia wanted to trade by sea. A rare exception to the principle of land trade was Captain Krusenstern, who traded in Canton in 1805. He made harbour at Canton on his way back to Russia after negotiations with Japan, and requested the right to dock at Canton.[6] Whilst in Canton he indulged in trade but he did not sell the most expensive sea-otter furs there because he could get a better price in Moscow.[7] China was clearly not a good market for the best sea-otter furs, and when he traded, the fur price in Canton dropped. He noted that American ships were coming every month with furs from the Pacific coast of North America.[8] So the opening of Canton to trade by sea caused prices to fall.

The British and American fur trade

Fur export to China by Great Britain and the United States grew rapidly at the end of the eighteenth century. The British began the fur trade to China later than

Russia. It was Cook's expeditionary party that started the fur boom with the British. During the third sailing in 1776–80, they obtained sea-otter furs in the North Pacific and exchanged them for large quantities of silk and cotton at Canton. So the British realized that sea-otter furs could be sold for high prices in China, and many British ships headed there.[9] On the way back from his audience with Emperor Ch'ien-lung in 1793, the British envoy Macartney saw a shop in Hangchow stocked with furs. He reported that most of them were probably brought to Canton by British ships.[10] Although the British fur trade with China expanded rapidly, it did not last long, because the British East India Company banned British maritime traders from selling Chinese goods at home. So in 1803, British ships disappeared from the North Pacific trade to China.[11]

American ships took over the fur trade from British ships. Table 3.1 and Table 3.2 show the fur trade with China by American ships in the first half of nineteenth century. Table 3.1 shows the quantity of imported furs from 1804. At the beginning of the nineteenth century, more than 10,000 sea-otter furs and more than 100,000 seal skins were imported by China nearly every year. Table 3.2

Table 3.1 The number of furs imported into China by the Americans

Years	Sea-otter	Seal	Nutria	Beaver	Rabbit	Fox	Land-otter
1804/05	11,003	183,173	67,200	8,756			
1805/06	17,445	140,297		34,464	3,400		
1806/07	14,251	261,330		2,368			
1807/08	16,627	100,000		11,750		2,009	
1808/09	7,944	34,000		5,170			3,400
1809/10	11,003			20,000		3,500	15,000
1810/11	9,200	45,000	4,800	14,200		4,500	15,000
1811/12	11,593	173,886	145,000	20,000			12,000
1812/13	8,222	109,189	1,200	2,330	4,736		2,000
1813/14– 1814/15	6,200	59,000		3,928		284	7,045
1815/16	4,300	109,000		168		12,553	14,364
1816/17	3,650	27,000	17,000	1,579		9,952	5,467
1817/18	4,177	47,290		15,067	300	350	9,400
1818/19	7,327	88,240		15,570	15,042	3,020	9,885
1819/20	3,902	19,520		14,677		8,031	10,678
1820/21	5,540	15,229			2,374	8,895	6,017
1821/22	3,507	111,924		17,778		17,084	9,716
1822/23	2,953	11,380	1,294	21,451	6,126	20,410	16,318
1823/24	3,547	12,909	117,684	4,588	100	17,986	10,855
1824/25	1,921	52,043		2,532	6,267	19,479	18,552
1825/26	2,550	32,521		4,886	1,010	10,108	14,883
1826/27	1,926	36,822		4,950		12,852	14,525
1829/30	700	11,902				19,683	12,884
1830/31	329	6,022				5,263	6,454
1831/32	1,591	71		1,828		9,367	11,722

Sources: BPP (1829) p. 195, (1833) p. 244.

Table 3.2 Importation of skin into Canton,
by American ships, 1804–18

	Number	Dollars
Sea-otter	133,385	4,001,550
Seal	1,371,232	2,056,848
Nutria	195,000	390,000
Beaver	149,389	746,945
Rabbit	22,336	16,613
Fox	25,752	51,504
Land-otter	101,462	507,310
Total		7,770,770

Source: BPP (1821) p. 416.

shows the amount and value of seven kinds of imported furs (sea-otters, seals, nutrias, beavers, rabbits, foxes and land-otters) during the period 1804–18. The value was 7,770,770 Mexican dollars, of which sea-otter furs accounted for 4,001,550 Dollars or more than half.[12]

The trade to China by sea was more profitable than that over land. According to Krusenstern, it took the Russians two years to carry furs overland from the North Pacific Area to Kyakhta where trade with China was permitted. But in 1805, he sailed from Petropavlovsk in Kamchatka on 9 October and he arrived at Macao on 20 November.[13] As imports by sea increased, the fur price at Canton fell. Before Great Britain and the United States began to send furs by sea, the price of sea-otter fur in China was determined by furs brought overland from Russia. When the trade began by sea, the situation completely changed. Chinese fur merchants were able to buy the same furs at much lower prices than at Kyakhta.[14] Cook's party described the trade of sea-otter furs in Canton in 1779, as follows: 'One of our seamen sold his stock alone for eight hundred dollars; and a few prime skins, which were clean and had been well preserved, were sold for one hundred and twenty each.'[15] In 1805, Krusenstern wrote about the trade in Canton as follows: 'But the most valuable sea otter skins were reshipped, each of them being worth two and three hundred roubles a piece at Moscow, while the highest price of them here was only twenty piasters.'[16] Although these two accounts use different currency units, the dollar and the piaster, they actually had the same value, and it can be seen that the price at Canton had fallen substantially.

The Japanese fur trade

The leading item in the British and American fur trade to China was sea-otter fur. They had an advantage over Russia because they could carry fur by sea. But the first to deliver fur to China by sea was Japan. As early as 1483 it was noted that sea-otter fur was a profitable export to China.[17] And, at the beginning of the seventeenth century, there was an expression in Japanese, 'someone as smooth as sea-otter fur' meaning an opportunist or someone far too 'smooth'.[18] So, the quality of sea-otter fur was known widely.

At the beginning of the eighteenth century, sea-otters appeared in an encyclopedia named *Wakansannsaizue*, which said furs were exported to China via Nagasaki, and the Chinese were eager to buy them.[19] In those days, China only imported a few sea-otter furs from Russia, and those from Japan were of greater importance. There is a record of the Nagasaki trade written in 1780, which says that sea-otter furs were exported to China in place of 15 kg of silver.[20] So sea-otter fur was an ancient export from Japan to China.

Although the Japanese had sea-otter fur, sea-otters did not live in Japan. To get sea-otter furs, the Japanese had to trade with the Ainu who lived in Ezochi. The Ainu hunted sea-otters on Ulup Island where the animals lived, or obtained them by trading with the people of the northern islands. During the eighteenth century, products from Ezochi gradually increased in Japan, and Japanese merchants started to obtain a great deal of manure there which was used to grow rice, cotton, indigo and many other crops in western Japan. International relations with Ezochi also changed at this time. In the second half of the century, the Russians expanded their activities south of the Kamchatka peninsula and the Kuril Islands and established contact with the Ainu. They also began to go to Ulup Island to hunt sea-otters. However, it was difficult for the Russians to obtain food and provisions, and to solve this problem, Russia hoped to obtain supplies from Japan. So control of Ezochi and Kuril Islands became an important political objective for the Tokugawa government.

The importance of Ezochi increased economically and politically. At the turn of the century, the price of sea-otter furs fell in the trade between Japan and the Ainu. Table 3.3 shows prices in the trade in eastern Ezochi (the area farthest from Japan) in 1786, and in 1809 and 1813. It shows the prices of four articles, fish oil, knitted tree fibre cloth, seal skin and sea-otter fur, goods typical to the trade. Fish oil was greatly in demand in Japan, and tree fibre cloth was part of the traditional life of the Ainu. Sealskin was cheap fur, and sea-otter fur expensive fur. Of these four articles, only sea-otter fur fell in price, and the others were stable or rose in price. The Japanese government wanted to bring the Ainu under their control, and not allow them to fall under Russia control. To maintain their domination over Ezochi, the government needed to make the trade favourable to the Ainu, so they

Table 3.3 Prices at the eastern Ezochi, in the later eighteenth century and early nineteenth century

1786	Year	1809 or 1813
68.5	Fish oil (1.8 litre)	67
48	Cloths of tree fiber (1 sheet)	224
72	Seal skin (1 sheet)	448
37,294	Sea-otter skin (1 sheet)	22,400

Sources: Mogami (1979) pp. 27–30; Aarai (1991) pp. 172–3, Kaga (1989) pp. 368–71.

Note
Currency unit: mon.

would maintain their relations with Japan and break with Russia. What happened to the prices of the above items met this aim except that of sea-otter fur. So, why did the price of sea- otter fur fall? We know Japan imported sea-otter furs from the Ainu and exported them to China, and the cause of the fall in prices was not due to trade with the Ainu. It lay instead in the trade with China. There is a note about sea-otter fur written in 1805, which says the Chinese preferred land-otter fur to sea-otter fur, so land-otter fur had recently been sent to Nagasaki.[21] It was probably a misunderstanding that the Chinese preferred land-otter fur because we know of the record by Krusenstern and the interaction in Table 3.2 referred to in the previous section. It probably means that the Chinese were not as keen as before in buying Japanese sea-otter fur. So the fall in the price of sea-otter fur in China caused prices to decline in the trade between Japan and the Ainu.

The interaction between the fur trades of the major countries

The previous section has shown that the Japanese fur trade was influenced by the fur trade of Russia, Great Britain and the United States. But what did Japan think of the fur trade of these countries, and what did they in turn think of the Japanese fur trade?

Japan was well aware of the Russian fur trade. Mogami Tokunai, a member of the first team to study Ezochi for the Tokugawa government in 1785, wrote

> The Kuril Islands belong to Japan. Sea-otter fur is the best product of Ezochi. It has been sent to Nagasaki to be sold to Chinese ships since the old days. However, in recent years, the Russians have come to collect sea-otter furs and sell them to Beijing as a Russian product. This is a shame and a serious problem for Japan.[22]

So Mogami reveals that Russians exports to China were thought to be a serious problem. Aizawa Seishisai was an observer in Mito and knew of Mogami's report. He said that, because sea-otter fur was specifically a Japanese product, the fact that the Russians were exporting it to China showed Japan had lost control of the Kuril Islands.[23] The background to this opinion was the fact that the specific area under Japanese control was not clearly defined in those days. Some of those in charge of the Ezochi policy of the Tokugawa government thought that Kamchatka was within the Japanese sphere of influence.[24] But now because of the Russian fur trade, sea-otter furs clearly had an important political significance.

Other countries did not ignore the Japanese fur trade. In a piece about the North Pacific Area in 1788 written by Britisher, John Mears, there is a description of the sea-otter; 'It is however said in China, that the skins of this animal taken in the Corean and Japan seas, are superior to those of Russia or the North Western Coast of America.'[25] Sea-otters are not actually found around Korea, but only in the Kuril Islands near Japan, and sea-otter furs were exported from Japan to China through Korea. According to a record of the Lord of Tsushima, sea-otter furs were included in the exports to Korea.[26] Sea-otter furs exported to China via Japan from the Kuril Islands were highly regarded in China. Merchants in the British fur trade between the North Pacific and China knew of the Japanese fur trade and thought of Japan as a market for their fur.[27] Russia also hoped to export furs to Japan. The pattern of trade with Japan as envisaged by Russia was that Russia would provide supplies to sustain its activities in the North Pacific Area, and fur would be obtained as a result, with Japan as one of the markets for their fur.

The Japanese were well aware of the Russian fur trade. The fur traders of Russia, Great Britain and the United States thought of Japan both as a supplier and as a market. In those days, Japan had little foreign trade and no direct trade with these countries. But she was nonetheless connected with them through the fur trade.

Notes

1 Innis (1930); Shimoyama (1993, 1994, 1995, 1996, 1997).
2 Kojima (1994); Kawakami (1997).
3 Sasaki (1996); Kishigami (2001).
4 Yoshida (1963) pp. 43–50.
5 Cochrane (1825) p. 169.
6 Yoshida (1963) p. 50.
7 Krusenstern (1973) Vol. 2, p. 290.
8 Ibid., Vol. 2, pp. 330–1.
9 Gibson (1988) p. 379.
10 Cranmer-Byng (1962) p. 179.
11 Gibson (1988) p. 380.
12 BPP (1821) p. 416.
13 Krusenstern (1973) Vol. 2, pp. 257–77.
14 Mears (1967) p. lxxxiv.
15 Barrow (1941) p. 470.
16 Krusenstern (1973) Vol. 2, p. 290.
17 Tsuzi (1933) p. 491.
18 Kojima (1994) p. 75.
19 Terashima (1980) p. 545.
20 Nagasaki Prefecture (1965) p. 85.
21 Tounei (1969) p. 40.
22 Mogami (1969) pp. 466–7.
23 Kurihara (1993) p. 128.
24 Habuto (1803).
25 Mears (1967) pp. 243–4.
26 Tashiro (1981) p. 262.
27 Mears (1967) p. lxxxiv.

References

English

British Parliamentary Papers (BPP) (1821) (476) VII. 'Reports by the Lords select committee appointed to inquire into the means of extending and securing the foreign trade of the country', *Area Studies, China 36*, pp. 9–428. Shannon: Irish University Press.

British Parliamentary Papers (BPP) (1829) (285) XXIII 'Papers respecting the trade with India and China, etc', *Area Studies, China 40*, pp. 153–224. Shannon: Irish University Press.

—— (1833) (229) XXV. 'Papers respecting the East India and China trade', *Area Studies, China 40*, pp. 235–268. Shannon: Irish University Press.

Barrow, J. (ed.) (1941) *Captain Cook's Voyages of Discovery*. London: Dent, New York: EP. Dutton.

Cochrane, J. D. (1825) *Narrative of a Pedestrian Journey through Russia and Siberian Tartary, from the Frontiers of China to the Frozen Sea and Kamtchatka* London: S. Bentley and R. Bentley.

Cranmer-Byng, J. L. (ed.) (1962) *An Embassy to China: Being the Journal kept by Lord Macartney during his Embassy to the Emperor Ch'ien-lung, 1793–1794.* London: Longmans.

Gibson, J. A. (1988) 'The maritime trade of the North Pacific coast'. In W.E. Washburn (ed.) *History of Indian–White Relations (Handbook of North American Indians Vol. 4)*, pp. 375–90. Washington, DC: Smithsonian Institution Press.

Innis, Harold Adams (1930) *The Fur Trade in Canada*. New Haven, CT: Yale University Press.

Krusensutern (1973) *Voyage Round the World, in the Years 1803, 1804, 1805, & 1806, by Order of His Imperial Majesty Alexander the First, on Board the Ships Nadeshda and Neva, Under the Command of Captain A. J. von Krusenstern, of the Imperial Navy.* Japan: Tenri University Press.

Mears, John (1967) *Voyages Made in the Years 1788 and 1789, from China to the North West Coast of America*. New York: Da Capo Press.

Japanese

Habuto, Masayasu (1803) Hensakushiben (『辺策私弁』) Unpublished).

Kawakami, Jun (1997) 'Trade of Rasshua Island Ainu in Bunka period, the iron pot and the sea otter fur'. *The Memoirs of the Preparative Office of Nemuro Municipal Museum 11*, pp. 77–93.

Kishigami, Nobuhiro (2001) 'Indigenous trade of resources in the northern regions of North America: with a special focus on the fur trade and its impacts on aboriginal societies'. *Bulletin of National Museum of Ethnology 25(3)*, pp. 293–354.

Kojima, Kyoko (1994) 'Rakkokawato Ezonisikino Michi'. ('Road of Sea-Otter Akin and Ezonishiki'.) In Akira, Yoshida (ed.) *Rekishinomichi Saihakkenn* (Rediscovery of Historical Road) Vol. 1 (「ラッコ皮と蝦夷錦の道」『歴史の道・再発見　第1巻』) pp. 71–99. Osaka: Forum A.

Kurihara Shigeyuki (1993) 'Chishima-ibun strange tales of Chishima (reproduction)'. *Journal of Atomi Gakuen Women's University 26*, pp. 105–141.

—— (1969) 'Ezokokuninnjouhuuzokunokoto'. In Takakura, Shinichirou (ed.) *Nihon Syominn Seikatsu Shiryou Syuusei* (Historical Records of Japanese Common People's Life) *Vol. 4* (「蝦夷国人情風俗之沙汰」『日本庶民生活史料集成　第四巻』) pp. 439–84. Tokyo: San'ichishobo.

Mogami Tukunai (1979) 'Ezozoushi Beturoku'. In Matsumae Town (ed.) Matsumaechoushi Siryouhenn (History of Matsumae Town, Historical Records) vol. 3, (「蝦夷草紙　別録」『松前町史　史料編　第三巻』) pp. 13–40, Hakodate: Daiichiinsatsu shuppanbu.

Nagasaki Prefecture (1965) 'Nagasakikaisyogosatumono Vol. 2'. In *Nagasaki Kenshi Siryouhen* (History of Nagasaki Prefecture Historical Document) Vol. 4, (「長崎会所五冊物　二」『長崎県史　史料編　第四』). Tokyo: Yoshikawakoubunnkan.

Sasaki, Shiro (1996) *Hoppoukara Kita Kouekimin* (Traders from North: Silk and Fur with 'Santan' People) (『北方から来た交易民　絹と毛皮とサンタン人』). Tokyo: Japan Broadcast Publishing.

Shimoyama, Akira (1993, 1994, 1995, 1996, 1997) 'A study on the history of fur trade in relation to the "World Frontier" and racial slavery(1)–(5)'. In Institute for the Study of Humanities and Social Sciences, Doshisha University (ed.) *The Social Sciences. Vols. 51,52,54,57,58.*

Tashiro, Kazui (1981) *Studies on the History of the Diplomatic Relations and Trade between Japan and Korea in 17th and 18th Centuries.* Tokyo: Soubunsya.

Terashima, ryouann (1980) 'Wakannsannsaizue 1'. In Endo, Shizuo (ed.) *Nihon Syominn Seikatsu Shiryou Syuusei* (Historical Records of Japanese Common People's Life) *Vol. 28* (「和漢三才図会 1」『日本庶民生活史料集成　第二十八巻』) pp. 23–44. Tokyo: San'ichishobo.

Tounei, Gennsin (1969) 'Toukaisantan'. In Takakura, Shinichirou (ed.) *Nihon Syominn Seikatsu Shiryou Syuusei* (Historical Records of Japanese Common People's Life) *Vol. 4* (「蝦夷国人情風俗之沙汰」『日本庶民生活史料集成　第四巻』). Tokyo: San'ichishobo.

Tsuzi, Zennnosuke(ed.) (1933) *Daijoin Jisha Zojiki. Vol. 7* (『大乗院寺社雑事記　第七巻』) Tokyo: Sankyo Shoin.

Yoshida, Kinichi (1963) 'Trade between Russia and Chin China'. *The Toyo Gakuho 45(4)*, pp. 39–86.

4 The Japanese acquisition of maritime technology from the United Kingdom

Masami Kita

In the middle of the nineteenth century, American wooden sailing ships were very active in the Asia-Pacific area and virtually dominated trade in the Yantze (Haviland, 1958). Britain was then at war with both India and China. British ships were also made of wood so it was difficult for them to make the long voyage to the Far East. The invention of the iron steamship and the screw propeller led to the end of the wooden sailing ship. In 1854, the British navy held a trial to compare the efficiency of the paddle wheel and the screw propeller. The screw won (Cucari and Angelucci, 1975).

There were opportunities for Scottish business men in the Asian market as it opened up. Due to the rapid progress and expansion of the Scottish iron industry, Glasgow became the centre of world pig-iron production. This was the result of J.B. Neilson's hot blast smelting method. The West of Scotland was the heart of British heavy industry. At that time Britain was the workshop of the world (Moss and Hume, 1977).

From the middle of the nineteenth century, when the monopoly of the British East India Company was abolished and the Opium War was over, many business opportunities arose in Asia and Scottish merchants flocked to take advantage of the new openings from India to the Far East (Kita, 1998). Trade across the Atlantic region was controlled by merchants from Liverpool, Bristol and elsewhere in England, so Asia was a lucrative new market Scottish traders could explore to their advantage. They could benefit from the progress of Scottish iron smelting, railway engineering and shipbuilding and the most recent technological developments made at Anderson College, Glasgow, and Glasgow and Edinburgh universities (Moss and Hume, 1979).

By the late nineteenth century, Japan under the Tokugawa regime had followed a policy of 'Sakoku' for over two centuries, closing itself to all foreign trade except that of the Dutch and Chinese at the port of Dejima in Nagasaki (Umemura and Yamamoto, 1989). But Western powers gradually and increasingly sought to open trade. In June 1853, Commander M.C. Perry of America came to Uraga with five ships to ask the Japanese government to open their ports. The following month, Commander Putiatin Efim V. of Russia's Far East fleet came to Nagasaki to ask for a treaty (Yokoi, 1988). Sir J. Stirling of the British East India Company fleet also sought a treaty in October 1854 (Miyanaga, 1981).

In September 1853, recognizing the superiority of Western vessels, the Tokugawa government abolished the prohibition on building vessels over 500 *koku* (50 tons) and established the first official shipyard at Uraga. The first ship, *Hoshou-maru*, was launched the following year. Then the Tokugawa government started an iron works at Akiura, Nagasaki, a shipyard at Kamitsukuri, Nagasaki and engineering works at Yokohama and Yokosuka. They wanted to produce their own ocean-going ships but were not successful (Teratani, 1989). They established shipyards at 14 local *han* (clans) to produce their own ocean-going vessels without success. Japan lacked the necessary knowledge and experience. Under the Tokugawa government's closed-door policy, Japanese shipwrights were not permitted to make large ships for overseas trade and could only make flat-bottomed ships for carrying rice over short distances. A breakthrough came for the ship workers of Japan when the Russian vessel, *Diana*, drifted ashore at Heta on the Izu Peninsula in November 1854 and Japanese workmen were used to repair it under the supervision of a Russian naval architect. Those engineers and workers at Heta were to become the naval engineers of the Meiji government (Ishii, 1989).

The international environment around Japan

In 1859, J.B. Harris of America and Lord Elgin of the UK signed an Amicable and Trade Agreement with Japan, and the seaports of Nagasaki, Yokohama, and Hakodate were opened to foreign ships and people (Oliphant, 1860). W. Keswick of P&O rushed from Shanghai to Nagasaki to open the first trade route between Shanghai and Nagasaki and appointed T.B. Glover, an Aberdonian, to represent Jardine & Matheson at Nagasaki (Howarths and Howarths). A French Navigation Company, MI (Cie des Services Maritimes des Messageries Imperiales), came to Yokohama in 1862 and, in 1865, and sent an officer to explore the possibility of a route between Shanghai and Yokohama. The company changed its name to Cie des Messangeries Maritimes (MM) in 1873. In 1863, an American company, Pacific Mail (PM) opened a route from San Francisco to Yokohama and Hong Kong and this was extended to Shanghai (Imazu, 1989). America originally wanted to use Hakodate as a base port for the American Pacific trade. This American initiative affected the British and French Shanghai routes considerably. But fortunately for Britain and France, the American Civil War hit America's trade in the Pacific (Yamamoto, 1980; Isii and Sekiguchgi, 1982).

International factors lay behind the opening of a new phase of commerce with Asian countries in the late nineteenth century. The opening of the Suez Canal in 1869 and the completion of the trans-America railway speeded up the movement of goods and people to Asia. Consequently, two new steamship companies were established in the Far East. The formation of Hambourg American (HA) Line in 1872 and Occidental & Oriental Steam Ships (O&O) in 1875 caused fierce competition on the regular route from San Francisco to Hong Kong via Yokohama. In addition, the telegraph was introduced at that time. Both The Great Northern Telegraph via Siberia and the Great Eastern Telegraph via India were extended to the Far East (Tsunoyama, 1988). Lord Kelvin laid the cable line to America across the Atlantic in 1866. In 1871, the sea cable between Shanghai, Nagasaki and Vladivostock was laid and in 1872 the cable line between India and Australia was completed. The telegraph network began in London and ended in Tokyo, ushering in a new era of transport and communication (Hosoya and Tanaka, 2000; Herman, 2002).

The technological transition from feudal Japan to modern Japan

A Dutch doctor, Dr P.F.B. Siebold of the Dutch East India Company's Japan branch, who stayed in Japan from 1823 to 1829, made Japan aware of what was happening abroad. He also enabled Westerners to learn about Japan (Miyazaki, 1997). Under his influence, the Tokugawa government tried seriously to learn about the advanced technologies of the Western powers and asked the Netherlands to help. In 1855, the Tokugawa government set up the Nagasaki naval school using the paddle-steamer *Soembing*, presented by the Dutch government. These Japanese ratings were taught by Dutch naval officers like P. Rijicken and Huijssen Van Kattendijke. There were about 70 Japanese ratings there such as Rintaro Katsu, Tomoatsu Godai and Takeaki Enomoto who became leaders in Meiji Japan after the Restoration (Mizuta, 1974). In 1857, the ship *Kanrin-maru* together with the equipment for repairing ships was presented to the Nagasaki naval college. Engineers were also sent headed by H. Hardes. However it soon closed and the Kaigun Sourensho (navy training academy) was moved to Edo. In 1856, the Chikusho-chosho (school of learning) was established to teach Western knowledge. In 1863 it changed its name to the Kaisei school (Oukubo, 1986). In 1863, the Tokugawa government sent the *Chitose-maru* to Shanghai to begin trade there. France in collaboration with the Tokugawa government, sent engineers, led by F.L. Verny, to build the first Western lighthouse at Kannonzaki in 1869. It also sent instructors to start a new Japanese army (Brunton, 1900). After the Meiji Restoration, the new Japanese government favoured British technology and engineers. R.H. Brunton, a Scottish engineer, was the first 'Oyatoi' (foreign employee) of the new government. He was invited to Japan with E. Gilbert from the Stevenson Company of Edinburgh, where the Northern Light Commission

Table 4.1 The Oyatoi of the Meiji government (1871–98)

Year	Britain	America	France	Germany	Total numbers in Japan
1871	119	16	50	8	214
1875	277	56	98	33	527
1879	132	37	33	22	262
1883	65	16	7	21	132
1887	76	37	11	43	195
1891	63	31	10	29	155
1895	31	16	8	12	70
1898	37	14	10	22	100

Source: Umemura, N. (ed.) (1985) *Kindaika-no-suishinsha-tachi* (Leaders of Industrialisation of Modern Japan after Meiji), p. 203.

Table 4.2 Distribution of Oyatoi among governmental departments in the Meiji period (1868–1900)

	Kobu (industry)	Monbu (education)	Fuken (local gmt)	Kaigun (navy)	Naimu (interior)	Rikugun (army)	Kaitakusi (pioneer)	Okura (finance)	Daijyokan (cabinet)	Others	Total
Britain	533	86	119	118	26	2	4	38	11	77	1,034
France	90	39	27	69	2	75	1	20	59	19	401
America	13	105	94	12	15		56	13	3	35	351
Germany	24	93	38	8	43	16	5	6	1	43	279
China	46	7	17	1	5		13	1		4	95
Philippines	69			4						3	76
Dutch		12			21	5	3	2		7	51
Italy	10	2	2		1	7		2		3	27
Russia		8			1		5	1		2	16
Canada		3	7							1	11
Austria	1	2	1		1	1	1	3	4	0	11
Switzerland	1	3	4	1			1			1	10
Denmark	8	1	1								10
Portugal	1			2	1						6
Belgium		3				2		2			5
Malaya	1		4								5
Sweden	2				1						3
Korea		2									2
Spain		1									1
Norway	1										1
Finland	1										1
Mongol	1										1
Others	2		1								3
Total	825	367	315	215	117	108	88	88	83	194	2,400

Source: Umetani, N. (ed.) (1990) Kindaika no Suisinsyatachi (Promoter of Modernization of Japan), pp. 202–4; Umemura, N. (1985) Kindaika-no-suishinsha-tachi (Promoters of Industrialization of Japan), p. 218.

Note
Britain includes Australia and New Zealand; Austria includes Hungary; Portugal includes Goa and Macau.

was in charge of the lighthouses in Scotland. They were to establish a number of lighthouses in Japan. Then, Brunton asked A.R. Brown from P&O to help him complete 28 lighthouses around Japan between August 1869 and March 1870 (TOKOKAI, 1969).

Tokugawa Japan also sent young men to study abroad to gain the latest knowledge and information. In 1862, 15 young samurai (young warriors) were sent to the Netherlands for 5 years. In 1865, 6 were sent to Russia and 14 were sent to Britain. In 1867, 11 were sent to France. The Tokugawa government also sent delegations to foreign countries in several occasions. In 1860, the first delegation was sent to America to collect information. The largest group of 25 people was sent to Paris for the International Exhibition in 1867 (Yoshida, 1986). Apart from the Tokugawa government, local *han* like the Satsuma-han and Choshu-han (who dominated politics after the Meiji Restoration) sent groups of samurai to Britain. Their efforts were supported by Scottish merchants and engineers. T.B. Glover at Nagasaki was a key person in this Scottish network in Japan. So there was a very efficient and able network of diplomats, missionaries, teachers and engineers with links to the prosperity of Victorian Scotland (Kita, 1984). For example, the British Association of Advanced Sciences, set up by Scottish scholars and engineers, was central to the exchange of useful information with Japan. With respect to Western knowledge, it must be stressed that the Japanese government decided precisely what was to be studied and in which country, before sending their students overseas and employing foreign 'Oyatoi'. The Meiji government also had an effective policy of employing brilliant young employees from foreign countries on very good salaries for periods of three to five years (Kaigairyugaku-kisoku, 1981).

The Kobu-sho (Ministry of Public Work) and Kobudaigakukko (Imperial College of Engineering)

The Meiji government was advised by E. Morell, a Scottish engineer who came to Japan after working in the Indian railways. He established the Ministry of Public Works in 1870. Its purpose was to industrialize all fields of engineering, including railways, lighthouses, dockyards, harbour construction, shipyards, manufacturing plants, printing presses etc. (Umetani, 1987). At the same time, domestic businesses were reorganized to transform a feudal society to a modern industrial society. Consequently, Japan was accepted as a member of the International Post Treaty in 1877 and a member of the International Telegraph Treaty in 1879 (Umino, 1982). Under Kobu-sho (the Ministry of Public Works), five major institutes were established, Kogaku-sho (Engineering), Tetudo-sho (Railway), Kozan-sho (Mining), Denshin-sho (Telegraph), Todai-sho (Lighthouse) and Seisaku-sho (Manufacturing). A number of Oyatoi, foreign employees, (mostly British and especially Scottish) were employed (Umetani, 1990). At its height in 1875, 3,000 employees worked for the government. Together with appointments in the private sector, their number was over 5,000 in 1878–83. The largest number of Oyatoi were employed by Kobu-sho.

Table 4.3 Distribution of Oyatoi to departments among Kobu-sho (1868–1900)

	Hon-kyoku (Head office)	Kouzan-kyoku (Mining)	Tetsudo-kyoku (Railway)	Denshin-kyoku (Telegraph)	Kousaku-kyoku (Manufacturing)	Kyoiku (Education)	Todai-kyoku (Lighthouse)	Total
Britain	41	133	1,070	301	192	201	439	2,377
France		136	9		187	3		335
Philippines			2				169	169
China							122	122
Germany		52	15	4	10			81
America		7	26	2	4		6	45
Italy			6		2	24	3	35
Denmark			10	9				19
Sweden			6					6
Portugal			5					5
Finland			5					5
Swiss					3			3
Australia							2	2
Norway			2					2
Dutch		1						1
Malaya		1						1
Mongol							1	1
Others							9	9
Total	41	330	1156	316	398	228	751	3,220

Source: Toyohara, J. (1964) *Kibusho-to-Oyatoi-gaikokujin* (Ministry of Public Works and Foreign Employees), in Kobe Shodai Ronshu (Journal of Kobe Commerce College), No. 60-1, pp. 35–6.

Note

Manufacturing includes office staff and that of Tomyo-maru, Thiebold-maru and Meiji-maru.
Manufacturing includes the Dept of Maintenance; lighthouse includes the Dept of Maintenance; lighthouse includes office staff and that of Tomyo-maru, Thiebold-maru and Meiji-maru.

Table 4.4 Number of Japanese youth going overseas (1867–74)

	America	Britain	Germany	France	Russia	China	Austria	Belgium	Hong Kong	Italy	Dutch	Swiss	Total
Before													
1867		26											26
Meiji Restoration													
1868	3	6		3								1	13
(Meiji 1)													
1869	5	5	2								1		13
1870	69	55	32	25	4								187
1871	80	71	34	17	4	7		2		1			218
1872	44	18	7	15	1		1	2	2				86
1873	2	10	6				4			1			23
1874	6	3	1										10
Total (from 1868)	209	168	82	60	9	7	5	4	2	2	1	1	550

Source: Ishibu, M. (1972) *Kindai-Nippon Ryugaku-shi* (Historical Record of Japanese Youth Abroad in Modern Times), pp. 151–4.

Under the Kobu-sho project, the Kobu-daigakko (originally the Kogaku-sho) was established as the first Engineering College of Western technology. Supported by the leaders of the early Meiji period, the core group of ex-Choshu han were trained in the UK (Miyoshi, 1979). The plan for this Engineering College was drawn up by Yozo Yamao of the Choshu five who had worked at the Napier shipyard and had taken evening classes at Anderson College (currently, Strathclyde University) at Glasgow from 1866 to 1867 (Kita, 1984). This plan was successfully implemented by Henry Dyer, a Glasgow University graduate who had been a classmate of Yamao at Anderson College and who had spent nine years as the principal of the Engineering College. He was assisted by colleagues from Britain, most of whom were Scottish. Western technology was adopted successfully in Japan and increased the skills of Japanese people because even in feudal times there had been a high standard of general education (Dyer, 1890). In addition, several training schools were launched using the best technocrats, who produced skilful assistants and workers for the newly trained engineers. Two kinds of educational bodies combined to make a success of the industrial revolution in Japan.

The philosophy of engineering

Meiji Japan appreciated the advanced technology brought from Scotland and also the attitudes of the Victorian Scottish. The Scots believed that engineers should be considered equal to lawyers, medical doctors and priests (Dyer, 1909). This philosophy and conviction was held in Glasgow and carried to every corner of Britain through the mechanics institutes movement of the industrial revolution. It was thought that engineers should be social leaders and study and work throughout life (Dyer, 1883). This philosophy of commitment and diligent work was new in Meiji Japan. Previously there had been a feudal ethic based on the caste system of Shi-No-Ko-Sho, based on a social hierarchy in descending order of warrior, farmer, craftsman and merchant. This needed to be replaced with a new ethic, suitable for the new industrial society. This attitude was a characteristic of the Scottish experts and was their most valuable contribution to Meiji Japan (Kita, 1995).

Japan abandoned her old feudal ethic within 40 years, a magnificent example of the speed of Japanese national evolution. It was a major factor by which Meiji Japan became the most modernized country in Asia. The teachers for the Kobu-daigakko were recruited mainly from Glasgow University through Lord Kelvin, one of the greatest figures in the British scientific world. He linked the Scottish network of engineering colleges with the mechanics institutes movement across the country. Massachusetts Institute of Technology (MIT) in America and the Kobu-daigakko of Japan were considered the most successful of their overseas affiliations (Dyer, 1912).

The Kobu-daigakko began in Autumn 1875, made up of six departments with six-year courses in civil engineering, mechanical engineering, telegraphy, architecture, practical chemistry, mining and smelting. To begin with, naval architecture came under mechanical engineering but in 1879 became an independent subject (Obituary Notices of the Royal Society of London, 1942, 1969). Three

Table 4.5 Introduction of iron and steel technology to Japan

Foreign countries	Japan
1730 Derby & his son 　invention of coke furnace 1740 Huntsman 　invention melting pot of steel 1783 H.Cort 　puddling process at forge 1828 J.B. Neilson 　invention of hot-blast furnace	1846 Translation of *Western method of Iron* 　*smelting* written by U. Huguenin
1855 H. Bessemer 　invention of revolving furnace 1856 W. Siemens (Germany) 　invention of open hearth	1850–51, reflecting-furnace (Saga, Tikuji) 1852–54, furnace (kagoshima, Iso) 1854–55, reflecting-furnace (Izu, Nirayama) 1854–56, reflecting-furnace (Mito, Anaminato) 1857–61, furnace (Nanbu, ohashi)
Meiji Restoration	
	1871 furnace (Nakakozaka-1882) 1875 mining office at Hiroshima
1873 Deaton 　invention of forge of mixed 　iron & steel 1877 Thomas 　patent of steel making	1880 furnace (kamaishi) using 　25 tons of imported iron ore 1882 melting pot of steel (Navy arsenal) 1883 abolition of governmental business
1879 W. Siemens (Germany) 　invention of electrical open hearth 　in arch method	(Kamaishi)
1885 Mannesman 　invention of seamless steel pipe	1885 furnace of iron pig production 　(Tanaka ironwork) 　steel-making forge 　(Koishigawa ironwork)
1886 K.E. Thomson 　invention of electrical welding 1887 　America becomes the leading 　world steel producer	1890 acid open hearth (Yokosuka & Osaka 　artillery arsenal) Steel production overtakes 　that of traditional Tatara
	1896 government Yahata ironwork established 　by law 1901 Yahata steel production initiated 1901 coke furnace started at Tanaka iron work

Source: Kobayashi, M. (1977) *Kindai sangyo Gijyutsu no Dounyu* (Introduction of Modern technology to Japan), in Miyamoto, M. and the Hakagawa, K. (ed.) *Kogyoka to Kigyosya-katudou* (Entrepreneurial Activity and Industrialization of Japan), pp. 156, 163.

people contributed greatly to Japanese marine engineering education. These were Shozi Sakurai of the Naval Ministry who was from the pre-Meiji Satsuma-han and had been to University College, London. Also Shinrokuro Miyoshi, a brilliant graduate of Kobu-daigakko who had been educated at Glasgow University. Lastly, C.D. West with whom Miyoshi had worked on a wide-ranging programme of naval education for Japanese youngsters. There was a very close relationship

Table 4.6 Introduction of the technology of naval architecture to Japan

Foreign countries	Japan
1802 W. Symington construction of steamer	
1807 R. Fullton (Scottish American) invention of paddle steamer	Kimizawa-kei at Toda, Ishikawajima 1859 Akiura-maru at Akiura, Nagasaki
1837 patent of screw propeller	1862 steam warship, Chiyoda-kei at Ishikawajima
1862 production of steel merchant ship	
Meiji Restoration	
	1871 ironship, Kousan-maru at Osaka
1873 (France) production of steel warship	
1879 Parsons production of ship with steam turbine	
1884 Parsons invention of steam turbine	1884 iron warship, Atago & Takao at Yokosuka
1885 Mannesman invention of seamless steel pipe	
1886 K.E. Thomson invention of electrical welding	1887 ironship of Yugao-maru at Mitsubishi
1887 America became leading world steel producer invention of Diesel engine	1890 first steel warship, Chikughigawa-maru at Mitsubishi
1895 Curtis (America) invention of steam turbine	first steel warship of Yaeyama at Yokosuka
1895 Germany became second largest world steel producer	
	1904 arrival of Parson's turbine engine 1906 warship, Aki, with Curtis turbine 1907 arrival of Curtis's turbine engine first Japanese turbine ship, Tenyo-maru 1908 Sakura-maru with Japanese made turbine 1924 first Danish made Diesel ship in Japan

Source: Kobayashi, M. (1977) *Kindai sangyo Gijyutsu no Dounyu* (Introduction of Modern technology to Japan), in Miyamoto, M. and the Hakagawa, K. (ed.) *Kogyoka to Kigyosya-katudou* (Entrepreneurial Activity and Industrialization of Japan), pp. 156, 163.

between Glasgow University and the development of Japanese naval education. In 1883, the first chair of naval architecture at Glasgow University was offered to F. Elgar, who had been invited in 1879 for one year to advise Japanese dockyards and shipyards. His successors, Dr J. Biles and Dr Hilhouse held the chair later when they in turn came back from Japan (Kita, 1984). There were also many Scottish naval engineers who worked for shipyards in Japan. They lived the rest of

Table 4.7 The names and careers of Oyatoi from Glasgow University to Kobu-da i gakko and others

Glasgow University	Work in Japan	Career after Japan
H. Dyer 1868–72 BSc	Principal & Professor of Civil Engineering, and Mechanical Engineering of Kobu-da i gakko (Imperial College of Engineering), 1873–82	Governor of Glasgow and West of Scotland Technical College Chairperson of Glasgow School Board
W.G. Dixon 1872–75 MA	Professor of English and English Literature at ICE 1876–79	Lecturer of Theology of Almond College in Australia. Moderator of Presbyterian Church at New Zealand
T. Gray 1874–78 BSc	Professor of Telegraphy at ICE 1878–81	Engineer of the Atlantic Cable, Assistant to Lord Kelvin. Prof. of Power Engineering of Rose Poli-Technic at Indiana, USA
T. Watson 1870–74 BSc	Assistant Professor of Mechanical Engineering at ICE 1875–78	Lecturer of Civil Engineering of GWSTC, Professor of Mechanical Engineering of Poona College in India
T. Alexander 1868–72 BSc	Professor of Mechanical Engineering at ICE 1879–87	Professor of Mechanical Engineering of Trinity College at Dublin
P.A. Hillhouse 1877–88 BSc	Professor of Naval Architecture at Imperial Univ. 1888–90	Professor of Naval Architecture of Glasgow Univ.
J. Struthers 1890–94 MA	Lecturer of Agriculture and Chemistry of Tokyo Agricultural Univ. 1895–1905	Lecturer of GWSTC
J. Perry 1874–75 (Graduate of Queen's University) BE 1870	Professor of Civil and Mechanical Engineering at ICE 1874–75	Professor of Mathematics and Mechanical Engineering of ICT Chairman of English Electrical Engineers
W.E. Aryton 1870–71 (University College London graduate 1867–68)	Professor of Telegraphy at ICE 1873–78	Professor of Mechanical Engineering of Univ. College, London President of British Physics Association

Source: Calendars of Glasgow University, between 1872 and 1895, Glasgow University Archives.

Table 4.8 The names and careers of Oyatoi from Edinburgh University to Kobu-da i gakko and others

Edinburgh University	Work in Japan	Career after Japan
D.H. Marshall 1866–69 MA	Professor of Mathematics at ICE 1878–81	Honorary Professor of Physics of Queen's Univ. at Ontario, Canada
J.A. Ewing 1876–77 BSc	Professor of Mechanical Engineering of Kaisei-gakko and Imperial College 1878–83	Professor of Mechanical Engineering at Dundee Univ., and later of Cambridge Univ., Vice-Chancellors of Edinburgh Univ.
G.C. Knott MA 1867 MB 1873	Professor of Natural Philosophy of College of Science of Imperial Univ.	Professor of Applied Mathematics of Edinburgh Univ.
J.M. Dixson 1874–75 after St Andrew's graduation	Professor of English and English Literature at ICR 1880–85	Professor of English Literature of Washington Univ., and later of Southern California of America
W. Renwick MA 1870	Chief Engineer to Imperial Mint of Japan and to Ministry of Railway, Chief Engineer of Takashima coal mine, 1876–83	Not to be traced

Source: *Calendars of Edinburgh University, between 1866 and 1895*, Special Collection of Edinburgh University Library.

Table 4.9 The names and careers of Oyatoi from Imperial College of Techonology & Science (Royal College of Mines, Science and Chemistry amalgamated)

RCS, RCC	Work in Japan	Career after Japan
W. Gowland 1868–70	Chief Engineer of Mint of Japan and Adviser to Metallurgy of Army 1872–88	Chief Engineer of Boulton Mining Co., Honorary Professor of Metallurgy of Royal College of Mines
E.F. Monday 1868–71	Professor of Drawing and Metallurgy at ICE 1873–78	Professor of Science of Colleges in Calcutta and later in Dacca at Bengal
E. Divers 1852–53	Chief Engineer to Mint of Japan 1872–75	Engineer of Metallurgy at Liverpool
J. Milne 1871–72	Professor of Geology at ICE & Tokyo University	Director of Seismological Research Institute at Isle of Wight, Britain

Source: *Calendars and Matriculation of Royal Colleges of Mines, Science & Chemistry*, at the Library of Imperial College of Science & Technology.

Table 4.10 The names and careers of Oyatoi from University College, London

UCL	Work in Japan	Career after Japan
J. Conder 1871–75	Professor of Architecture at ICE and Imperial Univ. 1876–88	Lived in Japan until his death in 1920. Honorary President of Architects in Japan
R.W. Atkinson 1863–67 (RCS) 1867–72 BSc	Professor of Chemistry of Minami-ko and Science College of Tokyo Univ. 1874–81	Lecturer of Univ. College London
J.E. Manning 1868–72 BA	Medical Engineer to Governmental Hospital and Engineer to Ministries of Railway & Public Work 1877–1883	Maritime engineer to Liverpool Shipyard
P. William 1870–1874 BSc	Chief Engineer to Railway Bureau of Japan, 1876–79	Professor of Civil Engineering of Elphinston College of Bombay, India, Professor of Civil Engineering of Univ. of London

Source: *Calendars of the University College of London, between 1872 and 1876* at the University College Archives.

their lives in Japan, like C.D. West who had helped over 25 years in recruiting 111 marine engineers to the Naval and Telegraph ministries, as well as various shipyards, dockyards and shipping companies (Nippon Yusen Kabushikikaisya, 1985).

A.R. Brown and Japanese shipping and shipbuilding

When the Iwakura Mission visited Britain in Autumn 1872, A.R. Brown, who worked for R.H. Brunton of the Lighthouse Bureau, returned home briefly to guide delegation members around factories in Glasgow and Edinburgh (Kume, 1978; Tanaka and Takada, 1993; Nishikawa and Matsutomi, 1995). It must have been a major point in Brown's life, when in early 1874 he was asked by Yataro Iwasaki, the founder of Mitsubishi, to supply the ships to carry the Japanese army to Taiwan. This was in response to an incident in which Japanese sailors had drifted ashore on a wrecked ship and had been killed there. The Meiji government first asked America and Britain to provide ships but they were afraid to become involved in this international conflict and declined the request (Kita, 1984). Brown was asked by the government to gather the required number of ships for the army. Brown provided 13 steamships from Shanghai and Hong Kong for the Mitsubishi Steamer Company between May 1874 and March 1875, in collaboration with Mr Glover (Bush, 1969). In 1875, Brown returned from Scotland on the ship, *Meiji-maru*, a steamship built at the Napier shipyard in Glasgow, to survey sites for lighthouses constructed by Brunton. During this trip to Britain, he also bought some ships with his own money and sold them when he returned to Japan.

That year, Brown was asked by Hisoka Maejima (who had trained at Glasgow central post office and is known as 'the father of the Japanese post') to serve on the newly established marine bureau to regulate Japanese navigation. Later, under a new policy supported by the Minister of Interior, Shigenobu Okubo, which encouraged private shipping companies, Brown resigned from the government to join the Mitsubishi Steamer Company (Nippon Yusen Kabushikikaisya, 1936; Kobayashi, 1995). Under Brown in October 1875, Mitsubishi took over Nipponkoku Yubin Jyokisen Kaisha, bought the Yokohama and Shanghai lines from both P&M (Pacific Mail Steamship Company) and P&O (Peninsular and Oriental Navigation Company) and initiated a new line to the Ryukyu Islands. In November, he set up the Mitsubishi Mercantile Shipping Company training school which operated two training courses: a five-year course for ocean shipping and a three-year course for domestic shipping. These training courses were set up to produce marine officers, and later became the basis of the Tokyo Shosen Daigaku (Tokyo Mercantile Maritime University) (Kobayashi, 1980). In December, Mitsubishi built an ironworks at Nagasaki, half financed by the Boyd Company of Shanghai, and designed by the famous maritime architect, J.F. Calder from the Lobnitz Company of Western Scotland (Kita, 1984). In 1876, there were two incidents, the Korean Kokashima Affair in January and the Hagi Revolt in October. Brown supplied the necessary ships for the government. During the course of the year, Mitsubishi took over a P&O route from Hong Kong and Shanghai to Yokohama. At the end of the year, they opened a route to the Ogasawara Islands (Wray, 1984). In the Seinan War of 1877, Mitsubishi had the opportunity to display the company's commitment to suppress the rebellion at Kagoshima. Mitsubishi offered all its ships to the government except those on the Shanghai route. They also sent Brown to Britain in February 1878 to pick up nine more ships for the government. Brown also helped frame the regulations for almost all Japanese ships when Takashi Masuda launched the Mitsui Maritime Insurance Company in August 1879 (Nippon Keieishi Kenkyusho, 1979).

Then came two incidents which affected the political environment and the business of Mitsubishi. The Minister of the Interior, Okubo, was assassinated in May 1878 and in October 1881, the Minister of Finance, Shigenobu Okuma, resigned from the political decision-making group. As a result, the influence of Iwasaki was drastically reduced. Mitsubishi's opponents set up a new shipping company named Kyodo-unyu Kaisha under Rear Admiral Mankichi Ito, and this affected Mitsubishi's dominance (Fukumoto, 1981). A fierce competition took place between the two companies. Apart from these events, in 1881, E.H. Hunter, who worked for the Scottish firm Kilby House in Kobe, set up the Osaka Ironworks jointly with Saburohyoue Uchida, and, in May 1884, the shipping company, Osaka-shosen Kaisha, was established (Inoue, 1990). Several other local shipping companies were set up about this time. Interestingly, when Ito went to Britain to buy ships, Brown, who was supposed to be working for his rival Mitsubishi, also visited Britain and helped him procure the necessary 16 ships for Kyodo-unyu. Brown also bought 8 ships for himself and sold them to Mitsubishi on his return (Nippon Keieishi Kenkyusho, 1988). In July 1885, the Meiji government recommended that the two companies be amalgamated before there

Table 4.11 Japanese students at Glasgow University (1880–1915)

Year	No. of students
1880–81	4
1881–82	1
1882–83	3
1883–84	0
1884–85	1
1885–86	1
1886–87	1
1887–88	1
1888–89	4 (2)
1889–90	4 (1)
1890–91	2 (1)
1891–92	2 (1)
1892–93	1 (1)
1893–94	2 (1)
1894–95	1 (3)
1895–96	1 (2)
1896–97	2 (2)
1897–98	4 (3)
1898–99	5 (3)
1899–1900	5 (2)
1900–01	7 (1)
1901–02	6
1902–03	4 (1)
1903–04	4 (1)
1904–05	1 (1)
1905–06	2 (1)
1906–07	1 (2)
1907–08	3 (1)
1908–09	5 (1)
1909–10	1 (1)
1910–11	0 (2)
1911–12	1 (1)
1912–13	2
1913–14	1
1914–15	1
Total	84 (35)

Source: *Matriculation cards from 1880 to 1915* at Glasgow University (GU) Archives.

Notes
1 ( ) means extra (Summer) or special (single) matriculation card.
2 Before 1880, Y. Yamao was at Anderson College, N. Taniguchi and R. Matsuda at GU for two years 1876–78, and K. Kawada, for one year at GU 1878–79.

Table 4.12 The names of Japanese recipients of degrees from Glasgow University

Year	Recipient
1878	Reisaku Matsuda, Bachelor of Science & Certificate in Engineering Science
	Naosada Taniguchi, BSc and CE
1886	Kaichi Watanabe, BSc and CE
1893	Buyata Iwasa, CE
	Richard (Ryotaro) Hirano Hunter BSc and CE
	(Scottish Japanese born at Kobe, later naturalized to be Japanese)
1895	Nagakata Yamamoto, BSc
	(Recipient of Glasgow University honorary doctorate in 1910)
1902	Koji Sato, BSc
1904	Sanpachi Fukuzawa, BSc
1905	Tomochika Iwane, BSc
1909	Shigeya Kondo, BSc
1913	Edward Hunter, BSc
	(Ryotaro's younger brother, and later to be British)
1916	Taizo Shozo, BSc
	Yoshinobu Kakura

Source: *Calendars of Glasgow University, between 1878 and 1918* at Glasgow University Archives.

was a commercial disaster. In September, both Mitsubishi with 29 steamers and 1 sailing ship and Kyodo-unyu with 29 steamers and 10 sailing ships were amalgamated as Nippon Yusen Kaisya (NYK) (Nippon Yusen Kabushikikaisya, 1956). A.R. Brown was appointed a director. In February 1886, NYK opened a route to Tengchung from Nagasaki and extended it to Kobe. In May, NYK agreed to do freight business with P&M and O&O (Occidental and Oriental Steamship Company), collaborating in carrying cargoes to their final destination. Early in 1887, NYK dispatched Brown to Glasgow to order six ships and he was accompanied by Japanese engineers who came to observe the process of ordering ships under construction. In April, Asano Kaisobu was formed, and in August Osaka-shosen was declared eligible to receive government aid. Osaka-shosen invited a marine engineer, J.G. Reid, from Glasgow to design the first large steel ship ever built in Japan. It was of 7,000 tons and had triple expansion engines (Riddell, 1970). In June 1887, NYK took possession of the Nagasaki shipyard it had been using, as a result of the new government policy of privatization. In March 1889, Mitsubishi opened a route to Vladivostock. In April, NYK was reorganized in accordance with the Meiji government's decision to use Japanese staff instead of foreigners. Because of this, Dyer, Principal of Kobu-daigakko, went back to Glasgow in 1883. Brown also resigned from Mitsubishi and returned to Britain. In June, Brown was invited to the Imperial Court to receive the honour of being appointed Japanese Consul in Glasgow (Japan Gazette, 1889). When he returned to Britain in October 1883, Brown had an audience with Queen Victoria (Salisbury & Manchester Journal, 1889). Then, he started a large-scale maritime business together with his son, and his friend, G. McFarlane, to deal with all kinds of marine engineering supplies (Brown, 1896).

Table 4.13 Names of vessels purchased by A.R. Brown (May 1874–March 1875)

No.	Name	Original name	Year built	Company, country	Materials	Tons	HP
1	Tokyo-maru	New york	1864	New York, USA	Wood	2,117	350
2	Niigata-maru	Behale	1885	Bankhead, Glasgow, Scotland, UK	Iron	1,603	300
3	Hyogo-maru	Min	1874	Robert Thompson, Sunderland, UK	Iron	1,411	200
4	Kyusyu-maru	Viola	1862	Cork, UK	Iron	839	112
5	Sharyo-maru	Shaftesbury	1862	Hartlepool, UK	Iron	800	110
6	Shinagawa-maru	Charles Albert	1872	John Bremer, Sunderland, UK	Iron	1,169	120
7	Sumida-maru	Unknown	1875	Sunderland, UK	Iron	1,411	200
8	Tamaura-maru	Muriel	1874	James Ring & Sons, Sunderland, UK	Iron	877	110
9	Tokai-maru	Acanthus	1870	Roley, Glasgow, UK	Iron	1,047	180
10	Toshima-maru	Yentai	1873	William D. Ford & sons, Sunderland, UK	Iron	946	150
11	Tsuruga-maru	Luzon	1864	Blackwood & Gordon Glasgow, UK	Iron	929	110
12	Kinsei-Maru	Madras	1852	Glasgow, UK	Iron	1,185	275
13	Takasago-Maru	Delta	1859	London, Thames Iron Works, UK	Iron	2,121	400

Source: Iwasaki family (1980) *Iwasaki-Yanosuke-Den.* Vol. 1, pp. 153–7; NYK (1935) *Nippon-Yusen-Gojyunen-Shi,* pp. 629–33.

Note
All these ships except of Tokyo-maru to Nippon-yubin was sold down to Mitsubishi Steamer in September Meiji 10 (1877).

Table 4 14 British ships purchased by A.R. Brown for Mitsubishi during Meiji 10 (1877)

No.	Name	Original name	Year built	Company, country	Material	Tons	HP
1	Wakanoura-maru	Canada	1854	Blackwell, London, UK	Iron double engine	2,125	300
2	Kanko-maru	Sakana	1869	Henderson, Courban, Renfrew, Scotland, UK	Iron and wood	298	70
3	Kumamoto-maru	Gadshill	1875	C. Mitchell, Newcastle, UK	Iron	1,913	200
4	Suminoe-maru	Duna	1871	Atkin & Mandell, Glasgow, Scotland, UK	Iron	1,320	150
5	Takachiho-maru	Lotus	1873	C. Mitchell, Newcastle, UK	Iron	2,152	200
6	Akitsushu-maru	Montgomeryshire	—	Govan, Scotland, UK	Iron	1,750	200
7	Kokonoe-maru	King Richard	—	South Shields, UK	Iron	1,825	200
8	Atago-maru	Massila	—	Glasgow, UK	Iron	1,640	400

Source: Nipponyusen (1935) *Nipponyusen-Gojyunen-shi*, pp. 629–32.

Table 4.15 The vessels purchased by A.R. Brown for Kyodo Unyu during Meiji 16 (1883)

No.	Name	Original name	Year built	Company country	Material	Tons	Engine
1	Ise-maru	Craig Mount	1883	H. McKintyre, Paisley Scotland, UK	Iron	1,185	Double
2	Owari-maru	—	1883	Henry Murray, Glasgow, Scotland, UK	Iron	1,125	Double
3	Echigo-maru	Petlisco	1883	London & Glasgow Eng., Glasgow, Scotland, UK	Iron	1,015	Double
4	Daiichi-tomi-maru	—	1883	Robert Thompson & Sons, Sunderland, UK	Iron	1,840	Double
5	Yamashiro-maru	—	May 1884	Armstrong & Mitchell, Newcastle, UK	Iron	2,528	Double
6	Daiichi-oumi-maru	—	July 1884	Armstrong & Mitchell, Newcastle, UK	Iron	2,473	Double
7	Mutsu-maru	—	July 1884	Henry Murray, Glasgow, Scotland, UK	Iron	890	Double
8	Daiichi-sagami-maru	—	1884	Armstrong & Mitchell, Newcastle, UK	Iron	1,885	Double
9	Satsuma-maru	—	1884	Napier, Shank & Bell, Glasgow, Scotland, UK	Steel	1,866	Double
10	Kii-maru	—	August 1884	London & Glasgow Eng., Glasgow, Scotland, UK	Iron	1,355	—
11	Higo-maru	—	September 1884	London & Glasgow Eng., Glasgow, Scotland, UK	Iron	1,354	Triple
12	Mino-maru	—	1884	Henry Murray, Glasgow, Scotland, UK	Iron	893	—
13	Izumo-maru	—	1884	H. McKintyre, Paisley, Scotland, UK	Iron	720	—
14	Suruga-maru	—	1884	H. McKintyre, Paisley, Scotland, UK	Iron	677	Double
15	Harima-maru	—	1884	H. McKintyre, Paisley, Scotland, UK	Iron	677	Double
16	Daiichi-nagato-maru	—	1884	Napier, Shank & Bell, Glasgow, Scotland, UK	Steel	1,810	Double

Source: NYK (1935) Nipponyusen-Go jyunen-shi, pp. 631–4.

Table 4 16 The vessels purchased by A.R. Brown for Mitsubishi during Meiji 16 (1883)

No.	Name	Original name	Year built	Company, country	Material	Tons	Engine
1	Daini-Nagoya-maru	Woolpack	December 1883	David & William Henderson, Glasgow, Scotland	Iron	2,835	—
2	Daiichi-Yokohama-maru		1884	London & Glasgow Eng., Glasgow, Scotland, UK	Steel	2,305	Double
3	Daiichi-Mikawa-maru	Gratitude	1884	Robert Thompson & Sons, Sunderland, UK	Iron	1,940	Triple
4	Daini-Wakayama-maru	Chinnoo	March 1885	Sir L. Dixon Co., Middlesbrough, UK	Iron	2,510	Triple
5	Fushiki-maru		1885	Tyne Iron Shipyard, Wellington, UK	Iron	1,919	Double
6	Matsuyama-maru	Kaishaw	December 1885	Joseph L. Thompson & Sons, Sunderland, UK	Steel	3,160	Triple
7	Daiichi-Otaru-maru	Dardness	May 1886	R. & W. Horthorn Leslie, Newcastle, UK	Steel	2,374	Triple
8	Daiichi-Tenshin-maru	Wooster	February 1887	William Gray Co., West Hartpool, UK	Steel	2,908	Double

Source: NYK (1935) *Nipponyusen-Go jyunen-shi*, pp. 631–4.

The growth of shipbuilding and shipping of Japan

In the middle of the nineteenth century, because of the enormous gap between the advanced maritime technologies of the Western powers and Japan, the Japanese government put to one side its ambition to build ocean-going steamships itself and decided to buy ready-made Western ships. On the other side of the world, the Clyde shipbuilding area of western Scotland had became the world centre for making iron railways, locomotives, engineering products and shipbuilding. Glasgow was said to be the second largest city after London, in terms of population, and was the capital of the engineering industries. Many of the new technologies related to railways and shipbuilding were invented and operated by Glasgow companies (Burrow, 1932; Kita, 1999).

As far as Japanese shipbuilding was concerned, there were three major shipyards: the Mitsubishi Shipyard set up by Yataro Iwasaki, the Kawasaki Shipyard started by Shozo Kawasaki and the Ishikawajima Shipyard established by Tomiji Hirano (Iida, 1982). Although it was one of the top shipping companies as a result of Brown's efforts, Mitsubishi did not have its own shipyard. To repair ships, it used the Yokosuka government shipyard or facilities in Hong Kong and Shanghai. In July 1884, Mitsubishi started its own repairing services by borrowing the Nagasaki government shipyard (Yokosuka Kaigun Kousho, 1979). As for Kawasaki he moved into shipbuilding after he had made his fortune in the national rice trade. Approved by the Treasury Ministry in 1874, he built his own shipyard at Tukiji in 1878 (Mishima, 1997). Mr Hirano however came to the shipbuilding business after success in the printing industry, operated by an old friend at Nagasaki since feudal days. When Shozo Motoki became successful at Tukiji Printing House, Hirano, supported by Yozo Yamao, rented the Isikawajima dockyard, and in October 1876 renamed it the Ishikawajima Shipyard, the first private shipyard in Japan (Yamashita, 1984; Teratani, 1989). Hirano also integrated the Yokohama Ironworks

Table 4.17 The vessels purchased by A.R. Brown for his personal business in March Meiji
26 (1887)

No.	Name	Year built	Year arrived Japan	Company, country	Material	Tons	Engine
1	Sakata-maru	June 1887	September 1887	Andrew Leslie Co., Newcastle, UK	Iron	1,856	Triple
2	Miike-maru	March 1888	May 1888	Robert Thompson & Sons, Sunderland, UK	Iron and steel	3,308	Triple
3	Saikyo-maru	June 1888	August 1888	London & Glasgow Eng., Glasgow, Scotland, UK	Steel	2,913	Triple
4	Kobe-maru	1888	October 1888	London & Glasgow Eng., Glasgow, Scotland, UK	Steel	2,901	Triple
5	Sendai-maru	1889	December 1889	Lobnitz, Renfrew, Scotland, UK	Steel	1,717	Triple
6	Musashi-maru	1889	March 1890	Unknown, UK	Steel	2,714	Triple

Source: Two volumes of *A.R. Brown's Scrapbooks of the newspapers* (Glasgow University Archives).

Table 4.18 The vessels built in Scotland purchased through A.R. Brown for NYK after his return to Glasgow (all ships made by steel)

No.	Name	Year built	Arrived Japan	Company, country	Engine	Tons
1	Daini-Genkai-maru	1891	July 1891	Napier, Shank & Bell, Glasgow, Scotland, UK	Triple	1,427
2	Benten-maru	1896	—	Russell & Co., Glasgow, Scotland,UK	Triple	3,668
3	Kanagawa-maru	October 1896	March 1897	David & William Henderson Glasgow, Scotland, UK	Two triple	6,151
4	Hakata-maru	December 1896	May 1897	David & William Henderson Glasgow, Scotland, UK	Two triple	6,151
5	Kawachi-maru	January 1896	August 1897	Napier, Shank & Bell, Glasgow, Scotland, UK	Two triple	6,099
6	Wakasa-maru	March 1897	August 1897	David & William Henderson, Glasgow, Scotland, UK	Two triple	6,266
7	Sanuki-maru	April 1897	September 1897	Napier, Shank & Bell, Glasgow, Scotland, UK	Two triple	6,117
8	Inba-maru	June 1897	November 1897	David & William Henderson, Glasgow, Scotland, UK	Two triple	6,192
9	Tanba-maru	August 1897	February 1898	Napier, Shank & Bell, Glasgow, Scotland, UK	Two triple	6,192
10	Bingo-maru	August 1897	March 1898	David & William Henderson, Glasgow, Scotland, UK	Two triple	6,241
11	Kasuga-maru	December 1897	September 1898	Robert Napier & Sons, Glasgow, Scotland, UK	Triple	3,797
12	Futami-maru	April 1898	February 1899	Robert Napier & Sons, Glasgow, Scotland, UK	—	3,841
13	Yahata-maru	May 1898	March 1899	Robert Napier & Sons, Glasgow, Scotland, UK	—	3,818
14	Etorofu-maru	1898	—	Russell & Co., Glasgow, Scotland, UK	—	4,116
15	Hakuai-maru	October 1898	April 1899	Lobnitz Co., Glasgow, Scotland, UK	—	2,629
16	Kousai-maru	December 1898	June 1899	Lobnitz Co., Glasgow, Scotland, UK	—	2,627
17	Santo-maru	January 1899	—	Hall & Russell Co., Aberdeen, Scotland, UK	—	2,032
18	Shinano-maru	January 1900	—	David & William Henderson, Glasgow, Scotland, UK	Two triple	6,388

(continued)

Table 4.18 Continued

No.	Name	Year built	Arrived Japan	Company, country	Engine	Tons
19	Kumano-maru	June 1901	November 1901	Fairfield Shipbuilding Co., Glasgow, Scotland, UK	Two triple	5,076
20	Daini-Sagami-maru	June 1902	—	Grangemouth & Greenock Co., Scotland, UK	—	1,934
21	Takeshima-maru	March 1902	—	Ramsay & Ferguson, Leith, Scotland, UK	—	2,673
22	Awaji-maru	August 1906	—	Grangemouth & Greenock Co., Grangemouth, Scotland, UK	—	2,045
23	Chikuzen-maru	February 1907	—	David & William Henderson, Glasgow, Scotland, UK	—	2,578
24	Chikugo-maru	April 1907	—	David & William Henderson, Glasgow, Scotland, UK	—	2,563
25	Rangoun-maru	June 1908	—	Russell & Co., Glasgow, Scotland, UK	—	5,348
26	Daini-Omi-maru	April 1912	—	Napier & Miller Co., Glasgow, Scotland, UK	—	3,582
27	Renan-maru	November 1912	—	Russell & Co., Scotland, UK	—	5,280
28	Tokushima-maru	July 1913	—	Russell & Co., Scotland, UK	—	6,055
29	Tottori-maru	August 1913	—	Russell & Co., Scotland, UK	—	6,057
30	Tsushima-maru	September 1914	—	Russell & Co., Scotland, UK	—	6,724
31	Takada-maru	October 1914	—	Russell & Co., Scotland, UK	—	6,728
32	Nagasaki-maru	March 1922	—	William Denny & Brothers Co., Glasgow, Scotland, UK	Geared-turbine double	5,272
33	Syanhai-maru	August 1922	—	William Denny & Brothers Co., Glasgow, Scotland, UK	Geared-turbine double	5,259
34	Asuka-maru	July 1924	—	David & William Henderson, Glasgow, Scotland, UK	Internal combustion double engine	7,524
35	Atago-maru	July 1924	—	Lithgow Co., Glasgow, Scotland, UK		7,544

Source: NYK (1935) Nippon-Yusen-Gojyunen-shi, pp. 640–57, Two volumes of A.R. Brown's Scrapbooks of the newspapers, and various documents at Glasgow University Archives as well as at that of NYK.

Notes
There were 266 vessels owned by NYK until the spring of 1935. The number of British made was 125, American 7, Germany 5, Norway 2 and Japanese 125. Among the British made, there were 70 vessels built in Scotland, composed by 55 at Glasgow, 6 at Renfrew, 4 at Paisely, 2 at Grangemouth, 1 at Leith, 1 at Aberdeen and 1 at Greenock 49 vessels were made in England, composed of 19 at Sunderland, 15 at Newcastle, 8 at Middlesburgh, 3 at Hartlepool, 2 at London, 2 at Stockton, 1 at Cork and 1 at Warrington.

as a part of the Ishikawajima shipyard. He employed A. King, a Scottish engineer, when his contract expired with Kobu-daigakko and began to build many small and medium-sized ships at his shipyard (Miyamoto and Nakagawa, 1977).

To come to terms with modern maritime technology, the Japanese government decided to encourage the building of ships with steam or combustion engines rather than sail. In 1881, it drew up a twenty-year plan for naval construction but early the following year, because of political tension in Asia, decided to examine and revise the programme every 8 years to ensure rapid expansion. In 1886, the programme was changed to a 3-yearly review to catch up with international competition (Teratani, 1989). In 1888, the first phase of naval expansion resulted in 6 cruisers, 4 patrol ships, 5 gunboats, 2 survey ships, 2 training ships and 18 torpedo boats. A battleship, a gunboat and all the torpedo boats were produced at the Ishikawajima Shipyard. Hirano was convinced his company's future lay in producing a variety of marine and general engineering goods and increased the company's range of items to include all kinds of iron and steel goods. In 1881, he found a profitable market in small modern ships suitable for Tokyo Bay and he became a pioneer in this field of ship production (Osaka Shosen Mitsui Kabushikikaisha, 1966).

In March 1896, the Meiji government issued two Acts of Zosen-shoreiho (ship-building support) and Koukai-syoreiho (shipping support). They did not subsidize any particular company but helped any company which could actually build ships. This encouraged a number of local industrialists to start naval architectural projects (Bush, 1969). Before the Sino-Japanese War, no shipyard in Japan could make a vessel of 7,000 plus tons. Many ships bought during the war were old second-hand ships, which needed to be repaired or to be modified for further use. These Acts were proposed by members of the Japanese cotton spinning association in order to import raw cotton from India and by the Tokyo Chamber of Commerce to create the necessary transport system for their industrial and commercial activities. Under the shipbuilding support act, grants were given to Japanese shipyards to make ships of iron and steel over 700 tons. The Kawasaki shipyard produced the 727-ton *Iyo-maru* in 1897 and the 1,694-ton *Daigen-maru* in 1899. The same year, Mitsubishi produced the 1,519-ton *Tsukishima-maru*, the 1,898-ton *Hitachi-maru*, as well as the 6,172-ton *Awa-maru* which were of the largest international class. However, many shipping companies took advantage of the shipping support act, which gave grants to buy within five years foreign ships over 1,000 tons, and purchased bigger vessels. NYK ordered 12 ships: 10 from Britain and only 2 from the Mitsubishi shipyard. The other shipping companies followed NYK in favouring overseas builders. Then the government cut the subsidy to shipping by half to stimulate large vessel production at home. So Japanese international shipping companies began ordering from domestic shipyards (Nakanishi, 1982). A new era of Japanese shipbuilding began. Mitsubishi received orders for ships over 5,000 tons from NYK. It provided *Kaga-maru* and *Iyo-maru* in 1901, *Aki-maru* in 1902, *Nikko-maru* and *Suzuran-maru* in 1903, *Tango-maru* in 1905, *Hitachi-maru* in 1906 and *Atuta-maru* with two others of the same class in 1907. Kawasaki received orders from Osaka-shosen for medium and smaller size ships of around

2,000 tons for China and coastal navigation. It built *Daigen-maru* for the Yangtze River in 1899, *Dairi-maru* and *Daijin-maru* in 1900, *Keiji-maru* in 1902 and two more vessels in 1903, one in 1904, one in 1905 and one in 1906 (Teratani, 1988). Osaka Tekkosho received orders for ships for the South China trade in 1901 from Osakasyosen and supplied them with *Daigi-maru* and *Gaikichi-maru* (Hitachi Zosen). Mitsubishi occupied the outstanding position among Japanese shipyards in terms of building bigger vessels. Kawasaki caught up a decade later in 1908 in producing *Mishima-maru* and *Miyazaki-maru*. But Mitsubishi had already built two sister vessels over 10,000 tons, the world's largest class, for the Toyo-kisen company, *Tenyo-maru* and *Chiyo-maru*.

In 1907, the shipping support act was abolished and a new Act supporting ocean navigation was passed. As a result of the previous Acts, Japanese shipbuilding was now well established. Gross shipping produced in Japan was greater than imported tonnage. But as regards ocean ships over 2,000 tons, NYK continued to depend on Scottish shipyards, as they could offer more favourable prices, terms of construction, advanced equipment and payment conditions than their counterparts in Japan (Kita, 1984).

The First World War was another turning point in the history of Japanese shipbuilding. In 1914, Japanese shipping was of minor importance because of the decline in trade with European countries. But gradually Allied countries started ordering items from Japan, mainly armaments, munitions and food. Also, China, India and the Pacific Islands became markets for Japanese goods which replaced European goods no longer available. With an increased volume of overseas trade and rising prices, almost all heavy industries in Japan were stimulated into further development. In 1916, the total tonnage of ships made by Japanese shipyards rose above 100,000 tons and reached a level of 640,000 tons in 1918. During the War, encouraged by the war boom, the number of shipyards equipped to produce ships over 1,000 tons increased from 5 to 52, dockyards from 17 to 157 and workers from 16,000 to 107,000. The influence of the war had a beneficial impact on the shipping industries, and Japanese shipyards made sufficient progress to maintain their ability to make larger vessels. Then in July 1917, the grants to home ship-yards were suspended and the following year, the Act of shipbuilding support disappeared (Muroyama, 1984; Teratani, 1988).

Conclusion

In the middle of the nineteenth century, when Japan abandoned the closed-door policy which it had maintained for over two centuries, it was still a feudal society. But by the time H. Dyer, the first principal of Kobu-daigakko, wrote *Dai-Nippon, Britain of the East: A Study in National Evolution* in 1904, Japan had successfully transformed itself into one of the most influential industrialized countries in Asia. It had defeated China and would soon go to war against Russia, backed by the Anglo-Japanese Treaty of 1902 (Dyer, 1904). There are many reasons why the Japanese could learn modern technology so quickly. The high standard of Japanese education in the feudal period was one of the major reasons as it provided a foundation for modernization (Lehmann, 1982).

The contribution of Scottish scientists, educators, merchants and their financial experience was very important in this process. One of the best examples was A.R. Brown, who was asked by R.H. Brunton to work for the light house organization of Japan, as captain of their survey ship. Japanese shipping and shipbuilding was in its primitive stage when Brown arrived in Japan as a P&O captain and started to work for the lighthouse authority. As Japan could not make her own ocean-going vessels, Brown and Glover went to Shanghai and Hong Kong to purchase second-hand ships for Japan. At this time all education related to shipping was undertaken by Scottish engineers and teachers. In the next phase, Kobudaigakko and other higher educational colleges, and affiliated training schools were started, and private shipping companies were set up. These were the formative days of Japanese shipbuilding and shipping history. Brown arranged to supply two ships from the North of England and Scotland for the Mitsubishi and Kyodo-unyu companies (Zosen Kyokai, 1974). Then in the following phase, NYK was created though the amalgamation of two rival companies. As a director of the new company, Brown took young engineers to Glasgow and other shipyards to see the process of vessel construction, when he went there to order the latest ships. At the same time, he was an adviser in the selection of Glasgow naval architects who were invited to come to Japan at the request of the Japanese shipyards. Gradually, Japanese engineers acquired the knowledge and technology to be able to make the hulls of vessels (Mitsubishi Zosen, 1957). In the final stage, supported by national policy, it was decided that Japanese ships must be made by Japanese shipyards, and shipping must be organized by Japanese marine engineers. Because of this, Brown decided to return to the UK as consul for Japan at Glasgow as well as agent for Mitsubishi (Nippon Keieishi Kenkyusho, 1988). Brown started trade in marine engineering goods with G.M. McFarlane and exported the latest inventions such as engines and rigs to his counterparts in Japan. He supplied his old friends in Japan with whatever they requested for the shipbuilding and shipping business (Bush, 1969). So it is important to stress the influence of Scottish diplomats, teachers, engineers and merchants in Japan since feudal times. Their influence enabled Japan to learn the new technology although it had previously been significantly behind the West. It was all due to the good relationship between those teachers from Scotland and the hard-working students of Japan.

References

Brown, A.R. (1896) *A. R. Brown, M'Farlane & Co. Ltd., Consulting Engineers and Naval Architects*, pp. 4–6.

Brunton, R.H. (1900) *Pioneer Engineering in Japan: A Record of Work Helping to Re-lay the Foundation of the Japanese Empire (1868–1870)*, pp. 36–8.

Burrow, J. (1932) *A Shipbuilding History, 1750–1932*, p. 84.

Bush, L. (1969) *The Life and Times of Illustrious Captain Brown, A Chronicle of the Sea and of Japan's Emergence as a World Power*, pp. 59–60, 94–9.

Cucari, A. and Angelucci, E. (1975) LE NAVI, p. 125.

Dyer, H. (1883) 'Valedictory Address to the Students of the Imperial College of Engineering', *Imperial College of Engineering*, p. 6.

Dyer, H. (1890) 'On a University Faculty of Engineering', *Transaction of the Institution of Engineers & Shipbuilders, Scotland, 1889–1890*. Vol. 33, p. 21.

Dyer, H. (1904) *Dai Nippon* (The Britain of the East, a study in National Evolution) London: Blackie & Son, pp. 6–9.

Dyer, H. (1909) 'Western Teaching for China', *Nature*, 25 March 1909, p. 99.

Dyer, H. (1912) *Education and National Life*, pp. 87–8.

Fukumoto, K. (1981) *Nippon Kogyo Senkakusya Shiron* (Essays on Pioneers of Industries of Japan), pp. 69–71.

Haviland, E.K. (1958) *American Steam Navigation in China, 1845–1878*. Vol. 15–18, pp. 16–18.

Herman, A. (2002) *The Scottish Enlightenment: The Scots' Invention of the Modern World*, p. 383.

Hitachi Zosen, *Hitachi Zosen Hiyakunen-shi* (100 Years of Hitachi Shipbuilding), p. 34.

Hosoya, C. and Tanaka, T. (ed.) (2000) *Nichiei Koryu-shi, 1, 1600–2000, Seiji-Gaiko* (History of Britain and Japan, Political and Diplomatic Relationship), pp. 88, 89.

Howarths, D. and Howarths, S. (1994) *The History of P & O, The Peninsular and Oriental Steam Navigation Company*, revised edition, pp. 102–5.

Iida, K. (1982) *Gijyutsu no Syakaishi 4* (Social History of Technological Progress in Japan), pp. 252–5.

Imazu, K. (1989) *Kindai Nippon no Gigyututeki Jyoken* (Fundamental Conditions of Receiving Modern Technology to Japan), pp. 184–5.

Inoue, Y. (1990) *Nippon Kindai Zousengyo no Tenkai* (Development of Modern Shipbuilding of Japan), pp. 50, 73, 74.

Ishibu, M. (1972) *Kindai-Nippon Ryugaku-shi* (Historical Record of Japanese Youth Abroad in Modern Times), pp. 151–4.

Ishii, K. (1989) *Kaikoku to Ishin* (Opening of Japan to Meiji Restoration), p. 31.

Isii, T. and Sekiguchgi, H. (ed.) (1982) *Sekaishijyo to Bakumatsu Kaikou* (Relationship of World Market and Opening of Feudal Japan), pp. 78–84.

Japan Gazette, 18 May, 1889.

Kaigairyugaku-kisoku (1981) *Nippon Kagaku-ghijyutu Shi Taikei* (History of Development of Science and Technology), p. 36.

Kita, M. (1984) *Kokusai Nippon wo Hiraita Hitobito* (Who Contributed to Make the Modern Industrialized Japan), pp. 26–8, 57–60, 97, 110, 170, 185–8, 224, 230, 247.

Kita, M. (1995) 'Transfer in Shipbuilding Technology from Scotland through Education in the Late 19th Century', *Papers on the History of Industry and Technology of Japan*. Vol. 1, p. 197.

Kita, M. (1998) *Kindai Sukottorando Iminshi Kenkyu* (Study of the Modern Scottish Emigrants), p. 98.

Kita, M. (1999) *Kindai Sukottorando Tetudo Kaiungyousi* (Study of Modern Scotland's Railways and Shipping History), pp. 13–15.

Kobayashi, M. (1977) *Kindai sangyo Gijyutsu no Dounyu* (Introduction of Modern technology to Japan), in Miyamoto, M. and the Hakagawa, K. (ed.) *Kogyoka to Kigyosya-katudou* (Entrepreneurial Activity and Industrialization of Japan), pp. 156, 163.

Kobayashi, M. (1980) *Kaiungyo no Roudou Mondai* (Study of Labour Problem of the Japanese Shipping Industries), p. 63.

Kobayashi, M. (1995) *Seifu to Kigyo* (Government and Enterprises of Japan), p. 81.

Kume, K. (1978) *Tokumei Zenken Taishi Beiou Kairan Jikki* (Narrative of Iwakura Mission). Vol. 2, pp. 192–226, 382.

Lehmann, J.P. (1982) *The Roots of Modern Japan*, pp. 115, 129.

Mishima, Y. (1997) *Zousenou Kawsakishozo no Shougai* (Life of the Founder of Kawasaki Shipyard), p. 98.

Mitsubishi Zosen, (1957) *Sougyo Hiyakuen no Nagasaki Zosensho* (Nagasaki Shipyard's One Century), pp. 45–51.

Miyamoto, M. and Nakagawa, K. (1977) *Kogyoka to Kigyosya-katudou* (Entrepreneurial Activity and Industrialization of Japan), p. 93.

Miyanaga, T. (1981) Commander Perry (The Expedition to Japan and His Life), pp. 96–8.

Miyazaki, M. (1997) *Siiboluto to Sakoku Kaikoku Nippon* (Life of P.F. Siebold and Feudal Japan), pp. 10–28.

Miyoshi, N. (1979) *Nippon Kogyo-Kyouiku Seiritsu-si no Kenkyu* (Study of Industrial Education in Japan), p. 229.

Mizuta, N. (1974) *Nagasaki Debssyusho no Hibi* (Days of Nagasaki Dutch Maritime Training School), pp. 6–9.

Moss, M.S. and Hume, J.R. (1977) *Workshop of the British Empire, Engineering and Shipbuilding in the West of Scotland*, p. 33.

Moss, M.S. and Hume, J.R. (1979) *Beardmore: The History of a Scottish Industrial Giant*, p. 81.

Muroyama, M. (1984) *Kindai Nippon-no Gunji to Zaisei* (Historical Study of Finance to Armament in Modern Japan), pp. 122–7.

Nakagawa, N. and Yui, T. (1985) *Business History of Shipping, Strategy and Structure*, p. 89.

Nakanishi, H. (1982) *Nippon Kindaika no Kisokatei sita* (Study of the Foundation of Japanese Moderization, latter part, 1885–1900), p. 175.

Nippon Yusen Kabushikikaisya (1936) *Nippon Yusen Gojyunenshi* (50 Years of NYK), p. 111.

Nippon Yusen Kabushikikaisya (1956) *Nippon Yusen Nanajyunenshi* (70 Years of NYK), p. 18.

Nippon Keieishi Kenkyusho (1979) *Tokyo Kaijyo Hoken Kabushikikaisya* (History of Tokyo Maritime Insurance Company), p. 72.

Nippon Yusen Kabushikikaisya (1985) *Nanatu no Umide Isseiki* (History of NYK for One Century over the Seven Seas), p. 660.

Nippon Keieishi Kenkyusho (1988) *Kindai Nippon Kaiunseisei Shiryo* (Historical Documents of Japanese Shipping History), pp. 456, 457.

Nippon Keieishi Kenkyusho (1988) *Nippon Yusen Hiyakunenshi Shiryo* (Historical Documents of NYK for a Century), p. 73.

Nishikawa, N. and Matsutomi, S. (1995) *Beioukairanjikki wo Yomu* (Study on Iwakura Mission), pp. 78–82.

Obituary Notices of the Royal Society of London (ONRSL) (1942).

Obituary Notices of the Royal Society of London (ONRSL) (1969).

Oliphant, L. (1860) *Narrative of the Earl of Elgin's Mission to China and Japan in the years of 1857, '58, '59*, pp. 45–53.

Osaka Shosen Mitsui Kabushikikaisha (1966) *Osaka Shosen Hachijyunen-shi* (80 Years of OSM Company), p. 25.

Oukubo, T. (1986) *Rekishi Chosakushuu 5* (His Historical Views Collection), pp. 71–85.

Riddell, J.F. (1970) *Clyde Navigation: A History of the Development and Deepening of the River Clyde*, p. 95.

Salisbury & Manchester Journal, 20, July 1889.

Tanaka, A. and Takada, S. (ed.) (1993) *Beioukairanjikki no Gakusaiteki Kenkyuu* (Interdisciplinary Study of Iwakura Mission), pp. 54–6.

Teratani, T. (1989) *Nippon Kindai Zousenshi Jyosetsu* (The Formative Days of Japanese Shipbuilding), pp. 3–4, 44, 166–8.

Teratani, M. (1988) *Nippon Kindai Zousenshi Jyosetsu* (The Formative Days of Japanese Shipbuilding), pp. 359, 166–8.

TOKOKAI (1969) *Nippon Todai Shi* (One Hundred Years of Lighthouses in Japan), pp. 26–8.
Toyohara, J. (1964) *Kobusho-to-Oyatoi-gaikokujin* (Ministry of Public Works and Foreign Employees), pp. 35–6.
Tsunoyama, S. (1988) *Tsushou Kokka Nippon no Jyohosenryaku* (Information Strategy of Modern Japan through the Consular Reports), pp. 42, 43.
Umemura, N. (ed.) (1985) *Kindaika-no-suishinsha-tachi* (Leaders of Industrialisation of Modern Japan after Meiji), p. 203.
Umemura, M. and Yamamoto (ed.) (1989) *Kaikou to Ishin* (Opening and Reformation of Japan), p. 14.
Umetani, N. (ed.) (1990) *Kindaika no Suisinsyatachi* (Promoter of Modernization of Japan), pp. 202–4.
Umetani, N. (ed.) (1987) *ZaYatoi* (The Foreign Employee by Meiji Government), pp. 169–72.
Umino, F. (1982) *Ghijyutu no Syakaishi 3* (Social History of Technology), pp. 23, 34–6.
Wray, W.D. (1984) *Mitsubishi and the NYK, 1870–1914*, pp. 87–92.
Yamamoto, H. (1986) *Koutsu-Unyu no Hattatsu to Ghijyutu Kakushin* (Development of Transport and Communication and Technological Change), pp. 317–26.
Yamashita, Y. (1984) *Kaiungyo to Zousengyo* (Historical Relationship of Shipping and Shipbuilding of Japan), p. 113.
Yokoi, K. (1988) *Ajia no Umino Daieiteikoku* (The Great Maritime British Empire), pp. 91–7.
Yokosuka Kaigun Kousho (1979) *Yokosuka Kaigun Senshoushi* (History of Yokosuka Navy Arsenal), pp. 160–5.
Yoshida, M. (ed.) (1986) *Bankoku Hakurankai no Kenkyuu* (Study of the World Expositions), p. 22.
Zosen Kyokai (ed.) (1974) *Nippon Kinsei zosenshi-Meiji Jidai* (History of Modern Japanese Shipbuilding in Meiji Era), pp. 45–51.

Further reading

Banbury, P. (1971) *Shipbuilders of the Thames and Medway*.
Checkland, O. (1989) *Britain's Encounter with Meiji Japan, 1868–1912*.
Dougan, D. (1968) *The History of North East Shipbuilding*.
Dyer, H. (1879) *The Education of Engineers, Imperial College of Engineering*.
Dyer, H. (1880) *The Education of Civil and Mechanical Engineers*.
Dyer, H. (1904) *Dai Nippon, The Britain of the East, A Study in National Evolution*.
General Report of Imperial College Engineering, 1873–1877 and 1883.
Grant, G. (1950) *Steel & Ships, The History of John Brown (1877)*.
Hyde, F.E. (1975) *Cunard and the North Atlantic 1840–1973, A History of Shipping and Financial Management*.
Kattendyke, W.J.C.R.H. (1860) *Kattendyke gedurende zijn verblijf in Japan in 1857, 1858 en 1859*.
Kita, M. (1984) 'A. R. Brown (1839–1913); Servant of Japan', in *Proceedings of the British Association for Japanese Studies*. Vol. 9, pp. 58–61.
Kobe Chronicle, (1918) The Japan Chronicle, History of Kobe, Jubilee Number 1868–1918, in Japanese translation.
Lehmann, J.P. (1982) *The Roots of Modern Japan*.
Peebles, H.B. (1997) *Warship building on the Clyde: Naval Orders and the Clyde Shipbuilding Industries, 1889–1939*.
Roll of Institutes of Naval Architecture (RINA) *Salisbury & Manchester Journal* (1889).

5 Inter-Asian competition in the world silk market: 1859–1929

Shinsuke Kaneko

As Asia modernized, it did not compete directly with the West in economic terms because the goods it produced were so different,[1] so Asia was able to make remarkable progress.[2] Asian industrialization was based on the Asian market, and also on the demand from the West. The silk industry is a prime example. Raw silk (thread direct from the cocoon)[3] was the most important export of both Japan and China,[4] and it featured greatly in the industrialization of Japan. Japan survived intense inter-Asian competition[5] from India and China in the world silk market from the middle of the nineteenth century, and, in the twentieth century, captured the raw silk market of the United States, the largest consumer of raw silk.[6] The trade provided the basis for Japanese industrialization. This chapter examines the relationship between the Asian economy and the West and investigates inter-Asian competition in the silk industry.

Inter-Asian competition in raw silk

In the world silk market,[7] the leading suppliers of Asian raw silk changed during the nineteenth century and the first half of the twentieth century. Indian raw silk[8] was the main Asian raw silk in the first half of the nineteenth century, Chinese raw silk[9] was popular in the second half of the nineteenth century, and Japanese raw silk came to the fore in the first half of the twentieth century.[10]

After Japan's ports opened, from the 1860s to the 1880s, Indian, Chinese, and Japanese raw silk competed vigorously in the European market.[11] But Chinese raw silk outstripped Indian and Japanese raw silk, and Indian silk production declined and she became a raw silk importer.[12] So the Japanese silk industry switched its main export target to the United States,[13] and Japanese raw silk drove Chinese raw silk from that market.[14] The 1890s to the 1920s saw a split in the world silk market in which Chinese raw silk dominated in Europe, and Japanese raw silk in the United States.[15] The Japanese silk industry grew in line with the expansion of the United States market during these years.[16] But the Chinese silk industry began to stagnate relatively,[17] because the European market for silk slowed down.[18] This explains why Japanese raw silk exports exceeded Chinese raw silk exports by the beginning of the twentieth century.[19] After the depression, through the 1930s, Japanese raw silk dominated the world silk market,[20] because of the decline in the Chinese silk industry.

It is possible to explain this inter-Asian competition in the world silk market by the difference in silk worm voltinism in each production region.[21] High-, middle-, and low-quality raw silk was made, respectively, from univoltine, bivoltine (or F1-hybrid), and multivoltine silk worms. The univoltine silk worm has one cocoon harvest per year, the bivoltine has two harvests per year, and the multivoltine has more than three harvests per year. In Japan, most of the F1-hybrid silk worms were created from the univoltine and bivoltine.[22] While univoltine raw silk has a few small knots (made by sericin[23]) and great strength, multivoltine raw silk has lots of small knots and is brittle.[24] The quality of bivoltine (and F1-hybrid) raw silk lies somewhere between that of univoltine and multivoltine raw silk (Tables 5.1–5.4a,b). Indian raw silk was of two types: Kashmir raw silk was made from univoltine, while Bengal raw silk was made from multivoltine (Table 5.5). Chinese raw silk also had two types: Shanghai raw silk of univoltine[25], and Canton raw silk of multivoltine.[26] Japanese raw silk was generally bivoltine, and in Japan, the F1-hybrid silk worm became popular rapidly after the First World War. All European raw silk was univoltine.

In Europe, Shanghai and Kashmir raw silk competed directly with each other, as they were of similar quality, and so did Canton and Bengal raw silk.[27] Chinese and Japanese raw silk was white, whereas Indian and European raw silk was yellow.[28] Each color has particular advantages and suits particular purposes; white raw silk is best suited for light shades and a pure white background; on the other hand, yellow raw silk is better suited for darker shades and a black background. In the United Kingdom, white raw silk was preferred to yellow, owing to the demand for lighter shades.[29] So Indian yellow raw silk was at a disadvantage to Chinese white raw silk in the UK market, and Indian raw silk exports to the UK decreased (Tables 5.6 and 5.7). In the French market, attention was drawn to the numerous defects in Indian raw silk. For instance, big knots resulted in large

Table 5.1 The quality of main countries' raw silk

	Class	Denier	Chop mark	Big knot	Small knot	Strength (g)	Strength (%)
Bengal filatures	SA	13–15	5	8	357	3.54	19.4
Canton filatures	SA	16–20	13	10	890	3.31	—
Canton filatures	A	9–11	12	1	517	3.52	18.0
Canton filatures	A	18–22	5	17	1,745	3.93	19.2
Japan filatures	—	13.5–17	5	1	146	3.25	19.6
Japan zaguri	—	13.5–17	6	1	131	3.33	19.6
Shanghai filatures	SA	13–15	2	1	112	3.89	20.6
Shanghai filatures	A	13–15	2	2	105	3.73	20.8
Shanghai filatures	SA	9–11	3	1	66	3.77	19.8
Shanghai filatures	A	9–11	7	1	78	4.15	20.4
Tsatlees	A	—	4	28	112	—	19.2
Italy (yellow)	SA	11–13	6	2	86	4.11	22.0
Italy (white)	A	10–12	4	1	41	3.89	19.4

Source: Imamura (1935), pp. 315–18.

Table 5.2 The quality of Chinese raw silk

Regions	Rank	Big knot	Middle knot	Small knot	Strength (g)	Strength (%)
Shanghai	The grand double extra	0.3	0.7	50.0	3.68	20.9
	The extra A	0.2	1.1	56.5	3.72	21.0
	The extra B	0.0	1.1	101.0	3.45	18.7
	The extra C	0.2	9.5	39.0	3.69	20.9
	The good A golden load	0.2	2.0	93.0	3.66	20.7
	The new model re-reels	1.5	3.4	105.0	3.63	16.7
	The new model re-reels	0.8	1.5	119.5	3.80	19.9
Canton	The old model double extra	0.6	3.2	2,392.5	3.10	17.0
	The old model extra	1.5	3.3	2,395.0	3.37	17.4
	The old model special star	1.0	1.8	2,670.0	3.12	16.4
	The new model star special	1.0	4.2	3,195.0	3.00	16.4
	The new model best no.1	0.5	2.7	3,190.0	2.93	15.3

Source: Toua Kenkyu-jo (1943), pp. 332–9.

Table 5.3 The New York market's average price in 1914

	Price (dollars)
Italy	4.18
Shangai filatures	4.12
Japan filatures	3.66
Canton filatures	3.18

Source: Toua Kenkyu-jo (1943), pp. 409–10.

Note
Price was per 1lb.

Table 5.4a Relative prices of silks in New York market (Italy = 100)

	1898/01	1910/13
Shangai filatures	103.6	105.5
Japan filatures	92.5	87.7
Canton filatures	79.0	79.8

Table 5.4b Relative prices of silks in Lyons market
(Italy = 100)

	1898/1901	1910/13
Shangai filatures	100.5	97.2
Japan filatures	94.7	91.3
Canton filatures	76.8	78.7
Bengal filatures	73.6	75.0

Source: Federico (1997), p. 230.

Table 5.5 The raw silk export of Indian regions (1,000 kg)

Year/region	Bengal	%	Kashmir	%	Total
1905	226		54		280
1906	270		55		325
1907	290		60		350
Average	262	82.4	56	17.6	318
1908	190		60		250
1909	180		55		235
1910	154		76		230
Average	175	73.5	64	26.9	238
1911	108		116		224
1912	50		118		168
1913	27		86		113
Average	62	36.9	107	63.7	168

Sources: Noushoumu-shou (1912), p. 71; (1916a), p. 103.

Table 5.6 Indian raw silk in the European market: 1869–74 (lbs)

	UK	%	France	%	Total
1869–70	1,892,480	79.9	383,040	16.2	2,368,452
1870–71	1,679,104	78.8	263,147	12.3	2,131,399
1871–72	1,581,507	83.5	180,279	9.5	1,893,322
Average	1,717,697	80.6	275,489	12.9	2,131,058
1872–73	1,458,884	65.4	512,877	23.0	2,231,578
1873–74	1,314,627	59.1	458,091	20.6	2,223,917
1874–75	1,009,705	61.0	450,258	27.2	1,656,015
Average	1,261,072	61.9	473,742	23.3	2,037,170

Sources: *British Parl. Papers* (1875), pp. 74, 114; (1876), pp. 86, 126.

Table 5.7 Indian raw silk in the European market: 1910–14 (lbs)

Country/year		1910–11	11–12	12–13	Average	13–14	14–15
Raw	UK	58,049	22,105	11,214	30,456	19,299	55,210
silk	France	411,417	358,065	369,827	379,770	140,636	27,14
	Total	494,035	381,677	382,081	419,264	160,22	82,712
Waste	UK	260,516	263,330	255,239	259,695	205,017	165,082
	France	808,884	750,748	627,166	728,933	539,678	148,823
	Total	1,147,243	1,092,764	943,143	1,061,050	909,077	347,754
Total		1,641,278	1,474,441	1,325,224	1,480,314	1,069,299	430,466
	Total of UK	318,565	285,435	266,453	290,151	224,316	219,292
	%	19.4	19.4	20.1	19.6	21.0	50.9
	Total of France	1,220,301	1,108,813	996,993	1,108,702	680,314	175,965
	%	74.4	75.2	75.2	74.9	63.6	40.9

Source: *British Parl. Papers* (1916), pp. 96, 138, 139.

Note
Waste is "Chasam or Waste," Chasam was the Indian handmade raw silk.

numbers of "chop marks" and raised costs because they slowed down the machines. Chop marks are the marks which result from knotting strands of silk when they have broken. There was also a huge loss in "boil off" which is the weight decrease in raw silk after it has been boiled to remove the extra sericin. With ordinary raw silk, the boil off is 18–23 percent.[30] But the boil-off with Kashmir raw silk is 30 percent.[31] The lack of strength of Kashmir raw silk made it unsuitable for machine-made products.[32] So the quality of Indian raw silk was inferior to that of Chinese raw silk. The Indian silk industry declined, especially in Bengal,[33] and from the 1870s India's raw silk imports began to exceed her exports (Tables 5.8 and 5.9). The Chinese types of raw silk, Shanghai and Canton, were preferred in Europe to the Indian types, Kashmir and Bengal, and Chinese raw silk dominated even in India with a share of about 70 percent (Tables 5.10 and 5.11). So the Indian raw silk industry lost both the European market and its own domestic market.

Japan's share of the Indian raw silk market was less than 10 percent in these years apart from the 1910s and the 1930s (Tables 5.10, 5.15), but the European share of the Indian market was more than 30 percent in its best year.[34] The share of Chinese and European raw silk in the Indian market was about 90 percent from 1905 and about 80 percent between 1910 and 1914. High-quality and low-quality raw silk dominated the Indian market, providing more than 70 percent of the market (Tables 5.12, 5.13, 5.14). Indian consumers preferred high-class silk, so the market for middle-quality raw silk was very small. This was similar to the situation in the European market,[35] and was in sharp contrast to the US market, where Japanese middle-quality raw silk had the highest share. The Indian silk industry used only univoltine and multivoltine silk worms and so produced no middle-quality raw silk.[36] The share of Japanese bivoltine middle-quality

Table 5.8 The export and import of raw silk in India (lbs) (£)

Year	Export		up	Import		up
	(lbs)	*(£)*		*(lbs)*	*(£)*	
1851/55	1,458,205	640,890	44.0	—	—	—
56/60	1,636,258	825,810	50.5	—	—	—
61/65	1,345,516	874,975	65.0	—	—	—
66/70	2,342,070	1,328,051	56.7	1,885,043	703,613	37.3
71/75	1,980,424	982,168	49.6	2,187,952	733,161	33.5
76/80	1,592.804	686,526	43.1	1,978,964	689,492	34.8
81/85	1,448,125	367,818	25.4	1,984,380	852,484	43.0

Sources: *British Parl. Papers*, "Statistical Abstract for the Several Colonial and other Possessions of the United Kingdom," "Statistical Abstract Relating to British India," "Statement of the Trade of British India with British Possessions and Foreign Countries."

Note
up is the unit price per 100 lbs.

raw silk was less than China's in the Indian market, and the same was true in the European market.

From the 1890s to the 1920s, Chinese raw silk dominated the European and Indian markets, and Japanese raw silk dominated the US and Australian markets. Japanese raw silk took nearly 100 percent of the Australian market.[37] In the Australian silk fabric market,[38] Japanese silk fabric was overwhelmingly predominant, being more than 60 percent of the total, and China supplying less than 1 percent.[39] The US and Australian markets were large middle-quality raw silk markets, while the European and Indian markets took little middle-quality raw silk.[40] So, Japanese middle-quality raw silk from the bivoltine/F1-hybrid silk worms predominated in both the US and Australian markets, and Chinese univoltine high-quality raw silk and multivoltine low-quality raw silk dominated the European and Indian markets.

Silk production links in Japan and China

Silk worm voltinism determines raw silk quality and also silk fabric quality. The sericultural industry is affected by the natural environment, and the needs of the domestic silk fabrics industry it serves, which in turn is shaped by the character of domestic demand. This chapter calls these "silk production links." The world silk market was divided because silk production links in Japan and China were different.[41] Chinese silk production links were of two types: Central China's silk production was of high-quality expensive fabrics,[42] made from high-quality raw silk using univoltine silk worms, while Southern China's silk production involved low-quality cheap silk fabrics,[43] made from low-quality raw silk using multivoltine silk worms. Japanese silk production by contrast was of middle-quality silk fabrics, made from middle-quality raw silk using bivoltine/F1-hybrid silk worms (Table 5.16).

Table 5.9 The export and import of raw silk and waste in India (lbs) (£)

Year	Total export		Raw silk unit price	Raw silk		Raw silk unit price	Waste unit price	B/A	Import		Unit price
	(lbs) (A)	(£)	(£)	(lbs)(B)	(£)	(£)	(£)	%	(lbs)	(£)	(£)
1886/90	1,622,199	497,379	30.7	486,217	374,273	76.9	10.8	30.0	2,229,753	1,011,150	45.3
1891/95	1,610,528	587,972	36.5	601,171	489,460	81.4	9.8	37.3	2,693,310	1,181,949	43.9
1896/00	1,648,764	458,094	27.8	602,996	397,706	66.0	5.8	36.6	2,163,690	787,189	36.4
1901/05	1,708,932	397,358	23.3	623,667	340,156	54.5	5.3	36.5	1,964,660	504,555	25.7
1906/10	1,817,836	376,957	20.7	617,025	319,827	51.8	4.8	33.9	2,759,966	808,457	29.3
1911/14	1,074,858	191,017	17.8	251,673	145,539	57.8	5.5	23.4	3,780,034	1,139,280	30.1

Sources: *British Parl. Papers*, "Statement of the Trade of British India with British Possessions and Foreign Countries," "Tables relating to the Trade of British India with British Possessions and Foreign Countries," "Statistical Abstract for the several British Colonies, Possessions, and Protectorates," "Tables rebles to the Trade of British India with the British Empire and Foreign Countries."

Table 5.10 The import of raw silk and silk yarn to India (lbs)

Year/ country	Total import	Chinese		European		Japanese	
		Import	%	Import	%	Import	%
1905/09	2,681,464	1,826,705	68.1	566,244	21.1	178,296	6.6
10/14	3,633,050	2,470,362	68.0	507,564	14.0	546,306	15.0

Notes
1 Chinese raw silk includes Singapore.
2 Silk yarn is "Silk Yarn, Noils, and Warps."

Table 5.11 The composition of Chinese raw silk imports to India (lbs)

Year/region	Canton		Shanghai		Singapore	
	Import	%	Import	%	Import	%
1900/04	821,900	42.3	707,075	36.4	367,974	19.0
05/09	705,370	36.7	887,584	46.1	202,506	10.5
10/14	626,115	23.9	1,649,597	62.8	138,763	5.3

Sources: *British Parl. Papers*, "Tables relating to the Trade of British India with British Possessions and Foreign Countries," "Statistical Abstract for the several British Colonies, Possessions, and Protectorates," "Tables relating to the Trade of British India with the British Empire and Foreign Countries."

Table 5.12 Change in the ranking of imported raw silk in the Indian market

1905	1909	1913
① Canton (rs) 29.9% £24.5)	① Shanghai (rs 43.5% £32.5)	① Shanghai (rs 46.8% £35.6)
② Shanghai (rs 21.2% £24.5)	② Canton (rs 20.5% £21.3)	② Canton (rs 14.4% £25.9)
③ Italy (sy 20.6% £22.7)	③ Italy (sy 11.4% £23.6)	③ Japanese (sy 13.9% £33.0)
④ UK (sy 3.9% £37.1)	④ Japanese (sy 7.0% £29.6)	④ Italy (sy 10.0% £17.2)
⑤ Japanese (rs 3.4% £10.4)	⑤ U.K (sy 3.0% £39.7)	⑤ UK (sy 1.8% £31.8)

Note
£ is unit price per 100 lbs rs is raw silk, sy is silk yarn.

Table 5.13 The price zone of the main raw silks and silk yarns to India

Price zone/year	1905 (%)	1909 (%)	1913 (%)
Above £30	25.1	49.9	62.5
Below £25	53.9	36.0	25.8

Note
In 1913, "Below £25" includes Canton of £25.9.

Table 5.14 The unit price of the main raw silks and silk yarns imported to India

Year/region	Shangai		Japan		Italy		Canton	
	Unit price (£)	Share (%)	Unit price (£)	Share (%)	Unit price (£)	Share (%)	Unit price (£)	Share (%)
1905/09	36.7	33.1	32.0	3.7	24.4	13.1	24.0	26.3
1910/14	34.7	45.4	31.8	11.8	22.0	10.1	24.8	17.2

Sources: *British Parl. Papers*, "Tables relating to the Trade of British India Possessions and Foreign Countries," "Statistical Abstract for the several British Colonies, Possessions, and Protectorates," "Tables relating to the Trade of British India with the British Empire and Foreign Countries."

Note
Shangai and Canton are raw silk, Japan and Italy are silk yarn.

Table 5.15 The import of raw silk and silk yarn in India (1,000 lbs)

Year/region	China	%	Japan	%	Italy	%	Total
1926–27	1,990	66.3	182	6.1	398	13.3	3,000
1927–28	2,652	71.4	289	7.8	406	10.9	3,714
1928–29	2,118	50.7	451	10.8	832	19.9	4,178
1929–30	2,332	56.5	513	12.4	731	17.7	4,131
1930–31	2,318	68.9	255	7.6	432	12.8	3,364
Average	2,282	62.1	338	9.2	560	15.2	3,677
1931–32	1,872	57.2	150	4.6	622	19.0	3,273
1932–33	3,348	54.0	1,352	21.8	862	13.9	6,196
1933–34	2,716	61.6	1,034	23.5	249	5.7	4,407
Average	2,645	57.2	845	18.3	578	12.5	4,625
1934–35	1,791	32.5	2,732	49.6	348	6.3	5,510
1935–36	1,047	18.0	4,002	68.8	284	4.9	5,819
1936–37	1,368	31.0	2,731	61.8	239	5.4	4,419
Average	1,402	26.7	3,155	60.1	290	5.5	5,249

Source: *British Parl. Papers*, "Statistical Abstract for the British Empire."

Table 5.16 Silk production links in China and Japan

	Silk worm	Quality of raw silk	Price of silk fabric
Central China	Univoltine	High-quality	Expensive
Japan	Bivoltine/ F1-hybrid	Middle-quality	Medium-price
Southern China	Multivoltine	Low-quality	Cheap

The multivoltine silk worm lives in the tropics, whereas univoltine and bivoltine silk worms line in temperate zones.[44] So the kind of silk worm used in southern China's silk production link was determined by her tropical environment. But Japan and central China have temperate climates. The Japanese sericultural industry used univoltine silk worms before her ports opened, but after they opened, bivoltine silk worms were used increasingly, and F1-hybrid silk worms became more and more popular from the 1910s. This is because silk fabrics became popular[45] with the growth of the middle class in Japan. But central China's sericultural industry used univoltine silk worms until 1930 because silk fabrics maintained their high-quality character in China, where society's privileged elite also flourished. Then sericulturists were forced to use F1-hybrid silk worms as part of the modernization policies of the Nanking government. In Japan, both the domestic raw silk market[46] and the domestic cotton cloth market[47] expanded after her ports opened, because raw silk exports increased the income of sericulture and silk-reeling farmers.[48] The expansion of these domestic textile sales stimulated an increase in production of new silk-cotton mixed-weave fabric.[49] These were an inferior substitute for middle-quality silk fabrics and matched the output of silk fabrics temporarily.[50] The new silk-cotton mixed-weave fabrics popularized bi-voltine, which was reared in the autumn.[51] This made the output of the Japanese silk industry unsuitable for the European market, but very suitable for the United States.[52] In central China, the Nanking government forced sericulturists to use F1-hybrid silk worm in the 1930s, but many sericulturists protested violently.[53] This change of silk worm resulted in the loss of the European raw silk market, and the Chinese silk industry declined.[54]

Conclusion

The world silk market in these years, can be roughly divided into two types of market. In China, Europe, and India, consumers preferred high-quality silk. But in Japan, the United States, and Australia consumers preferred middle-quality silk.[55] This was largely because the former were elite societies, while the latter were mass-consumption societies.[56] The main competitors in the world market for raw silk were Japan and China. The producing and exporting regions were connected to importing regions which consumed cloths of a nature similar to that of their own home markets. So, the factors behind Japan's victory in the inter-Asian competition for raw silk were the popularization of Japanese society and the relative similarity between the Japanese market and the US market. The world economy was divided not only between Asia and the West but also between mass consumption societies and elite societies.

Notes

1 Kawakatsu (1991).
2 Hamasita and Kawakatsu (1991); Sugihara (1996).
3 Raw silk is a thread made from silk cocoons. Raw silk is directly used for cheap silk manufactures. Silk yarn is twisted raw silk, and is used for expensive silk manufactures.
4 The principal exports of Japan and China were as follows. In 1868/72, the main Japanese exports were raw silk (36.1 percent) and tea (19.8 percent), Chinese exports were tea (53.7 percent) and raw silk (34.0 percent) (Shibahara (1985), p. 172). After that, the situation in China reversed for tea and raw silk. In 1898, raw silk was 27.99 percent, tea was 18.15 percent. In 1913, raw silk was 19.88 percent, tea was 8.41 percent (Latham (1978), p. 87).

5 Hamasita and Kawakatsu (1991); Latham and Kawakatsu (1994).
6 In 1927/31, the United States' share accounted for 68.2 percent of raw silk imports (quantity) in the world (Toua Kenkyu-jo (1942), pp. 8–11).
7 The pioneering works dealing with the world/international silk markets, are Isii (1972); Sugiyama (1979, 1988); Ueyama (1983), and others. Recent works are Ikawa (1992); Ko *et al.* (1993); Nakabayashi (1994, 2001, 2003); Federico (1997); Negishi (1998); Kaneko (2002a,c, 2003), and others.
8 The principal works on the Indian silk industry are, Kumar and Raychaudhuri (1983); Bag (1989).
9 The principal works on the Chinese silk industry, are Kiyokawa (1975); Shih (1976); Li (1981); Eng (1986); So (1986); Suzuki (1992); Soda (1994); Ikawa (1998); Bell (1999); Ma *et al.* (2000). In addition, the principal work, dealing with commercial networks and modern filatures, is by Motono (2000), and the pioneering work, dealing with the mulberry industry, is by Tajiri (1999).
10 The share (quantity) of Asian raw silk in the world markets was as follows: in 1825/30 Indian raw silk 18.1 percent and Chinese raw silk 11.7 percent. In 1873/77 Chinese raw silk 54.0 percent, Japanese raw silk 10.7 percent, and Indian raw silk 32 percent. In 1926 Japanese raw silk 66.5 percent, Chinese raw silk 21.7 percent, and Indian raw silk 0.2 percent (Federico (1997), p. 200).
11 In Japan, the pioneering works, which deal with the French silk trade and the French silk industry, are Hattori (1971); Matsubara (2003).
12 Kaneko (2001, 2002c).
13 Japan exported 50.5 percent of the total raw silk imports to the United States in 1884 (Yokohama (1980), p. 181).
14 In the US market, the share (quantity) of Chinese and Japanese raw silks was in 1876/80, 53.7 and 29.2 percent, respectively. Then, in 1886/90 their shares reversed, China 21.7 percent, and Japan 52.8 percent (Sugiyama (1988), p. 104).
15 In 1925/29, the share of Chinese raw silk was 53.9 percent in the French market and, the share of Japanese raw silk was 7.9 percent while in the US market, China was 15.1 percent and Japan 81.5 percent (Federico (1997), pp. 214, 216).
16 The total raw silk exports of Japan were 4,850 quintals (= 100 kg) in 1860. This then increased rapidly ×16 to become 80,820 quintals in 1909 (Federico (1997), pp. 197–98).
17 During the period concerned, the average annual growth rate of Chinese raw silk exports was 2.45 percent, while the average annual growth rate of Japanese raw silk was 7.08 percent (Ko *et al.* (1995)). Kiyokawa (1975) points to the relative stagnation of the Chinese silk industry's technology. Ikawa (1998) points out the relative stagnation of the Chinese sericultural industry. However, the total raw silk exports of China rose from 38,142 quintals in 1860 to 79,311 quintals in 1909 (Federico (1997), pp. 197–8). The pioneering work, on the development of the Chinese silk industry, is Li (1981).
18 In 1884/88, the raw silk consumption of the French market and the US market was 3,586 tons and 1,923 tons. Then, in 1925/29, France 3,772 tons, and the United States 33,289 tons (Federico (1997), p. 213).
19 The year Japan raw silk exports exceeded those of the Chinese was 1909 according to Yamada (1934), p. 41, and 1906 according to Kiyokawa (1975), p. 241. In 1929, the total raw silk exports (quantity) of China and Japan were 115,637 quintals and 344,910 quintals (Federico (1997), p. 199).
20 The shares of Japanese and Chinese exports in 1934 were 82.3 and 7.5 percent, respectively, of world raw silk production (quantity) (Toua Kenkyu-jo (1942), p. 2).
21 Kaneko (2002c).
22 Ibid.
23 Sericin is gelatin of raw silk.
24 Therefore, multivoltine raw silk cannot be used for the warp of silk fabrics even now (Kaneko (2002c), p. 43). Bivoltine (F1-hybrid) raw silk could be used for stockings,

but multivoltine raw silk and rayon could not be used for silk stockings, and nylon could be used only for inexpensive stockings in the 1930s (Toua Kenkyu-jo (1942), pp. 17–23).

25 White raw silk exported from Shanghai was called "Chinas" (Rawlley (1919), pp. 15–16). This paper excludes yellow raw silk, which was exported from Shanghai. Yellow raw silk's share of the total raw silk exports (excluding wild silk) was 12.5 percent in 1868/1911 (Ko *et al.* (1994), pp. 394–5. Yellow raw silk's share of the total raw silk exports (including wild silk) was 15.2 percent in 1912/49 (Hamazaki *et al.* (1995), p. 15).

26 The shares of Shanghai and Canton raw silk production were estimated at about 50 and 30 percent, respectively, of total raw silk production (quantity) in the 1920s (Shenbao (1934), p. K-27). In 1946 the former was 56.3 percent, the latter was 12.9 percent (Zhu(Si) (1947), p. 312).

27 Rawlley (1919), pp. 29–31.

28 Rawlley (1919), pp. 14–16, 23, 28.

29 Rawlley (1919), pp. 23, 25.

30 Rawlley (1919), p. 21.

31 Ghosh (1949), p. 115.

32 Noushoumu-shou (1916b), pp. 335–46; Rawlley (1919), pp. 15, 18, 21, 27, 75, 77; Ghosh (1949), p. 115.

33 In Bengal, there were 97 filatures employing about 12,000 workers in the 1870s (*British Parl. Papers* (1874), p. 29), but in 1904, there were 75 filatures employing 9,526 workers. In addition, cocoon rearing and mulberry areas also decreased (Ghosh (1949), p. 12). Works which point out the first decline of the Bengal silk industry and Bengal raw silk exports in the 1830s, are those by Kumar and Raychaudhuri (1983), p. 321; Bag (1989). The principal reasons for this first decline were as follows. First, imports of fancy English cotton goods in huge quantities reduced internal silk demand in India after the 1820s. Second, the East India Company's silk trade ceased in 1835 (Bag (1989), pp. 398–401).

34 The share of European raw silk was 34.1 percent in 1905 (*British Parl. Papers* (1911), p. 49).

35 In the French market, the shares (quantity) of the main raw silk producing countries were as follows: in 1884/88 French raw silk 19.9 percent, Italian raw silk 24.1 percent, Chinese raw silk 30.0 percent, and Japanese raw silk 10.0 percent. In 1925/29 French raw silk 7.8 percent, Italian raw silk 22.3 percent, Chinese raw silk 53.9 percent, and Japanese raw silk 7.9 percent (Federico (1997), p. 216).

36 Bivoltine silk worms can be found in the Himalayan mountainous area, but they were not used (Asia Kyoukai (1959), pp. 7–8).

37 The share of Japanese raw silk (value) in 1924/28, 98.6 percent (Toua Kenkyu-jo (1939), p. 113).

38 The Australian silk fabrics market had low customs duties, and was in sharp contrast to the US silk fabrics market, which had high customs duties. Import penetration (value) from the main countries into the Australian silk fabrics market in 1928 was as follows: Japanese silk fabrics 63.7 percent, French silk fabrics 14 percent, Swiss silk fabrics 11 percent and United Kingdom's silk fabrics 4 percent (*British Parl. Papers*, (1937), pp. 166, 167).

39 In the Australian silk fabrics market, the share (quantity) in 1937 of Chinese silk fabrics was 0.95 percent (Nihon Yushutsu Kinu Jinken Orimono Kumiai (1940), p. 94).

40 European silk fabrics were of two types: high-quality expensive silk fabrics made of high-quality raw silk by machine-looms in Lyon city and low-quality inexpensive silk fabrics made of low-quality raw silk by handlooms in farming villages (Ohno (1984), pp. 5–10). So, there was big demand for multivoltine low-quality raw silk in the European market.

41 Kaneko (2002b, 2003).

42 Toua Kenkyu-jo (1943), pp. 165–7, Noushoumu-shou (1899), pp. 22–33; Zhu (xin) (1985), pp. 151–8.

43 Noushoumu-shou (1921), p. 5 and Sanshi-gyo Dougyo Kumiai (1929), p. 24.

44 Yasugi *et al.* (1996), p. 219.

45 Utida (1997).

46 A recent estimate of domestic raw silk consumption (and the domestic consumption rate) was 2,467 tons (81 percent) in 1874, 6,888 tons (71 percent) in 1900, and 14,586 tons (30 percent) in 1929 (Utilda (1995), p. 36).

47 Tanimoto (1998).

48 Incomes per head of sericulture and silk-reeling farmers were 3 ryou and 1.5 ryou in the 1860s (Saito and Tanimoto (1989), p. 235).

49 After Japan's ports opened, the quality of silk-cotton mixed-weave fabric greatly changed (Kaneko (1999)).

50 Production (quality) of the silk fabric and the new silk-cotton mixed-weave fabric was as follows: Silk 3,495,712 tan, Silk-cotton mixed-weave 3,230,970 tan in 1887. Silk 13,621,979 tan, Silk-cotton mixed-weave 13,216,494 tan in 1910 (for each year of the "Noushoumu Toukei Hyou"). Tan is the old Japanese unit of cloth. 1 tan = cloth for 1 person.

51 The share of summer and autumn cocoon harvests in the total harvests of a year was 28.8 percent in 1886, 43.5 percent in 1913, and 50.4 percent in 1929 (Nourin-shou (1961), pp. 8–11).

52 Most of the silk-reeling factories in Nagano prefecture aimed at the production of middle-quality raw silk (Ueyama (1988)).

53 Some sericulturists rioted (Bennou (1993)).

54 In the French market, the shares (quality) of Chinese raw silk diminished from 55.4 percent in 1925, to 35.0 percent in 1936 (Toua Kenkyu-jo (1943), pp. 406–7). The total raw silk exports of China diminished from 160,461 piculs in 1929, to 52,738 piculs in 1934 (Toua Kenkyu-jo (1943), p. 55).

55 In the United States, readymade silk clothes were popular in the early twentieth century (Takatori (1924), p. 87), which accounted for the high consumption of middle-quality raw silk. But tailor-made silk clothes were popular in Europe.

56 In Japan, mass consumption society developed after the 1920s (Nakamura (2002), pp. 27–30). Before the Second World War, one person (average man and woman) had four items of clothing in the United Kingdom, seven items of clothing in the United States, and 24 items of clothing in Japan. In Osaka Japan, one middle-class lady (average) had 40 items of clothing. In Japan, according to an investigation, one ordinary young career woman had about 25 items of silk clothing in 1935 (Yagi (1978), pp. 103–5).

References

Bag, Sailendra Kumar (1989) *The Changing Fortunes of the Bengal Silk Industry: 1757–1833*, Calcutta: Pradip Kumar Banerjee Manasi Press.

Bell, Lynda S. (1999) *One Industry, Two Chinas: Silk Filatures and Peasant-Family Production in Wuxi County, 1865–1937*, Stanford, CA: Stanford University Press.

British Parl. Papers (1874) Vol. 68 (C. 982-I) "Report on Silk in India."

British Parl. Papers (1875) Vol. 55 (C. 1373) "Statement of the Trade of British India with British Possessions and Foreign Countries for the Five Years 1869–70 to 1873–74."

British Parl. Papers (1876) Vol. 57 (C. 1616) "Statement of the Trade of British India with British Possessions and Foreign Countries for the Five Years 1870–71 to 1874–75."

British Parl. Papers (1911) Vol. 56 (Cd. 5608) "Tables Relating to the Trade of British India with British Possessions and Foreign Countries, 1905–06 to 1909–10."

British Parl. Papers (1916) Vol. 21 (Cd. 8343) "Tables Relating to the Trade of British India with British Possessions and Foreign Countries, 1910–11 to 1914–15."

British Parl. Papers (1936–37) Vol. 27 (Cd. 5298) "Statistical Abstract for the British Empire for each of the ten years 1926 to 1935."

Eng, Robert Y. (1986) *Economic Imperialism in China: Silk Producution and Exports, 1861–1932*, Berkeley, CA: Institute of East Asian Studies, University of California.

Federico, Giovanni (1997) *An Economic History of the Silk Industry, 1830–1930*, Cambridge: Cambridge University Press.

Ghosh, C.C. (1949) *Silk Production and Weaving in India*, India: Council of Scientific and Industrial Research.

Kumar, Dharma and Raychaudhuri, Tapan (eds) (1983) *The Cambridge Economic History of India. Vol. 2: c.1757–c.1970*, Cambridge: Cambridge University Press.

Latham, A.J.H. (1978) *The International Economy and the Undeveloped World 1865–1914*, London: Croom Helm Ltd (First published in the United States Rowman and Littlefield).

Latham, A.J.H. and Kawakatsu, Heita (eds) (1994) *Japanese Industrialization and the Asian Economy*, London: Routledge.

Li, Lillian M. (1981) *China's Silk Trade: Traditional Industry in the Modern World 1842–1937*, Cambridge, MA: Harvard University Press.

Ma, Debin (2000) "Europe, China, Japan: Transfer of Silk Reeling Technology in 1860–95," in Latham, A.J.H. and Kawakatsu, Heita (eds) *Asia Pacific Dynamic 1550–2000*, London and New York: Routledge.

Motono, Eiichi (2000) *Conflict and Cooperation in Sino-British Business, 1860–1911: The Impact of the Pro-British Commercial Network in Shanghai*, London: Macmillan Press.

Rawlley, Ratan C. (1919) *The Silk Industry and Trade: A Study in the Economic Organization of the Export Trade of Kashmir and Indian Silks, with Special Reference to their Utilization in the British and French Markets*, London: P.S. King & Son, Ltd.

Shih, Min-hsiung (1976) *The Silk Industry in Ch'ing China*, Michigan: The University of Michigan Center for Chinese Studies.

So, Alvin Y. (1986) *The South China Silk District: Local Historical Transformation and World-System Theory*, Albany, NY: State University of New York Press.

Sugiyama, Shinya (1988) *Japan's Industralization in the World Economy 1859–1899*, London: The Athlone Press.

Japanese references

Asia Kyoukai (1959) *Indo Sanshi-gyo eno Kyouryoku* (Cooperate to the Indian Silk Industry), Asia Kyoukai Hakkou.

Bennou, Saiichi (1993) "Tyugoku no Nougyo Kindai-ka ni Taisuru Teikou: 1920–30nendai Sekkou-shou no Sanshu Kairyou ni Miru" ("The Resistance to Agricultural Modernization in China: A Case Study Based on the Zhejiang Silkworm Egg Improvement Campaign of the 1920s and 1930s") *Shakai-Keizaishigaku*, No. 59-1.

Hamasita, Takesi and Kawakatsu, Heita (eds) (1991) *Asia Koueki-ken to Nihon Kougyou-ka 1500–1900* (Intra-Asian Trade Area and Japan Industrialization: 1500–1900), Riburopoto.

Hamazaki, Minoru, Ko, Kokutatsu (Gu, Guoda), Uyama, Mitsuru (1995) "Minkoku-ki (1912–1949) ni Okeru Tyugoku Kiito Yushutsu no Kenkyu" ("Study of Chinese Raw Silk Export in the Republic of China (1912–1949): Factors in Fluctuations in Quantity in Producing Districts of Chinese Raw Silk Export") *Kyoto Kougei Seni Daigaku Seni Gakubu Gakujutsu Houkoku*, No. 19.

Hattori, Haruhiko (1971) "19seiki France Kinu Kougyou no Hatten to Sekai Shijo" ("French Silk Industry and the World Market in the Nineteenth Century") *Shirin*, No. 54-3.

Ikawa, Katsuhiko (1992) "Seisi-gyo to America Sijo" ("The Silk reeling Industry and the American Market"), Takamura, Naosuke (ed.) *Kigyo Bokko: Nihon Shihonshugi no Keisei* (The Rise of Firms: The Formation of Japanese Capitalism), Mineruva Shobo.

Ikawa, Katsuhiko (1998) *Kindai Nihon Seishi-gyo to Mayu Seisan* (Modern Japan Silk Industry and the Cocoon Production), Tokyo Keizai Jyoho Shuppan.

Imamura, Shouzo (1935) *Sekai Seni-kai to Sanshi* (The Fiber Industries in the World and Silk), Meibundou.

Isii, Kanji (1972) *Nihon Sanshi-gyo-shi Bunseki* (Analysis of Japanese Silk Industry), Tokyo Daigaku Shuppan-Kai.

Kaneko, Shinsuke (1999) "Kaikou-go no Oume ni Okeru Yunyu Menpu no Bouatsu" ("Competition Between the Import and Oume Cotton Goods, from the 1860s to the 1880s'), *Tihoushi Kenkyu*, No. 279.

Kaneko, Shinsuke (2001) "Senzen-ki India Sanshi-gyo Kenkyu Josetsu" ("The Silk Industry in British India, 1899–1936"), *Yokohama Siritu Daigaku Daigakuin Insei-ronshu*, No. 7.

Kaneko, Shinsuke (2002a) "Kaiyo Asia no Thiiki-kan Kyoso to Sekai Sijio; Kindai ni Okeru Nihon Tyugoku India no Sanshi-gyo wo Tyushin-ni" ("Intra-Asian Competition in the World Markets: Modern Silk Industries of Japan, China, and India"), Kawakatsu, Heita (ed.) *Global History ni Mukete* (Towards a Global History), Fujiwara Shoten.

Kaneko, Shinsuke (2002b) "Senzen-ki Tyugoku Sanshi-gyo Kenkyu Josetsu" ("The Silk Industry in China, 1901–1941"), *Yokohama Siritu Daigaku Daigakuin Insei-ronshu*, No. 8.

Kaneko, Shinsuke (2002c) "Senzen-ki no Sekai Kiito Sijyo wo Meguru Asia-kan Kyoso" ("Intra-Asian Competiton in raw Silk for the World Markets, 1859–1929"), *Aziya Kenkyu*, No. 48-2.

Kaneko, Shinsuke (2003) "Kiito wo Meguru Nitthuu Tiiki-Kan Kyousou to Sekai Shijou: Sumiwake to Mayu Kiito Hinshitsu tono Renkan wo Tyusin-ni" (Competition Between Japan and China in the World Raw Silk Market"), Kawakatsu, Heita (ed.) *Asia Taiheiyou Keizaiken-shi: 1500–2000* (Economic History of the Asian Pacific Ocean: 1500–2000), Fujiwara Shoten.

Kawakatsu, Heita (1991) *Nihon Bunmei to Kindai Seiyo* (Japanese Civilization and the Modern West), Nihon Hoso Shuppan-kyokai.

Kiyokawa, Yukihiko (1975) "Senzen Tyugoku no Sanshi-gyo ni Kansuru Jakkan no Kousatsu (1)" ("A Consideration on the Technology of the Silk Reeling Industry in Pre-liberation China), *Keizai-gaku Kenkyu*, No. 26-3.

Ko, Kokutatsu (Gu, Guoda), Hamazaki, Minoru, Uyama, Mitsuru (1993) "Kindai Kiito Sekai Shijo no Seiritsu Youin to Sono Jukyu Kankei (1842–72nen)" ("The Materialization Factors in the Modern World's Raw Silk Market and the Relation Between Demand and Supply: 1842–72"), *Nihon Sanshi-gaku Zasshi*, No. 62-5.

Ko, Kokutatsu (Gu, Guoda), Uyama, Mitsuru, Hamazaki, Minoru (1994) "Shin Makki ni Okeru Tyugoku Yushutsu Kiito no Santi Bunseki no Suikei (1868–1911)" ("Districts Exporting Chinese Raw Silk During the Late Ch'ing Dynasty: 1868–1911"), *Nihon Sanshi-gaku Zasshi*, No. 63-5.

Ko, Kokutatsu (Gu, Guoda), Hamazaki, Minoru, Uyama, Mitsuru (1995) "Shin Makki ni Okeru Tyugoku Kiito Yushutsu-ryou Hendo no Youin Bunseki (1868–1911)" ("Factor Analysis of the Chinese Raw Silk Export in the Late Ch'ing Dynasty: 1868–1911"), *Nihon Sanshi-gaku Zasshi*, No. 64-2.

Matsubara, Takehiko (2003) *France Kindai Kinu Kougyou-shi Ron* (A Study of the French Silk Industry's History), Kouyou Shobou.

Nakabayasi, Masaki (1994) "Yousan-gyo no Saihen to Kokusai Shijo: 1882–1886nen" ("The Reconstruction of Sericure and the International Market: 1882–1886"), *Toti-Seidoshigaku*, No. 145.

Nakabayashi (2001) "Daikibo Seisi Koujo no Seiritsu to America Shijyo" ("The Formation of Large Silk-reeling Factories and the United States Market: A Case Study of the Growth of the Okaya Silk Reeling Co. and the Establishment of its Brand"), *Shakai-Keizaisigaku*, No. 66-6.

Nakabayashi (2003) *Kindai Shihon-shugi no Soshiki: Seishi-gyou no Hatten ni Okeru Torihiki no Touti to Seisan no Kouzou* (An Organization in Modern Capitalism: the Governance of Trade and the System of Production in the Development of the Silk Reling Industry), Tokyo Daigaku Shuppan-kai.

Nakamura, Muneyoshi (2002) "Nihon no Taishu Shouhi Shakai" ("Mass Consumption Society in Japan") Oosugi, Yuka, Katohno, Takeshi, Saito, Shinji, Nakajima, Masato, Nakamura, Muneyoshi, Watabe, Shigeru (eds), *Dai 2 han: Nihon Keizai no Keizai-gaku* (The 2nd Edition: Economics of the Japanese Economy), Gakubunsha.

Negishi, Hideyuki (1998) "Kindai Ikou-ki no Nihon Kiito to Europe Shijo" ("Japanese Raw Silk and the European Market in the 1870s and 1880s"), *Asahi Daigaku Keiei-ronshu*, No. 13-1.

Nihon Yushutsu Kinu Jinken Orimono Kumiai Rengo-kai (1940) *Nihon Yushutsu Kengyou Toukei Gairan* (Overview of Japanese Silk Exportation Statistics).

Nourin-shou Nourin Keizai-kyoku Toukei Tyousa-bu (1961) *Yousan Ruinen Toukei Hyou* (Sericulture Statistics), Nourin Toukei Kyoukai.

Noushoumu-shou Shoukou-kyoku Shouji-ka (1899) *Shinkoku Senshoku-gyou Shisatsu Hukumei-sho* (A Report of the Textile Industry in the Ch'ing Dynasty), Yurin-dou.

Noushoumu-shou Seisai Tyousa-kai (1910) *Sekai no Sanshi-gyou Narabini Jinzou Kenshi-gyou* (The Silk and Artificial Silk Industry in the World).

Noushoumu-shou Noumu-kyoku (1912) *Noumu Isan Dai 26: Sekai no Sanshi-gyou Narabini Jinzou Kenshi-gyou (Dai 2 ji)* (The 2nd Edition: The Silk and Artificial Silk Industry in the World).

Noushoumu-shou Noumu-kyoku (1916a) *Noumu Isan Dai 26: Sekai no Sanshi-gyou Narabini Jinzou Kenshi-gyou (Dai 3 ji)* (The 3rd Edition: The Silk and Artificial Silk Industry in the World).

Noushoumu-shou (1916b) *Ihutsu no sanshi-gyou* (The Silk Industries in Italy and France), Meibun-dou.

Noushoumu-shou Noumu-kyoku (1921) *Shina Seishi-gyou Tyousa Hukumei-sho* (The Investigative Report of the Chinese Silk Industry).

Ohno, Akira (1984) "Oushu Kengyo to Beikoku Kengyo no Hikaku Kousatsu" ("The Comparative History of the European Silk Industries and the American Silk Industry"), *Kwansei Gakuin Keizai-gaku Kenkyu*, No. 17.

Saito, Osamu and Tanimoto, Masayuki (1989) "Zairai Sangyo no Saihensei" ("Reorganization of the Traditional Industries"), Umemura, Mataji and Yamamoto, Yuzo (eds), *Nihon Keizai-si3*, Iwanami Shoten.

Sanshi-gyo Dougyo Kumiai Tyuohkai (ed.) (1929) *Shina Sanshi-gyo Taikan* (Overview of the Chinese Silk Industry), Okada Nitiei-dou.

Shibahara, Takuji (1985) "Nittyu Ryoukoku no Menseihin-Kiito Boueki (1868–92) to Sono Haikei" ("The Cotton-Silk Trade in Japan and China, 1868–92"), *Oikonomika*, No. 21-2, 3, 4.

Soda, Saburo (1994) *Tyugoku Kindai Seishi-gyo no Kenkyu* (Research of the Chinese Modern Silk Industry), Kyuko Shoin.

Sugihara, Kaoru (1996) *Azia-kan Boueki no Keisei to Kouzou* (Formation and Structure of Intra-Asian Trade), Mineruva Shobou.

Sugiyara, Sinya (1979) "Bakumatu, Meiji Shoki ni okeru Kiito Yushutu no Suuryou-teki Saikentou" ("Quantitative Review on Japan's Raw Silk Exports from 1859 to the Mid-1870s") *Shakai-Keizaishigaku*, No. 45-3.

Suzuki, Tomoo (1992) *Yomu Undo no Kenkyu* (A Study of Westernization Movement in China), Kyuko Shoin.

Tajiri, Tosi (1999) *Shindai Nougyo Shougyouka no Kenkyu* (Research into Agriculture Commercialization in the Ch'ing Dynasty), Kyuko Shoin.

Takatori, Youkou (ed.) (1924) "Oushu no Kengyo to Kiito no Shouhi" (Consumption of Raw Silk and the Silk Industry in Europe"), *Sanshi-gyo Dougyo Kumiai Tyuoukai Houkoku Gougai*.

Tanimoto, Masayuki (1998) *Nihon ni Okeru Zairai-teki Keizai Hatten to Orimonogyo* (Traditional Economic Development and the Textile Industry in Japan), Nagoya Daigaku Shuppankai.

Toua Kenkyu-jo (1939) *Nitigou Boueki Gaikan* (A Survey of Japan–Australia Trade).

Toua Kenkyu-jo (1942) *Shina Kiito no Sekai-teki Tii* (Status of Chinese Raw Silk in the World).

Toua Kenkyu-jo (1943) *Shina Sanshi-gyo Kenkyu* (Research of the Chinese Silk Industry), Oosaka Yagou Shoten.

Ueyama, Kazuo (1983) "Daiitiji Taisen Mae ni Okeru Nihon Kiito no Taibei Shinshutu" ("Export of Japanese Raw Silk to the USA before the First World War"), *Josai Keizai Gakukai-si*, No. 19-1.

Ueyama (1988) "Sanshi-gyo ni Okeru Tyutou-ito Seisan Taisei no Keisei" ("Formation of the Middle-quality Raw Silk Production System in the Japanese Silk Industry"), in Takamura, Naosuke (ed.) *Nitiro Sengo no Nihon Keizai* (Japanese Economy After the Japan–Russia War), Sima Shobo.

Utida, Kanao (1995) "Senzen-ki Nihon no Kiito Kokunai Shijo" ("Domestic Market of Raw Silk in Prewar Japan: An Estimate and Quantitative Analysis of Silk Consumption"), *Keiei-sigaku*, No. 29-4.

Utida, Kanao (1997) "Zairai Sangyo to Dento Shijo: Meiji Zenki no Nishijin Kinu Orimono Genryo-ito Shijo wo Megutte" ("Traditional Industry and the Traditional Market: The Raw Silk Market for Nishijin Silk Fabric in the First Half of Meiji"), in Nakamura, Takahusa (ed.) *Nihon no Keizai Hatten to Zairai Sangyo* (Japanese Economic Development and Traditional Industry), Yamakawa Shuppansha.

Yagi, Akio (1978) *Seikatu Keizai-si* (Economic History of the Living), Hyouron-sha.

Yamada, Moritarou (1934) *Nihon Sihon Shugi Bunseki* (Analysis of Japanese Capitalism).

Yasugi, Ryuiti, Kozeki, Haruo, Huruya, Masaki, Hidaka, Tositaka (eds) (1996) *Iwanami Seibutu-gaku Jiten* (Iwanami Biology Dictionary, The 4th Edition), Iwanami Shoten.

Yokohama-shi (1980) *Yokohama-shishi: Siryou-hen 2: Zouteiban* (Yokohama City History: Data Book 2: The 2nd Edition).

Chinese references

Shenbao (1934) *Minguo 23 nian Shenbao Nianjian* (Almanac of the Republic of China in 23).

Zhu, Si huang (1947) *Minguo Jingji-shi* (The Economic History of the Republic of China: Volume 1), Ynhang Xuehui.

Zhu, Xin, yu (ed.) (1985) *Zhejiang Sichou-shi* (History of the Silk Industry in Zhejiang), Zhejiang Renmin Chubanshe.

6 Inter-Asian competition in the sugar market, 1890–1939

Takashi Kume

Introduction

We are all aware of sugar as a food, but before the nineteenth century, in East Asia, sugar was only used for medicine and high-class confectionaries.[1] After the opening of East Asian ports to Western nations, sugar emerged as a very popular commodity for the people of this region, with the modern sugar industry establishing itself in Hong Kong and Japan. The sugar market there expanded rapidly, but until the 1880s, people preferred brown sugar made in the traditional way. As people's tastes gradually changed, demand for refined white sugar increased. From the 1880s, in addition to cane sugar from Mauritius and Java, beet sugar was brought to Asia from Europe in large quantities, resulting in a reorganization of the sugar industry there. This chapter will discuss inter-Asian competition for sugar in these years, focusing in particular on Japan, China, and India.

Various treaty restrictions at first made it impossible for these three countries to introduce a protective tariff on imported sugar, resulting in the domination of their markets by imports. However, upon the revision of the relevant treaties, Japan established effective tariffs in 1899, China in 1929, and India in 1932. The subsequent fall in sugar imports was drastic, with the sugar industry in those countries becoming increasingly competitive. While Japan and China developed a modern sugar refining industry, India concentrated instead on its traditional sugar industry. What factors lay behind these differences?

The Japanese market

In the late 1870s and the first half of the 1880s, British capital set up two major modern sugar refining companies in Hong Kong: the China Sugar Refining Co. and the Taikoo Sugar Refining Co., the former being established by Jardine, Matheson & Co. and the latter by John Swire & Sons. Both companies targeted the Chinese and Japanese markets.

In the 1860s and 1870s the Japanese market was very small, importing mainly unrefined brown sugar from southern China and Formosa (Table 6.1).

Yet beginning in the latter half of the 1880s, as the white sugar market in Japan expanded, sugar from these two companies, along with beet sugar from Germany

Table 6.1 Imports of sugar to Japan 1868–95 (1,000 piculs)

	Sugar, brown	Sugar, white	Sugar, bar	Sugar, crystal
1868	171	55	1.5	3.6
1869	235	69	0.7	7.6
1870	527	89	1.3	4.75
1871	522	107	1.2	4.97
1872	333	83	1.3	5.17
1873	373	82	1.6	7.5
1874	470	91	1.2	7.93
1875	623	115	1.7	8.34
1876	583	84	1.9	7.5
1877	456	85	0.9	7.68
1878	416	76	2.6	7.9
1879	492	108	2.6	8.81
1880	559	121	1.0	9.32
1881	487	172	2.2	8.9
1882	601	189	1.2	8.78
1883	604	231	1.2	7.6
1884	825	351	1.8	7.06
1885	612	414	2.4	4.53
1886	506	566	2.0	3.43
1887	754	566	3.6	1.67
1888	732	723	2.8	0.65
1889	617	591	2.4	1.33
1890	835	824	2.8	0.67
1891	722	894	1.8	0.12
1892	817	1,083	1.6	0.01
1893	960	1,092	1.8	0.01
1894	1,138	1,093	1.6	0.03
1895	1,119	1,295	2.5	0.04

Source: *Dainihon Gaikoku Bôeki Nenpyô* (Annual Return of the Foreign Trade of the Empire of Japan). Department of Finance, 1882–96.

and Austria–Hungary, began to dominate the market. In 1868, Japanese domestic sugar production was estimated to be about 510,000 piculs,[2] whereas imported sugar amounted to about 231,100 piculs. In 1885, domestic production was about 680,000 piculs[3] while imported sugar stood at about 1,033,000 piculs. In 1892, about 90 percent of the Japanese white sugar market was foreign refined sugar.[4]

In those days, although brown sugar was widely consumed in the Japanese market, white sugar called *Sanbontô* was the main domestic product, of the Dutch standard between Nos 11 and 15 (under the Dutch standard, "lower grade" is sugar ranked between Nos 11 and 18; "high grade" indicates a ranking exceeding No. 18).[5] *Sanbontô* was produced in a traditional way and strictly categorized by the Dutch standard, but the actual quality was over No. 15.[6] By comparison, imported white sugar from Hong Kong was mainly between standard Nos 15 and 21[7] and imported beet sugar from Germany and Austria between Nos 18 and 21.[8] These three kinds of sugar competed fiercely with each other in the Japanese white sugar market.

In order to compete with foreign sugar, modern refining companies were established in Tokyo and Osaka in 1896. In addition, as a result of a new treaty between Britain and Japan which took effect in 1899, the Japanese government was able to raise its tariff. However, the tariff increase was confined to raw sugar below No. 15 on the Dutch standard.[9] As a result, Japanese refined white sugar was still in keen competition with foreign refined sugar in the Japanese market. In 1902, by reinstating import taxes on imported raw sugar, the Japanese government enabled domestic refining companies to gain a larger foothold in the market[10] (Table 6.2). It was from this time that Japanese refined white sugar began to drive out imported sugar.

It is also worthy of note that British refined sugar from Hong Kong was more expensive than that from Germany or Austria–Hungary, so British sugar was unable to sustain its position in the Japanese market (Table 6.3). The development of the beet sugar industry in Germany and Austria–Hungary was supported by export subsidies, but these were abolished under the Brussels agreement on sugar in 1902. After that, beet sugar from those countries was no longer competitive.

However, the greatest factor driving foreign sugar from the Japanese market was the Japanese possession of Formosa, as a result of the Sino-Japanese War.

Table 6.2 Imports of white sugar to Japan 1899–1905 (piculs)

	Hong Kong	Austria	Germany
1899	730,927	107,145	251,068
1900	1,097,324	430,505	404,313
1901	1,001,470	473,929	1,089,472
1902	193,346	167,717	480,105
1903	124,391	420,280	391,941
1904	187,154	28,072	158,795
1905	19,790	845	37,178

Source: *Dainihon Gaikoku Bôeki Nenpyô* (Annual Return of the Foreign Trade of the Empire of Japan). Department of Finance, 1900–06.

Table 6.3 Price of imported white sugar in the Japanese market 1899–1905 (yen per picul)

	Hong Kong	Austria	Germany
1899	8.49	7.14	7.42
1900	8.61	7.08	7.27
1901	8.83	7.39	7.48
1902	7.56	6.53	6.15
1903	7.64	5.92	6.29
1904	7.96	6.63	7.12
1905	8.99	7.10	7.21

Source: *Dainihon Gaikoku Bôeki Nenpyô* (Annual Return of the Foreign Trade of the Empire of Japan). Department of Finance, 1900–06.

The Japanese government backed up Mitsui, setting up as part of its national policy the Taiwan Sugar Refining Co. in 1901. Following this, several other modern refining companies were established there. The consequence of such activity was that foreign white sugar was effectively driven from the Japanese domestic white sugar market by the 1910s.

The Chinese market

After their exit from the Japanese market, from the 1910s British modern refining companies in Hong Kong concentrated on China. The sugar market in China comprised three main product categories: high-grade refined white sugar, a lower-grade refined white sugar, and an unrefined brown sugar. The unrefined brown sugar market was dominated by Chinese sugar produced in the traditional way. The lower-grade white sugar market was dominated by sugar from Java, but in the high-grade white sugar market, sugar from Hong Kong competed with sugar from Japan, together fully satisfying demand in the 1910s.

In Japan, the government extended its support to the sugar industry, refining the sugar obtained from Taiwan for domestic use and the sugar from other areas for export use. Taiwanese raw sugar was more expensive than Java raw sugar by 4.5 yen per picul on average from 1924 to 1929 (Table 6.4). The government charged import taxes on foreign raw sugar to protect Taiwanese raw sugar. Nevertheless, the government refunded import taxes to the Japanese sugar industry only in refining the raw sugar obtained from Java (Nos 11 to 15 under the Dutch standard) for export. With the refining companies in Hong Kong also using raw sugar from Java,[11] the Japanese government reinstated import taxes on foreign raw sugar. However, a change in the quality of Java raw sugar (from Nos 11 to 15 under the Dutch standard to Nos 16 to 21) led the government to revise its tariff again in 1927 (Table 6.5). Before the revision of the tariff, the Japanese government did not classify sugar over No. 18 as a raw material, so import taxes could not be refunded to the Japanese sugar industry under the reinstated import taxes policy. Consequently the Japanese sugar industry fared poorly against Hong Kong during the first half of the 1920s. However, following the revision of the tariff, the Japanese government

Table 6.4 Production cost of sugar from Java and Taiwan (yen per picul)

	Java (No. 16–21) (A)	Taiwan (B)	Differential (B – A)
1924–25	7.710	10.385	2.675
1925–26	6.769	10.707	3.938
1926–27	5.655	12.046	6.391
1927–28	5.395	9.871	4.476
1928–29	5.000	9.750	4.750
Average	6.016	10.552	4.446

Source: Kawano Shinji, *Nihon tôgyô hattatsushi (Shôhihen)* (The History of the Development of the Modern Japanese Sugar Industry (Consumption)). Tokyo: Maruzen, 1930, pp. 501–2.

Table 6.5 The revision of the tariff on sugar imported to Japan (yen per picul)

July in 1911		April in 1927		Differential
Type I (under No. 11)	2.50	Type I	2.50	
Type II (under No. 15)	3.10	Type II	3.95	+0.85
Type III (under No. 18)	3.35	Type III	3.95	+0.60
Type IV (under No. 21)	4.25	Type IV	3.95	−0.30
Type V (over No. 21)	4.65	Type V	5.30	+0.65
Sugar, crystal and others	7.40		7.40	

Source: Naigai Togyô Chôsasho Chôsabu (Naigai Research Center for the Sugar Industry) (ed.) *Satô torihiki Nenkan* (Sugar Year-Book of Japan) Tokyo: Bungadô, 1924, p. 390; 1928, p. 236.

Table 6.6 Quantity and value of refined sugar from Hong Kong and Japan at Shanghai market

	1920		1921		1922	
	Hong Kong	Japan	Hong Kong	Japan	Hong Kong	Japan
Quantity (piculs)	165,613	392,966	988,594	406,899	501,771	967,014
Value (HK$)	1,859,083	3,491,138	10,792,043	4,249,533	4,651,338	8,258,901
HK$ per picul	11.23	8.88	10.92	10.44	9.27	8.54

Source: Naigai Togyô Chôsasho Chôsabu (Naigai Research Center for the Sugar Industry) (ed.) *Satô torihiki Nenkan* (Sugar Year-Book of Japan) Tokyo: Bungadô, 1924.

Table 6.7 White sugar imported to China (piculs)

	1925	1926	1927	1928
Java	4,375,579	3,042,595	4,457,930	5,624,834
Japan	2,669,912	2,933,808	2,587,390	3,428,992
Hong Kong	1,727,176	1,826,440	726,364	526,378

Source: Kawano Shinji, *Nihon tôgyô hattatsushi* (*Seisanhen*) (The History of the Development of the Modern Japanese Sugar Industry (Production)). Tokyo: Maruzen, 1930, p. 515.

classified sugar up to and including No. 21 as raw material, resulting in the Japanese sugar industry benefiting once more from the import taxes policy. Owing to this, the price of Japanese white sugar exported to China fell to 10.1 yen per picul on an FOB basis in 1928, compared with 19.7 yen per picul in 1921.[12]

As a result, the market share of Japanese sugar increased, greatly exceeding that of Hong Kong in the Chinese market in the latter half of the 1920s (Tables 6.6 and 6.7). However, in 1929 a protective tariff was imposed in China on imported sugar. This tariff, in combination with a boycott of Japanese sugar and a disadvantageous situation in which the Guangdong provincial government had established a special relationship with dealers in Java, Japanese white sugar could not compete in the lower-grade white sugar market in China in the 1930s.[13]

The Indian market

There are several notable points of contrast in the sugar market of India vis-à-vis those of Japan and China. In Japan and China, many modern refining factories utilizing the latest technology were built, resulting in the gradual decline of the indigenous sugar industry. However, in India, because plantation white sugar continued to be imported from Mauritius and Java, the modern sugar industry was unable to establish itself firmly. Instead, the indigenous traditional sugar industry became more competitive.

The sugar market in India was also divided into three submarkets: a white sugar market, a higher-grade *gur* market, and a lower-grade *gur* market (*gur* being an unrefined sugar produced in a traditional way, containing molasses in addition to sucrose). While higher-grade *gur* could be consumed as it was, lower-grade *gur* was generally of poor quality resulting in it being used primarily as raw sugar for refining.[14] Some argue that there was a high degree of substitution between *gur* and refined sugar, but this remains a point of contention among historians.[15] It seems most likely that there was not a high degree of substitution insofar as *gur* was not used for sweetening tea or coffee but as a raw ingredient in confectioneries or other food. For sweetening tea, the ratio of white sugar to *gur* was about 7:1 during 1935–39, but for sweetening milk, *gur* and white sugar of average quality were used in a relatively equal ratio.[16]

According to Figure 6.1, as imports of white sugar increased rapidly during the 1920s, domestic prices for all types of sugar fell substantially, with the price differential between *gur* and white sugar also decreasing. Kiyokawa argues that, had the differential continued to fall, the *gur* manufacturing industry would have become uncompetitive with the modern sugar industry, as the quality of *gur* was low. However, this probably applied to lower-grade *gur*, and insofar as there existed a usage difference between high-grade *gur* and white sugar, a high degree of substitution did not occur between the two.

The white sugar market was exposed not only to competition between Asian countries but also to wider international competition. In the early 1860s, India exported sugar to Europe, but the development of the beet sugar industry in Germany and Austria–Hungary in the 1880s resulted in the exclusion from Europe of cane sugar from India and Mauritius. Beet sugar even flowed into the Indian market, with India ceasing to be a net sugar exporter, becoming instead a net sugar importer (Table 6.8).

The development of the European beet sugar industry was supported by export subsidies, but these subsidies were abolished as a result of the Brussels agreement on sugar in 1902, as noted earlier. When European beet sugar was eliminated, white sugar from Java and Mauritius moved in to dominate the Indian white sugar market. As the habit of drinking tea or coffee took root among ordinary people at the beginning of the twentieth century, the white sugar market continued to grow. There was no protection from imported sugar until the Sugar Industry Protection Act of 1932. Furthermore, sugarcane was grown by small-scale farmers, resulting in conditions which made it impossible for the modern sugar refining industry to develop in India.

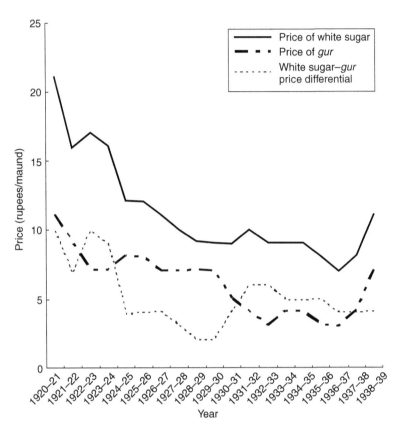

Figure 6.1 Trends in the final consumption price of white sugar and *gur* (rupees per maund).

Source: Yukihiko Kiyokawa and Akihiko Ohno, "Technology and labour absorption in the indigenous Indian sugar industry: an analysis of appropriate technology." In Peter Robb (ed.) *Local Agrarian Societies in Colonial India*, Delhi: Manohar, 1997, p. 352 (figure 3).

Original source: Government of India, *Report on the Marketing of Sugar in India and Burma*, Delhi, 1943, pp. 428–9.

Note
1 maund = 37.3 kg.

Whereas a constant supply of sugarcane was needed over a sustained period of time to meet the processing capabilities of the modern refining factory, in India many farmers grew cane on only part of their holdings, averaging less than half an acre. A modern factory in the early 1930s could crush on average up to 500 tons of cane per day, meaning that more than 10,000 farmers would have to supply sugarcane to the typical factory. What actually happened is that the indigenous *gur* refining industry grew gradually in a slowly expanding traditional domestic sugar market. The large price differential between *gur* and white sugar, and the poor quality of lower-grade *gur*, worked in favor of the traditional industry.

Table 6.8 Indian imports and exports of sugar (thousands of cwts)

Years (average)	Imports	Exports
1874–79	550	577
1880–84	998	1,106
1886–90	1,840	1,058

Source: George Watt, *The Commercial Products of India*, London: John Murray, 1908, p. 959.

Note
1 cwt (one hundred weight) is 50.8 kg.

Table 6.9 Percentage of cane used in the production of the different types of sugar

Year (average)	White Sugar (%)	Gur (%)	Price differential between white sugar and gur (per maund)		
			Rs.	A	P
1926–30	2.4	67.6	2	13	0
1930–31	3.9	66.4	4	2	0
1931–32	4.2	67.8	5	12	0
1932–33	6.8	65.9	5	12	0
1933–34	9.4	66.7	4	9	0
1934–35	12.1	65.3	4	9	0
1935–36	16.0	62.8	4	12	0
1936–37	17.4	61.7	3	12	0
1937–38	17.7	61.2	3	15	0
1938–39	19.2	57.3	4	4	0

Source: Government of India, *Report on the Marketing of Sugar in India and Burma*. Delhi: Manager of Publications, 1943, p. 69, pp. 428–9.

Conclusion

What emerges from this brief history, is that in the Japanese and Chinese sugar markets, industrial policy determined market competitiveness. Specifically, in the case of Japan, the sugar industry association, a cartel, was established in 1910; even before this, the Japanese government had taken these steps to protect the industry. In addition, what enabled the Japanese government to take these steps was the fact that Japan was outside the Brussels agreement, which had been concluded by Britain, France, Belgium, Germany, Austria, Netherlands, Russia, Spain, Portugal, and Australia. In contrast, a Sugar Committee was not established in India until 1917, and, even then, the committee was not a cartel but rather a committee for investigation and advice. Besides, the taste of the Indian consumers for sugar and for *gur* were so very different that the elasticity of substitution was quite small between sugar and *gur* within normal price ranges (Table 6.9). Therefore, it is not too much to say that in India, where the free market was operative, technological problems and the conservative tastes of ordinary people determined the market outcome.

Notes

1 Tsunoyama Sakae, *Karasa no bunka, amasa no bunka* (Culture of the Piquancy, Culture of the Sweet). Tokyo: Dôbunkan, 1987, pp. 197–205.
2 Higuchi Hiroshi, *Nihon tôgyôshi* (The History of the Japanese Sugar Industry). Tokyo: Naigai keizaisha, 1956, pp. 173, 531.
3 Nakajima Tsuneo (ed.), *Gendai nihon sangyô hattatsushi* (*Shokuhin*) (The History of the Development of Modern Japanese Industry (The Food Industry)). Tokyo: Kôjunsha, 1967, pp. 90, 95.
4 Higuchi, 1956, p. 533.
5 Kawano Shinji, *Nihon tôgyô hattatsushi* (*Shôhihen*) (The History of the Development of the Modern Japanese Sugar Industry (Consumption)). Tokyo: Maruzen, 1930, p. 58.
6 Kawano, 1930, p. 290.
7 Kawano, 1930, pp. 30, 58–9, 291.
8 Shadan Hôjin Tôgyô Kyôkai (ed.), *Kindai nihon tôogyôshi* (The History of the Sugar Industry in Modern Japan), Vol. 1. Tokyo: Keisô shobô, 1962, pp. 355–9.
9 Kawano Shinji, *Nihon tôgyô hattatsushi* (*Seisanihen*) (The History of the Development of the Modern Japanese Sugar Industry (Production)). Tokyo: Maruzen, 1930, p. 38.
10 Nihon Tôgyô Rengôkai, *Shina no tôogyô – koto ni nanshi saikin no tôgyô jijyô ni tsuite* (The Sugar Industry in China – Especially the Recent Condition of the Southern Part of China), Tokyo: Nihon Tôgyô Rengôkai, 1939, pp. 8–10.
11 Sugiyama Shinya, "Jûkyû seiki kôhanki ni okeru higashi ajia seitô shijô no kôzô" ("The Structure of the Sugar Market in East Asia in the Latter Half of the Nineteenth Century"). In Hayami, Saitô, Sugiyama (eds) *Tokugawa shakai kara no tenbô*, Tokyo: Dôbunkan, 1989, p. 342.
12 Calculated from data in Yokohamashi, *Yokohamashishi* (*Shiryôhen Vol. 2*) (The History of Yokohama City (Statistics Vol. 2)). Yokohama: Yokohamashishi Hensanshitsu, 1980.
13 Nihon Togyô Rengokai, 1939, pp. 15–31.
14 Government of India, *Report of the Indian Sugar Committee 1920*. Simla: Superintendent, Government Central Press, 1921, pp. 527–9.
15 Yukihiko Kiyokawa and Akihiko Ohno, "Technology and Labour Absorption in the Indigenous Indian Sugar Industry: An Analysis of Appropriate Technology." In Peter Robb (ed.) *Local Agrarian Societies in Colonial India*. Delhi: Manohar, 1997, p. 344.
16 Government of India, *Report on the Marketing of Sugar in India and Burma*, Delhi: Manager of Publications, 1943, pp. 170–80.

Bibliography

English

Amin, Shahid, *Sugarcane and Sugar in Gorakhpur: An Inquiry into Peasant Production for Capitalist Enterprise in Colonial India*. Delhi and New York: Oxford University Press, 1984.

Galloway, J.H, *The Sugar Cane Industry: An Historical Geography from its Origins to 1914*. Cambridge (England) and New York: Cambridge University Press, 1989.

Gandhi, M.P, *The Indian Sugar Industry: Its Past, Present and Future*, Calcutta: The Book Co., 1934.

Government of India, *Report of the Indian Sugar Committee 1920*, Simla: Superintendent, Government Central Press, 1921.

Government of India, *Report of the Indian Tariff Board on the Sugar Industry: Calcutta, 1931*. Delhi: Manager of Publications, 1932.

Government of India, *Review of the Sugar Industry of India during the Official Year 1934–35*, Delhi: Manager of Publications, 1936.

Government of India, *Report of the Indian Tariff Board on the Sugar Industry: Delhi, 1938*. Delhi: Manager of Publications, 1939.

Government of India, *Report on the Marketing of Sugar in India and Burma*, Delhi: Manager of Publications, 1943.

Robb, Peter (ed.), *Local Agrarian Societies in Colonial India*, Delhi: Manohar, 1997.

Watt, George, *A Dictionary of the Economic Products of India: Volume 6*. Calcutta: Central Printing Office, 1883.

Watt, George, *The Commercial Products of India*, London: John Murray, 1908.

Japanese

Cristian, Daniels, "Chûgoku satô no kokusaiteki ichi – Shin matsu ni okeru zairai satô shijô ni tsuite" ("Chinese Sugar in the World and Domestic Sugar Markets in the Late 19th and Early 20th Centuries"). In *Shakai Keizai Shigaku* (The Socio-economic History) Vol. 50, No. 4, 1985.

Akira Hayami, Osamu Saitô, Shinnya Sugiyama (eds), *Tokugawa shakai kara no tenbô* (The Perspectives from the Japanese Society in Tokugawa Era). Tokyo: Dôbunkan, 1989.

Higuchi, Hiroshi, *Nihon tôogyôshi* (The History of the Japanese Sugar Industry). Tokyo: Mitô shoya, 1956.

Itô, Jûrô (ed.), *Taiwan seitô kabushiki kaisha shi* (The History of the Taiwan Seitô Co. Ltd.). Tokyo: Taiwan Seitô Co. Ltd., 1939.

Kimura, Masutaro, *Shina no satô bôeki* (Foreign Trade of Sugar in China). Tokyo: Tôgyô kenkukai, 1914.

Kawano, Shinji, *Nihon tôgyô hattatsushi* (*Shôhihen*) (*Seisanhen*) (The History of the Development of the Modern Japanese Sugar Industry (Consumption) [Production]). Tokyo: Maruzen, 1930.

Kume, Takashi, "Ryôtaisenkanki no chûgoku satô shijô wo meguru ajiakan kyôsô" ("Inter-Asian competition in the Sugar Market of China 1914–1930"). In Kawakatsu, Heita (ed.) *Ajia Taiheiyô keizaikenshi 1500–2000* (Economic History of Asia and the Circum-Pacific Region in the Modern Era 1500–2000). Tokyo: Fujiwara shoten, 2003.

Naigai Togyô Chôsasho Chôsabu, (Naigai Research Center for the Sugar Industry), (ed.) *Satô torihiki Nenkan* (Sugar year-book of Japan). Tokyo: Bungadô, 1924.

Nakajima, Tsuneo (ed.), *Gendai nihon sangyô hattatsushi* (*Shokuhin*) (The History of the Development of Modern Japanese Industry (Food Industry)). Tokyo: Gendai Nihon Sangyô Hattatsushi Kenkyûkai, 1967.

Nishihara, Yûjirô (ed.), *Nittô saikin jûnen shi* (The Recent Ten year's History of Dainihin Seitô Co. ltd.). Tokyo: Dainihin Seitô, 1919.

Ôkurashô Kanzeikyoku (Department of Finance), *Dainihon Gaikoku Bôeki Nenpyô* (Annual return of the foreign trade of the Empire of Japan), 1882–1896, 1900–1906 (Annual). Tokyo: Ôkurashô.

Seitô, Kenkyûkai (ed.), *Tôgyô Binran* (The Sugar Handbook). Tokyo: Seitô Kenkyûkai, 1937.

Shadan Hôjin Tôgyô Kyôkai (ed.), *Kindai nihon togyo-shi*, Vol. 1 and 2 (The History of the Sugar Industry in Modern Japan), Tokyo: Keisô shobô, 1962, 1997.

Sugiyama, Sinya and Grove, Linda (eds), *Kindai ajia no ryûtsu network* (Commercial Networks in Modern Asia), Tokyo: Sôbunsha, 1999.

Tsunoyama, Sakae, *Karasa no bunka, amasa no bunka* (Culture of the Piquancy, Culture of the Sweet), Tokyo: Dôbunkan, 1987.

Yanagisawa, Haruka, *Minami indo shakai keizaishi* (Socio-Economic Change in South Indian Rural Society: The 1860s to The 1980s), Tokyo: University of Tokyo Press, 1991.

7 Rival merchants

The Korean market in the late nineteenth century

Sooyoon Lee

Introduction

In the late nineteenth century, Korea entered into a series of treaties of commerce with foreign countries, and opened trade with Japan in 1876. In the pre-colonial period Korea chiefly exported rice, beans, hides, and gold bullion and in return imported cotton textiles. But exchange rates fluctuated widely due to the absence of a modern monetary system, and this destabilized foreign trade. Prices varied in response to harvests and around the open ports were subject to chronic inflation.

A number of attempts have been made by scholars to examine the problems of Korean society in this transition period; but there is room for further investigation. Most discussion about the modern economic history of Korea has concentrated on its ties with Japan, and scholars have focused on the economic penetration of Japan into Korea in the late nineteenth century. Undoubtedly Japan's role in modern Korean history was overwhelming. But, Japan was not the only influence in the Korean economy particularly before the Sino-Japanese War of 1894–95. China also had an impact on Korea from the time of *Imogunran*, a rebellion of the Korean army in 1883. The Chinese were linked with the Korean market through the commercial network between Shanghai, Korea, and Japan.

So Korea was not simply absorbed into the Japanese market. After its ports were opened to international trade, there was still a separation between each country's markets, and consequently price differentials between them. Merchants were aware of these differentials, and therefore maintained links between Korea, China and Japan.

This chapter discusses the competition among merchants at Korean treaty ports, which spurred Korea to link itself with outside markets. Chinese financial networks in east Asia will be examined via gold outflows and competition between foreign merchants and their commercial networks in Korea. This will reveal the role of Korean merchants in both domestic and foreign trade. In this way, a better insight will be gained into the east Asian regional economy in the nineteenth century.

Gold outflow

Few works discuss the outflow of gold from Korea and how it was connected with the internal commercial network. Much attention has been paid to Japan's imports

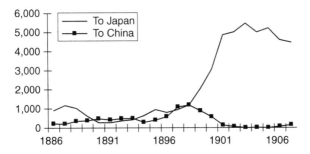

Figure 7.1 Gold exports from Korea.

Source: 1885–93, China, Imperial Maritime Customs, *Returns of Trade and Trade Reports*, Appendix II: Corea; 1894–1907, *Kabusikikaisha daiichi-ginko kankoku kakushitem shucchosho kaigyo irai eigyo jokyo* (*The Activities of Branches of Daiichi Bank Co., Ltd. in Korea since their start-up*).

of Korean gold, which accounted for nearly all of Japan's gold imports, and was the rationale for those who sought to introduce the gold standard in Japan in 1897. It has also been said that the inflow of Korean gold was essential to Japanese industrialization.[1] Japanese bank notes were exchanged for Korean copper coins to buy gold from Korea.[2] This was how the Japanese private bank *Daiichi ginko*[3] began to circulate Japanese currency in Korea.[4]

But these arguments ignore the fierce competition between Japanese and Chinese merchants for the gold trade from the 1880s (see Figure 7.1). As the Chinese also smuggled out gold, the outflow to China was even greater than it appeared.[5]

Gold was mostly obtained in exchange for goods sold to Korea such as cotton or silk textiles, so the basis of the gold outflow differed from port to port. At Incheon, the nearest port to China, three quarters of the gold went to China in 1891.[6] Wonsan, the biggest gold-export port, also sent more gold to China than to Japan because cotton goods were imported from Shanghai.[7]

Gold exports to China also depended on the price of gold in Shanghai. In 1892 and 1893 about $260,000[8] worth of gold was sent to China from Incheon but only $90,000 worth to Japan. The price of gold in Shanghai had risen sharply because of the fall in the price of silver, which suggests that Chinese merchants were taking advantage of the difference in the price of gold across the Yellow Sea. However, at Pusan, which had the closest economic relations with Japan during the Chosun dynasty, gold exports were influenced mostly by the exchange rate between Korean copper coins and Japanese silver yen.

The relationship between gold exports and the domestic economy must also be considered. The value of gold exported fell from $1,388,269 in 1887 to $689,078 in 1891. Indeed, Korean gold production actually declined at this time. This was not due to exhaustion of the goldfields, but to good crops, which paid better wages than gold washing.[9] Most of the gold produced in those days was in the form of gold dust, produced by panning. To sum up, the high rate of exchange for copper cash and the sudden rise in open-port wage rates in years of good harvests may explain the decrease in the shipment of gold. In a good crop year, labour abandoned gold panning to rush to a settlement where they could get a good job as a coolie to ship rice and beans. Also, the relatively low price of gold in exchange for copper cash restricted gold production.[10] Therefore the export of gold from nineteenth century Korea was inversely related to rice and bean exports.

Gold exports were also linked to the exchange rate of copper cash *Yopgeon* against foreign currencies. The devaluation of the *Yopgeon* may have made buying gold with copper cash more profitable. For example, in 1888, although very few goods were exported from Incheon to Japan, the fall in the value of copper cash resulting from excess supply led to a large sum of gold being sent from Incheon.[11] In this case, an excess supply of cash was caused by inactivity in the commodity exports trade, which made the gold price in copper cash relatively cheap. The same year, gold exports to Japan from Pusan increased by $91,064 over the previous year. The decline in the value of copper cash made Japanese merchants purchase gold more readily to 'balance Japanese trade at Pusan'.[12]

But the fall in the value of copper cash in Pusan in 1892 was not just due to a poor harvest. When the price of copper cash was at its peak in 1890 and 1891 in Pusan due to a good harvest, a large amount of *Pyongyang-geon* worth only one-fifth of indigenous copper coins, was minted and flowed into Pusan via Korean, Japanese, and even Chinese merchants.[13] An inflow of substandard coins as well as inactive export trade caused the devaluation of copper cash against foreign currencies like silver yen and consequently caused a gold outflow.

Korean gold was, usually, exported in exchange for imports and had an inverse relation with harvests until about 1890. The movements of labour and the exchange rates of copper cash against foreign currencies were barometers indicating gold production, and rice and beans export. However, from 1890, gold exports were affected by two new factors. One was the change in the relative overseas price between gold and silver, and the other was the decline in the value of copper cash as a result of excessive minting. These changes signify that Korean trade was closely linked to the open ports around Korea, and the Korean economy had integrated with the commercial network and monetary system of East Asia.

Foreign merchants in the ports

The foreign merchants in Korea were mostly Japanese and Chinese. In the early days after Korea opened its ports, Japan dominated the Korean market until Korea started making treaties with other countries in 1882. A striking feature of Japanese trade in the early period was that more than half the Japanese exports to Korea were goods of foreign origin, such as English shirting, and that the Japanese were more interested in buying produce from Korea than selling Japanese goods there. Table 7.1 shows this aspect.

Table 7.1 Japanese trade with Korea 1877–82 (1,000 yen)

Year	Imports from Korea	Exports to Korea	Origin of exports	
			Japan	Others
July1877–June1878	119,538	228,554	87,149	141,405
July1878–December1878	154,707	142,618	29,332	113,286
1879	677,061	566,953	55,647	511,306
1880	1,373,671	978,013	116,130	861,883
1881	1,882,657	1,944,737	1,742,668	202,069
January 1882–June1882	897,225	742,562	47,519	695,043

Source: The ministry of Agriculture and Commerce, *Kankokushi* (*The Journal of Korea*) 1904: pp. 112–13.

The Chinese made inroads in the Korean market from 1883 taking advantage of a Korean military revolt known as *Imogunran*. China competed with Japan, which was the only other active foreign trader at the Korean open ports. Incheon became a base for Chinese commercial activities in Korea due to its proximity to both China and Seoul. The main articles China supplied were luxury goods such as Chinese-made silk goods, calico, and dyes, which had been imported over land during the Chosun Dynasty. The Koreans liked these goods, and because the Chinese now brought them directly by sea from Shanghai they could provide them more cheaply than previously and increase their sales. The Chinese goods were brought to Seoul and then distributed to local areas by peddlers.[14] The merchants used their own distribution system linking the merchants at the open port to the local Chinese peddlers. There was a central organization of Chinese peddlers in Seoul, and in some provincial towns they were locally supervised and managed.[15]

Chinese immigration to Korea increased in the late 1880s, mostly from Shandong, Guangdong, and Zhejiang. Although imports from China at Incheon exceeded those from Japan in 1888, they remained relatively low in Korea as a whole. This was because, as a Japanese Consular report points out, the Chinese took gold in exchange for goods and smuggled it from the coast.[16] The situation was similar at Wonsan. At this port, the Japanese previously had nearly all the market, but in 1887, a handful of Chinese came in. Chinese imports at Wonsan, worth only $30,000 in 1886, leaped tenfold in 1889 to $320,000. This was 40 per cent of the port's total imports, and the gold they took away in exchange surpassed that to Japan, which was worth $300,000.[17] As the Chinese flooded the foreign-origin cotton textile market in Wonsan, the Japanese switched from cotton textiles to the Korean coastal trade, dealing in cow hides, beans, dried fish, and so on.[18] Goods brought by the Chinese in the 1880s were mostly English and American cotton textiles similar to those of the Japanese, but they could supply them more cheaply direct from Shanghai.

Both the Japanese and the Chinese brought calicos and silk goods, and exported rice, beans, cowhides, and gold dust. Japanese merchants concentrated on the export trade from Korea, but the Chinese placed emphasis on imports and domestic peddling. It was often reported that the Japanese were short of copper cash to buy goods from Korea while the Chinese had enough copper cash to purchase gold dust at high prices and had an advantage. The Chinese would also exchange surplus copper cash into Japanese bank notes and send them to Nagasaki or Kobe in notes or as a draft. Their branch in Japan converted them into silver yen or used it as another flow of money. The Japanese banks then lent these bank notes to Japanese merchants to make payment for rice, beans, etc. purchased in Korea.[19]

The Chinese merchants used Chinese peddlers and also the Korean distribution system of wholesalers and shippers. When the Chinese handed goods to Korean fabric wholesalers, they accepted cash. But Korean merchants considered reliable were allowed credit. If a debtor could not pay his debts, the merchants had the right to claim the debtor's house, with the support of the Chinese consulate.[20] So until the Sino-Japanese War Chinese merchants were backed by the political and military support of the Chinese authorities in Korea.

Korean brokers

From the eighteenth century, about a thousand local markets were established as a result of the growth in agricultural production. In addition, a step was taken in 1791 to limit the exclusive rights given to certain merchants to deal in particular goods. This encouraged others to improve their own networks to carry commodities between the capital and local areas. Now new principle traders emerged who controlled small local traders and established their own branches in the main ports. This system connecting the centre and its periphery was called *Gaekju*, which was the word for the principal merchant who managed the system. This became the dominant commercial system in the late Chosun dynasty.[21]

When Korea opened its ports, its trade increased sharply. Trade with Japan averaged ¥130,000 per year between 1873 and 1876 and grew to ¥380,000 by 1881. The distribution system had to be transformed to link the open ports to the interior. So, after establishing their internal networks upcountry, a number of *Gaekju* merchants moved to the treaty ports. Figure 7.2 shows how goods flowed through the Gaekju system up to 1876.

Until the early 1880s, only Korean merchants were involved in this new domestic distribution system because, according to the treaties, foreigners were not allowed to trade inland. Figure 7.2 shows some of the developments which occurred after 1876. The merchants in charge of the distribution of products and goods between the ports and the interior were called *Gaehangjang-Gaekju*, or 'open-port brokers'.[22] At first, the open-port brokers comprised a few big merchants from Pusan, Pyongyang, and Kyongkang (Seoul). Those based in Pusan and Pyongyang had had previous dealings in foreign trade at the border under government permit, and those from Kyongkang had dealt chiefly with the rice trade to Seoul.[23] The open ports and the local areas were connected through their own commercial network. So Korean brokers used this network to export

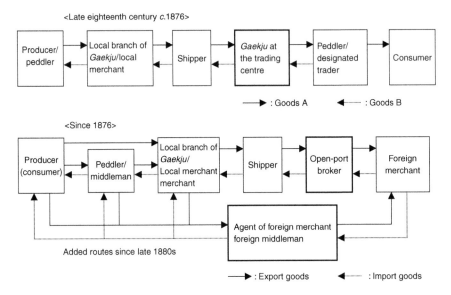

Figure 7.2 The Korean distribution system.

Source: Lee (2001): p. 6.

products from the open ports and to distribute imports locally. Figure 7.2 shows how they conveyed goods. An intermediary trader under the control of an open-port broker hired boats to carry goods such as rice collected by peddlers at the rural centre and consigned them to a broker in the open-port for sale. By controlling this distribution system the open-port brokers connected the local traders and the foreign merchants.

Even after restrictions on peddling by foreigners in the interior were eased, links with Korean brokers at the ports remained important. Foreigners were restricted from occupying or leasing any real estate except in the concession area, and were prohibited from anchoring at non-open ports, and so could obtain very little information about the hinterland.[24] Brokers received commission from both foreign and local traders for facilitating trade. The commission rate varied by port and by article but was generally 1–5 per cent by quantity.[25]

Direct deals by foreigners in the interior increased gradually. The Japanese in particular caused frequent trouble over the commission paid to the brokers and tried to cut them out by purchasing products directly from rural areas. This was a threat to Korean merchants and also the local governor. As the demand for imported cotton goods grew, Koreans sold increasing amounts of agricultural products even in bad crop years. Many local governors strove to stop the grain outflow from particular provinces by prohibiting the export of grain. The government also tried to keep control of the distribution system by strengthening the open-port brokers' privileges and limiting their numbers.[26]

Competition and changes

Although several steps were taken to guarantee privileges to Korean brokers and prevent foreign traders from reaching the interior, the exclusive right of brokers to deal in particular goods and receive commission actually accelerated foreigners' commercial activities in the hinterland.

As mentioned previously, Chinese merchants entered Korea when a military rebellion broke out in 1882. These merchants were originally mainly small peddlers, and most of them returned to China as soon as the rebellion was suppressed. The Chinese made inroads into Korea in earnest in the late 1880s and from around 1890 increased their trade and further extended their commercial networks in the interior.[27] Chinese commercial activities in the 1880s were for the most part illicit. Junks from Shandong were often observed as smugglers on the west coast of the Korean peninsula in provinces like Pyongang and Hwanghae. A Japanese diplomat in Korea estimated that the number of Chinese in the Pyongyang area in 1888 was around two thousand to three thousand, of which traders who had immigrated legally via Inchoen and Seoul accounted for just 10 per cent.[28]

The Chinese developed their business by concentrating on cotton goods like calico, a favourite fabric for upper class clothing, and this enabled their commercial network to extend smoothly. During the Sino-Japanese War, they apparently returned to China. But when the war ended, they came back to Korea and began to supply goods cheaply and regularly as before.[29] They maintained their dominant position in imports and the sale of calico until 1900. Then there was an anti-foreign movement in China, which resulted in the Chinese halting calico exports from Shanghai to Korea. This was a turning point, and the Chinese now gave way to Japanese merchants who gained the advantage in selling calico in Korea.[30] At the same time, the Chinese merchants turned from selling luxury goods to selling miscellaneous goods like matches, yarn, and narrow-width cotton cloth for the ordinary people. They set up shops at key points in local areas, and were connected through business associations to particular areas or the same type of trade. Now that they could operate in their own networks and without a wholesaler, the local branches of the Korean open-port brokers were faced with notable competition.

Japanese merchants were more interested in exports from Korea than imports to Korea, so they had to rely on the Korean commercial network to buy items such as rice. From the later 1880s they operated in the hinterland on their own, buying export goods without using the open-port brokers.[31] They were small-scale traders who mainly bought rice to export to Japan. The Sino-Japanese War (1894–95) provided a turning point for them. Japanese peddlers, who also supplied weapons, stayed in the interior along the route of its army and sold a variety of goods. Once the Japanese commissariat was established, the army hired labourers and horses within the vicinity and used convertible notes as payment. So the Koreans began spending Japanese bank notes to buy Lancashire cotton goods at the peddler's shops in the Japanese bases.[32] The Japanese who stayed inland after the war subsequently switched their business links from the army to the open ports.[33] At newly opened ports such as Mokpo (1897), Chinmanpo

(1897), and Gunsan (1899), Japanese merchants were virtually the only ones to deal in exports and imports. This emergence of the Japanese was helped by the retreat of the Chinese from Korea. Since 1900, liner services between Shanghai and Inchoen had been halted, resulting in a fall in imports from Shanghai. Some Chinese merchants continued to import goods from Shanghai via Japan using their Japanese branches. A Japanese observer noted that from 1900 to 1901 cotton goods imported by the Chinese in Inchoen increased even when the liner services from Shanghai were absent.[34]

As inland connections were developed by foreign merchants, the practices of Korean merchants changed. Local traders and shippers, previously under the control of open-port brokers, began expanding and gradually broke away from their management. Some local traders established their own branches in the open ports, and themselves operated virtually as open-port brokers.

In the midst of these changes, internal trade between the open ports was stimulated. When several additional ports were opened, the import volume of Incheon in 1901 increased by 45 per cent compared to the previous year. About half the goods imported were sent to the port from Gunsan and Mokpo because of the lack of a proper financial organization and because the open-port brokers in Inchoen opened branches in the new open ports.[35] As the open ports increased in number, the distribution of goods such as narrow-width cotton fabrics and dried fish grew using the merchants' commercial networks and liner services.

Conclusion

Earlier studies have suggested that the outflow of gold from Korea was a symbol of Japanese Imperialism, for after the Korean ports were opened in 1876 Japan encouraged colonization. It has been argued that the Korean economy had exclusive bilateral relations with Japan, and from 1910 its distribution system was integrated with Japan through colonization. But, the latest study shows that there were two market networks in the period of Japanese rule 1910–45.[36] Certainly, Korea began to have close relations with east Asian markets. But there were still separate sections in each market. Within these divisions, the Japanese and the Chinese competed in the Korean open ports using separate commercial networks.

With the opening of the ports, Korea was integrated into the east Asian regional economy. This was the result of both Korean and foreign merchants' commercial activities in the interior. The use of modern liner services stimulated Korean trade in the interior. Circulation of copper cash between the ports increased and so did trade between Wonsan and Pusan. At the same time the Korean distributors had to compete with foreign merchants. To begin with, local merchants had the advantage of familiarity with the hinterland, which enabled them to be the main dealers in the open-port trade. But, after 1894 they faced severe competition in the interior from well-organized Chinese and Japanese merchants. The Korean government and Korean merchants tried to counter this by strengthening their guild merchant system.

Table 7.2 The share of the Korean brokers' guild in rice exports from Incheon (unit: 1,000 Koku)

	Year				
	1928	1929	1930	1931	1932
Total rice export	1,484	1,165	1,224	1,897	1,527
Share of Korean brokers' guild	542	502	657	823	571
(%)	36	43	51	42	36
Share of Japanese brokers' guild	598	479	610	940	688
(%)	40	41	49	49	45

Source: *Jinshenfushi* (*The History of Incheon Prefecture*) 1933: pp. 934, 1176–7.

Note
1 Koku = 180 litre.

After 1910, the Korean market was connected to Japan more closely by modern transport, communications, and the fiscal and monetary system. The number of Korean broker-merchants continued to decrease. However in Table 7.2 we can see that Korean brokers dealt with about 40 per cent of the grain exports from Inchoen even in the 1930s. So the indigenous distribution system operated by Korean brokers continued to exist even during the colonial period. Previously, it has been said that the Korean market was integrated into the regional economy of East Asia through the Japanese market after the opening of the ports in 1876, and this process accelerated after Korea was annexed by Japan in 1910. But it seems the Korean market was isolated to some extent even four decades after the opening of ports in 1876, and that Korean traders were actually stimulated by the connection with the East Asian commercial network. Even after 1910 this modernized indigenous system was able to compete with the modern financial and distribution system introduced by Japan.

Notes

1 Nakatsuka 1968; Choi 1971; Murakami 1973a.
2 Kang 1966.
3 *Daiichi ginko* was the first Japanese private bank to establish a branch in Korea. Its Pusan branch was established in 1878, and Wonsan 1880, Incheon 1882, and Seoul 1888. Because of its contract in 1884 with the Korean government as maritime custom duty agency, *Daiichi ginko*'s bank bills could be used in paying duty, fees and fines in the open ports. In 1902, the bank gained the right to circulate its convertible note and drove other currencies out of Korean market. Consequently in 1905 the bank became the National bank of Korea and after annexation in 1910 succeeded as *Chosen Ginko* (Colonial central bank in Korea). See *Shibusawa eiichi denki shiryo* (*the shibusawa collection*) Vol. 16: pp. 11, 215–16, 260–5.
4 Takashima 1978; Murakami 1973b.
5 China, Imperial Maritime Customs, *Returns of Trade Reports for the Year 1887*, hereafter CIMC: 508.
6 CIMC 1891: p. 633.
7 CIMC 1890: p. 625.

8 Mexican dollar, the dollar in which the customs revenue and all values are stated, is equivalent in American money (gold) to $1.28; in Hongkong$, $1.52, at the average for 1885.
9 CIMC 1891: p. 619.
10 CIMC 1890: p. 612.
11 *Tsushohokoku* (*The Commercial Reports*) 89, 21 November 1888: p. 12.
12 CIMC 1892: p. 648.
13 *Nihongaikomonjo* (*The Diplomatic Documents of Japan*) Vol. 24, 1891: pp. 176, 379.
14 *Tsushohokoku* (*The Commercial Reports*) 55, 9 March 1888: p. 18.
15 Nobuo: 25.
16 *Tsushohokoku* (*The Commercial Reports*) 71, 7 July 1888: p. 16.
17 *Tsushohokoku* (*The Commercial Reports*) 78, 30 August 1888: p. 9.
18 *Tsushohokoku* (*The Commercial Reports*) 118, 2 August 1889: p. 11–12.
19 *Nihongaikomonjo* (*The Diplomatic Documents of Japan*), Vol. 24, 1891: p. 384–5.
20 Chosen sotokuhu (The Government General of Korea) ed., *Chosen ni okeru sinajin* (*The Chinese in Korea*) 1924: pp. 42–3.
21 Na: pp. 26, 33.
22 Yoshino: p. 40.
23 Takao: p. 20.
24 *Kankokushi*: p. 126–7.
25 *British Parliamentary Papers*, 1894 (*c*.6856–66), 'Commercial Condition of the Ports of Pusan and Wonsan', p. 6.
26 BPP, 1894, (*c*.7293–87), 'Report for the Year 1893 on the Trade of Korea', p. 5.
27 Lee 2001: p. 9.
28 *Nihongaikomonjo* (*The Diplomatic Document of Japan*), Vol. 22, 1889: p. 381.
29 *Tsushoisan* (*The Commercial Reports*), Vol. 109, 8 September 1898: pp. 53–7.
30 Ha 1994: p. 78.
31 *Tsushoisan* (*The Commercial Reports*) 8, Appendix, August 1894: p. 13.
32 *Tsushoisan* (*The Commercial Reports*) 52, an extra, 2 November 1894: pp. 59–60.
33 *Tsushoisan* (*The Commercial Reports*) 196, 10 August 1901: p. 69.
34 *Tsushoisan* (*The Commercial Reports*) 195, 25 July 1901: p. 8.
35 *Tsushoisan* (*The Commercial Reports*) 195, 25 July 1901: p. 18.
36 Cha 2000: pp. 86–93.

References

Cha, Myung-Soo (2000) 'The Colonial Origins of Korea's Market Economy', in A.J.H. Latham and Heita Kawakatsu (eds), *Asia Pacific Dynamism*, London and New York: Routledge.

Choi, Yoo-Gil (1971) 'A Study on the Establishment of the Gold-Standard System in Japan and Korea', in *The Socio-Economic History* (*Shakai-keizai shigaku*), Vol. 36, No. 6.

Furuta, Kazuko (1999) 'Chinese and Japanese Merchants in Korean Trade and the Shanghai Network – The early 1890s', in *Mita Journal of Economics*, Vol. 92, No. 1.

Ha, Myung Saeng (1994) 'Commercial Activities of Overseas Chinese in Korea – Case of the Overseas Chinese in Seoul and Incheon from 1882 to 1897', in The Graduate School of Economics Kanagawa University (ed.), *Annal of Economics* (*Kenkyu-Ronshu*), No. 23.

Kang, Duk-Sang (1966) 'Consolidation of the Korean Currency System', in *Sundai Historical Review (Sundaishigaku)*, No. 17.

Lee, Sooyoon (2000) 'A Feud Between Chinese, Japanese and Korean Traders in the Korea Open Ports in the Pre Sino-Japanese War Period', in *The Japanese Colonial History (Nihon Shokuminchi Kenkyu)*, No. 12.

——(2001) 'Changes in the Trade Mechanism of Korea During the Port-Opening Period: Korean Brokers in the Open Ports and Foreign Merchants', in *Waseda Economic Studies*, No. 53.

Murakami, K. (1973a) 'The Absorption of Gold from the Colonies During the Industrial Revolution', in *The Journal of Economic Studies (The University of Tokyo)*, No. 16.

——(1973b) 'The Korea Affiliate of the Dai-ichi Bank and Colonial Finance', in *The Journal of Agrarian History (Tochiseido Shigaku)*, 61, Vol. 16, No. 1.

Na, A. J. (1998) *Hanguk gundae haeunupsa yongu (A Study on the History of the Shipping Industry in Modern Korea)*, Seoul: Gukhakjaryowon.

Nakatsuka, A. (1968) *Nissin senso no kenkyu (A Study on the Sino-Japanese War)*, Tokyo: Aoki-shoten.

Nobuo, J. (1901) *Kanhanto (The Korean Peninsular)*, Tokyo: Tokyodeshoten.

Takashima, M. (1978) *Chosen ni okeru shokuminchi-kinyushi no kenkyu (A Study on the Colonial Financial History of Korea)*, Tokyo: Oohara-sinsei-sha.

Takao, N. (1917) *Gensan hattenshi (the development history of genene)*, Genson: Gensanjodo.

Yoshino, M. (1975) 'On the Exports of Korea Since the Opening of its Country to Foreign Trade', in *Bulletin of the Society for the Korean Historical Science (Chosenshi kenkyukai ronbunshu)*, No. 12.

8 Tan Kim Ching and Siam "Garden rice"

The rice trade between Siam and Singapore in the late nineteenth century

Toshiyuki Miyata

Introduction

The rice export economy of Siam developed substantially in the late nineteenth century and Siamese rice exports played an important part in the growth of "Intra-Asian Trade."[1] Singapore was one of the most important rice markets for Siam rice and the volume of Siamese rice exports to this city increased more than to other areas in these years. This chapter examines the growth of Siamese rice exports to Singapore, and focuses on the high quality of Siamese rice, and the development of the rice trade network between Siam and Singapore.

A type of Siamese rice called "Garden rice" (*khaao naa suan* in Thai) was regarded as a high quality rice in Singapore and other Asian rice markets during the late nineteenth century. In the early twentieth century its quality was also recognized in the European rice markets. Middlemen, millers and exporters in Bangkok, and dealers in foreign rice markets called this high quality transplanted rice Siam "Garden rice." It was preferred to both Saigon and Rangoon rice in Singapore for its good taste, long grain and white color, and was in great demand and sold at the highest price. The good reputation and popularity of Siam "Garden rice" lead to an increased demand for Siam rice in general in Singapore. There was keen competition between the different kinds of Asian rice[2] in the Asian market creating an inter-Asian rivalry.[3] However, ultimately Siam rice came to be regarded as the best rice.

The development of the rice trade between Siam and Singapore promoted the rapid growth of the Siamese economy. This chapter also examines the activities of Tan Kim Ching (Figure 8.1), who was a Straits Hokkien Chinese merchant and a Siamese royal agent and later Siamese Consul General in Singapore. His rice mill and rice exporting company in Bangkok was the first to introduce Siamese "Garden rice" to Singapore. Tan Kim Ching extended his rice trade network by importing rice to Singapore from both Bangkok and Saigon, but Bangkok was the most important base of his business. In the Singapore rice market, "Garden rice" imported by Tan Kim Ching's company was one of the most reputed and expensive rices.

Many studies have been made of the development of the Siamese rice export economy from the viewpoint of the structural changes in the international rice

Figure 8.1 A portrait of Tan Kim Ching (陳金鐘).

Source: S.O. Siang, *One Hundred Year's History of the Chinese in Singapore* (San Francisco: Chinese Materials Center, 1975 [1923]), p. 92.

trade. James C. Ingram pointed out that:

> The Suez Canal may have had an important indirect influence on the market for Thai rice, however, in that Burmese rice exports may have been diverted from Asian to European markets, thus increasing the demand in Asia for Thai rice.... The foreign demand for Thai rice may perhaps be better explained by the development of cheap ocean transportation which enabled Thailand to compete in Asian markets and by the development of economies in Asia which depended on large regular imports of rice, e.g., Malaya.[4]

Suehiro on the other hand argues more convincingly that an increasing demand for Siam rice from Southeast Asia and southern China was a key factor in the rapid expansion of rice exports from Siam.[5] The development of colonial enterprises in Southeast Asia, with large-scale rubber plantations and tin-mining in the Malay Peninsula, required a large number of immigrant wageworkers. Suehiro emphasizes that all these immigrant workers, regardless of their ethnic backgrounds or nationality, were "rice-eating people."[6] In line with the growth in the number of immigrant workers in the Malay Peninsula, rice imports to the port of Singapore increased quickly.[7] Paradoxically, both in the Malay Peninsula to which immigrants were coming and southern China from where immigrants were departing[8] the demand for foreign rice rose tremendously at the turn of the century. Under these circumstances, rice-growing areas such as Burma were hard pressed to supply enough rice. This was because Burmese rice was traditionally exported westward mainly to the European market and later to the Indian market where it was preferred. Likewise, Cochin-China rice was exported mainly to France and the French colonies as well as other Asian markets, including Hong Kong and the Philippines (Table 8.1). So Siam became the most important supplier to the "rice-eating wage labourers" of Southeast Asia and China, especially those of Chinese origin.

However, little research has been conducted on the kind of Siam rice that was exported to Singapore and how it was regarded in the Singapore market. The purpose of this chapter is to reexamine the background of the growth of Siam rice exports to Singapore. It is important to recognize the high quality of Siamese rice for "Garden rice" was one of the most crucial factors in stimulating the rice exports of Siam. It is also important to note the development of the rice trade network between Siam and Singapore, particularly Tan Kim Ching's activities. He played one of the key roles in promoting high quality "Garden rice" as an international commodity and so contributed to the growth of the Siamese rice export economy.

"Garden rice" and the development of Siam rice exports to Singapore

During the late nineteenth century and early twentieth century Siam experienced a rapid growth of rice exports. According to Table 8.2, the average annual export value of rice exports from Bangkok increased from 0.29 million pounds of silver in 1856–76 to 4.8 million silver pounds in 1901–10. The export value of Siam rice in the early twentieth century was about 16 times as great as in the mid-nineteenth century. As shown in Table 8.2, the ratio of rice to total commodity exports rose from 35 percent in 1856–70 to 75 percent in 1901–10.

Rice trade figures for Siam, Burma and Cochin-China in Table 8.1 reveal that Siam rice export volumes to Singapore increased from 53,000 tons in 1871–80 to 315,000 tons in 1902–10. Singapore rapidly became one of the most significant rice markets for Siam, and was a redistribution center like Hong Kong, another major market. In the period of 1902–10 Siam rice exports to Singapore rose to nearly six times as much as they were in 1871–80, while those to Hong Kong rose about four times. Table 8.1 shows that Siam was the most important supplier of rice to Singapore, and the average volume of Siam rice imported to Singapore in 1902–20 was greater than that from either Burma or Cochin-China.

Siam rice exports to Singapore included paddy, white broken rice, cargo rice (half-milled rice), and others, but milled white rice was the most important of all. Table 8.3 shows that during the period between 1902 and 1910, the average annual export volume of white rice to Singapore from Siam amounted to 216,368 tons, which was 57 percent of Siam's total white rice export and 69 percent of

Table 8.1 Rice export volumes of Siam, Burma, and Cochin-China: 1871–1910 (Unit: 1,000 tons)

	Period	Total	Asian market					European market				Others[c]
			Asia total	Singapore[a]	Hong Kong/China	India	Others	England	Germany	France[b]	Others	
Burma	1871–80	811	185	67	1	114	3	511	5	—	12	98
Cochin-China	1871–80	283	266	25	188	5	48	—	—	10	1	6
Siam	1871–80	165	152	53	87	—	12	—	—	—	3	10
Total		1,259	603	145	276	119	63	511	5	10	16	114
Burma	1881–1900	1,222	474	188	1	261	24	260	222	—	247	19
Cochin-China	1881–1900	500	420	45	287	—	88	—	—	45	14	21
Siam	1881–1990	364	290	116	168	—	6	—	—	—	35	39
Total		2,086	1,184	349	456	261	118	260	222	45	296	79
Burma	1901–1910	2,169	1,156	274	12	607	263	154	334	—	304	221
Cochin-China	1901–1910	708	509	31	179	1	298	—	—	122	25	52
Siam	1902–1910	854	719	315	398	1	5	20	35	—	76	5
Total		3,731	2,384	620	589	609	566	174	369	122	405	278

Sources Burma: Cheng Siok-Hwa, *The Rice Industry of Burma 1852–1940* (Kuala Lumpur: University of Malaya Press, 1968), pp. 201–17; Cochin-China Coquerel A., *Paddys et riz de Cochinchine*, Lyon, 1911; Horiguchi Kenji, *Nanyo no kome* (*Rice in Southern Sea*), Nanyokyokai, 1921, pp. 157–8; *Toyo oyobi nanyosyokoku no kokusaiboueki to nihon no chii* (*Japanese Position in the International Trade among the East and Southern Sea*), Mitsubishikeizai kenksusyo, 1933, pp. 283–4; *Nanyososho kaitei fu-tsury oindoshina hen dai 2kan* (*French Indochina, Southern Sea Research Series Vol. 2*), Mantetsu Toakeizai Chosakyoku, 1941, pp. 136–7. Siam: British Consular Reports in British Parl. Papers (1871–1900); "Shakoku oyobi Saigon chiho sanshutsumai joukyou," *Tsushoisan* ("*Rice Production in Siam and Saigon delta*," *Japanese Consular Reports*), No. 63, 1907, pp. 1–9; Foreign Trade and Navigation of the Port of Bangkok (1908–12); A.J.H. Latham and Larry Neal, "The International Market in Rice and Wheat, 1868–1914," *Economic History Review*, Vol. 36, No. 2, 1983, p. 279.

Notes
a Singapore, Penang, Malacca, and British Malaya.
b France and French Colonies.
c Africa, Latin America, and others.

Table 8.2 The   average   annual   value   of
total exports and rice: 1856–1910
(unit: million pounds of silver)

Period	Total (a)	Rice (b)	(b % a)
1856–70	0.81	0.29	35
1871–80	1.60	0.97	61
1881–90	2.19	1.47	67
1891–1900	2.89	2.05	71
1901–10	5.96	4.68	75

Source: British Parl. Papers, Commercial Reports on
Siam, various years.

Table 8.3 Export volumes of various types of Siam rice (unit: tons)

Types	Total	Singapore	Hong Kong/ China	Asia/ Oceania	Europe	America	Others
Period 1902–10							
White rice	382,683	216,368	120,674	3,207	37,706	2,101	2,627
White broken rice	187,261	37,321	113,229	1,779	34,407	445	81
Cargo rice	171,779	19,595	100,823	1,220	50,039	102	0
Others	112,249	41,356	62,761	487	7,646	0	0
Total	853,972	314,640	397,487	6,692	129,797	2,648	2,708

Sources: "Shakoku oyobi Saigon chiho sanshutsumai joukyou," *Tsushoisan* ("Rice production in
Siam and Saigon delta," *Japanese Consular Reports*), No. 63, 1907, pp. 1–9; *Foreign Trade and
Navigation of the Port of Bangkok* (1908–12).

Table 8.4 Average monthly price trends of white rice of Siam, Burma, and Saigon in
Singapore: September 1892–September 1895 (unit: straits dollar per picul)

Average price of month	Siam white rice No.1	Siam white rice No.2	Rangoon white rice	Saigon white rice
September–December 1892	2.93	2.88	2.70	2.65
January–December 1893	2.88	2.84	2.59	2.46
January–December 1894	3.19	3.15	2.72	2.69
January–September 1895	3.24	3.20	2.74	2.71
September 1892–September 1895	3.07	3.03	2.68	2.61

Source: "Ei, Futshuryo, Indo narabini Syamu beisaku no keikyo," *Tsushoisan* ("Situations of Rice
Production in British India, French Indo-China and Siam," *Japanese Consular Report*), No. 31, 1895,
pp. 10–13.

Siam's total rice export to Singapore. So Singapore was the most important
market for Siam white rice, and Siam was the supply base for white rice as the
staple food for Singapore. However a large amount of white rice was reexported
to the Malay Peninsula and the Dutch East Indies.

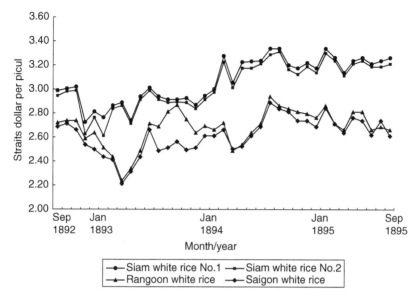

Graph 8.1 Average monthly price trends of white rice of Siam, Burma, and Saigon in Singapore: September 1892–September 1895.

Source: "Ei, Futshuryo, Indo narabini Syamu beisaku no keikyo", Tsushoisan ("Situations of rice production in British India, French Indo-China and Siam," Japanese Consular Report), No. 31, 1895, pp. 10–13.

Siam white rice in Singapore sold at much higher prices than Rangoon or Saigon rice. In a Japanese Consular Report (*Tsushoisan*) of February 1890, a record of the average monthly prices of rice in the Singapore market in December 1889 shows that Siam white rice No. 1 was sold at S$ (Straits Dollar) 2.93 per picul (60 kgs), Saigon white rice No. 1 at S$ 2.68, and Rangoon white rice at S$2.70. These figures show that the market price of Siam white rice was higher than the others. According to this table, during the period from September 1892 to September 1895, the average monthly price of Siam white rice No. 1 in Singapore was S$3.07 per picul, whilst that of Rangoon white rice was S$2.68, and that of Saigon white rice was S$2.61. Table 8.4 and Graph 8.1 supports this data. This trend continued during the 1920s and the early 1930s, as shown in Table 8.5 and Table 8.6.

What was the cause of the high price of Siam white rice in Singapore? It was probably because Siam rice was of such good reputation in Singapore. The type of Siam rice classified as Siam white rice No.1 in the rice trade in Bangkok was mostly "Garden rice." It was grown as seedlings and then transplanted by the farmers and was regarded by rice dealers, rice millers, and rice exporters in Bangkok as the best quality rice. This was because its grain was long, thin, translucent, strong, and when well-matured, gave only a small percentage of broken grains when milled.[9] In Bangkok, "Garden rice" was preferred to "Field rice"

Table 8.5 Average annual price trends of Siam rice, Rangoon rice, and
Saigon rice in Singapore during 1923 and 1929 (unit: straits dollar
per picul)

Year	Siam rice No.1	Rangoon rice No.1	Saigon rice No.1
1923	8.53	6.00	6.67
1924	10.46	7.06	7.79
1925	9.82	6.86	7.33
1926	11.13	7.47	7.85
1927	10.95	6.90	7.42
1928	9.90	6.23	4.54
1929	9.95	6.39	6.96

Source: Otani Toshiharu, *Nanpokeizaisigensouran dai 6 kan Malay no keizaisigen*
(*Economic Resources in Malay, South Sea Research Series, Vol. 6*), Toaseikeisya,
1943, pp. 455–6.

Table 8.6 Average weekly price trends of Siam rice, Rangoon rice, and
Saigon rice in Singapore during March and May in 1932 (unit:
straits dollar per picul)

Month/year	Siam rice No.1	Rangoon rice No.1	Saigon rice No.1
March 7, 1932	4.75	4.00	4.05
March 14, 1932	4.63	4.20	4.30
March 21, 1932	4.65	4.15	4.30
March 31, 1932	4.50	4.00	4.20
April 4, 1932	4.25	3.80	4.10
April 11, 1932	4.38	3.95	4.15
April 19, 1932	4.33	3.93	4.00
April 25, 1932	4.30	3.95	4.00
May 5, 1932	4.18	3.85	3.90

Source: "Siam market-notes on current trade during the June quarter 1932," The
Record, Vol. 12, No. 1, p. 65.

(*khaao naa muang* in Thai). "Field rice" was usually cultivated by the broadcasting
technique and sold as the lowest quality of milled rice, because its grain was short
and broad, opaque, hard, and inclined to be brittle, especially when not well-
matured. The typical "Field rice" plant matures as the water level rises and ripens
while floating on the surface of deep water and can be reaped from boats.

In the Singapore rice market, the reason why the Siam white rice No.1 "Garden
rice" was sold at a much higher price than Rangoon or Saigon rice was that it
suited the tastes of the Singapore people, especially the Chinese. This hypothesis
is strongly supported by Cheng Siok-Hwa's observation.

The principal reason for the domination of Siam [rice] in the Malayan market
was due to the large Chinese population, who preferred Siam qualities,
especially the 'garden' Siam type, to rice from the other two countries. It was

noted that in the import market of Singapore, what is known as Siam No. 2 rice is consistently more expensive than those termed Rangoon No.1 or Saigon No. 1. Despite the cost, the consumer was willing and able to pay for Siam rice.[10]

A.J.H. Latham and Larry Neal also point out,[11] "Siam qualities were preferred by the growing numbers of Chinese miners and plantation workers in the Straits Settlements and in the Dutch East Indies." In the early 1920s, a Japanese observer in Singapore, Kohei Mizuno, also confirmed the high reputation of Siam "Garden rice."[12] He wrote,

> the transplanted rice ["Garden rice"] is treated as the highest quality of rice in Singapore. Even the general type of Siam "Garden rice" is valued more than Saigon "Baixaw" rice by Singapore Chinese and is usually sold at 10 percent higher prices than Saigon rice.

It is clear from these observations that Siam rice, especially "Garden rice" was preferred in Singapore. This strong preference for Siam rice resulted in the high-price of Siam white rice No. 1 produced from "Garden rice."

Turning to Siam rice exports to Europe in the late nineteenth century, two features can be indicated. First, partly milled cargo rice constituted about 70 percent of total exports and only 20 percent was milled white rice. This was very different from Siam rice exported to Singapore where milled white rice predominated. Second, "Field rice", which constituted most Siam rice exported to Europe, was used for starch and spirits. Although "Garden rice" was introduced to Europe with the development of steamship lines between Siam and Europe, and in the early twentieth century gradually became more popular,[13] its export really only began to increase in the 1910s.[14] In the late nineteenth century European rice millers generally ranked Siam rice as a lower and cheaper grade than Burmese rice, Bengal rice or Japanese rice.

According to a Japanese Consular Report (*Tsushohoukoku*) from Liverpool in 1891, Siam rice was classified lower than Saigon or Japanese rice.

> Both Siam rice and Saigon rice are mostly exported as cargo rice. On the one hand, the quality of Saigon rice is as good and strong as Burmese "Passiin rice." As the way of loading of Saigon rice has improved and become more careful recently, the quality of it is better than before. On the other hand, Siam rice is usually of poor quality. No rice is more inclined to be brittle than Siam rice.... It is said that the rice miller can gain nothing by dealing in Siam rice, because the different grains are often mixed and Siam rices are exported with minute black substances which cannot be removed.... As Japanese rice is ranked as a high grade of rice and is suitable for consumers to eat, there is no doubt that the demand for Japanese rice will increase more.[15]

A Japanese Consular Report (*Tsushohoukoku*) from London in 1891 reported that the price of Siam rice was very low in the London rice market.[16] Siam rice was sold at only 7s. per ctw (51 kg), whereas Japanese rice sold at 11s., Bengal high quality rice at 10s. 9d., Rangoon rice at 7s. 2d., and Saigon rice at 7s. 2d. These prices indicate the lower reputation of Siam rice. This is also evidenced by a commentary on the Hamburg rice market reported in A Commercial Report from Japanese Legations and Consulates (*Koshikan oyobi ryoji houkoku*) in 1893.[17] It reported that Siam rice was sold at 5s. $4\frac{1}{2}$d.–6s. per cwt. while Rangoon rice was purchased at 6s. $7\frac{1}{2}$d., Arrakan rice at 6s. 3d., and Saigon rice at 5s. $10\frac{1}{2}$d. In European continental rice markets as well as in London, Siam rice, most of which was "Field rice," was ranked as a lower grade and generally traded at a lower price.

Many kinds of Siam rice were exported to foreign markets. In rice milling grades, rice was divided into paddy, cargo rice, white rice, white broken rice, and others (see Table 8.3). But "Garden rice" and "Field rice" were classified separately based on their methods of cultivation. This classification was in accordance with the grades of rice used by millers, exporters, and consumers. There were great differences in the types of Siam rice exported to different foreign markets based on demand. White rice produced from the famous high quality "Garden rice" was the larger part of total rice exports to Singapore. However most Siam rice exports to Europe in the late nineteenth century were "Field rice."

The rice trade network of Tan Kim Ching

In the development of white rice milling in Bangkok and the export of white rice to foreign markets, a vital role was played by a Straits Hokkien Chinese, Tan Kim Ching (陳金鐘 1829–92), a British subject and a Baba Chinese of Malacca. He was a well-known exporter of best quality rice, Siam white rice No. 1, to the Singapore market, as well as a pioneer of white rice milling in Bangkok. Although Tan Kim Ching had a cluster of political, social, and business activities based in Singapore, he succeeded in expanding his network of political and business activities to the Malay Peninsula, Bangkok, Saigon, and Hong Kong. C.D. Cowan referred to Tan Kim Ching as "a perfect example of the cosmopolitan Straits merchant."[18]

Figure 8.2 reveals that in the early 1890s just before his death, Tan Kim Ching had developed his business network linking Singapore, Bangkok, Saigon, and Hong Kong. In Bangkok and Hong Kong, he had branches of his mercantile firm, and he had rice mills in Bangkok and Saigon. He had his own steamships, "Singapore" and "Siam" and was also a marine insurance agent. He accomplished a complete vertical integration of his rice business, by rice dealing, rice milling, rice exporting, and by running a steamship service and marine insurance service in Southeast Asia.

Tan Kim Ching's activities in the late nineteenth century were summarized by Song Ong Siang, a famous Singapore Chinese intellectual.[19] Mr. Tan Kim Ching, the eldest of the three sons of Tan Tock Seng (Figure 8.3), was born in Singapore in 1829, and his father was a famous Straits born Chinese merchant in Singapore who died in 1850. The following year, the firm of "Tan Tock Seng" was changed

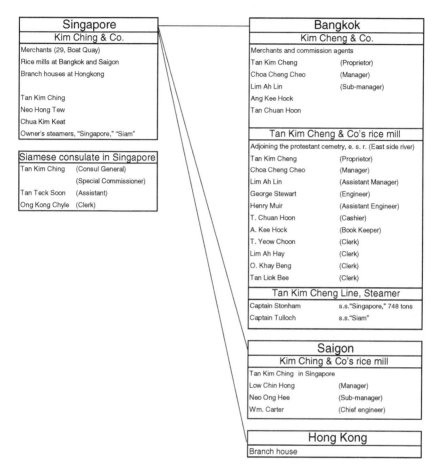

Figure 8.2 Business activities of Tan Kim Ching (陳金鐘): 1891.

Sources: "Singapore Directory," *The Chronicles & Directories for China, Corea, Japan & c. for 1892* (Hong Kong: Daily Press, 1892), pp. 326, 335; "Bangkok Directory," *The Chronicles & Directories for China, Corea, Japan & c. for 1892* (Hong Kong: Daily Press 1892), p. 314; "Saigon Directory." *The Chronicles & Directories for China, Corea, Japan & c. for 1892* (Hong Kong: Daily Press, 1892), p. 298; *The Directory for Bangkok and Siam for 1890* (Bangkok: Bangkok Times, 1890), p. 208; *The Directory for Bangkok and Siam for 1892* (Bangkok: Bangkok Times, 1892), pp. 297, 305.

to "Tan Kim Ching." His business, which became known as Kim Ching & Co. chop Chin Seng (振成行) attained considerable success, owning rice mills in Saigon and Bangkok. As a head of the Hokkien Huay-kuan (association), located in the Chinese temple "Thian–hok-kiong" in Telok Ayer Street (Singapore), he acted as "Captain China" in the Hokkien Chinese society. He gave timely assistance in 1852 to the Hospital (The Tan Tock Seng General Hospital) founded by his father financing extensions to the Hospital buildings at a cost of $2,000 and was made

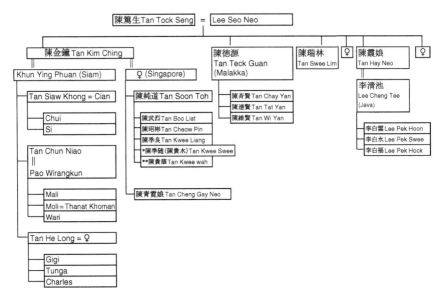

Figure 8.3 陳篤生 (Tan Tock Seng) family.

Sources: Nopphapon ruangsakun lae Orawan Siudom, "Chum chon cinbaba nai krungthep," ("Baba Chinese Community in Bangkok"), Warasansetthasatculalongkon, Vol. 3, No. 3, 1991, p. 355 (in Thai); Kua Bak Lim, *Who's Who in the Chinese Community of Singapore*, Singapore Federation of Chinese Clan Associations, 1995, pp. 82–3, 86 (in Chinese); Song Ong Siang, *One Hundred Years' History of the Chinese in Singapore*; Singapore Chinese Chamber of Commerce & Industry, 1993 [1923], pp. 465–90 (in Chinese, originally in English).

Notes
This figure is mainly based on Kuo Buk Lim (1995).
 * means that in Song Ong Siang (1993), the Chinese character of Tan Kwee See is 陳貴水 which is different from 陳季隨 in Kuo Buk Lim (1995).
** means that the Chinese character 陳貴華 of Tan Kwee Wah is from Song Ong Siang (1993).

a Justice of Peace in 1865 and recognized as a "Respectable Chinese" by the Straits Settlements government. One reason for this was that the government wanted him to help them in their dealings with Chinese society in the Straits Settlements. He was a "faithful agent" in Singapore of King Rama IV of Siam and Consul General and Special Commissioner for Siam in the Straits Settlements and in 1885 was conferred[20] the high ranking Siamese title, Phraya Anukunsiamkitupanikkasitsiamrat, by King Rama V. He was perhaps the most powerful Chinese leader in the nineteenth century with great influence on the Chinese in the Siamese–Malayan borders namely Kelantan and Patani, and he figured most prominently in Perak affairs prior to the signing of the Pangor Treaty in 1874. He both persuaded the Triad leaders to accept Government arbitration, and influenced the Malay chiefs.

This chapter examines in detail Tan Kim Ching's rice business in Bangkok and his rice trade networks. Until recently little has been known about the role of his rice mill in Bangkok and his rice trade network between Singapore and Bangkok, although his rice mills in Bangkok and Saigon were mentioned in historical studies of the Singapore Chinese, such as Song Ong Siang's work.

Tan Kim Ching invested in his rice mill Tan Kim Ching's Rice Mill (also called Tan Kim Cheng's Rice Mill in Bangkok) and a branch of his firm, Kim Ching & Co., in Bangkok in order to export white rice to Singapore. His rice mill and firm were very famous in the rice business circles of Bangkok, because Kim Ching's Rice Mill was a pioneer company that milled a high grade of white rice, and Kim Ching & Co. was the first exporter of "Siam white rice No.1" to Singapore. In 1894 Charles S. Leckie of the Borneo Company, which also conducted rice milling and trade in Siam, made a brief reference to Tan Kim Ching in recounting the development of the Bangkok rice mill industry.

> The Europeans have taught the Chinese to mill rice by steam, and, with the Chinaman's trading ability, backed by the wealth of the Siamese, John Chinaman has gained the hold on the rice trade of Siam, which the Europeans of 40 years ago looked to secure to themselves. The European in the East generally gives himself the credit of leading, and the Chinaman is supposed to follow. In Bangkok we have an instance of the white rice industry being pioneered by a Singapore Chinaman, a British subject, supported by his Scotch engineers, and, after some years, the European millers in Bangkok followed his lead.[21]

European predominance in the rice industry seems to have been clearly demonstrated in the development of modern rice milling in its early stages. However, the first steam-powered rice mill in Siam was established in 1858 by an American firm.[22] After that, British and German firms followed by building steam-powered rice mills. Generally, the Europeans traded semi-milled cargo rice because it did not deteriorate over the long distance to the European markets.[23] Against this background Tan Kim Ching pioneered the "white rice industry" in the 1870s and the export of white rice to Singapore. In the 1870s, his firm in Bangkok began to export high-grade white rice to Singapore. Other Chinese and European rice millers and exporters followed his lead by milling white rice and exporting it mainly to Singapore and Hong Kong, because white rice was a higher value-added product than cargo rice.[24] The following quote by A.E. Stiven is useful for understanding the activities of Tan Kim Ching. It is by a contemporary European businessman in Bangkok in 1908, 16 years after Tan Kim Ching had passed away. He was a manager of the Borneo Company, Ltd, a rice mill in Bangkok, and wrote a report about "Rice" in Siam. He explained the history and activities of the Kim Cheng Rice Mill (also called Tan Kim Ching Rice Mill) as follows:[25]

> Established some thirty-six years ago on the banks of the Menam Chow Phya, this mill has the distinction of being the first to have produced No. 1 white rice in Bangkok. To keep pace with the great advance that has been made in recent years in the methods of rice milling, the Kim Cheng Mill was, some years ago, equipped with the latest Scotch milling machinery, with

patent furnaces for burning the paddy husk, thereby occasioning the saving of about 100 per cent in the cost of fuel. The mill is devoted solely to the production of the first quality of white rice, and shipments by this company have, for years past, invariably realised the highest price in the Singapore market, while exhibit by the firm of white rice at the St. Louis Exposition was awarded a bronze medal. The mill has an output of 1,000 bags of No. 1 rice per day of twenty-four hours, and works continuously during separate periods of three months.

The mill is part of the estate of the late Tan Kim Cheng, of Singapore, and is under the management of Mr. Lim Teck Lian, who has general charge of the business in Siam. Like many of the leading Chinese businessmen in Bangkok, Mr. Lim Teck Lian comes from the Swatow district of China. He has had many years' experience in the rice-milling industry. The working of the mill is under the immediate control of Mr. W. Sidney Smart, the super-intendent engineer, who has been connected with Bangkok rice mills for the last nineteen years.

At the back of the Kim Cheng Mill there may still be seen two immense freestone rollers, now long since replaced by modern machinery, which are reputed to be the first of their kind used in Bangkok. These relics of already antiquated methods illustrate in a striking manner the great progress that has been made in rice milling even during a comparatively small number of years.

Mr Stiven noted that the high quality of the white rice, "Siam White Rice No.1" exported by Tan Kim Ching's rice mill was ranked highly and sold at the highest prices in Singapore. According to him, while Tan Kim Ching, a Hokkien Chinese usually lived in Singapore, Teochew Chinese (潮州華僑: the major Chinese dialect group in Siam) rice experts[26] such as Lim Teck Lian, mentioned earlier, managed his rice mill and his firm in Bangkok, and a European engineer like Mr W. Sidney Smart supervised technological matters in his rice mill. Mr Smart was a well-known rice mill engineer in Bangkok, as can be seen in the following quotation. "He has, during his stay in Siam, been prominently associated with the rice milling industry, and has erected and equipped with modern machinery no less than nine large mills."[27] And on February 13, 1929, the article mourning his death in Australia where he spent the rest of his life, appeared in the *Bangkok Times Weekly Mail* –

A shrewd and capable engineer, he held the confidence and esteem of his employers of many years, the firm of Kim Cheng and Co., who until their mill was burnt down, milled rice for the Singapore market and had a reputa-tion second to none for its products...In addition to looking after this mill Mr. Smart represented various rice engineering manufacturers in Europe and his advice was frequently sought by Chinese about to build mills.[28]

It will be clear from these quotations that Tan Kim Ching's rice mill and firm was a great success in the rice business in Bangkok. This was because although they were owned by Tan, a Hokkien Chinese, they were well managed by a Teochew Chinese rice expert who had a close commercial network with the other Teochew merchants and millers in Bangkok and "a shrewd and capable" European engineer who supervised the rice mill.

Tan Kim Ching's rice mill had the largest capacity of any mill in Bangkok in its day. As shown in Table 8.7, the production capacity of Tan Kim Ching's rice mill in 1898 was as much as 300 tons per day of which 120 tons was fully milled white rice and 180 tons partly milled cargo rice. These figures reveal that Tan Kim Ching's rice mill had a capacity equal to the Guan Seng rice mill of the Phra Phisanbut family and Tan Huang Lee's rice mill.

According to Table 8.8, Tan Kim Ching's firm in Bangkok exported as much as 8,000–10,000 tons of rice to Singapore in 1889 and 1890. Even though Table 8.8 covers the volumes of rice exported only for two years, it tells us that the average annual export volume of rice by his firm to Singapore during

Table 8.7 The production capacity of rice mills in Bangkok: 1898 (unit: tons per day)

Group	Owner	Rice mill	Cargo rice	White rice
European Trading Houses	A. Markwald & Co.	A. Markwald	150	90
	Windsor & Co.	Windsor	150	90
	The Arracan Co. Ltd.	The Arracan	150	—
	Owner/Manager			
Chinese tax farmers	Late Tan Kim Ching (Phraya Anukun: 陳金鐘)	Tan Kim Ching's rice mill	180	120
	Phra Phisan	元豐盛	60	30
		元盛	180	120
		元利	150	72
	Phra Phibunpattanakon	乾利棧	150	—
		常記棧	150	60
	Akon Teng (張宗煌)	金成利	150	72
	Phra (劉繼賓) Phakdipattarakon	源裕泰	150	90
	Phra Boribunkosakon	Lee Tit Kuan	150	120
	Owner			
Chinese merchants	Mah Hua & Co. or Koh Mah Wah & Co.	元得利	120	60
		元豐盛	150	72
	高媽和、高暉石	元和盛	180	—
		Kuan Heng Huat	72	36
	Hiap Yuu	廣合盛	150	72
	Tan Tsu Huang 陳「釁利」	Bangkok rice mill	120	60
	Tan Tsu Huang 陳「釁利」	隆興利	180	120
	Lao Bang Seng 老萬成	老萬成	150	72
	Lee Thye Hoa	華興盛	150	72

Sources: Suehiro Akira, *Capital Accumulation iin Thailand 1855–1985* (Tokyo: The Center for East Asian Cultural Studies, 1989), p. 51; Phannii Bualek, *Sayaam nai krasaethaan haeng kaanplianplaeng: Prawattisaat thai tang tae samai ratchakaanthii 5 (Siam in Transition: Thai History after the Reign of King Rama V)* (Bangkok: Muang booraan, 1998), p. 97.

Table 8.8 Rice exporters from Bangkok to Singapore: 1889–90 (unit: tons)

No.	Exporter	Type	1889	1890	Average
1	Tan Kim Ching (Phraya Anukun[a])	Tax farmer, Singapore Chinese	8,787	10,318	9,553
2	Luang Boribun	Tax farmer, Bangkok Chinese	n.d.	n.d.	n.d.
3	Luang Charoen	Tax farmer, Bangkok Chinese	n.d.	n.d.	n.d.
4	Phraya Samut	Officer of rice export tax, rice mill owner	n.d.	n.d.	n.d.
5	Nguan Heng Yu	Bangkok Chinese	1,565	344	955
6	Ban Hong	Bangkok Chinese	6,954	1,604	4,279
7	Huang Li	Bangkok Chinese	4,216	n.d.	4,216
8	Lao Bang Seng	Bangkok Chinese	11,132	9,396	10,264
9	Ma Hua	Bangkok Chinese	5,859	6,908	6,384
10	Thai Hua Li	Bangkok Chinese	n.d.	n.d.	n.d.
11	Markwald and Co.	European	15,960	8,058	12,009
12	Borneo Co.	European	1,912	n.d.	1,912
13	Windsor Clarke	European	n.d.	n.d.	n.d.
14	Windsor Rose	European	71,564	62,787	67,176
		Total	127,949	99,415	113,682

Sources: C.M. Wilson, "Ethnic participation in the export of Thai rice 1885–90," in Karl L. Hutterer (ed.), *Economic Exchange and Social Interaction in Southeast Asia* (Michigan: Center for South and Southeast Asian Studies, The University of Michigan, 1977) pp. 245–71.

Original source: "Phasi Khao Krungtheb lae Chachoengsao" ("Rice tax in Bangkok and Chachoensao"), in Records of the Krasuan Phra Khlang Mahasonbat, R.5. Kh. (Kho Khwai) 6 and Kh. 17.2k (Bangkok: National Archives).

Notes
n.d. means no data.
a The full name of Phraya Anukun, one of the Siamese titles, was Phraya Anukunsiamkitupanikkasitsiamrat.

the two years amounted to 9,553 tons. This came next in order after 12,009 tons by Markwald and Co. and 10,264 tons by Lao Bang Seng. It is clear that Tan Kim Ching's firm played an important role in expanding rice exports to Singapore.

After Tan Kim Ching passed away in 1892, his daughter, Tan Cheng Gay Neo (陳青霓娘) inherited his huge fortune in Singapore, Bangkok, and other places. Several years later, his grandchild, Tan Boo Liat (陳武烈) succeeded as head of the business. In Bangkok, even after Tan Kim Ching's death, Teochew Chinese experts like Lim Teck Lian and European engineers continued to manage his rice mill and firm. In the early twentieth century, according to the article in the *Bangkok Times Weekly Mail* mentioned earlier, Tan Kim Ching's rice mill was burned down. As his rice mill and firm cannot be found in the "Bangkok Directory"[29] of 1913, it seems that a fire broke out in 1912 or 1913 causing the family of the late Tan Kim Ching to withdraw from the rice business in Bangkok (Figure 8.4).

	Name	Company	Dominancile of origin	Property (Straits $)	Business
1	陸裕	興隆	廣東	30,000,000	Tin mining, coconut plantation, rubber plantation
2	陳若錦	豐興	福建	8,000,000	Real estate agent, loan office
3	李俊源	振裕	福建	3,000,000	House rent, loan office, Director of Chinese Commercial Bank
4	余連成		潮州	2,000,000	House rent
5	余東旋	余仁成	潮州	1,000,000	Pharmacy, remittance office, loan office, tin mining
6	余北成		潮州	1,000,000	House rent
7	林秉祥	和源	福建	1,000,000	Steam shipping, sugar, miscellaneous goods, rubber plantation, President of Chinese Bank, President of Chamber of Commerce
⑧	陳武烈 Tan Boo Liat	振成	福建	1,000,000	Rice import from Annam, but not from Siam
9	阮荔邨	朱廣蘭	廣州	800,000	Tobacco, miscellaneous goods
10	林霽	鼎盛興	福建	600,000	Wholesale of rubber and wheat
11	郭 王炎	通合	潮州	500,000	Rice import from Annam
12	劉長意	榮豐	潮州	400,000	Rubber, cotton textile dealer
13	朱權	朱有蘭	廣州	400,000	Tobacco, miscellaneous goods
14	藍金盛	裕盛棧	潮州	300,000	Consignment sale of Siam rice
15	陳鶴珊	陳生利	潮州	300,000	Consignment sale of Siam rice
16	廖正興	萬德興	潮州	250,000	Wholesale of piece goods, President of Four Seas Bank
17	陳先進	吉美	福建	200,000	Rice import from Rangoon
18	劉隆鎮		潮州	200,000	Tax farmer of gambling
19	陳敏廷	三盆	廣東	200,000	Dry goods dealer, money exchanger
20	劉少愚	萬裕隆	潮州	150,000	Wholesale of rubber and piece-goods

Figure 8.4 Singapore major businessmen: Tan Boo Liat's property and business in 1914.

Source: Department of Research of Taiwan Bank, "Important persons of property in Singapore," *Overseas Chinese in the South Sea* (*Nanyo niokeru kakyo* in Japanese), Taiwan Bank, 1914, pp. 74–7.

Tan Kim Ching's strategy of having experts manage his rice mill and firm was a crucial factor in his success in the rice business in Bangkok. He could expand his rice trade connections with the Teochew Chinese merchants by hiring Chinese experts like Lim Teck Lian and could produce high quality rice with the guidance of a trained European engineer like Mr S.W. Smart. This strategy allowed his firm to have access to market information about rice and allowed his rice mill to use the latest technology in rice milling. This enabled him to become the pioneer of the milling and exporting of high quality white rice to Singapore.

In this way he became one of the most important rice merchants in Singapore. The main purpose of his investment in rice milling in Bangkok was to import rice to Singapore and to reexport it to Johore, Riau, and other places near Singapore. This was noted by C. Trocki who states, "Tan Kim Ching was, moreover, the lightning rod for animosity as a result of his attempt to corner the Singapore rice market and to force up the price of foodstuffs in the colony."[30] He acquired a thorough knowledge of rice trading in Singapore and had good access to information on the rice markets and crop situation in Siam.

His close connection with the Siamese Kings and the Siamese government cannot be ignored. Like his father Tan Tock Seng, who had been a private agent of King Rama IV, Tan Kim Ching was a "faithful agent" of the Siamese Kings and the Consul General in Singapore. In addition he invested in a tin mining company with King Rama IV and was appointed as a "tax farmer" and Governor in south Siam by the Siamese government.[31] In 1877 when there were crop failures in Siam, King Rama V sent a letter to Tan Kim Ching showing concern about his rice mill in Bangkok and the poor rice harvest in Siam.[32] As historical data on this point are limited, the only thing that can be noted here is the indirect influence of the Kings and government in promoting Tan Kim Ching's rice business in Bangkok.

Notes

1 Kaoru Sugihara, *Asiakanboueki no kouzou to keisei* (*The Structure and Formation of Intra-Asian Trade*) (Tokyo: Minerva shobo, 1996). See also A.J.H. Latham, *International Economy and the Underdeveloped World*, 1865–1914 (London: Croom Helm,1978), pp. 77, 94, where the concept of intra-Asian rice trade is first mentioned.
2 Sakae Tsunoyama, "Asiakan kome boueki to nihon" ("Japan in the intra-Asian rice trade"), *Shakaikeizaishi* (Vol. 51, No. 1, 1986), pp. 126–40.
3 Heita Kawakatsu, "Nihon no kogyoka wo meguru gaiatsu to ajiakankyosou," in Takeshi Hamashita and Heita Kawakatsu (eds), *Asiakouekiken to nihonkougyouka 1500–1900* ("Foreign Pressure and Asian rivalry in the context of the Japanese industrialization," *Asian Trade and Japanese Industrialization 1500–1900*) (Tokyo: Libroport, 1991), pp. 181–93.
4 J.C. Ingram, *Economic Change in Thailand, 1850–1970* (Stanford, CA: Stanford University Press, 1971), pp. 42–3.
5 Akira Suehiro, *Capital Accumulation in Thailand, 1855–1985* (Tokyo: The Center for East Asian Cultural Studies, 1989), pp. 28–9.
6 Cheng Siok-Hwa, *The Rice Industry of Burma, 1852–1940* (Kuala Lumpur: University of Malaya Press, 1968), p. 14.
7 A.J.H. Latham and Larry Neal, "The International Market in Rice and Wheat, 1868–1914," *Economic History Review* (Vol. 36, No. 2, 1983), pp. 279–80.
8 China, especially southern China, traditionally suffered rice shortages due to frequent natural disasters and overpopulation. Moreover, British colonial intervention after the Opium War immediately gave rise to anti-colonial movements in southern China, and in turn brought about deteriorating economic conditions including rice shortages (Suehiro, op. cit., p. 29). But also see A.J.H. Latham, "Rice is a luxury, not a necessity", in Dennis O. Flynn, Lionel Frost, and A.J.H. Latham (eds) *Pacific Centuries: Pacific and Pacific Rim History since the Sixteenth Century* (London: Routledge, 1999), pp. 110, 122.
9 "Note on the classification of Padi," *The Record* (No. 34, 1929), pp. 311–12.
10 Cheng Siok-Hwa, op. cit., pp. 215–16.
11 A.J.H. Latham and Larry Neal, op. cit., p. 262.
12 Kohei Mizuno, "Siam no kome (4)," *Nanyokyokaizashi* ("Siam rice (4)," *Journal of South Sea Association*) (Vol. 8, No. 5, 1922), p. 69.
13 *British Parl. Papers 1908*, Vol. 115, Cd.3727-21: "Diplomatic and Consular Reports, Siam, Report for the year 1906 on the Trade of Bangkok," p. 6.

14 The average amount of Siam rice exported to Europe from 1913 to 1915 was about 18,000 tons per year. But a few years after WWI, from 1922 to 1924 it declined to about 4,300 tons per year. At this period R.S. le May, the Acting Adviser of the Ministry of Commerce was concerned about this serious fall. In order to investigate its causes, he consulted semi-officially with Mr Graham, the Adviser of Lands and Agriculture and three persons of the major rice exporting companies in Bangkok, Mr Stiven of the Borneo Company, Mr Bjorling of the East Asiatic Company, and Mr Scott of the Anglo-Siam Corporation. And he also received opinions of the principal rice dealers in London, the London–Rangoon Trading Company, Messrs. Jackson, Son, & Co., Messrs Lockie, Pemberton & Co. through Mr. Scott of the Anglo-Siam Corporation. Most of them suggested that most important reason for the decline in the demand for Siam rice to Europe was the steady decline in the quality of Siam rice shipped from Bangkok, in other words, the mixing of inferior grains. Messrs Lockie, Pemberton & Co. reported as follows:

> when we talk about Siam Rice, we always remember that the quality was beyond reproach a few years ago and stood in a class of its own when compared with other Long Grained Rice, particularly Saigon No.1 – in fact, the old Siam Rice as we knew it a few years ago was nearer to the highest quality of Long Grained Rice known as Patna coming from Calcutta. Today, however, Siam Rice is ridiculously unlike Patna and . . . it won't be long before Siam Rice is as low, if not lower, as Saigon Rice . . . .

According to these opinions as mentioned above, two points can be indicated. First, in the 1910s and the period before 1922 Siam rice, especially, Siam "Garden rice" was of high repute. Secondly, the main causes for the decline of Siam rice export to Europe was mostly the mixing of the inferior rice with Siam "Garden rice" and the decrease of the standardization of the quality of Siam "Garden rice," not the deterioration of the grain itself. (R.S. le May, Acting Adviser of Ministry of Commerce, "The export of Siam rice to Europe: a report on its decline, and the cause alleged therefore," compiled in the file of (Ko.Kho.0301.1.28/16) at Thai National Archives.)

15 "Eikoku beikoku shikyo," *Tsushohoukoku* ("The British rice market," *Japanese Consular Report*) (No. 2337, 1891).

16 "London beikoku shokyo," *Tsushohoukoku* ("The rice market in London," *Japanese Consular Report*) (No. 2613, 1892).

17 "Hamburg beikoku shokyo," *Koshikan oyobi ryoji houkoku* ("The rice market in Hamburg," *A Commercial Report from Japanese Legations and Consulates*), (No. 2961, 1893).

18 C.D. Cowan, *Nineteenth-Century Malaya* (London: Oxford University Press, 1962 (reprinted)), p. 56.

19 Song Ong Siang, *One Hundred Years' History of the Chinese in Singapore* (San Francisco, CA: Chinese Materials Center, 1975 (1923)), pp. 92–3.

20 In 1888 Japan also conferred on him the award of the 3rd Class Decoration of the Order of the Rising Sun for his service to Prince Komatsu of Japan who was on a diplomatic mission to Siam via Singapore (Song, ibid., pp. 92–3).

21 Charles. S. Leckie, "The commerce of Siam in relation to the trade of the British Empire," *Journal of the Society of Arts* (Vol. 42, No. 2168, 1894), pp. 651–2.

22 Suehiro, op. cit., pp. 47–8.

23 Suehiro, op. cit., p. 103.

24 Suehiro, op. cit., p. 103.

25 A.E. Stiven, "Rice," in Arnold Wright and Oliver T. Breakspear (eds), *Twentieth Century Impressions of Siam* (Bangkok: White Lotus, 1994 [1908]) pp. 157, 160–1.

26 It is confirmed that managers in Tan Kim Ching's rice mill in Bangkok were Choa Cheng Cheo (1889–93), Lim Ah Lin (1894), Chua Boon Quay (1894–96), Lim Teck

132   *Toshiyuki Miyata*

Lian (1896–1910), Chua Boon Quay (1902–03), Bay Swee Him (1904–05), Chua Boon Poh (1911–12) in the Bangkok Directory.

27 C. Lamont, "Engineering," in Arnold Wright and Oliver T. Breakspear (eds), *Twentieth Century Impressions of Siam* (Bangkok: White Lotus, 1994 [1908]) , p. 198.

28 "Death of Mr W. S. Smart," *The Bangkok Times Weekly Mail* (February 13, 1929), p. 29.

29 "Bangkok Directory," *The Chronicles & Directories for China, Corea, Japan &c. for 1913* (Hong Kong: Daily Press, 1913), p. 1272.

30 Carl A. Trocki, *Opium and Empire: Chinese Society in Colonial Singapore, 1800–1910* (Ithaca, NY: Cornell University Press, 1990), p. 116.

31 Jennifer W. Cushman, in Craig J. Reynolds (ed.), *Family and State: The Formation of A Sino-Thai Tin-Mining Dynasty 1797–1932* (Singapore: Oxford University Press, 1991), pp. 32–7.

32 Nathawut sutthisongkhram, *Chiwit lae ngankongsulthai khong phrayaanukunsayamkit upanikkasitsayamrat (tan kim ceng) kongsulyeneoral thai khon raek na muangsingkhapo* (krungthep: phim camnai nuang nai mahamongkonsamai khrawsomphot krungrattanakosin khroprop 200pi, 1982), p. 112, in Thai (*Life and Achievements of the First Siamese Consul General in Singapore, Phraya Anukunsayamkitupanikasitsyamrat (Tan Kim Ching)*.

9 *The Rangoon Gazette* and inter-Asian competition in the intra-Asian rice trade 1920–41

A.J.H. Latham

In the years before the Second World War, Burma was one of the greatest rice exporters in the intra-Asian rice trade, but it faced inter-Asian competition from Siam and French Indo-China. *The Rangoon Gazette and Weekly Budget* (hereafter *Rangaz*) reveals the crises and concerns of the Burma rice merchants in these years, for there were grave problems in the rice trade in the late 1920s and 1930s, coinciding with world depression (Latham (1981), pp. 176–8 (1986a), pp. 654–6, 663 (1988), pp. 94–5, 99–100). This chapter examines the information flow to those in the rice trade. How did they interpret the causes of their problems? Were they aware of the activities of their rivals in Siam and French Indo-China and did they relate their problems to the simultaneous overproduction crisis in world wheat markets?

1920–25

During the 1914–18 War, the government controlled the rice trade and also shipping, freight movements and freight rates. There was a fixed price for paddy (un-milled rice in the husk), and the Rice Controller set the price for milled rice. Exports ceased from Siam, there was famine in India and the Allies bought rice wherever they could obtain it, regardless of price (*Rangaz* 26 March (1923), p. 1). After the war the rice trade slowly returned to normal.

The year 1920 began with the failure of the crop in Siam, and the partial failure of the crop in Burma, which forced the Ministry of Food to raise its prices (*Rangaz* 8 March (1920), p. 24). But 1921 saw real excitement, in June *The Rangoon Gazette* ran the headline, 'The rice market goes panicky owing to a corner. Business suspended.' On Friday, 17 June, the price of milled 'special' rice reached an all time high of Rs 580 per 100 baskets. An Indian firm was thought to be trying to corner the market. It was believed that all paddy was in the hands of Indian and Chinese brokers who were holding out for higher prices. Business was suspended and Mogul street, centre of the rice trade, was crowded with excited throngs, all wondering if the Government would intervene. On Saturday paddy prices rose to Rs 225 (*Rangaz* 20 June (1921), p. 10). But it was not until a fortnight later by about 5 July that the 'bombshell' came that the Government was going to refuse all rice export licences except those to India. There would be no licences to Europe, which was the main market for specials, and none to the Far East (*Rangaz* 11 July (1921), p. 3). The Government said it had used price-control powers it had retained from war-time, because although half the estimated Burma crop had been allotted to India, the crop was less than expected. By banning exports to other markets it was hoped that prices would fall. No mention was made of the alleged corner (*Rangaz* 11 July (1921), p. 3).

In this way the corner was broken. Two weeks later No. 10 mill at Kanoungto was burnt with a loss of Rs 2 million. It belonged to the Indian company Ahmed Moola Dawood and Sons, but was leased to Jamal Brothers (*Rangaz* 25 July (1921), p. 14). On Saturday 30 July the market opened at Rs 580, but when the big millers sold at this price rather than buying, the market dropped to Rs 572–573 before steadying at Rs 575, with paddy at Rs 232–235 (*Rangaz* 1 August (1921), pp. 2, 25). A fortnight later specials were down to Rs 560 (*Rangaz* 15 August (1921), p. 4). But those who had sold when the corner was broken, lost out when there was a 'dead cat's bounce' and new demand from Bombay and Calcutta pushed specials to highs of Rs 590, with new crop in line at Rs 445 for February–April 1922 delivery (*Rangaz* 22 August (1921), p. 20). By 29 August specials were quoted at Rs 622–628 for August and September, and one big miller sold 200,000 tons of specials at Rs 620 for August and September delivery to Bombay. Paddy was steady at Rs 250 (*Rangaz* 29 August (1921), p. 29). The trend was still up and on 2 September deals were done at Rs 640 for specials before the market dropped back to Rs 620 (*Rangaz* 5 Septmber (1921), p. 1). Demand was falling from India, and by the end of the month white rice was at Rs 645–655 for September delivery, and Rs 647–648 to Rs 635 for October (*Rangaz* 3 October (1921), p. 4). A fortnight later business was slack at Rs 635 for October and small mills specials at Rs 626 but no business (*Rangaz* 17 October (1921), p. 3). By November prices were down to Rs 613–618 to 610 (*Rangaz* 7 November (1921), p. 2). Attention was focussing on New Crop specials and on 25 November 2,000–3,000 tons of New Crop specials were sold at Rs 475–495 for December delivery. Then came rumours that the Government was going to allow 100,000 tons to be shipped to foreign countries other than India, and much speculation was done at Rs 460 to Rs 472–478 for January, and Rs 452–458 to Rs 462–468 for February–April 1922 delivery. The rumours turned out to be true (*Rangaz* 28 November (1921), p. 26). On 2 December (1921) the market was quiet, and although Old Crop could now be exported to foreign countries, no business was reported (*Rangaz* 5 December (1921), p. 28).

So 1921 was an eventful year, and revealed all the volatilities of the rice market. The *Gazette* commented in its review of the year that a new element had entered the Burma rice trade, with certain operators attempting to hold up stocks of rice to get better prices. In June a large operator had come out as a 'bull' forcing the market to Rs 590 for Big Mills specials, but panic had hit the market in July when the Government refused to issue export licences to certain freight destinations, and prices had immediately dropped 40 points (*Rangaz* 6 March (1922), p. 23).

So who was behind this 'corner' if corner it was? An old Burma Chinese told the author in Singapore some years ago that it was thought to be the Burma

Chinese merchant Lim Chin Tsong (Latham (1986b), pp. 11–13 (1988), pp. 98–9). No one in Burma cut a figure like Lim Chin Tsong, and in November 1920 he and his wife entertained Mon. Clemenceau, the French statesman, at his new Rs 2,200,000 'palace' in Kokine (*Rangaz* 29 November (1920), p. 18). The case against Lim is not proven, but after the corner was broken everything went wrong for him, and following a bout of influenza, he died in his sleep from a heart attack two years later on 2 November 1923 at the age of 56 (*Rangaz* 5 November (1923), p. 1). His estate was declared insolvent on 10 June 1924 (*Rangaz* 26 December (1927), p. 27). It was hopelessly encumbered, some estimates suggesting liabilities of Rs 20,000,000 against assets of only Rs 10,000,000. In the last years of his life Lim had been borrowing desperately from wherever he could (*Rangaz* 11 May (1925), p. 26). It has been said that the heart attack was triggered by a threat from the telephone company to disconnect him for not paying his bill (Corley (1983), p. 155).

The ban on rice exports to countries other than India was finally lifted on 1 April 1922 (*Rangaz* 20 March (1922), p. 11). Although this coincided with huge flows of rice to Shanghai and other Chinese ports, where crops had failed, Japan seems to have supplied most of China's needs and Burma did not benefit much (*Rangaz* 2 April (1923), p. 22). These large movements of rice to Hong Kong continued into 1923, with a number of Japanese ships being chartered to carry rice from Bangkok and Saigon, Burma's great rivals. There was also a brisk movement of rice from the Straits Settlements, particularly Singapore, which was a re-distribution centre in the rice trade, nearly every ship leaving there carrying varying amounts of rice to China. Some of this must have originated in Burma, but there was also a good crop in southern Siam, and supplies were adequate (*Rangaz* 4 June (1923), p. 21).

Burma does not seem to have benefited much from this heavy demand from China. In February 1923 came another disaster on the waterfront in Rangoon when No. 1 building and several godowns belonging to the Ally Moolla Corporation was destroyed by fire (*Rangaz* 12 February (1923), p. 25). This corporation only dated back to December 1920 (*Rangaz* 20 December (1920), p. 27), but its rice manager had indulged in heavy speculation resulting in a criminal charge against the manager and big claims against the company (*Rangaz* 30 April (1923), p. 3). Had the mill been deliberately set on fire for the insurance money? The firing of mills was a classic indication of trouble in the rice trade, and there was a rash of mill fires at this time, particularly among Chinese-owned mills (*Rangaz* 4 June (1923), pp. 6, 12).

Problems continued into 1924, and in February there were petitions to wind up the Ally Moolla Corporation (*Rangaz* 18 February (1924), p. 7). Also C.T. Johnstone, a director of Anglo-Burma Rice, was convicted of fraud in a rice mill, following a lengthy trial (*Rangaz* 18 February (1924), pp. 10–14, 20, 25 February (1924), pp. 10–12, 3 March (1924), pp. 7–11, 17 March (1924), pp. 7–12, 14 April (1924), pp. 18–20, 25–8). Then came the liquidation of D. Jan Mahomed & Co. and Darwood Ally Co., declared insolvent by their own petition. No balance sheets had been drawn up since 1918. They had engaged in rash and hazardous speculation in rice long after 1921, when Darwood Ally Jan Mahomad, Senior Partner and active head, must have known his firm was insolvent (*Rangaz* 9 January (1928) between cover and p. 1).

1925–30

The years 1925 and 1926 were relatively quiet years in the rice trade, suggesting good business conditions, and there is little of significance reported in the *Gazette*. Then came 1927, a year of turmoil in the rice trade. In January there was a fire at one of the Chinese mills at Kanoungto (*Rangaz* 31 January (1927), p. 3), and then the news of a big fire on 17 February in Bangkok, in which three mills were burned to ashes, making a total of four destroyed there in three months, costing the insurance companies nearly a million ticals (*Rangaz* 14 March (1927), p. 10). Note the references to insurance companies and the comment already made that when things start to go wrong in the rice trade there is a rash of mill fires. Note also that the *Gazette* kept its readers well informed of news from their milling rivals in Bangkok. Then there was a strike at Bulloch Bros.' mill at Hteedan, Kemmendine (*Rangaz* 18 April (1927), p. 12, 25 April (1927) p. 9). In June came an order to wind up M.E. Mulla and Sons Ltd., who owned shares in the now defunct Ally Moolla Industrial Corporation (*Rangaz* 27 June (1927) p. 11). This was on the application of the Chartered Bank of India, to whom they owed Rs 800,000 (*Rangaz* 25 July (1927), p. 19). On 5 September there was a 'tumultuous disturbance' at about 6 p.m. in the compound of mill No. 3 at Kanoungto, the Eng Beng Hwat mill. An 'unlawful assembly' armed with saws, axes, knives and carrying shields had come to assault the mill hands. Many were arrested, tried, convicted and sentenced to rigorous imprisonment, some for one month, others for two (*Rangaz* 19 March (1928), p. 20). This was the first sign of trouble at Eng Beng Hwat, but there was to be more!

Things had taken a turn for the worse in the rice trade. The year 1928 opened with more fires, one at Anglo-Burma's mill at Upper Pazundung, with over Rs 700,000 of damage (*Rangaz* 9 January (1928), p. 1) and another at No. 12 mill in Kemmendine owned by Sulieman Hajee Brothers, damage estimated at over Rs 300,000 (*Rangaz* 12 March (1928), p. 1). In April, Steel Brothers, the leading British rice millers in Burma, reported a fall in net profits from £563,128 in 1926 to £443,517 in 1927 (*Rangaz* 23 April (1928), p. 12). In June the *Gazette* noted that *The Times Trade Supplement* of 26 May 1928 reported that A.W. Bibby of the famous Liverpool shipping line had written to *The Times* saying that the Burma rice trade to Britain had declined, because during the war the Government had bought Burma rice at low prices and sold it in Britain at extortionate prices. As a result British consumers had turned to rice from Japan, America, Italy and Spain, etc. with lasting effect. The *Supplement* also reported that Burma's rice exports to Europe were now mainly to Germany and the Netherlands, these countries taking 481,000 tons in 1925–26 and 268,000 tons in 1926–27, Britain only taking 102,000 and 77,000 tons in these years (*Rangaz* 25 June (1928), p. 5). In the same edition of the *Gazette*, Tha Zin blamed the poor quality of Burma rice for the problems and said that the Agricultural Department should rectify this. Meanwhile the export duty on rice ought to be temporarily suspended (*Rangaz* 25 June (1928), p. 10).

In July the *Gazette* discussed the May edition of the *International Crop Report and Agricultural Statistics* published by the Institute of Agriculture in Rome. This noted that in Burma 'the low level of prices and falling off of exports had brought about a state of depression which had not been felt for years'. However it did note that Burma was holding its own against competitors, and if exports to India were included, exports had risen by about a million tons between 1913 and 1927 (*Rangaz* 9 July (1928), pp. 26–7). Later that month it was reported that the Burma vernacular papers, especially the *Sun*, had been denouncing the export duty since January (*Rangaz* 30 July (1928), p. 26). Then came news in August that Japan, Korea and Formosa had banned rice imports from Burma and French Indo-China, although the Chamber of Commerce thought this would not have much impact as Burma did not export much there anyway (*Rangaz* 13 August (1928), p. 25). The Burma legislative council passed a resolution to press for the abolition of the export duty on rice (*Rangaz* 13 August (1928), p. 25). But the Indian Government took no action and the duty remained.

Now the depression really began to bite. Early in September Chinese rice millers Khoo Beng Ok were judged insolvent with liabilities of Rs 3,700,000 but assets under Rs 100,000 (*Rangaz* 3 September (1928), p. 15). The following week the major Chinese millers Beng Hwat and Co. (where the riot had been in September 1927) were declared insolvent, owing the Netherlands Bank about Rs 5,000,000, Lloyds Bank Rs 3,200,000 and the Hong Kong and Shanghai Banking Corporation Rs 450,000, a total of over Rs 8,650,000 (*Rangaz* 10 September (1928), p. 10). The following week another Chinese company, Chip Moh and Co., went under with debts of Rs 1,000,000 (*Rangaz* 17 September (1928), p. 10).

These dramatic events were the outcome of a bitter struggle between British and German millers for control of the rice trade to Europe. In 1906 Bulloch Bros., Steel Bros., the Arracan Co. and Mohr Bros., had combined to form The General Rice Co., London, known as 'London shippers'. Up to 1914 they handled 80 per cent of the rice trade to Continental Europe, and they even manufactured starch in Poland. Prior to 1906 the Hamburg and Bremen millers had bought from these companies individually, but they did not like the monopoly of the new consortium. So they decided to try to break its grip by buying through brokers and agents from the various small Burma mills, many of them Chinese owned, and they even began to acquire mills of their own in Burma (Thiessen (1968), pp. 44–5, Braund (1975), pp. 42–3). Then in 1909 F.A. Luthke built a new rice mill in the Veddel in Hamburg. It was one of the biggest in the world, capable of finishing 300,000 tons a year, at a time when Steels were finishing 1,000,000 tons from all their mills in total. Two-thirds of Luthke's rice went to Cuba, Russia and Czechoslovakia (Luthke (1985a)). In retaliation 'London shippers' built their own mill at Hamburg, the Allgemeine Reisgesellschaft, followed by another in Breslau (Wroclaw) in Poland. During the 1914–18 War the Allgemeine Reisgesellschaft properties in Germany were seized by the German authorities, and the British likewise seized the German mills in Burma. But when the war was over, German millers again appointed agents to buy from the small Burma millers, and 'London shippers' replied by founding the New General Rice Co., with a subsidiary in Hamburg, the Neue Allegemeine Reisgesellschaft mbH, selling as before direct to German consumers (Theissen (1968), pp. 44–5, Braund (1975), pp. 42–3). Georg Luthke (born 1905) recalls that as a young man his father sent him to Burma to work in the office of his leading supplier Beng Hwat, to learn the trade. He was actually there in Beng Hwat's office in 1928 on the day they ceased trading, and accepting defeat with a good face went straight to Steels to ask for a job, starting there that very day at 6 p.m. Henceforward Luthke's were to buy from Steels (Luthke (1985a)). Beng Hwat had overdone their credits to other small Burma millers, and gone under with debts of *c*. Rs 12,000,000 (Luthke (1985b)). In the subsequent insolvency case, total liabilities were given as Rs 10,341,064–9–1 (*Rangaz* 31 March (1930), p. 2, 7 April (1930), p. 2).

So the collapse of Beng Hwat and the other Chinese companies in September 1928 was a victory for the British companies, now operating in a shadowy consortium known as the Bullinger Pool (more properly the Bullenger Pool, Clark (1984a)). This echoed the old 'London shippers' and was made up of Bulloch Bros., Steel Bros., Ellerman's Arakan Rice and Trading Co. and the Anglo-Burma Rice Co., and had been set up in 1921 (Cheng (1968), p. 67, fn. 49). According to 'Nobby' Clark, one of Steel's head buyers, the whole purpose of the Pool was to fight off the competition from the small Chinese and Indian mills, and he remembered the many fires at Chinese mills at this time (Clark (1984a)). So the Bullenger Pool had succeeded, but their victory was to presage a bitter campaign of vilification against them (see also Diokno, pp. 60–5).

Meanwhile the levy on rice exports imposed by the Indian government continued, and the Japanese ban on rice imports was extended to the end of the year (*Rangaz* 15 October (1928), p. 21). There was a fire at the Anglo-Burma Rice Co., mill at Kanoungto (*Rangaz* 29 October (1928), p. 27). The question of the export levy was taken up by E.H. Solomon, economics lecturer at Rangoon University College, when he spoke to the Burma Economic Society in November. Referring to the recent depression in the rice trade, he said that exports to India and Ceylon were rising, but were offset by a fall to large markets like Europe, the Far East, the Straits Settlements, the Dutch East Indies and Australasia. Partly this was because of increased production there, and because freight rates were higher than from Saigon. But the real reason was the high f.o.b. (full-on-board) cost of Burma rice compared to her rivals in Siam and French Indo-China due to the rice export duty, which was higher than the similar levies of her rivals. Saigon actually exported to France duty free. He hoped that Burma might be exempted from the levy if the next Indian budget showed a surplus. (*Rangaz* 12 November (1928), p. 11).

Despite the success of the Bullenger Pool in forcing Beng Hwat into liquidation, it was not able to protect its own members from market forces. The extent of the depression was revealed in December, when one of their members, Ellerman's Arracan Rice and Trading Co., announced that they were getting out of the rice trade and that in future all their rice business would be handled by Steel Bros. (*Rangaz* 10 December (1928), p. 18). Their cessation belies the argument that the Bullenger Pool controlled the Burma rice trade and were responsible for all its ills. Ellerman's was not the only Pool member which found itself in difficulty at this time.

The depression in the rice trade continued. Lawrence Dawson was proprietor of Dawson's Bank, which made loans to paddy farmers against the collateral of their land. Speaking at the Bank's annual general meeting in December he noted that Burma rice exports to Egypt, Spain, Italy and America had fallen because of increased production there. Exports to Britain had also fallen, but there had been a rise to Continental Europe. The East was Burma's most important market, more than three times greater than Europe. Yet this was where Burma was losing sales, down by 353,000 tons for the year. This was a price sensitive market, and they were losing share to Saigon and Siam, and these countries were even selling rice in Burma's long-established markets in Southern India. French Indo-China exports carried lower export duties than those from Burma and those to France and her colonies were actually duty free. So clearly there was a strong case for removing the export duty on Burma rice (*Rangaz* 24 December (1928), p. 4). In this he was echoing E.H. Solomon's lecture to the Burma economic society, and it is clear that Burma rice men were only too aware of the activities of their Asian rivals.

In 1929 the situation continued to deteriorate, and there was another rash of bankruptcies in August and September, now amongst the Chettyar firms and some of their Parsi clients. Bad trade in the paddy business was blamed (*Rangaz* 12 August (1929), p. 12, 19 August (1929), p. 6, 16 September (1929), p. 6).

Things were so bad that there was an official enquiry into the situation. The Chamber of Commerce stated that in 1914 Italy, Spain, Egypt and America had only produced 600,000 tons of rice but that now Italy alone produced 700,000 tons. Spain produced another 350,000 tons, Egypt 200,000 tons and America a massive 800,000 tons, giving a total of 2,050,000 tons, more than three times the pre-war figure. That was why Burma's sales to Europe were falling. Meanwhile Siam and French Indo-China had made big strides in production and quality, with Saigon exporting roughly 1,500,000 tons and Bangkok 1,000,000 tons. They were competing with Burma in the important Cuba market, and in 1928 Saigon had even been active in the India market. Significantly, the Chamber also drew attention to the fact that wheat had fallen to its pre-war price level, but rice remained far above it. So wheat was displacing rice in countries where rice was previously the staple, like China and Japan. Another factor was the exchange rate which had been fixed at 1s 6p rather than 1s 4d, which increased the price of Burma rice in Europe by about 1s per cwt (*Rangaz* 16 September (1929), p. 5). Elsewhere the Chamber continued to press for the abolition of the export duty on rice (*Rangaz* 30 September (1919), pp. 5, 18).

1930–35

The gloom continued into 1930 and in February the Commissioner told an agricultural conference in Bassein that the state of the rice trade was very unhappy.

It had been caught up in the widespread depression, and prices were falling so low one wondered when the bottom would be reached, and if there would be any profit left for cultivators and traders (*Rangaz* 10 February (1930), p. 7). In March the Chamber of Commerce was that told that crop just harvested was good, with an exportable surplus of 3,050,000 tons, but rice prices were still falling, and even in England farmers were being hit by falling grain prices like those in Burma (*Rangaz* 3 March (1930), p. 3).

That month D. Hendry spoke to the Rotary Club about the kinds of rice in the Burma rice trade. He pointed out that most of the rice exported was a medium bold grain called *Ngasein* as in Burma No. 2, but the softer, fuller, round and opaque *Medon* was preferred locally and in the eastern market (*Rangaz* 24 March (1930), p. 17). Then came a fire at Fairweather and Richards rice mill at Kemmendine in April (*Rangaz* 28 April (1930), p. 2). In May there was a severe earthquake in Rangoon, followed by serious rioting and disorder between Indians and Burmese through into June (*Rangaz* 10 May (1930) p. 1 Photos, 12 May (1930), p. 19, 2 June (1930), p. 20, 30 June (1930), p. 6).

Against this background the Simon Commission recommended that Burma separate from India (*Rangaz* 30 June, p. 11). The slump in the rice trade continued, and in November there was a large protest meeting at Taikki attended by over 3,000 locals including landowners, rice millers, farmers and a few Chinese and Chettyar bankers. Current prices were Rs 110–118 for old paddy and Rs 70 for new. They resolved to demand Rs 180 and put paddy in store rather than sell for less. The Chettyars had virtually stopped lending money, and the meeting urged the Government to open a farmers' bank so that poorer farmers would not be forced into the hands of the moneylenders (*Rangaz* 24 November (1930), p. 8). December saw a meeting at Myoma to find ways to counter the unprecedented slump in rice and paddy prices. U. Thwin, a mill owner, took the chair and said the slump in the rice trade had begun soon after the earthquake on 1 May. Previously competition between the European millers and Beng Hwat and others had kept prices up. But now that the Chinese companies had gone, the Germans who had dealt with them had joined the Bullenger pool and prices had fallen. But the Government would not intervene as it would be against British interests. Another meeting was called to discuss a resolution that paddy should not be sold until prices rose to Rs 160 per 100 baskets of 46 lbs, and that the Government should defer collection of land revenue until the following June (*Rangaz* 29 December (1930), p. 10).

On 4 January 1931 the Burmese Chamber of Commerce convened a meeting in the Jubilee Hall. It openly attributed the current depression in the rice trade to the Bullenger Pool, and called on all present to withhold the sale of paddy until a Rangoon price of 100 (160?) could be obtained for *Ngasein* quality. This was the staple of the Bullenger Pool and the European market (*Rangaz* 12 January (1931), p. 9). In the Pool's defence the Burma Chamber of Commerce released correspondence about the situation. They had received a letter the previous November from the Council of National Associations of Burma. It said the fall in paddy prices had been greater than the fall in the price of milled rice in India and in foreign markets, and the price of paddy was now below its cost of production. They believed the Bullenger Pool was solely responsible for this and the general state of panic in the country. The Chamber had replied that they thought the Council misunderstood the causes of the low price of rice and paddy. The Bullenger firms only exported about 30 per cent of the 1929–30 crop, proving that they were not the sole buyers and could not control market movements. The Chamber's members were themselves seriously hit by the depression, but they could not influence the Bullenger Pool, and nothing that Bullenger Pool could do would have any effect. Siam and Saigon, as well as Burma were likely to have heavy crops in the current year. In Japan, Korea and Formosa crops were so large that although Japan normally imported foreign rice, that year she was trying to sell 400,000 tons of reserve stock in Burma's usual markets, India, China, Java and Europe. India's buying power was crippled by economic and political troubles, and according to the Government of India there was a surplus of wheat in the country of over a million tons, which it could not sell in India or abroad. Important markets like Ceylon, Malaya, Java and Sumatra were likely to take less rice in 1931 because of the depression in the rubber and planting industries. Prices and sales of rice in Europe and other Western markets were determined by the low price of wheat and other similar foodstuffs, so there was no immediate remedy (*Rangaz* 12 January (1931), p. 21). Meanwhile disturbances continued (*Rangaz* 12 January (1931), pp. 23, 26).

A special correspondent now reviewed Burma's position in the world rice trade. For 1931 Burma had an estimated surplus of 3,500,000 tons compared with actual exports in 1930 of 3,420,000 tons. Siam had a surplus of 1,950,000 tons compared with 1,040,000 tons the previous year, and Saigon a surplus of 1,700,000 tons compared with 1,050,000 tons. So in 1931 the three great Asian exporters had together a projected surplus for export of 7,150,000 tons compared with 5,510,000 tons in 1930, an increase of 1,640,000 tons or 29.7 per cent. Prices for Burma No. 2 per cwt f.o.b. on 16 January 1930 were 10s 3d, but on 16 January 1931 were down to 6s 8½ d. Siam No. 1 spells were down from 13s 5d to 9s 1d, and Saigon No.1 from 10s 4d to 6s 8½d. So volume was up nearly 30 per cent and prices down nearly 35 per cent. At the same time, crop forecasts in India (the major market) were good, and other Indian cereals were also plentiful. Demand from other big markets like Ceylon, Malaya, Java, Sumatra and the West Indies was expected to be low because of the depression in the planting industries. Labour forces were being cut in these countries, and attempts were being made to grow more rice locally there. In Japan, Korea and Formosa, crops were up 2,000,000 tons, and the Japanese Government was trying to sell off its reserve of 400,000 tons to Java, India, China and Europe (*Rangaz* 26 January (1931), p. 12). A subsequent report for the year 1930–31 called it one of the darkest years ever (*Rangaz* 30 November (1931), p. 10).

In February there were more riots, now between the Burmese and Chinese (*Rangaz* 23 February (1931), p. 14). Despite all the evidence to the contrary, the Bullenger Pool continued to be vilified for the depression in the rice trade. In the Burma Legislative Council, Tharrawaddy U. Pu said the Bullenger Pool was mainly to blame for the depression in Burma and the very low price of paddy. To loud laughter, he asked the Home Member to intervene, suppress the Pool's activities and hang its members. But R.B. Howison, General Manager of Steel Bros., said that the Pool only milled 36.9 per cent of total Burma milling in 1925, 36 per cent in 1926, 31 per cent in 1927, 22.4 per cent in 1928, 28.7 per cent in 1929 and 30.4 per cent in 1930. Nonetheless a resolution was passed recommending that the Government control the paddy market and fix the price of paddy at Rs 180 per 100 baskets of Ngasein (*Rangaz* 23 February (1931), p. 23). Because of the agitation about the Bullenger Pool, a Committee was set up to investigate the situation, but it found that the low prices of the day were due to the general depression in cereal prices, rather than the activities of the Pool, although it admitted that the Pool's activities made things worse. It found no case for government interference (Cheng (1968), pp. 67–8).

Mr Howison was in the Chair when the Governor addressed the Annual General Meeting (AGM) of the Chamber of Commerce in March. The Governor said that the estimated exportable surplus of 1929–30 had been 3,050,000 tons, but actual exports had been 300,000 tons more than this. Paddy prices during 1930 began at Rs 150, down by about Rs 10 on 1928–29. There was moderate demand from the eastern market, but not much from India, and the western market took little because of the fall in the price of other cereals. Paddy prices had declined until March, when they were down to Rs 130. Then came a sudden demand from China, which became very great, and became the main feature of the year, China taking 650,000 tons. In consequence paddy prices had risen to Rs 170, but when China's demand stopped in June 1930 prices began to fall and by the end of the year were down to Rs 85. In 1930–31 the crop had been substantial and prices had continued to fall, with a drop of Rs 12–15 since the start of the new season (*Rangaz* 9 March (1931), p. 9, see also 5 October (1931), p. 13).

Now the government replied to the request from the Burma Legislative Council that the price of paddy be fixed at Rs 180 per 100 baskets. They said that Burma exported about 2,750,000 tons of rice, of which India took 1,000,000 tons, Ceylon 300,000 tons, Malaya 200,000 tons, Dutch East Indies 150,000 tons, Japan 150,000 tons, China 150,000 tons, Germany 250,000 tons, Holland 100,000 tons, Great Britain 100,000 tons, Central Europe 50,000 tons, Cuba 100,000 and others 200,000 tons. So the price of rice was determined by what these countries would pay, and the Government could not force them to pay Rs 180 for 100 baskets of paddy. Rice also had to compete with wheat, which was currently very cheap, and so plentiful that there was more than the world could take. The world wheat crop was estimated in the current year at 127,125,000 tons, which was 14,500,000 tons more that the world needed. As for Burma's usual markets, many of these produced crops like jute, tea, sugar and rubber, but the price of these had fallen too, so they were unable to buy as much rice as previously (*Rangaz* 30 March (1931), p. 4). Clearly the government was aware of the fact that the glut in both rice and wheat was plunging grain markets to desperate levels, and there was nothing they could do about it (see Latham (1981), pp. 176–8; Latham (1986a), pp. 654–6). But it was sympathetic to the plight of the cultivators and arranged for

Rs 2,000,000 to be made available in loans to farmers, with interest rates cut from 10 to 6¼ per cent (*Rangaz* 1 June (1931), p. 17).

Then in June came serious news. Dawson's Bank, which specialised in providing loans to paddy farmers, reported unsettled conditions in its half-year statement as at 31 October 1930. Lawrence Dawson, Chairman, said that early in October 1930 a heavy fall had taken place in the price of paddy. Agricultural land was the main collateral for loans given to farmers, and land prices did not normally reflect variations in the price of paddy from year to year. But with the outbreak of rebellion and civil disorder, paddy prices had collapsed and so had agricultural rents, and this was likely to continue. If so the Bank would have to call in its advances to cultivators. Should the Bank foreclose on its borrowers and sell their land it would not get even 60 per cent of its true value. If this happened, the Bank would have to go into compulsory liquidation, with losses to shareholders. So the Bank was preparing a statement on the situation, which they would publish (*Rangaz* 22 June (1931), p. 6). Meanwhile there were rumours of an Indian uprising in Burma (*Rangaz* 22 June (1931), p. 11). Disturbances continued through to July (*Rangaz* 6 July (1931), p. 17).

Now Dawson's passed a resolution to wind itself up voluntarily in order to reconstruct itself. A letter to creditors said the economic situation in Burma was unprecedented. Many cultivators had taken advantage of the situation to avoid paying any rent, had sold their crops secretly elsewhere and refused to pay their debts. The racial antagonism of the communal disturbances had caused many Indians to leave large areas of lower Burma, including the areas served by Dawson's Bank. Reconstruction of the Bank was practicable, and involved the Bank's depositors converting their deposits into debentures, which could if necessary be sold after the reconstruction had taken place. The alternative was liquidation, which would result in large losses (*Rangaz* 6 July (1931), p. 18).

The Government made more loans available to cultivators (*Rangaz* 13 July (1931), p. 1). The rebellion continued (*Rangaz* 20 July (1931), p. 4). Then the situation in the rice trade was detailed in an appendix to the Report of the Controller of Currency. It noted that paddy prices were considerably lower than in recent years, the price of Rs 73 in March 1931 being the lowest since December 1901, when it had fallen to Rs 75 (*Rangaz* 20 July (1931), p. 30). The crisis at Dawson's Bank continued with a three-hour meeting of creditors (*Rangaz* 28 September (1931), pp. 20–1).

In August there was a brighter tone in Mogul Street, with the price of paddy improving, due to fresh demand from India, and also from China, where there had been flooding. The rebellion was easing and anti-Indian feeling subsiding (*Rangaz* 17 August (1931), p. 9).

But affairs at Dawson's Bank continued to haunt the situation. An application for the compulsory winding up of the Bank was dismissed on the grounds that shareholders rights would be the same under either compulsory or voluntary liquidation (*Rangaz* 24 August (1931), p. 17). Further wranglings continued at the Bank in December (*Rangaz* 7 December (1931), pp. 18, 25, 14 December (1931), pp. 13–14). Despite opposition, the reconstruction scheme to convert deposits into debentures was still being pursued. In a telling letter to creditors, the Bishop of Rangoon spoke in favour of the reconstruction scheme as otherwise he stood to lose the money he had put aside for the education of his two boys at an English public school (*Rangaz* 14 December (1931), pp. 26–7). Yet another attempt to have the bank compulsorily wound up was dismissed (*Rangaz* 28 December (1931), pp. 5–6).

So ended 1931, a year of crisis in the rice trade in general, and Dawson's Bank in particular. But 1932 was not to be much happier. In March the proposal to reconstruct Dawson's Bank was rejected by a meeting of creditors (*Rangaz* 7 March (1932), pp. 11–12). Yet a successful reconstruction scheme did emerge. Copies of the *Gazette* are missing for 1933, but fortunately nearly ten years later, at the 25th AGM of the Bank in February 1941, Lawrence Dawson went over the details. With regard to the successful reconstruction of the Bank, deposits had been converted into Bearer and Registered Bonds, upon which interest was paid at 5 per cent. Bonds were issued to an amount of Rs 5,768,300 and by February 1941 Rs 2,000,000 had been redeemed. Before the issue and during the reconstruction, interest payments to depositors had been made. With the rise in the price of paddy in the later 1930s land prices had improved, returning value to the Bank's principal asset. He was able to announce that all arrears on preference share dividends had been paid, and the Bank was once again on the road to prosperity, with a recommendation to pay a dividend of 5 per cent on the ordinary shares (*Rangaz* 10 February (1941), p. 6). In this way Dawson's struggled through the 1930s and had turned the situation around just before war broke out!

March also saw an assessment of the 1931–32 crop, indicating that the acreage of paddy harvested was much less than the previous year. There was a huge increase in the amount of rice being shipped to China every week (*Rangaz* 7 March (1932), p. 24). But the strains in the rice trade were still evident and in April a prominent rice broker Tan Cheng Gwan aged 35 of Prome-road shot himself with a revolver (*Rangaz* 25 April (1932), p. 11). In another sign of the times, in June came the news of a bloodless revolution in Siam, with the King agreeing to the establishment of a constitutional monarchy (*Rangaz* 17 June (1932), p. 27). The last Gazette of the year reported that Burma landholders were badly hit by the aftermath of the paddy slump. There were proposals that cheap loans be made by the Government and that land tax be deferred (*Rangaz* 26 December (1932), p. 18).

Now came a massive blow to the rice trade. Bulloch Bros., a member of the Bullenger Pool, and one of the oldest names in the business, went into liquidation. Although copies of the *Rangoon Gazette* are missing for 1933, it seems Bullochs went into liquidation over the New Year holiday, as the 26 December (1932) edition of the Gazette still advertises Bullochs as freight agents for the Henderson Line (*Rangaz* 26 December (1932), frontpage). W.D. Fairclough, one of Steels' mill managers at Bassein vividly remembers being on the tennis court with another of Steels' managers, Christopher Lorimer, when they heard the news that Bullochs had collapsed. This would fit with the New Year holiday period. He also remembers that at the height of the depression there was nothing to be made on rice at all and the only profit was on the gunny bags the rice was packed in! (Fairclough (1985)). When Bullochs went 'Nobby' Clark recalled that it seemed as if Steels would go under as well, but they survived by putting a 10 per cent cut on all salaries from top to bottom, and this saved them (Clarke (1984a)). Theissen says Bullochs went into voluntary liquidation in 1932, and the Burma–Siam Rice Co., a subsidiary of the Anglo-Burma Rice Co., took their place in the New General Rice Co. Ltd (Theissen (1968), p. 45). An entry in the *Gazette* in 1934 reads 'Owing to Messrs Bulloch Bros. and Co., going into liquidation in January 1933, the old established Pazundaung Foundry and Shipyard had to close down' (*Rangaz* 30 August (1934), p. 23, see photo, 3 September (1934), p. 4). Bullochs liquidation puts into context the complaints about the Bullenger Pool, of which they had been a major member. This had not saved them from liquidation, just as it had not saved Ellerman's Arracan Rice and Trading Co., in 1928 (see earlier). To emphasise this point, the *Financial Times* reported that Steel Bros' net profits up to 1 December (1932) were down to £247,055 compared to £309,238 at 1 December (1931) (*Financial Times* 1 April (1933), p. 8).

The year 1933 was a year of almost 'unrelieved gloom' according to the Chairman of the Chamber of Commerce. He told the AGM in March 1934 that at no time in the present century had the surplus crop been sold at such a low average price. Paddy had opened at Rs 70 but declined steadily during the first four months to Rs 56. There was recovery during the next 3 months up to Rs 70, but apart from a short jump in November, the rest of the crop did not average over Rs 65, and at the close of the year the new crop was starting to be marketed at Rs 60. Import duties had been imposed by China and the Federated Malay States, and licences were required for imports to Japan and the Dutch East Indies, amounting virtually to a prohibition. Italy and Egypt had been subsidising their rice exports, and Germany had banned some kinds of low quality rice and bran. The revolution in Cuba had disrupted trade to this previously important market. Despite the principle of Imperial Preference introduced by the Ottowa agreement of 1932, Ceylon had not given preference to Empire grown rice such as Burma's, and like India, had bought rice from Indo-China, Siam and Japan (*Rangaz* 5 March (1934), p. 13).

But 1934 was even worse! 'Nobby' Clerk noted in his own handwriting on a typewritten list of annual prices from 1893 to 1934, 'The all-time low was reached in March, and I personally bought Ngatseing paddy at Rs 45 per 100 baskets (5,000 lbs) in Pyapon equalling 30/- (shillings) per ton' (Clark (1933)). In April Chan Chor Khine shot himself at his house in Brightlands, 82 Park road, at 10.20 in the morning. He was a prominent member of the Chinese Hokkien community, a big landlord and financier with large interests in paddy in the districts. He was 50, and a son of Chan Mah Phee, a millionaire merchant, and landowner, founder of the firm Taik Leong (*Rangaz* 6 April (1934), p. 28; 16 April (1934), p. 20; 30 April (1934), p. 15). One of his brothers had married Lim Chin Tsong's daughter (*Rangaz* 9 July (1929), p. 16).

In September R.B. Howison, Managing Director of Steels, gave a paper to the Geographical Society at the University of Rangoon, on the Burma rice trade.

Key points included the introduction of a steam driven rice mill in 1874 by an Australian. Bullochs built several in 1886. Originally they were coal fired, but later fuelled with rice husks, which made a great saving. In the early days rice was shipped as cargo rice, a mixture of four parts de-husked rice, and one-fifth still in husk. But from the 1880s cargo rice had been replaced by milled white rice. He also noted growth of the trade in par-boiled rice to countries where Indian workers were employed, this being a quality they preferred (*Rangaz* 24 September (1934), p. 21).

Towards the end of the year a new Indian owned rice company, the Burma Rice and Produce Limited opened business in 220 Strand Road, Rangoon, dealing in all kinds of paddy and rice products (*Rangaz* 1 October (1934), p. 5). Steels were able to report a profit of £295,113–6–4 for the year up to 31 December 1934, to which was added the balance brought forward from the previous year's account of £40,020–11–9, making a total of £335,133–18–1. They also registered a new company in Bangkok on 31 December 1934, Steel Brothers and Company (Siam) Ltd, to take over the activities of their Siam branch (*Rangaz* 29 April (1935), p. iii).

1935–41

The gloom in the rice trade continued into 1935, and in February, H.C. Whitehouse, general manager in India of Messrs Strauss & Co., one of the biggest seed and grain firms in India, was found dead at the foot of the staircase in the Taj Mahal Hotel, Bombay. He had been ordered by his London head office to cease trading, and he left a suicide note 'I cannot face the tangle' (*Rangaz* 4 February (1935), p. 16). In April another rice mill burned down, one at Ye-U, leaving only the chimney stack standing, and damage put at Rs 70,000 (*Rangaz* 15 April (1935), p. 2). In July, in a sign of the times, Professor J.R. Andrus of Judson College read a paper on 'Burma and World Economic Nationalism' to the Burma Economic Society. One of his points was that 75 per cent of Burma's rice crop came from just 13 Lower Burma districts (*Rangaz* 22 July (1935), p. 21). Then came a fire at the old Bulloch Bros. godown at Lower Pazaundaung, containing thousands of bags of rice and bran, damage estimated at Rs 489,000 (*Rangaz* 29 July (1935), p. 2, 5 August (1935), p. iii). The fact that Burma was still in difficulties is shown by the *Financial Tribunal's* report to the Burma Legislative council, which revealed that the Burma Railways Annual Report showed that the area under rice served by the railways during the year 1934–35 had declined by 220,000 acres (*Rangaz* 19 August (1935), p. 12).

The year 1936 began with the partial failure of the rice crop in Bengal, which led to sudden demand for Burma rice and busy scenes at Calcutta docks (*Rangaz* 10 February (1936), p. iv). But the rash of mill fires continued. At Moulmein, fire destroyed Chin Lee's mill in Coal Yard street, next to Mupan railway jetty, leaving a damage of about Rs 250,000 (*Rangaz* 23 March (1936), p. 1). Lawlessness was on the increase and in April three local paddy buyers were robbed of Rs 1,012–8 just after obtaining advances from Steels' head broker at Mezaligon, Henzada district. They were travelling in carts to a nearby village (*Rangaz*

20 April (1936), p. ii). By June rice prices were showing a marked improvement over the low levels of 1934, but they were not feeding through to the local economy and rents in Rangoon hit rock bottom (*Rangaz* 29 June (1936), p. 12, 23). In July there was an interesting piece on the early days of the Burma Chamber of Commerce, noting that Halliday, Bulloch & Co., who became the recently defunct Bulloch Bros. had been a founding member in 1861, with George Bulloch the first Vice President (*Rangaz* 13 July (1936), pp. 8, 21).

In November F.B. Leach gave a paper to the Burma Economic Society on the Burma rice industry. He noted that Burma was the world's biggest rice exporter, exporting more than Siam and French Indo-China added together. Yet many Indians living in Burma were wheat eaters, not rice eaters, and there were many parts of the country where maize and millet were eaten in addition to rice. Before the 1914–18 War, Europe, including Britain, had been the most important market for Burma rice, but the war disrupted the trade and it never regained its pre-war position. Consumption of rice in Europe had fallen because the purchasing power of the population had declined, and more recently because of trade restrictions imposed by many European countries. The main demand was now from Asia, although there was still considerable demand from north and east Africa, and the West Indies. The leading Asian buyers used to be China, Japan, Ceylon, Malaya, the Dutch East Indies, the Philippines and India, but now Japan and the Philippines took no Burma rice at all, and the Dutch East Indies less and less. China was an unreliable market, and the only other markets were Malaya and Ceylon. So India was now the main market for Burma. Up to 1932–33 India rarely took more than 1,000,000 tons but in 1933–34 she took 1,750,000 tons and in 1934–35, 2,140,000 tons, with 1,600,000 in the 10 months to October 1936. India would be the main market for Burma rice in the future, and Burma should produce qualities of rice suitable for that market, and only a limited quantity of high quality rice for the European market (*Rangaz* 23 November (1936), pp. 8, 21–22).

Then came the fateful edition of 14 December (1936), bringing the news of the abdication of King Edward VIII of England, and a photo of his brother, the new King George VI and the Queen and their daughters, including Princess Elizabeth, the future Queen Elizabeth II (*Rangaz* 14 December (1936), pp. 5, 23–5).

December closed with a piece on the Burma rice crop based on the Report on Agriculture and Animal Husbandry in India 1934–35. This maintained that if the export trade to Europe was to be maintained it would be necessary to produce rice similar to Spanish rices. So experimental breeding was taking place at the research stations at Hmawbi, Myaungmya, Akyab and Mandalay. Varieties from many countries were being grown and hybrids being produced by crossing local strains and exotic varieties (*Rangaz* 28 December (1936), p. 11). It is worth noting that this policy was at variance with F.B. Leach's recommendation that Burma should concentrate on the Indian market!

March 1937 saw a piece on the Report of the Burma Rice Export Trade Enquiry Committee, established by the Governor in August 1936. This pointed out that Burma was the dominant rice exporter to Ceylon and India, which together had taken between 1,500,000 and 2,500,000 tons annually over the last 5 years. This was well over half Burma's exports. Burma had an advantage in these markets, being close and having good contacts there. The rice was carried to India by 'Conference lines' such as the British India Steam Navigation Co., the Scindia Steam Navigation Co., the Asiatic Steam Navigation Co. and to Ceylon by the Bibby and City Lines. Freight rates were kept down, because shippers could charter their own ships if they wished. Siam and Indo-China had not been active in these markets in the past, but recently had tried to sell broken rice there, forcing India to impose duty on all foreign brokens of 12 annas per maund (82 2/7 lbs or Rs 20–6–8 per ton) to protect Burma's position as her traditional supplier. But this did not apply to Ceylon, where the situation was serious. As for Far Eastern markets, Siam and Indo-China were the nearest suppliers, and could use the numerous local steamship companies, charging cut-price rates with which Burma could not compete. Between 65 and 85 per cent of Siam's exports went to these markets, and often 35–55 per cent of Indo-China's exports also, total demand being about 2,000,000–2,500,000 tons. Of this, Singapore (Straits Settlements) took about 500,000 tons from Siam, and Hong Kong rather more than 500,000 tons from Indo-China. Burma and Indo-China were the leading suppliers to Europe, which took 1,000,000–1,500,000 tons. Burma supplied 500,000–750,000 tons and Indo-China rather less. The United Kingdom, Germany and the Netherlands were the main destinations in Europe for Burma rice, and France took up to 90 per cent of Indo-China rice. Other western markets rarely took more than 500,000 tons, most of which previously came from Burma, but now both Siam and Indo-China had entered the market (*Rangaz* 29 March (1937), p. 16). From this it is clear that the threat from Siam and French-Indo China to Burma's interests in Ceylon and India were well recognised, as were Burma's difficulties in penetrating the large markets of the Far East.

On 1 April 1937 Burma separated from India, to become an individual member of the British Empire (*Rangaz* 5 April (1937), p. 5, 27 September (1937), p. 15). There was a rice mill fire at Mandalay damaging over 20,000 tons of paddy and causing a loss of over Rs 50,000 (*Rangaz* 5 April (1937), p. iv).

More details were published from the Rice Export Trade Enquiry. Although Germany had been Burma's best market in Europe, it rapidly declined after 1932 because of a decree of that year that all imported rice be placed under Government 'Monopoly' control. Later (under the National Socialists) it was subject to 'Compensation trading' which ruled that imports from a country must be balanced by an equal value of exports. Imports to Holland had also fallen because 'cleaned' or husked rice (*loonzein*) had been milled there and exported to Germany. Exports to Poland and Belgium were also down, but the United Kingdom still took about 35,000 tons of 'cleaned' rice. Two-thirds of Burma's sales to the Dutch East Indies were handled by Indian merchants but had fallen from 157,000 tons in 1931–32 to 79,000 tons in 1935–36 due to the depression in the planting industries. Three-quarters of sales to the Straits Settlements were handled by Chinese merchants, but cleaned rice was down from 200,000 tons in 1931–31 to 120,000 tons. Siam rice dominated this market with 250,000–300,000 tons, because it was sweet and slow to digest. The Chinese also dominated the trade to the Federated Malay States, but Burma rice led Siam rice in this market. Chinese merchants also took Burma rice to Hong Kong, but this market had dropped from 60,000 tons in 1931–32 to 5,000 tons in 1935–36 because Hong Kong was used less as a transhipment market to Swatow and Amoy, and rice increasingly went direct. In any case, Siam dominated the Hong Kong market with 500,000 tons, more than half the total. Indo-China provided the remaining 300,000–500,000 tons, which remained after France had been supplied. Japan had been an important market but now no longer took rice from Burma, Siam or Indo-China. Japan wished to be self-sufficient in rice, and accordingly production had increased in Japan, Korea and Formosa. As for India, Burma's major market, Madras Presidency led with imports rising from 524,000 tons in 1931–32 to 956,000 tons in 1935–36. Bengal was self-supporting in a good year but took up to 750,000 tons in a bad year. Bombay took between 300,000 and 400,000 tons. Travancore had risen from 59,000 to 113,000 tons. Ceylon was steady at 300,000–350,000 tons, 95 per cent of it par-boiled. So only India and Ceylon were showing increased demand, but Siam and Indo-China were trying to get into this market. India had responded with a tariff favouring Burma, but Ceylon had not followed suit, and between January and September 1936 had taken 92,000 tons from Siam, a small but significant amount when compared with the Burma shipment of 284,000 tons (*Rangaz* 5 April (1937), p. 19–21). The Rice Export Trade report also included a very interesting section on the work of the experimental stations since 1907 in Burma to develop new strains of paddy, although by 1934–35 these improved paddies were only planted in about 9 per cent of the paddy area, indigenous varieties continuing to dominate (*Rangaz* 12 April (1937), pp. 20–1).

June carried a crucial report on Burma rice prices and their relationship with wheat. The monthly average price for Burma No. 2 had fallen to its lowest point in April 1934 (confirming Nobby Clark, see earlier), when the price was only 40 per cent of the highest monthly price for 1929. But from April 1934 the price had risen slowly to December 1936, when the average for Burma No. 2 reached a London price of 9 shillings per cwt, c.i.f., (cost, insurance and freight) the highest level since April 1932. This was related to the notable rise in wheat prices during the 1936–37 season. Three successive years of small crops in North America and the small 1935–36 crop in Argentina had resulted in the stocks being used up which for years had caused a glut in the wheat market. World stocks had fallen from 31,000,000 tons in August 1934 to 19,000,000 tons in August 1936. By 1 August 1937 they were expected to be less than 14,000,000. This followed drought in North America in 1936 and poor crops in Europe. The United States normally exported wheat but in 1936–37 had imported it (*Rangaz* 7 June (1937), p. 7). What is clear from this is that observers of the Burma rice trade were well aware of the relationship between rice prices and wheat prices and that the collapse of rice prices in the early 1930s was directly related to the wheat glut.

Cuba at this time was importing about 200,000 tons of rice a year in total but had recently imposed higher duties on Burma rice. After representations from

Burma they relented and put the same duty on all foreign rice, so that Burma and Indo-China were on the same footing (*Rangaz* 7 June (1937), p. 17, 12 July (1937), p. 16, 23 August (1937), p. 5).

Copies of the *Gazette* for January to June 1938 are missing, but on 1 August came news of fresh rioting in Rangoon (*Rangaz* 1 August (1938), pp. 6, 19, 22–5). This continued on and off through into September (*Rangaz* 8 August (1938), pp. 9, 11, 17, 19, 22–4, 15 August (1938), pp. 5, 7, 10, 21–22, 22 August (1938), pp. 5, 7, 9, 10, 22, 29 August (1938), p. 8, 5 September (1938), pp. 10, 21, 23, 12 September (1938), pp. 6, 7, 13, 14, 15, 24, 19 September (1938), p. 9). Burma's overseas trade in September was down 19 per cent on the previous September, although trade with India remained fairly steady. The decline was almost entirely due to the fall in rice exports from 203,000 tons in September 1937 to 158,000 tons in September 1938 (*Rangaz* 14 November (1938), p. 17).

That Dawson's Bank had indeed survived the crisis of the depression is revealed in a note in November on the Royal Commission on Agriculture in India, which said that Dawson's was the only joint-stock agricultural bank to have come to its notice, and it received no state assistance (*Rangaz* 14 November (1938), p. 15).

November also saw an article by P.M. Isaac on the Burma rice export trade to India. From the 1860s to the 1890s Europe had been the main market for Burma rice, then eastern markets became more important. From 1900 to 1914, 60 per cent of exports went to the east and only 40 per cent to Europe. The war disrupted the rice trade to Europe, and exports there fell after 1920. Some countries imposed restrictions on Burma rice, and Italy, Spain and the United States competed there with superior grades of rice. In future Burma would have to seek its markets in China, Japan, Ceylon, Malaya, the Dutch East Indies, the Philippines and India. During the depression Burma's trade with other countries had fallen badly, but had increased with India, without which the depression would have been a bigger disaster than it was (*Rangaz* 18 November (1938), p. 18). This article provoked several letters, particularly as it stressed the importance of India as a market, at a time when the Tamil Nadu Congress Party was seeking a ban by India on imports of rice from Burma because of the recent race attacks against Indians (*Rangaz* 28 November (1938), p. 3, 26 December (1938), p. 3).

In March 1939 there were further race riots after a man was stabbed to death in Fraser street (*Rangaz* 6 March (1939), pp. 3–6). In August there was an article on the world rice situation based on a report of the Imperial Economic Committee. World rice production had fallen from 94,000,000 tons in 1932–33 to 84,000,000 tons in 1934–35 due to poor harvests in China, Japan and Burma but then had recovered up to 1936–37. India and Burma accounted for about half the world acreage, but the bulk of exported rice came from Burma, Siam, Indo-China, Korea and Formosa, although the last two countries exported almost exclusively to Japan. Outside Asia only Italy and the United States had sizeable exports, although France and Germany had substantial re-exports after processing. Rice exports were affected by the world price for plantation crops, as this determined the buying power of plantation workers to whom rice was a staple food. About 9 per cent of world production entered world trade, which was mostly within Asia where rice was a basic food. During the 1930s Burma was the world's largest rice exporter, with an annual average of just over 3 million tons over the previous 8 years. During the years 1934–38 exports were at a lower level, with 1938 being particularly low. In 1937 and 1938 almost half of Burma's exports went to India, followed by Ceylon, Malaya and the Dutch East Indies, these three taking another quarter of her exports. India itself also exported to Ceylon, and to Arabia and Mauritius. Exports to Cuba from Burma, Siam and Indo-China had declined in 1938 due to preferential tariffs in favour of the United States, whose exports had increased. Italy's rice exports went chiefly to Germany, and these had increased substantially in 1938. Exports from the United States went mainly to her possessions, particularly Puerto Rico, followed by Hawaii, but her exports to foreign countries had increased in the last two years, with Cuba now the most important market (*Rangaz* 21 August (1939), p. 14).

Then on 4 September 1939 came the headline 'The nation at war' and the news that at 11.15 a.m. in London on the previous day the Prime Minister, Mr Chamberlain, had told the nation that Britain and Germany were at war (*Rangaz* 4 September (1939), p. 23).

In November there was a conference in Rangoon on the control and export of Burma rice, but the Indian Government did not participate because it thought it would not be affected by any decision that would be made (*Rangaz* 13 November (1939), p. 11). At the conference the Ceylon delegation complained that because of her rice purchases, Ceylon bought more from Burma than Burma bought from her. This could be corrected if Burma bought more tea, salt and coconut oil from Ceylon (*Rangaz* 11 December (1939), p. 10). Following the conference there was a piece on the supply of rice to Ceylon, pointing out Ceylon's heavy dependence on Burma rice. In 1914, after the outbreak of war, an embargo had been placed on exports of rice from Burma, which resulted in 1915 in the threat of famine in Ceylon, only averted when the embargo was lifted. In 1930 a dock labourers strike in Rangoon had pushed up prices in Ceylon considerably, prices only falling when 100,000 bags were allowed through. But Siam and French Indo-China had increased their rice exports to Ceylon and Burma was to expect further competition from these countries even though it still supplied 73 per cent of Ceylon's rice imports. However a good harvest in Southern India meant more rice would come from there, displacing Burma rice. A triangle of trade existed by which Ceylon exported tea to Britain, Britain exported machinery to Burma and Burma exported rice to Ceylon. Three major shipping lines carried rice from Burma to Ceylon (*Rangaz* 18 December (1939), p. 17).

With 1940 came the news that Japan intended to buy all the rice she could from Burma that year, and had already made big purchases in Rangoon, Saigon and Bangkok (*Rangaz* 5 February (1940), p. 5). Christopher Lorimer, one of Steel's buyers, remembers that Japan bought 1 million tons from Burma that year, and everyone was glad to get the business! (Lorimer (1984)). No one seems to have asked why Japan was buying all this rice!

March carried details of a talk to the Rotary Club on Burma rice by Rai Bahadur Virjee Daya, who referred to J.W. Grant's Agricultural Survey on Rice of

1932 (Grant (1932)). In the 1890s there had only been 54 steam-driven rice mills in Burma, 21 in Rangoon, and 26 in other coastal towns, the rest in the interior. Now there were about 640. Indian merchants had contributed to the development of the trade, and some of them had been in business for two generations, particularly in Moulmein. Parboiling of rice had been introduced to Burma about 20 years previously, following the fashion in Bengal, and it was now preferred by consumers in South India, Ceylon and the West Indies. Big Mills Specials (BMS) was the lowest grade of milled rice, and was milled from poor to medium grade paddy of the *Ngasein* group, and could contain up to 42 per cent brokens of various sizes, with a fair proportion of red grain. Small Mills Specials (SMS) was the main quality dealt with in Futures or Forward delivery, the 'speculative' transactions. It was also milled from poor to medium grade paddy of the *Ngasein* group. Here too 42 per cent brokens were allowed. In appearance, SMS was slightly superior to BMS. Then there was Small Mills Quality, Bazaar Quality, Straits Quality, the European Qualities and others, all milled from *Ngasein* paddy. Other qualities were listed, together with the boiled rices (*Rangaz* 25 March (1940), pp. 14–16).

April saw an article on world rice production, which said that the declaration of war the previous September had caused prices to rise sharply to Rs 253, particularly due to the keenness of Indian shippers, but the following week prices had fallen back to Rs 245. Japan shippers were very active purchasing Burma rice! (*Rangaz* 22 April (1940), p. ii).

August–September saw a sudden increase in the price of rice all over Burma, provoking a discussion in the House of Representatives. Retail prices were out of all proportion to those in the export market in Mogul street. This was said to be due to heavy purchases from Japan and China. However there were still large stocks of rice in Burma, and it was argued that it was lucky that Japanese and Chinese buyers were in the market, as the European market was closed due to the war. How else could Burma dispose of an un-exported surplus of 750,000 tons? A motion that the Government take steps to prevent the rise in prices was lost (*Rangaz* 23 September (1940), pp. 9, 11–13).

On 4 January 1941 the *Gazette* announced that an export duty of 2¼ annas per maund had been placed on Burma rice going to India. It was thought that in consequence prices would rise in the Indian market, and fall in Rangoon, but in fact they fell in Bombay and rose in Rangoon. Merchants took the view that the duty had been imposed as a revenue measure (*Rangaz* 13 January (1941), p. 6).

February saw the 25th Ordinary General Meeting of Dawson's bank, noted previously, which reported how the bank had re-structured to avoid liquidation, and had struggled through the difficult years of the 1930s, and was now going to recommend that 5 per cent be paid on ordinary shares (*Rangaz* 10 February (1941), p. 6). They had returned to profitability, just as war was to break out!

In March a motion was put before the House of Representatives that rice control be re-introduced. All export trade in rice would be controlled by the Government, which would sell direct to overseas markets and buy rice locally under a tender system. Any profits would be used for Rural Finance and

Education initiatives, the opening of new industries and the encouragement of existing cottage industries. The House was adjourned, but the Commerce Minister U Ba Than said Government would not shrink from its responsibilities, and in any case the needs of Empire must be held in mind (Rangaz 17 March (1941), pp. 13–14).

June saw a piece about the worthy record of the late C.A.H. Kam, who had put in half a century with Steel Bros., having joined them in 1878 when the firm was still known as W. Strang Steel & Co. (*Rangaz* 16 June (1941), p. 7). At this point the known archive copies of *The Rangoon Gazette and Weekly Budget* cease.

Conclusion

What then is to be learned from this detailed examination of Burma's rice trade, as seen through the files of the *Rangoon Gazette*? As regards inter-Asian competition in the intra-Asian rice trade, readers did clearly view the threat from Siam and French Indo-China with concern. That these two rice exporters dominated the markets of the Far East was understood, and their proximity to these markets, and China in particular, was recognised as a natural reason for their domination there. But as regards India and Ceylon, Burma was best placed as a supplier. So as the depression bit in, the major concern was that that Siam and French Indo-China were seeking to enter even these markets, which Burma saw as her own. As regards the depression itself, it is clear that increased world production of rice in the 1920s, and overproduction in the wheat world, was recognised at least by some as the fundamental problem affecting prices and sales.

References

Braund, H.E.W. (1975) *Calling to Mind: Being Some Account of the First Hundred Years (1870–1970) of Steel Brothers and Company Limited*, Oxford: Pergammon Press.

Cheng, Siok-Hwa (1968) *The Rice Industry of Burma 1852–1940*, Kuala Lumpur and Singapore: University of Malaya Press.

Clarke, J.B. (1933) Rangoon Ngatseing Paddy Rates 1891–1933, 6 April.

Clarke, J.B. (1941) Burma and Her Rice Export Trade, *Steel's House Magazine*, 3 April pp, 25–8; July, pp. 25–7; October, pp. 31–42.

Clark, J.B. (1984a) Interview by Latham, 17/18 November.

Clark, J.B. (1984b) Letter to Latham, 11 December.

Corley, T.A.B. (1983) *A History of the Burmah Oil Company 1886–1924*, London: Heinemann.

Diokno, Maria Serena I. (1983) British Firms and the Economy of Burma, with Special Reference to the Rice and Teak Industries, 1917–1937, PhD London (Unpublished).

Fairclough, W.D. (1985) Interview by Latham, 16 August.

Financial Times, London.

Grant, J.W. (1932) *The Rice Crop in Burma: Its History, Cultivation, Marketing and Improvement*, Agricultural Department, Burma, Agricultural Survey No. 17 of 1932, Rangoon: Suptd. Govt. Printing and Stationary, Burma.

Latham, A.J.H. (1981) *The Depression and the Developing World, 1914–39*, London: Croom Helm.

Latham, A.J.H. (1986a) 'The International Trade in Rice and Wheat since 1868: A Study in Market Integration', in Fischer, W., McInnis, R.M. and Schneider, J. (eds), *The Emergence of a World Economy 1500–1914*, Wiesbaden, GmbH: Franz Steiner Verlag, pp. 645–63.

Latham, A.J.H. (1986b) 'Ethnic Chinese Multinationals in the International Grain Trade before the Second World War', *South African Journal of Economic History*, pp. 1, 4–18.

Latham, A.J.H. (1988) 'From Competition to Constraint: The International Rice Trade in the Nineteenth and Twentieth Centuries', *Business and Economic History* 17, pp. 91–102.

Lorimer, Christopher (1984) Interview by Latham, 27 December.

Luthke, Georg (1985a) Interview by Latham, 11 June.

Luthke, Georg (1985b) Letter to Latham, 20 August.

Rangaz. See *The Rangoon Gazette and Weekly Budget.* SM54. At British Library, Oriental and India Office Collections, 96 Euston Road, London NW1 2DB.

Thiessen, Max (1968) Neue Allgemeine Reisgesellschaft mbh, Hamburg, *Steel's House Magazine* 20(1), pp. 44–8.

10 Japanese competition in the Congo Basin in the 1930s[1]

Katsuhiko Kitagawa

Introduction

Japan has recently built a sophisticated network of international relations. However, Africa has been a blind spot, because of the low level of economic interaction Japan has had with the countries there.[2] So to bring Africa into Japan's world view, it is necessary to investigate Japan's economic relations with Africa. This chapter is part of a wider study of Japan's trade relations with Africa in the inter-war period, based on pre-war British and Japanese consular reports about economic conditions in Africa.[3]

After the Great Crash in the late 1920s, Britain took measures to protect her colonial market, whilst simultaneously Japan tried to increase her exports to Africa where she had found new markets. In the mid-1930s, attention was concentrated in British East Africa, the Belgian Congo and nearby areas as new markets for Japanese exports. Because the Congo Basin is in the centre of the continent, it was recognized as being a commercially strategic area. Diplomatic moves by Britain and Japan involved an amendment to the Peace Treaty in Saint-Germain-en-Laye in 1919. This was based on the general protocol of the Berlin Conference of 1885, which gave free and equal opportunity of development, residence and trade to citizens of all countries in tropical Africa, including the Congo Basin area.

This chapter will consider the role of the Congo Basin Treaty as the framework which enabled Japan to advance in African markets in the mid-1930s and the Anglo-Japanese rivalries over its revision and abolition. To begin with, the contents and historical background of the Congo Basin Treaty will be examined. Then competition between British and Japanese merchandise in the African market in the 1930s will be discussed. Lastly the moves by Britain and her colonies to revise and abolish the Congo Basin Treaty, and the Japanese reaction to these developments will be considered.

The Congo Basin Treaty: the international framework for Japanese advance in Africa

Before examining the Congo Basin Treaty, it is necessary to discuss relations between Japan and Belgium prior to the Japanese economic advance into the

Belgian Congo. On August 1, 1866 Japan concluded a treaty of amity and commerce with Belgium, based largely on the Tax Revision Agreement (Kai Zei Yakusho) of June 25, 1866.[4] In this the 20 percent tariff rate fixed in the Five Country Agreement of the Ansei period[5] was reduced to 5 percent. So Japan had to accept what amounted to Free Trade and was afraid that the absence of an import barrier would prevent the rise of modern industry in Japan. So from 1871 the Meiji government sought to revise the treaty.

In 1894 there were negotiations with Britain by Foreign Minister, Munemitsu Mutsu, to revise the Treaty and it was agreed that some tariffs could be increased. Imports from Britain, France, Germany and the United States of more than ¥50,000 annually were listed as agreed items on which tariffs could be placed. On June 22, 1896, a new treaty of commerce and navigation with an attached protocol was signed between Japan and Belgium. This revised treaty came into action on July 17, 1899.[6] On January 17, 1900, a declaration of amity and residence between Imperial Japan and the Congo Free State was signed by Ichiro Motono, the Japanese Minister Extraordinary and the Belgian Ministry of Foreign Affairs.[7] In this, freedom of trade and navigation was agreed and the subjects of both countries were allowed equal rights to travel and reside, and buy and sell property. The agreement as revised by Foreign Minister Munemitsu Mutsu, was for 12 years and was to end on July 16, 1911. The second Katsura Taro Cabinet[8] hoped to regain complete tariff autonomy and went to the negotiations to try to revise the treaty and obtain equality and reciprocity. These negotiations with Belgium were unsuccessful, but both Japan and Belgium thought that an interim agreement should be made on July 8, 1911, rather than no agreement be reached.[9]

After the end of the First World War, the Japanese government began negotiations to conclude a new treaty, hoping to gain both a tariff and residence agreement. A new treaty was signed on June 27, 1924 by Mineichiro Adachi, the Japanese Ambassador to Belgium, and the Belgium Minister of Foreign Affairs. Japan went ahead with reciprocal trade liberation. The trade and navigation agreement with Belgium of 1924 was the first to be concluded under this policy. It introduced the mutual opening of coastal trade, and the Treaty was applied to the dependencies of both countries (Korea and Belgian Congo).[10] The Agreement was reached easily because equal opportunities to all in the Belgian Congo had been declared in the Berlin protocol in 1885 and the Brussels protocol of 1890, and Japan had signed the Congo Basin Treaty of September 10, 1919.

The Congo Basin Treaty and Japan

It was a general Protocol of the Berlin Conference of February 26, 1885 which established the principle of free trade and equal opportunity to foreigners in Central Africa in order to expand the spheres of influence of the European powers there. On April 26, 1884, an Anglo-Portuguese Treaty had been made to prevent France and Belgium from advancing into this region.[11] France, Belgium, Germany and other nations had protested vehemently against this move, which was why the Berlin Conference was held under the auspices of the Prime Minister of Imperial Germany. The resulting protocol secured freedom of trade and navigation in the Congo River Basin and its adjoining lands to all interested countries. The signatory nations included Germany, Austria, Belgium, Denmark, Spain, the United States, France, Britain, Italy, the Netherlands, Portugal, Russia, Sweden and Turkey.

At the Brussels Conference on July 2, 1890 this protocol was supplemented with a general protocol and declaration. It was amended by the Treaty concluded in Saint-Germain-en-Laye on September 10, 1919 at the end of the First World War, but the principle of equal opportunity to trade was confirmed. The Congo Basin Treaty was signed by the ministers of Japan, the United States, France, Belgium, Portugal, Britain and Italy. It was ratified by Italy and the United States respectively on October 14, 1931 and October 29, 1934.[12]

Although both Germany and Austria were involved directly with the Berlin and Brussels Protocols, they did not become members of the Congo Basin Treaty. However it was interpreted that the protocol also applied to them in spirit. Turkey was allowed to join the Congo Basin Treaty and ratify it in the Turkish Peace Agreement. The difference between the Congo Basin Treaty and the Protocol of the Berlin Conference was that although the protocol allowed complete freedom to trade, the treaty prohibited only discriminatory tariffs in the Congo Basin. In the case of the Berlin Protocol, all nations were treated equally but only the member countries benefited from the Congo Basin Treaty.[13]

Article 1 of the treaty established equal trading rights to those countries which signed. This applied to the basin of the Congo River and its tributaries, the attached coastal zone from latitude South 2' 30" to the mouth of the Loge River and the Congo Basin to the Indian Ocean coast from latitude 5' North to the mouth of the Zambezi River. In other words it applied to part of French Equatorial Africa and French Cameroon, the Belgian Congo, Belgian Luanda and Ulundi, part of Portuguese East Africa (Mozambique) and Angola in West Africa, part of British Northern Rhodesia, Nyasaland, Uganda, Zanzibar, British Kenya, British Tanganyika, part of British Somaliland, Southern Ethiopia and part of the Anglo-Egyptian Sudan.[14]

In the regions listed in Article 1 member nations could trade freely, both importing and exporting. There were no taxes, extra commissions or additional charges other than commission charges (Article 2 Clause 1). Citizens of member nations and their properties were protected in all areas. In their business activities the citizens of the member nations were treated exactly like citizens of the region, subject to the need to maintain public order and safety in the provinces in question (Article 3). Although each country could dispose of state-owned assets and exploit natural resources in the provinces in question, the right to do this was given to all member nations equally (Article 4).

Article 1 also allowed the ships of member nations to pass freely along the coast and to call at ports and harbors without discriminatory treatment. The navigation of the Congo, without excluding any of its branches or outlets, remained free for the merchant-ships of all nations equally, whether carrying cargo or ballast, for the transport of goods or passengers. In the exercise of this navigation the subjects and flags of all nations were to be in all respects treated on a footing of perfect equality, not only for direct navigation from the open sea to the inland ports of the Congo and vice versa, but also the great and small coasting trade, and for boat traffic on the course of the river. Consequently, on all the courses and mouths of the Congo there would be no distinction made between the subjects of Riverain States and those of not-Riverain States, and no exclusive privilege of navigation would be conceded to companies, corporations, or private persons whatsoever. The navigation of the Congo would not be subject to any restriction or obligation which was not expressly stipulated by the Act. It would not be exposed to any landing dues, to any station or depot tax, or to any charge for breaking bulk, or for compulsory entry into port. In all the extent of the Congo, the ships and goods in process of transit on the river would be submitted to no transit dues, whatever their starting-place or destination. This freedom of navigation also applied to the river Niger and its tributaries (Articles 5 and 6). The roads, railways or lateral canals which may be constructed with the special object of obviating the in-navigability or correcting the imperfection of the river route on certain sections of the course of the Congo, its affluents, and other waterways placed under a similar system would be considered in their quality of means of communication as dependencies of this river, and as equally open to the traffic of all-nations. And on the river itself, so tolls would be collected on these roads, railways and canals calculated on the cost of construction, maintenance and management and on the profits due to the promoters. As regards the tariff of these tolls, strangers and the natives of the respective territories would be treated on a footing of perfect equality (Article 7). Article 15 stated that ten years after the protocol was signed and passed, member nations were to have a conference to amend its provisions in the light of their experience. In this way the Treaty became a framework which made possible Japanese commercial advance in the Congo Basin in the 1920s and 1930s.[15]

Japanese commercial strategy in the Congo Basin textile market

In 1927 Yoshitaro Kato, embassy clerk at Cape Town, was sent to the Belgian Congo to investigate economic conditions. This is known from a letter of June 27 from Tadanao Imai, consul of Cape Town to Giichi Tanaka, Minister of Foreign Affairs. Kato returned to the Consulate at Cape Town on June 3, 1927 and submitted his report, which was later printed and published by the Ministry of Foreign Affairs' Bureau of Trade and Commerce.[16]

This report outlined the future of the Belgian Congo for Japanese exports. The market in general was not likely to expand rapidly because there were few Europeans there, but commodities like silk manufactures, cotton goods, fancy goods, earthenware, glassware and bulky goods (enameled ware for example) and canned fish seemed promising for Africans to buy. There were African workers in the mining towns, and small farmers in rural areas who grew raw cotton and coffee. The mine workers had incomes and purchasing power and the farmers would buy more if they could earn cash by collecting palm produce and growing cotton. In the towns, Africans wanted khaki shirts and shorts and cotton cloth for women (white pattern on blue cloth, red headkerchiefs with a white pattern or indigo with polka dots). Farmers in the rural areas also wanted cutlery, knives with handles, enameled ware, candles, matches, chinaware and aluminum ware.[17]

A trade strategy was suggested operating from Dar es Salaam in Tanganyika. There seemed to be three routes by which Japanese merchandise could flow into the Belgian Congo. There was the route from Beira to Elizabethville by the Rhodesian railway, the route from Dar es Salaam to Kigoma on the East Coast of Lake Tanganyika and on to Albertville in Katanga by waterways and the route from Mombasa via Uganda to the Northeast Congo. It was thought that the second route was most important as without a base in East Africa, the Congo could never be a market for Japanese goods. The Japan–East African shipping line had opened in 1926 and Mombasa was well known in the Japanese business world, but the importance of Dar es Salaam was not yet recognized. Tanganyika, where sisal, groundnuts, coffee, cotton and other agricultural products were cultivated, was of critical importance as a source of raw materials and an area for investment. Special attention was to be paid to cotton cultivation, and Japanese trading companies were encouraged to participate in the cotton market and Japanese investors to seek production estates and contribute to the development of East Africa. Tanganyika was an area classified as a "B" mandate territory of the League of Nations, that is, an area to be developed.[18] Thus the Export Promotion Association and the Chamber of Commerce and Industry were to plan to advance into East and Central Africa. Japanese traders interested in business with Africa were advised to study the aims, organization and activities of the British Cotton Growing Association and organize a Business Association for Africa to devise measures to encourage investment. Experts were to be sent to investigate opportunities in Tanganyika and the eastern Congo.[19]

In British East Africa, imports from Japan consisted of beer, pottery and chinaware, glassware (bottles, jars, tumblers and other domestic ware, lighting glassware, tableware, plates and mirrors), cement, tin plate, enameled hollow ware, iron and steel manufactures (cutler's wares, implements and tools, locks, knives), cotton piece-goods, cotton blankets, knitware, clothes and matches. So Japan's exports to East Africa were mostly miscellaneous merchandize and cotton piece-goods, and in contrast with Europe and the United States, Japan exported necessities for Africans, Indians and Arabs. The value of Japanese products in East Africa's cotton piece-goods imports increased rapidly from 1931, and in 1936 her share rose to 80 percent. Considering that cotton piece-goods from Britain, India and the Netherlands had most of the market in the 1920s, it is remarkable that in the 1930s, Japanese goods on average accounted for 65 percent of East Africa's imports of cotton piece goods[20] (see Table 10.1).

Japanese cotton goods mostly consisted of unbleached grey cloth between 1925 and 1939 in volume and value, but from 1932 imports of printed cloth, dyed cloth and yarn dyed cloth increased steadily. The Japanese share of unbleached grey cloth was up to 90 percent in the latter half of the 1930s despite the sharp

Table 10.1 Imports of cotton cloth to East Africa by countries, 1926–39 (£1,000)

Year	Total import	Japan	UK	India	Netherlands
1926	1,797	438	543	335	375
1927	1,958	436	592	335	462
1928	1,050[a]	—	—	—	—
1929	1,176[a]	—	—	—	—
1930	1,436	253[a]	227[a]	81[a]	178[a]
1931	1,183	503	237	196	204
1932	1,151	527	258	116	114
1933	1,188	675	220	77	114
1934	1,258	891	240	60	45
1935	1,478	1,109	263	57	38
1936	1,530	1,225	190	57	32
1937	2,026	1,612	195	103	78
1938	1,562	1,168	186	81	99
1939	1,457	1,087	146	63	63

Source: Consular Reports in *Overseas Economic Conditions*.

Notes
East Africa includes Kenya, Uganda, Tanganyika and Zanzibar, 1926–33: Total of Kenya, Uganda and Tanganyika; 1934–39: Total of Kenya, Uganda, Tanganyika and Zanzibar.
a Tanganyika not included.

decline in the Great Depression of 1930–33. Between 1926 and 1939, on the average, the Japanese share in this category was 67 percent. This grey cloth was manufactured by companies such as Toyo Boseki Co., Nihon Boseki Co., Senshu Textile Co. and Naigai Cotton Co. Demands fluctuated according to the income of the indigenous consumers, and the seasonal harvest of cotton and other agricultural crops. Japanese grey cloth was mainly used for African clothes like *Kanzu* and *Shuka*. In the case of bleached cloth, British and Dutch goods predominated from the latter half of the 1920s to early 1930s, and the Japanese share was around 20 percent. But in the mid-1930s as a result of innovations in bleaching technology in Japan, her share rose to about 80 percent. Between 1926 and 1939 the Japanese share of the bleached cloth was 41 percent on an average and used for *Kanzu, Shuka* and African underwear[21] (see Table 10.2).

In the case of printed cloth, British goods took the major share, but after 1934 Japanese goods gradually increased. Japanese goods consisted mostly of printed jeans and Japan could not match Britain in *Khanga*. Imports of Japanese dyed cloth increased in the 1930s and in the latter half of the 1930s the Japanese share of the dyed-in-the-piece exceeded 75 percent. This reversion of position between Japan and Britain in the East African market led to a trade conflict. These dyed-in-the-piece goods were *Kaniki*, black cloth for female hoods (*Buibui*) and *Shuka*, *Hodorunk* (dyed dark brown cloth, *Kanzu* for females), bleached calicos, khaki colored drill (clothes for Africans living in rural areas) and crepe (*Kanzu* for middle-class Africans and clothes for European children). In the case of yarn dyed cloth, Japan accounted for over 70 percent of the total. Yarn dyed cloth included striped cloth (for underwear for Africans, Indians and Arabians), striped drills,

Table 10.2 Imports of cotton cloth to East Africa by kinds, 1926–39 (£1,000)

Year	Unbleached	Bleached	Khanga	Printed	Dyed in piece	Yarn dyed
1926	669 (403)	149 (11)	—	233 (5)	397 (6)	349 (37)
1927	669 (390)	881 (20)	—	261 (16)	431 (9)	427 (78)
1928	265 (143)	96 (10)	—	135 (51)	266 (10)	288 (15)
1929	390 (346)	78 (17)	—	157 (61)	248 (11)	303 (87)
1930	423 (142)	93 (16)	—	124 (44)	181 (9)	186 (54)
1931	393 (163)	100 (22)	—	143 (65)[a]	282 (14)	143 (68)
1932	272 (96)	86 (18)	—	150 (30)[a]	269 (54)	213 (21)
1933	295 (86)	76 (22)	—	133 (39)[a]	303 (112)	229 (32)
1934	284 (261)	90 (59)	102 (6)	184 (163)	339 (207)	253 (187)
1935	362 (343)	115 (87)	141 (6)	245 (215)	376 (270)	241 (184)
1936	393 (374)	149 (124)	106 (13)	254 (233)	379 (285)	240 (188)
1937	426 (395)	195 (168)	155 (21)	284 (254)	581 (464)	276 (302)
1938	393 (384)	108 (82)	191 (51)	226 (196)	371 (262)	267 (193)
1939	374 (275)	121 (92)	112 (22)	225 (196)	452 (359)	191 (137)

Source: Consular Reports in *Overseas Economic Conditions.*

Notes
East Africa includes Kenya, Uganda, Tanganyika and Zanzibar, 1926–33: Total of Kenya, Uganda and Tanganyika; 1934–39: Total of Kenya, Uganda, Tanganyika and Zanzibar.
( ) Import of Japanese goods.
a Includes Khanga.

Kikoi for African men, *Kunguru* (for checked underwear for Africans), and *Kisuwa* (headkerchiefs for African women and turbans for Arab men)[22] (see Table 10.2).

According to the Consular Report by Chosaku Mogaki, resident at Mombasa, in the Belgian Congo the main items for indigenous Africans were cotton cloth and in the various districts of Stanleyville Province 60–80 percent of commodities in the shops for Africans were cotton textiles.[23] In the retailer outlets printed cloth was favored followed by dyed-in-the-piece, gray cloth, yarn dyed cloth and bleached cloth. Printed cloth consisted of *Kitenge*, a plain-weave printed cloth with a large pattern used for loincloths by Africans and *Mombaya Rordi* for women's clothes. *Kitenge* was classified into superior and inferior according to the quality of print-ing. The superior was a wax-block print made in Britain with beautiful colours and patterns and Africans found it expensive. It was similar to the *Khanga* of the British East African market. The inferior imitated wax-block print stuffs and was cheap enough for Africans. These stuffs were imported from Britain, Belgium and the Netherlands. Japanese traders tentatively sent chintz from Java to this market, but its price was similar to the products of other countries and the pattern was unpopu-lar among the Africans. The *Kitenge* market included the Belgian Congo and West Africa. Consul Mogaki in Mombasa reported that Japanese traders ought to study the framework weaving patterns of the Africans and send expert designers to the region, and cooperated with local middlemen. Consul Mogaki's reports suggested that printed cloth of red and deep blue was popular in Stanleyville and blue cloth with a large pattern like the Japanese *Yukata* sold well.[24] But ordinary printed cloth was cheap Japanese merchandise like those clothes exported to British East Africa. These were used for loincloths and women's clothes usually made of in *Kitenge*. This kind of cloth sold well, but attention had to be paid to changes in fashions. Cheap printed striped cloth for underwear was popular among Africans and printed cloth with stripes was welcomed for loincloths by the indigenous people of Luanda and Ulundi.[25] In the case of dyed-in-piece cloths only indigo drill and khaki drill was found in the Congo market. Indigo drill was mostly in demand for deep blue jeans, and was also used for men's shirts and women's loincloths. Standard goods manufactured by Texaf (Societe Textile Africaine) for the Belgian Congo was rough to touch. Japanese cloth made by Sugimoto & Co. in Nagoya entered this market and was imported via Mombasa. African men usually put on khaki shorts or long trousers. The suppliers of this cloth were Japan, Britain, Belgium and the Netherlands, but Japanese cloth was predominant in Stanleyville market. Unbleached cotton cloth, the coarse quality, was called Americani. This was mainly used for loincloths. In British East Africa unbleached cloth was imported mostly, but in the Congo more printed cloth than bleached was imported. Eighty percent of unbleached cloth was imported from Japan and Japanese cloth competed with Texaf in the Belgian Congo. Yarn dyed cloth was used for men's underwear. Gingham had not yet been introduced here. Besides the above, loincloths woven in red, yellow and white yarn were welcomed. Yarn dyed cloth from Japan took 64 percent of the market and those made in Belgium 24 percent[26] (see Tables 10.3 and 10.4).

Table 10.3 Imports of cotton cloth to the Belgian Congo by
countries, 1932–36 (£1,000)

Year	Total imports	Japan (%)	UK	Belgium
1932	49,578	3,082 (6)	25,316	16,381
1933	52,174	10,225 (19)	27,277	10,477
1934	53,367	18,183 (34)	22,857	6,565
1935	96,836	43,025 (44)	—	—
1936	125,296	83,473 (66)	—	—

Source: Consular Reports in *Overseas Economic Conditions.*

Table 10.4 Imports of cotton cloth to the Belgian Congo by kinds, 1932–36 (£1,000)

Year	Bleached	Unbleached	Printed	Dyed in	Yarn dyed piece
1932	988 (52)	5,081 (1,434)	23,507 (504)	19,392 (1,075)	—
1933	1,146 (192)	5,017 (3,464)	28,180 (3,318)	17,407 (3,208)	—
1934	2,473 (880)	6,040 (4,960)	25,222 (5,139)	12,620 (3,038)	6876 (4,128)
1935	3,619 (1,339)	8,037 (7,238)	54,185 (18,289)	17,535 (6,245)	13,462 (9,917)
1936	5,426 (3,371)	16,855 (15,662)	60,123 (34,176)	23,659 (15,329)	19,237 (14,937)

Source: Consular Reports in *Overseas Economic Conditions.*

Note
Figures in parentheses represent Import of Japanese goods.

Revision of the Congo Basin Treaty and Anglo-Japanese relations

The penetration of Japanese cotton goods into the East African market generated fear and discontent amongst British traders. W.H. Franklin, H.M. Senior Trade Commissioner in East Africa, reported,

> The most notable feature of competition generally during the period under review has been the rise in importance of Japan as a supplier to East Africa; consideration of price margins has the tendency to make observers extremely pessimistic as to the possibilities of competition with that source of supply.[27]

In East Africa, the debate on whether to alter or abolish the Congo Basin Treaty came to the boil even before the 1932 Ottawa conference, in which Britain changed her policy from free trade to protectionism. On June 14, 1932 the Nairobi Chamber of Commerce decided to press for the abolition of the Treaty. But the Mombasa Chamber of Commerce had already resolved on May 11 to support the continuation of the Treaty. The British traders wanted to press for a preferential tariff to protect their trade in East Africa. The British East African Settler Conference and the Annual Session of the Association of Chamber of Commerce of East Africa campaigned for preferential tariffs as part of their overall strategy for the formation of the Union of East Africa.[28]

However, S.H. Sayers, the president of the Mombasa Chamber of Commerce was not in sympathy with this movement. In October 1933 he came to Japan and on October 21, visited the Osaka Chamber of Commerce. During the reception party in his honor, he appealed to Japanese traders to trade with East Africa and to buy goods from East Africa according to the spirit of free trade. On the other hand, in Britain there were worries about the advance of Japanese cotton piece goods and general merchandize in the East African market and the Joint East African Board of Communication sent John Seidman Allen to investigate Japanese activities there.[29]

Conclusion

The Congo Basin Treaty originated in the general protocol of the Berlin Conference in 1885, and in September 1919 when the Peace Treaty was signed, Britain, the United States, Japan, France, Italy, Portugal and Belgium proposed an amendment to it. Essentially this gave free and equal opportunities of development, residence and trade in tropical Africa to signatories, especially in the Congo Basin. It even prohibited countries who had colonies in Africa from putting preferential or favorable discriminatory tariffs on their own products, in their own colonies. So in East Africa, countries that did not possess colonies were not discriminated against. The safety of their citizens and property was guaranteed, and they could buy, sell and transfer property at will.[30]

Japan had no influence in the region and was gravely concerned and wary of the motives behind the amendment of the Congo Basin Treaty. In May 1935,

Britain imposed Import Quotas on her colonies to protect British trade interests. On March 19, 1934, the Cabinet organized the Committee on Japanese Trade Competition on the advice of the Board of Trade. The first meeting, on March 27, considered the introduction of import quotas on Japanese goods in West Africa and the amendment or abolition of the Congo Basin Treaty and the Abolition of the Anglo-Japanese Commercial Treaty.[31] But East Africa with reluctance was excluded from the enactment and Japanese cotton piece-goods were not shut out of this market. Japan was saved by the Congo Basin Treaty. Amendments to the Congo Basin Treaty could not be made after July 1934. But Japan withdrew from the League of Nations in March 1935, which put her in a precarious position regarding the East African market. She was particularly worried about developments in the League of Nations mandatory territory of Tanganyika.[32]

This was a period when European metropolitan countries were consolidating their economic positions within their spheres of influence. Viewed through the Japanese Consular Reports, the inter-war period in Africa was a time when Japan tried to edge itself into a region where she was not wanted but in which she felt she deserved a place as a lifeline for her national economy. In the 1930s the term, "Economic Diplomacy," was used in government documents and the mass media in Japan. In the international economy at this time, ideas of trade liberalism changed towards bilateralism, reciprocity and compensationism. Exports from Japan created serious trade frictions with advanced industrial economies in markets they considered their own. In this regard, several commercial negotiations took place: the Anglo-Japanese Trade Negotiation of 1934, the Japanese–Dutch Trade Negotiation, the Japanese–American Trade Negotiation, the Japanese–Canadian Trade Negotiation, the Japanese–Egyptian Trade Negotiation and the Japanese–Australian Trade Negotiation of 1935.

This study is mainly based on prewar Japanese Consular Reports which throw light on the activities of the Japanese in East and Central Africa in the inter-war period. It tries to fill a gap in the historical record of Japan's relations with Africa, but because of the vast amount of scattered literature it must be regarded as a preliminary venture, and only outlines the broad trends in commercial relations between these countries.

Notes

1 This was a paper presented at the, 20th International Symposium on Asia in the Age of *Pax Britannica* and *Pax Americana* held at the International Research Centre for Japanese Studies on September 24–28, 2002.
2 In this regard, it is significant that the Third Meeting of the Tokyo International Conference on African Development (TICAD III) took place in October 2003. See Opening Remarks by Mr Yoshiro Mori, Chairperson of TICAD III, September 29 2003, Tokyo, Highlights of the Summary by the Chair of TICAD III, closing address by Mr Yoshiro Mori, chairperson of TICAD III, October, 1 2003, Tokyo, and TICAD Tenth Anniversary Declarations, October 1, 2003, Tokyo. See also Remarks by the President of the Republic of Indonesia at the First Asia–Africa Subregional Organization Conference (AASROC), Bandung, July 28, 2003 and Co-Chairs' Statement: Asia–Africa Subregional Organization Conference, Bandung, Indonesia, July 29–30, 2003.

3   With reference to Japanese Consular Reports in regard to Africa, see the following studies; K. Kitagawa, "A Study of Japan's Pre-War Economic Research on Africa: A Preliminary Investigation," Kansai University of Foreign Studies, *Kenkyu Ronshu*, No. 48, 1988; K. Kitagawa, "A Study of Economic Conditions in Africa in the Pre-War Period Seen through Japanese Consular Reports: An Analysis of *The Journal of Commercial Reports*," Kansai University of Foreign Studies, *Kenkyu Ronshu*, No. 50, 1989; K. Kitagawa, "A Study of Economic Conditions in Africa in the Pre-War Period seen through Japanese Consular Reports: An Analysis of *The Official Commercial Reports*," Japanese Association for African Studies, *Journal of African Studies*, No. 35, 1989; K. Kitagawa, "Japan's Economic Relations with Africa between the Wars: A Study of Japanese Consular Reports," Kyoto University, *African Study Monograph*, Vol. 11, No. 3, 1990; K. Kitagawa, "Japan's Economic Interests in South Africa in the Pre-War Period," Ryukoku University, *Annual Report of the Institute for Social Science*, No. 22, March 1992; K. Kitagawa, "Japan's Economic Relations with South Africa in the Post-War Period: Determinants of Japanese Perceptions and Policies toward South Africa," Shikoku Gakuin University, *Ronshu*, No. 86, 1994; K. Kitagawa, "Pre-War Japan's Economic Relations with East Africa," in Takashi Okakura and Katsuhiko Kitagawa (eds), *A Short History of Japan–Africa Exchange: From Meiji Period to the World War II*, Tokyo: Dobunkan, 1993; K. Kitagawa, *A Study in the History of Japanese Commercial Relations with South Africa*, International Research Centre for Japanese Studies, Monograph Series, No. 13, 1997; K. Kitagawa, "Japan's Trade with East and South Africa in the Inter-War Period: A Study of Japanese Consular Reports," *Kansai University Review of Economics*, No. 3, 2001; K. Kitagawa, "Japan's Trade with South Africa in the Inter-War Period: A Study of Japanese Consular Reports," in Chris Alden and Katsumi Hirano (eds), *Japan and South Africa in a Globalizing World: A Distant Mirror*, Hampshire: Ashgate, 2003.

4   Tatsunori Isomi, Fumitaka Kurosawa and Ryoju Sakurai, *A History of Japanese–Belgian Relations*, Hakusuisha, Tokyo, 1989, p. 209.

5   Ansei indicates the period from November 13, 1855 to March 18, 1860.

6   T. Isomi, F. Kurosawa and R. Sakurai, op. cit., p. 210. This new Japanese–Belgian treaty was signed by the Ministers Plenipotentiary, Shuzo Aoki and Paul de Favereau.

7   Letter on August 2, 1899 from the Minister Plenipotentiary at Belgium, Katsunosuke Inoue to the Minister of Foreign Affairs, Shigenobu Okuma, "Congo State and Treaty of Amity," Letter on March 9, 1900 from the Minister Plenipotentiary at Belgium, Ichiro Motono to the Minister of Foreign Affairs, Shuzo Aoki, "Exchange of the Declaration with Congo Free State," Letter on October 7, 1900 from Prime Minister, Aritomo Yamagata to Minister of Foreign Affairs, Shuzo Aoki, "Draft of the Declaration between Imperial Japan and Congo Free State," in the Diplomatic Record Office of the Ministry of Foreign Affairs, File 2-5-1-59, Belgium, Congo Commercial Treaty.

8   The second Katsura Taro Cabinet was in power from July 14, 1908 to August 29, 1911.

9   T. Isomi, F. Kurosawa and R. Sakurai, op. cit., pp. 211–13. Letter on April 18, 1911 from the Minister of Foreign Affairs, Jutaro Komura to the Minister at Belgium, Keijiro Nabeshima; Instruction on September 23, 1911 from the Minister of Foreign Affairs, Kaoru Hayashi to the Minister at Belgium, Nabeshima.

10   T. Isomi, F. Kurosawa and R. Sakurai, op. cit., pp. 214–15. See also "Revision of Japanese–Belgian Commercial Treaty," Diplomatic Record Office, File 2-5-1-43, 90, 111.

11   Ministry of Foreign Affairs, "An Outline of the General Protocol of the Berlin Conference (February 26, 1885) and the General Protocol and Declaration of the Brussels Conference (July 2, 1890)," p. 1, Diplomatic Record Office, File B-10-5-0-8; "International Treaty on the Revision of the General Protocol of the Berlin Conference and the General Protocol and Declaration of the Brussels Conference."

12   The Ministry of Foreign Affairs, "An Outline of the General Protocol," ibid., pp. 1–2.

13   The Ministry of Foreign Affairs' Bureau of Trade and Commerce, "A Study of Equal Trade Treatment in the Mandate Territories and the Congo Basin Treaty" (1938),

pp. 117–18, Diplomatic Record Office File B-10-5-0-8; "International Treaty on the Revision of the General Protocol of the Berlin Conference and the General Protocol and Declaration of the Brussels Conference."

14 The Ministry of Foreign Affairs' Bureau of Trade and Commerce, "A Study of Equal Trade Treatment," ibid., pp. 119–20. See also "Protocols and General Act of the West African Conference," presented to both Houses of Parliament by Command of Her Majesty, March 1885.

15 The Ministry of Foreign Affairs' Bureau of Trade and Commerce, "A Study of Equal Trade Treatment," ibid., pp. 120–4.

16 Letter on June 27, 1927 from Consul Tadanao Imai at Cape Town to the Ministry of Foreign Affairs, Giichi Tanaka "Dispatch of the Embassy Staff to the Belgian Congo," Diplomatic Record Office File E-1-2-0-X1-BE2; "Miscellaneous Matter on Fiscal, Economic and Financial Issues in Several Countires: A Part of Congo." See also The Ministry of Foreign Affairs' Bureau of Trade and Commerce, *Economic Conditions in the Belgian Congo*, 1927.

17 The Ministry of Foreign Affairs, *Economic Conditions in the Belgian Congo*, pp. 61–4. "The General Conditions in the Belgian Congo," in *Overseas Economic Conditions* (The Ministry of Foreign Affairs' Bureau of Trade and Commerce), No. 7, 1937, pp. 219–43.

18 The Ministry of Foreign Affairs, *Economic Conditions in the Belgian Congo*, pp. 64–71. See also Osaka Shosen Kaisha (OSK), *A History of African Line*, 1956, and *Report of Economic Conditions in East Africa*, 1924. The OSK decided to open the East–South Africa line on March 23, 1926 and Kanada–Maru (5780t) was sent on the first run. This African line was authorized by the Ministry of Communication and the Mekishiko–Maru (5800t) which departed from Kobe was the first authorized ship. Thus regular service was opened once a month to East Africa.

19 The Ministry of Foreign Affairs, *Economic Conditions in the Belgian Congo*, pp. 72–5. From the Ambassador Extraordinary and Plenipotentiary of Belgium, Mineichiro Adachi to the Ministry of Foreign Affairs' Bureau of Trade and Commerce, "Economic Conditions of the Belgian Congo" (October 11, 1927) *Overseas Economic Conditions*, No. 1062, January 1928, pp. 1424–6.

20 Katsuhiko Kitagawa, "Japan's Trade with East and South Africa in the Inter-War Period: A Study of Japanese Consular Reports," *Kansai University Review of Economics*, No. 3, March 2001, p. 15. See Japanese Consuls' Annual Reports on Research of Japanese Imports and Exports in East Africa published in *Overseas Economic Conditions* (The Ministry of Foreign Affairs' Bureau of Trade and Commerce).

21 Katsuhiko Kitagawa, "Japan's Trade with East and South Africa in the Inter-War Period," pp. 16–17.

22 Katsuhiko Kitagawa, "Japan's Trade with East and South Africa in the Inter-War Period," pp. 17–18.

23 "The Belgian Congo as Japanese Merchandize Market" (March 26, 1936, Chosaku Mogaki to the Ministry of Foreign Affairs' Bureau of Trade and Commerce) *Overseas Economic Conditions*, No. 15, August 10, 1936.

24 "The Belgian Congo as Japanese Merchandize Market" (March 26, 1936, Chosaku Mogaki to the Ministry of Foreign Affairs' Bureau of Trade and Commerce), pp. 128–9. *Economic Conditions in the Belgian Congo*, pp. 61–4.

25 "The Belgian Congo as a Japanese Merchandize Market" (March 26, 1936, Chosaku Mogaki to the Ministry of Foreign Affairs' Bureau of Trade and Commerce), p. 130.

26 "The Belgian Congo as a Japanese Merchandize Market" (March 26, 1936, Chosaku Mogaki to the Ministry of Foreign Affairs' Bureau of Trade and Commerce), pp. 132–5.

27 Department of Overseas Trade, *Economic Conditions in East Africa and in Northern Rhodesia and Nyasaland*, by W. H. Franklin, London, HMSO, 1832, p. 37.

28 "Decision on the Revision of the Congo Basin Treaty by the Association of Chamber of Commerce of British East Africa" (Telegraph on July 27, 1933 from Consul Kuga at Mombasa) *Overseas Economic Conditions*, No. 30, July 1933, p. 5. See also Osaka Commercial Museum, *Commercial Reports*, No. 316, November 1933.
29 "Issue of the Revision of the Congo Basin Treaty and the Opinions of the Settlers in British East Africa," *Overseas Economic Conditions*, No. 35, September 1932, pp. 66–8. Osaka Chamber of Commerce, *Monthly Reports*, No. 317, October 1933. See also Department of Overseas Trade, *Economic Conditions in East Africa*, London, HMSO, 1934, pp. 60–1. In 1934, C. Kemp, the Trade Commissioner in East Africa, reported:

> The steps taken by Japanese manufacturers to create and establish new lines against the competition of goods which, over a period of years, had obtained a goodwill in the market, the continuous care taken to improve the qualities of goods of which first shipments were poor, and the margins of possible price differentials even when the benefits of currency depreciation are lost, show that, technically speaking, Japan is now fully organized to meet the competition of the older manufacturing nations. Moreover, if Japanese goods with relatively considerable rises in prices can still be produced and sold within the limits of native purchasing power, they start with a heavy advantage in the race for markets.
>
> (p. 60)

30 The Ministry of Foreign Affairs' Bureau of Trade and Commerce, "A Study of Equal Trade Treatment in the Mandate Territories and the Congo Basin Treaty" (1938), pp. 117–18, Diplomatic Record Office File B-10-5-0-8; "International Treaty on the Revision of the General Protocol of the Berlin Conference and the General Protocol and Declaration of Brussels Conference."
31 Cabinet, "Committee on Japanese Trade Competition," March 19, 1934, March 27, 1934, April 11, 1934, CAB/27/568. See also K. Kitagawa, "Japan's Trade with West Africa in the Pre-War Period: A Study of Japanese Consular Reports," *Economic Review of Kansai University*, Vol. 42, No. 5, January 1993. Kweku Ampiah, "British Commercial Policies against Japanese Expansionism in East and West Africa, 1932–1935," *International Journal of African Historical Studies*, Vol. 23, No. 4, 1990. R.A. Bradshaw, "Japan and Colonialism in Africa, 1800–1939," PhD Thesis, Ohio University, June 1992, pp. 365–6, 379. From Mamoru Shigemitsu, the Minister Extraordinary and Plenipotentiary of Britain to the Ministry of Foreign Affairs, "The Issue of the Congo Basin Treaty" (July 24, 1939), *Overseas Economic Conditions*, No. 19, October 1939.
32 From Genichiro Omori, the Ambassador of Belgium to the Ministry of Foreign Affairs "The General Conditions of the Belgian Congo" (June 10, 1936), *Overseas Economic Conditions*, No. 7, 1937, pp. 1–3. The Ministry of Foreign Affairs' Bureau of Trade and Commerce, "A Study of Equal Trade Treatment in the Mandate Territories and the Congo Basin Treaty" (1938), pp. 117–18, Diplomatic Record Office File B-10-5-0-8; "International Treaty on the Revision of the General Protocol of the Berlin Conference and the General Protocol and Declaration of the Brussels Conference." The Ministry of Foreign Affairs' Bureau of Trade and Commerce, "Issue of the Revision of the Congo Basin Treaty and Opinion of the Settlers in British East Africa," *Overseas Economic Conditions*, No. 35, September 1932, pp. 66–8.

11 Shifting patterns of multilateral settlements in the Asia-Pacific region in the 1930s

Masafumi Yomoda

Introduction

One of the greatest changes in the late twentieth century was the rapid development of the Pacific countries. Recent articles have focused upon the Pacific economy as a whole and have discussed the historical processes by which it has emerged (Jones *et al.* (1993); Miller *et al.* (1998); Flynn *et al.* (1999)). Because more and more people have recognised the economic significance of the Pacific economy, a deeper understanding of its long-term history is needed.

Countries (or regions) in the Pacific are diverse, reflecting their cultures, historical origins, levels of economic development etc., and each can be analysed individually. But in discussing the economic factors that caused the development of the Pacific economy as a whole, the region can be treated as a unit where common changes occurred simultaneously. This will help us understand features common to the Pacific countries, and provide a common criteria of comparison between them.

The historical origins of the Pacific economy can be dated to the founding of Manila in 1571 and the galleon trade between the Philippines and Mexico (Flynn *et al.* (1999) Introduction). But it would be difficult to write a comprehensive history of the Pacific region since the sixteenth century, so this chapter focuses only upon the inter-war world economy. The focus is on this period, because this was when the role of the Pacific economy changed greatly. The Pacific economy previously was a sub-system sustaining the 'core' (i.e. Atlantic, with India) of the world-system, now it broke away and became more or less independent of the 'core', a situation triggered by the First World War (hereafter WWI).

This chapter focuses upon the changes in the pattern of intra-Asian settlements after WWI, and their significance in the evolution of the global economy. The following section 'The Depression in the 1930s – a starting point for analysis' will survey studies on the changes in international settlements caused by WWI and the Depression in the 1930s. The section, 'Estimation of intra-Asian settlements' will attempt to make rough estimates of intra-Asian settlements from 1913 to 1938, and the section, 'Changes in the positions of Asian countries in international settlements' will compare settlements before and after the Depression, and analyse changes in each individual Asian economy. The section

'Emergence of new patterns of settlement in the Pacific' will analyse the details outlined in the previous section to investigate the changes in the Asian economies, and the last section 'Political limits to the emerging Pacific settlements; Japanese and American commercial policies' will also discuss the political limitations of the emerging Pacific economy, which could not prevent the Pacific War.

The Depression in the 1930s – a starting point for analysis

The Depression has been a controversial issue among economic historians, and has been analysed from various viewpoints. Some historians attributed its causes to domestic factors, such as tight monetary policy, maladjustment of the gold standard mechanism and the failure of balanced-budget policies. Others have attributed the Depression to international factors, such as the instability brought about by the transition from the *Pax Britannica* to the *Pax Americana*, and the consequent disorganisation of the multilateral settlement network.[1]

With respect to the latter, the League of Nations (1942) was a pioneering report showing how important multilateral settlements were to the world economy before 1930, and how they collapsed in the Depression. Though others have made additional analyses, they have tended to treat the Depression as an event that occurred essentially in the Atlantic region, and have ignored the significant role that Asian economies had in multilateral settlement. Indeed, the patterns of intra-Asian settlements and changes within them were not examined in the report, because most of Asia was classified as the 'Tropics' together with Africa. The report underestimated the role of Asia in the world economy at that time.

The importance of Asia in international settlements was first pointed out by Saul (1960), then by Latham (1978, 1981) and others. Saul demonstrated Britain's ability to maintain a deficit on her visible trade with industrial Europe and the United States (US), because it was balanced by a surplus with the third world, especially India. After the Opium War, triangular settlements among India, China and the United Kingdom (UK) merged into more complicated 'multilateral settlements' covering the world (Saul (1960) pp. 44–5). Asia had a significant role in this and an increasing role until the 1930s.

India, in particular, served as a 'safety-valve' funding the British deficit with the industrial countries and stabilising international settlements. Saul indicated that India's massive deficit with the United Kingdom (in the form of trade deficit, the 'Home Charges' and investment returns) was balanced by her massive surplus with Continental Europe, the United States and other Asian economies. He demonstrated that the triangular settlements (UK → Europe and US → India → UK) played the most important role in reinforcing multilateral settlements and stabilising the global economy. India's surplus with Asia, in particular with Japan and China, was as important as other surpluses, in balancing her payments (Latham (1978) pp. 81–2); therefore, we can conclude that expansion of 'intra-Asian trade', made clear by Sugihara (1986), made large contributions to the expansion of multilateral settlements.

The above historians imply that India's role gradually declined after WWI and that this resulted in the collapse of multilateral settlements and contributed to the Depression. Taking Asia's importance into consideration, it may be asked if the Depression was caused by changes in the Asian economies and changes in the economic relationship between Asia and Europe and America. In addition, recently revisionists have emerged and criticised the orthodox view that the Depression had a more severe impact on Asia than the developed countries, and that Asia was a passive actor (for instance, Brown (1989); Boomgaard and Brown (2000). They have argued that developing regions clearly reacted to the drastic changes spontaneously and actively by showing that economic growth and industrialisation occurred in Asia. Asia had a different dynamism to other regions in the Depression.

The main aim of this chapter is to revise the orthodox Euro-centric or Atlantic-centric views on the Depression and to re-estimate the revisionists' views in the context of the International Economic Order (Akita and Kagotani (2001)). The following sections will focus upon changes in Asian patterns of settlements in more detail.

Estimation of intra-Asian settlements

This section attempts to estimate intra-Asian settlements to show how they changed after 1910.[2] However, the balance-of-payments statistics of Asian countries are of poor quality, and the available data, on invisible trade balances and capital movements in particular, are so rough that it is hardly possible to make highly accurate and reliable estimates. Even where available, the methods of calculation and estimation differ. Despite these limitations, rough estimates are made here by combining incomplete balance-of-payments statistics from various sources, to indicate roughly the changes that occurred in Asia.

Asia is divided into four sub-regions – India, Southeast Asia, China and Japan – and intra-Asian payments are estimated, plus those between these sub-regions and the developed world: the United Kingdom (UK), Continental Europe (CE) and the United States. The estimates are shown in the Figures 11.1 and 11.2. The estimates in Figure 11.1 include only trade balances, and Figure 11.2 takes into account trade balances, investment returns, emigrants' remittances and government transfer payments, which were of great significance to most Asian countries. Investment returns are divided according to their destinations and are distributed in proportion to foreign capital stocks in the corresponding countries (Lewis (1938)).[3] Shipping earnings and capital movements are excluded because the statistics are unavailable. But even without considering these items, changes in the pattern of settlements can be sketched. In interpreting the estimated figures, it must be borne in mind that most shipping earnings and other items related to the colonial authorities (the UK Netherlands, France and the US) and Japan, (which was less important) and that Asia's actual current payments to Europe and Japan must have been a little greater than Figure 11.2 shows. Furthermore, capital was moving to the third world before the Depression and

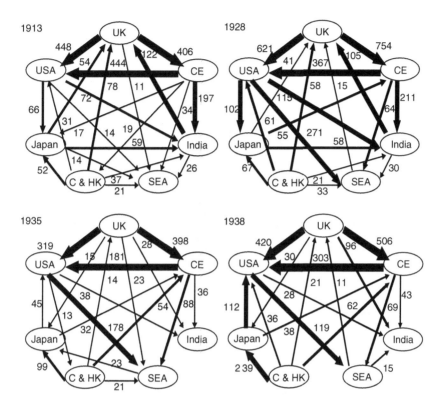

Figure 11.1 Patterns of settlements (trade balances only) (Unit: million US dollars ($1928)).

moving back to the creditor countries during the 1930s, judged from the statistics of the United States and the United Kingdom.

In order to analyse the influence of the Depression upon the patterns of settlements, the pattern in 1938 is usually compared with that in 1928 as in the League of Nations (1942). Here, patterns in 1935 are given in addition, because the first half of the 1930s was the period when the previous global economic order dissolved, and the second half was when it was being partially restored or reconstructed.

The pattern of settlements estimated by the above method is indicated in the figures. They show how the pattern of settlements in Asia changed from the 1910s to the 1930s. In the next section, the changes in settlements of each country are discussed in more detail.

Changes in the positions of Asian countries in international settlements

Asian economies, and particularly Japan, experienced drastic 'qualitative' changes in their patterns of settlement during the inter-war period. Perhaps no

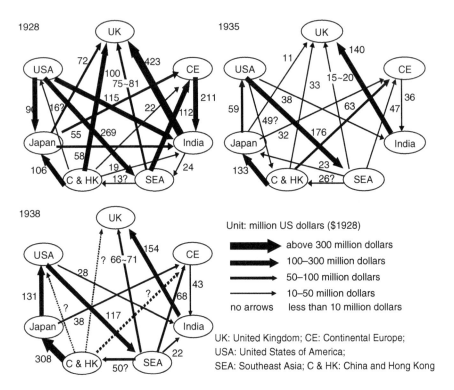

Figure 11.2 Patterns of settlements (inclusive of trade balances, investment returns, emigrants' remittances and government transfer).

other country underwent such drastic change as Japan did, although quantitative declines took place in most countries (regions). The Depression did not have the same impact on all regions, but different impacts according to regional characteristics. Its impact upon Asian economies was very different from that on other developing (or developed) economies. This section discusses the situation of each Asian country after WWI.[4]

India

As mentioned earlier, India had an important role in reinforcing multilateral settlements and stabilising the world economy. But Figure 11.1 suggests that India lost its pre-war importance after WWI. India's surplus with various countries including Asia, the Continental Europe, and the United States, was nearly balanced by her massive deficit with the United Kingdom before WWI as Saul (1960) demonstrated (see also Latham (1978) pp. 80–2). But, after the war, India's deficit with the UK and her surplus with the other countries stopped rising, as Figure 11.1 suggests (Latham (1981) pp. 94–6). India's surplus with

America, which became the most important axis in the world economy, was less important than Southeast Asia's and Japan's surplus with America. Hence, India's ability to increase her surplus was limited during America's prosperity and Europe's relative decline. The less was India's surplus, the weaker was India's ability to pay the United Kingdom. These changes weakened her role in maintaining the multilateral pattern of settlements and resulted in the relative decline of Britain's position.

In the 1930s, India's surplus fell even more. Figure 11.2 shows that her surplus with Continental Europe, the United States and Japan came to approximately US$ 380 million in 1928, 70 million in 1935 and 70 million in 1938. India's deficit with the United Kingdom fell as well. Our calculation indicates that India's net payment to the United Kingdom amounted to approximately US$420 million in 1928, 140 million in 1935 and 150 million in 1938. It appears that India's payment to the United Kingdom increased a little during the late 1930s. However, as 1935 was a year when India's government transfer payment decreased exceptionally (Banerji (1963) pp. 111–18), it is probably better to conclude that her net payments tended to fall continuously through the 1930s.

As mentioned earlier, the 1930s can be divided into a first phase when the previous international order dissolved and a second phase of partial revival and reconstruction. But India gradually diverged from her previous position in the world throughout this decade, and there was no return to the pattern of settlements before the Depression.

Reacting to this changing situation, the colonial authorities tried to increase India's exports to the United Kingdom and to cut her imports from the United Kingdom, also introducing an import-substitution policy, although this had been against Britain's national interests before WWI (Simmons (1987)). They sought bilateral settlements between the two countries inside the 'sterling bloc'. So, India completely lost her previous importance as a 'safety-valve' in the world economy. The percentage of India's exports in world trade fell from 4.3 per cent in 1913 to 3.0 per cent in 1938. India's 'multilateral trade dependency ratio'[5] fell from 11.6 per cent in 1928 to 6.0 per cent in 1935 and 4.2 per cent in 1938. These figures prove that India came to depend upon bilateral settlements as a result of trade contraction, contrary to the period before WWI. So India lost her position as a 'safety-valve' and as a major axis in 'intra-Asia trade', and virtually retreated into the 'sterling bloc'.

Japan

Japan had a complementary part in the multilateral settlement mechanism. Before the Depression, as indicated in Figures 11.1 and 11.2, Japan had a massive surplus with the United States (thanks to a dramatic increase in exports of silk, mainly silk thread) and had deficits with India and Southeast Asia (mainly because of a large increase in imports of raw cotton, rice, etc.). Overall, Japan served as a 'bye-pass' between India and the United States, and complemented India's role as a 'safety-valve' (Matsumoto (1996)). Moreover, rapid economic development in the United States during the 1920s helped Japan's exports grow more quickly than India's. Japan's trade expansion contributed to the stabilisation of multilateral settlements at a time when they were getting more unstable. However, Japan experienced dramatic changes in her balance of payments during the 1930s. Figures 11.1 and 11.2 show partly that directions of net payment between India and Japan, Southeast Asia and Japan, the United States and Japan all reversed compared to those in the 1920s. The changes suggest that her position in the world economy changed drastically as well.

The characteristics mentioned earlier reflected changes in her trade structure. Japan exported silk to the United States and cotton textiles to China; she imported raw materials and food stuff from India and Southeast Asia. But with the Depression as a turning point, Japan's trade composition underwent drastic changes. Japan exported textiles and miscellaneous articles to Southeast Asia and exported less to the United States and China, with both of which Japan had had a considerable trade surplus prior to 1930. In the 1930s, Japan imported raw cotton, petroleum and so on from the US,[6] and imported less from India, with which Japan had had a considerable trade deficit.

So the patterns of settlements around Japan changed, and her position in the world economy moved from reinforcing the Britain–India centred patterns of settlements to weakening them. Though Japan had served as a 'bypass' between India and the United States before the Depression, her complementary role now came to an end. Instead, the new emerging patterns worked against the previously dominant pattern, and Japan's export-oriented economic recovery played an opposing role. That is why trade frictions occurred in Southeast Asia and India, and were a source of dispute between the United Kingdom and Netherlands, and Japan.

Unlike India, the percentage of Japan's exports in world trade increased from 1.7 per cent in 1913, to 2.7 per cent in 1928 and 3.9 per cent in 1935. Furthermore, Shirakizawa (1999) has made it clear that Japan's 'multilateral trade dependency ratio' was increasing from 11.8 per cent in 1928 to 17.4 per cent in 1934. Japan increasingly depended upon multilateral (or triangular) settlements through trade expansion during the first half of the 1930s, unlike the world economy, which tended to depend upon bilateral settlements due to trade contraction. In particular, India depended upon more intra-bloc trade and less upon intra-Asian trade, while Japan did not depend on intra-empire trade, but on intra-Asian and Pacific trade until the mid-1930s. It is natural to think that maintenance of multilateral settlements was important to Japan even during the mid-1930s. One of the great changes in the Depression was India's retreat from an important position in international settlement and Japan's emergence as significant.

Southeast Asia

Southeast Asia's role in the world economy changed drastically after WWI. After the war, the prosperity of the US economy encouraged Southeast Asia's export of rubber and tin etc., and the United States trade deficit to Southeast Asia drastically increased from US$ 14 million in 1913 to approximately 270 million in 1928, as shown in Figure 11.1. Investment from foreign countries to Southeast Asia increased rapidly as well, stimulated by the increase in their exports to the United States. According to the statistics collected by Woodruff (1982), foreign capital in Southeast Asia as a whole increased from US$ 1.15 billion in pre-WWI to 4.1 billion in 1938; in India from 1.8 to 3.1 billion; in China from 1.6 to 2.5 billion; in Latin America from 8.9 to 11.3 billion. To sum up, foreign investment increased more rapidly in Southeast Asia than in other developing areas.

The increase in investment meant that Southeast Asia's dividend and interest returns, and its net payment to Europe in general also increased rapidly giving greater importance to Southeast Asia. Southeast Asia served as a 'link' between the United States and Europe, and contributed to the maintenance and stabilisation of multilateral settlements just as India had done. The region had the same important role that pre-1930 India did, though its net payments to the UK and CE were much less than India's.

India and Southeast Asia had almost the same role in the multilateral settlements from WWI to 1929, but their situations diverged during the 1930s. While India depended more and more upon bilateral settlements with the UK during the 1930s, Southeast Asia depended on more triangular (or multilateral) settlements during this decade and their authorities attempted to maintain them. The precipitous decline in the prices of its primary products was a severe blow to Southeast Asia's monocultural economy. In reaction to such hardship, the colonial authorities did not pursue an intra-bloc bilateral settlements policy, but maintained a much freer trade policy than they did in India.

The 'multilateral trade dependency ratios' in Southeast Asian regions showed no tendency to decline, unlike India. The ratios of British Malaya were 24.0 per cent in 1928, 21.5 per cent in 1935, and 25.1 per cent in 1938; Dutch East Indies, 6.3, 10.4, 9.7 per cent; Thailand, 18.4, 22.4, 19.2 per cent in the same years. Except for French Indo-China, no clear tendency toward bilateral settlement was seen. So the authorities in Southeast Asia did not seek bilateral settlement policies to overcome the Depression. Instead, they adopted a series of production restriction schemes and tried to raise prices of primary products by restraining production. The schemes mainly concerned staples produced in Asia, especially in Southeast Asia. For instance, the schemes in rubber and tin, principal staples in Southeast Asia, are said to have been more ambitious and radical than other restriction schemes. According to Churchill's comment, production restriction schemes were intended to 'make the Americans pay' (Latham (1981) pp. 109–15; Drabble (1991) pp. 150–8; Hillman (1988) pp. 246–7). As the United States became the largest creditor country after the war, the colonial authorities sought to increase the United States's net payments to Southeast Asia, and this policy was intended to alleviate a shortage of dollar liquidity and help to stabilise the world economy.

Figure 11.2 shows the United States's net payments to Southeast Asia continuously decreasing during the 1930s. But 1938 was a year when America experienced a severe recession again. Her net payments to Southeast Asia decreased exceptionally in 1938, and by 1937 her net payments had nearly recovered to the level of the late 1920s. Without the American recession in 1938, Southeast Asia's surplus with the United States would have kept increasing during the late 1930s, even if the recovery was very fragile. Seen from the balance of payments of the US, Southeast Asia's position as a region that 'made American pay' was more evident. According to Peek's estimate (Peek (1935)), America had a current deficit of US$ 90 million with Asia, of which her trade deficit with Southeast Asia amounted to 170 million in 1934. Her balance of payments with most other regions was favourable; hence, Southeast Asia had an exceptionally important role in spreading dollar liquidity to many countries with deficits with the United States. An estimate in *The Economist* suggests that the balance of payments in the British Empire as a whole was sustained by the massive trade surplus of British Malaya. The estimate must have exaggerated the importance of British Malaya in maintaining the empire's balance, because she had some deficits with countries outside the empire ('British–American Trade Agreement' in *Economist*, 26 November 1938). Nevertheless, British Malaya, rather than India, was helping to sustain the considerable deficits other regions in the British Empire had with the United States.

While India's surplus was absorbed by the United Kingdom, Southeast Asia's surplus could not be tapped by its colonial authorities. The estimates indicate that Southeast Asia's net payment to Europe amounted to approximately US$ 200 million in 1928, but fell to 60 million in 1935. Its net payments to China and Japan increased from almost nothing to US$ 50 million in the same years. In 1938, its net payments to Europe recovered to US$ 140 million dollars.[7] In addition, its net payments to China increased to 50 million, thanks to a rise in overseas Chinese remittances and their investments in their home country (Brown (1994) pp. 187–8). Southeast Asia's net payment to India also increased from virtually nothing in 1935, to US$ 20 million in 1938. The intra-Asian settlement network around Southeast Asia rapidly recovered and re-activated itself throughout the 1930s.[8] Increases in overseas Chinese and Indians' remittances, caused partially by the rapid recovery in the prices of primary products, played a crucial role in the recovery and growth of intra-Asian settlements. Such changes imply that the intra-Asian settlement network and production restriction schemes that had the intention of 'making the Americans pay' complemented each other.

In contrast, Japan's net receipts from Southeast Asia diminished to negligible amounts again, perhaps because of her export restrictions and her adoption of a wartime controlled economy. Japan began to rely upon new triangular settlements with Southeast Asia and in the early 1930s the United States, and her massive deficit with the United States was balanced by her increasing surplus with Asia and others. But because of the loss of her surplus with Asia, her imbalance of payments widened in the late 1930s. Had it not been for the Sino-Japanese War and the Pacific War, new patterns of settlements (the US → Southeast Asia → Japan → the US) might have emerged and grown. The next section discusses the emerging patterns of settlements in more detail.

Emergence of new patterns of settlement in the Pacific

It can be shown, from analyses of the balance of payments of individual countries, that new patterns of triangular settlements had emerged around the Pacific Ocean, replacing the pattern of settlements outlined by Saul (1960); (Kano (1995)).

So, was the Pacific trade vulnerable to the impact of the Depression? Due to worldwide trade contraction and severe deflation, it is extremely difficult to measure quantitatively whether Pacific trade was vulnerable or not during the 1930s. This study uses the percentage of Pacific trade in world trade, to discuss whether Pacific trade was vulnerable. Here 'Pacific trade' is defined as trade among East Asia, Southeast Asia and the United States and its percentage in the world trade total is calculated. Surprisingly, during the early 1930s, the relative share of Pacific trade did not decrease, despite the drastic fall in Japan's silk exports to the United States. The share of Pacific trade in world trade increased from 5.88 per cent in 1928 to 6.10 per cent in 1935 (calculated from League of Nations (1942) appendix III). The precipitous collapse in Japan's silk exports was compensated by an increase in Southeast Asia's rubber and tin exports and in Japan's export of miscellaneous articles. The share of trade between Europe and the American Continent diminished from 21.3 per cent in 1928 to 18.7 per cent in 1938. Overall, the absolute value of Pacific trade was difficult to reduce, and was relatively less vulnerable to and less influenced by the Depression than the Atlantic trade or elsewhere. Unfortunately, the percentage declined from 6.10 per cent in 1935 to 5.34 per cent in 1938 perhaps as a result of various countries' import restrictions against Japanese manufactures, and the Japanese wartime controlled economy.

As for Japan, her deficit with India and Southeast Asia was balanced by her surplus with the United States prior to 1930; hence she had a role in maintaining and re-inforcing Britain-centred multilateral settlements. However, as dramatic changes in the composition of Japan's trade took place during the early 1930s, patterns of settlements around Japan changed drastically. Her deficit with Southeast Asia became a favourable trade balance, and her surplus with the United States became a deficit. So new patterns of settlements emerged around Japan.

Dietrich, a contemporary economist studying Far Eastern economies in the Institute of Pacific Relations, emphasised that triangular trade between the US, Japan and Southeast Asia was of great significance to the Japanese economy, and that the triangular trade ought to be promoted by the US government to prevent economic and military conflict with Japan (Dietrich (1940) pp. 11, 93–4). This opinion was completely ignored, but the argument that the triangular trade was vital to the Japanese economy in stabilising her balance of payments was right. However, the patterns of settlements centred on Japan competed with those centred on Europe (US → Southeast Asia → Europe → US) in Southeast Asia. That gave rise to trade friction between Japan and other countries, because Southeast Asia was getting more important to the major countries (Kahn (1946) pp. 232–5).

Beasley pointed out:

> Certainly American economic interests in China do not seem to have been considerable enough to warrant full-scale confrontation. And it was only as Japanese moves towards south-east Asia were becoming a factor in Britain's ability to resist the Axis power that the United States began reluctantly to intervene.
>
> (Beasley 1987, p. 222)

Southeast Asia was of vital importance to the United States, and to the United Kingdom. The defeat of the United Kingdom would have meant that national interests of the US would be also vulnerable, because the United Kingdom and the United States were linked by Southeast Asia as abovementioned. As pointed out by a Japanese pre-war economist (Nawa (1937)), the Japanese economy in those years was vulnerable without the Pacific pattern of settlements. But Japan pursued the 'Great East Asia Co-prosperity Sphere (*Dai-Toa Kyoeiken*)' an expansion policy at the expense of the Pacific economy. However, the triangular trade, resembling that of the 1930s, revived in the 1950s, and helped Japan develop rapidly, by reducing her deficit on current account. Was its emergence in the 1930s a first sign of the post-war Asia-Pacific economy? Certainly, it is important to note that the triangular trade was vital to Japanese economic growth in the early 1930s. However, the Pacific War eventually broke this down. Why didn't the emerging Pacific triangular settlement prevent the Pacific War? The next section discusses the causes of the Pacific War by suggesting that there were gaps in perception between the United States and Japan.

Political limits to the emerging Pacific settlements; Japanese and American commercial policies

The Japanese economy during the early 1930s tended to depend upon multilateral (or at least triangular) settlements. Worldwide restrictions on imports from Japan prevented Japan's exports from increasing rapidly. So the Japanese government consistently argued for freer trade, and entered negotiations with various countries to eliminate restrictions on Japan's exports. Recent studies in the field of Japanese diplomatic history (Kato (1993) ch. 1; Inoue (1994); Kagotani (2000), chs 6–8, for example) criticise the orthodox view that Japan isolated herself from the world in the 1930s due to intermittent warfare with China. Instead, they emphasise that the Japanese government pursued a series of appeasement policies with the United Kingdom and the United States during the period between Japan's withdrawal from the League of Nations (1933) and the Sino-Japanese War (1937). These studies suggest Japan's position in international society did not get worse until the Marco Polo bridge incident (1937).

In 1934, Cordell Hull, Secretary of State in the United States, proposed a 'reciprocal trade agreement' and the United States abandoned her traditional protective tariff policy (e.g. the notorious Smoot-Hawley Act of 1930) in favour of freer trade. Hull attempted to persuade neighbouring countries to reduce their trade barriers. The concessions granted in these agreements, as a rule, were to be extended to all third countries ('most-favoured-nation treatment'). This policy was based upon bilateralism unlike the post-war GATT policies based upon multilateralism. Hull tried to avoid 'free riders' benefiting from free trade without paying its cost by taking advantage of 'most-favoured-nation treatment'. The United States granted concessions to 'chief suppliers' to avoid giving benefits to free riders (Tasca (1938)).

As Japan's increasing exports were confronted with trade barriers all over the world, Japan's Ministry of Foreign Affairs placed its hope upon Hull's moves to freer trade (Kato (1993)). Japan's attitude in favour of freer trade coincided with the new diplomacy of the United States and with Hull's idealism. The citation below reflects the Japanese government's expectations towards America's new trade policy.

Japan's unfavorable balance of visible trade with the United States in 1934 was Yen 370,000,000. Kurusu (= Japanese diplomat) believes and hopes that some way can be found to utilize this balance in counteracting the unfavorable balances prevailing with the South American countries. He quoted Secretary of State Hull as stating in one of his public utterances that he was definitively in favor of trilateral trade agreements. ... he sincerely believes that the inauguration of such a three-cornered trade agreement would not only prove mutually beneficial, (but) would serve as an excellent example to the world of one means of unraveling the present trade and economic tangle.
(*Foreign Relations of the United States, 1935*, Vol. III, p. 940)

Kurusu proposed to the US government that they should quickly make a trilateral agreement covering the two governments and the Latin American countries. Japan's balance of payments with Latin America was favourable like that with Southeast Asia, and Latin America's balance with the United States was also favourable; hence, maintenance of triangular settlements among the three regions through freer trade was favoured by Japan (it was less important than triangular settlements among Southeast Asia, Japan and the United States). Moreover, as Latin American countries were under America's powerful influence, the Japanese government judged this scheme as being more feasible. But Southeast Asia was under European dominance apart from the Philippines and Thailand, and its colonial authorities in these countries were outside Hull's scheme. So it made sense to assume that it would be time-consuming to conclude triangular trade treaties covering Southeast Asia by utilising Hull's policy.

Nevertheless, there were gaps in the perception of the two governments. The gap in perception was also rooted in another point, revealed below:

He (= Sayre, Assistant Secretary of State in the U.S.) cited as an example of multilateral trade the excess of exports of the United States to European countries, of European countries to Latin America, and of Latin American countries to the United States, and he showed how the trade between these three areas would be reduced if the principle of bilateral balancing were effectively carried out.

(Foreign Relations of the United States, 1936, Vol. IV, p. 898)

Sayre's comment suggests that the United States laid more weight upon recovery in trans-Atlantic triangular settlements among the United States, Latin America, and European countries, than the Pacific settlements that Japan considered important. All the countries that the United States signed treaties with were Latin American and European countries, and there were no Asian independent countries. His above comment coincided with the list of countries with which the United States signed treaties.

Why was there this perception gap? To explain it, the reason why the United States changed her foreign policy must be examined in some detail. Carr pointed out the background against which Hull determined changes in diplomacy.

Down to 1930, successive revisions of the United States tariff had been almost invariably upward; and American economists, in other respects staunch upholders of *laissez-faire*, had almost invariably treated tariffs as legitimate and laudable. But the change in the position of the United States from a debtor to a creditor Power, combined with the reversal of British economic policy, altered the picture; and the reduction of tariff barriers has come to be commonly identified by American spokesmen with the cause of international morality.

(Carr 1956, p. 75)

As Carr implied, the United States became the largest creditor after WWI, and changes in her international position induced Hull to change America's trade policy to freer trade. In insisting that the 'reciprocal trade agreement' was of significance to the United States, Sayre gave various reasons. The most important of them were that the United States must import more from debtor countries to promote the debtors' exports and to increase their payments of investment returns, and that American trade must assume 'striking triangularity' as bilateral balancing killed American trade (Sayre (1936)).

The 'reciprocal trade treaty' policy was adopted by the US authorities. Hull regarded free trade policy as a strategy essential to a creditor nation because it eventually maintained her foreign assets and promoted receipt of her investment returns. In negotiating and signing the treaties, the US government gave priority to Latin America; then to European countries; and lastly to Asia. This priority coincided in some degree with the distribution of America's foreign capital. According to Peek's estimate (Peek (1935)), investment returns receipt amounted to US$ 129 million from Canada, 110 million from Europe, 64 million from Latin America and only 28 million from Asia. Moreover, as the United States was a monopolistic investor in Latin America, mutual reduction of trade barriers by the United States and Latin America increased debtor Latin America's exports and so maintain investment returns paid exclusively to the US.

An attempt has been made to explore which factors determined whether the United States signed a treaty with a country or not, by using 'probit' analysis. The results suggest that the greater the country's ratio of investment from the United States (not the sum of investment), the lower the export–import ratio of the United States with the country, and the greater the sum of export and import values of the United States with the country, the higher was the probability that the two governments would conclude a treaty.[9] In particular, the first factor related to America's national interests as a creditor. The fact that the United States concluded treaties with a country with higher ratios of US investment means that she attempted to prevent other creditors from gaining benefit as free riders, and to gain as much benefit as possible. The second factor reflected exporters' interests in the United States and the government's intention to 'improve' their exports (Takamitsu (1996)). As far as Japan was concerned, the ratio of investment was low and the export–import ratio was high, so the probability that she would conclude a treaty with the United States was less.

Hull's reciprocal trade treaty policy reflected the economic interests of investors, and America's national interest as a creditor. The other side of the Pacific was not a principal destination of America's foreign investment, though as important a trade partner as Europe. Perhaps America's reluctance to conclude a treaty with Japan reflected industrial interests fiercely opposed to it; furthermore, it is important to point out that investors' and exporters' interests were relatively weak, as the above statistical analysis implies. Even if the United States had concluded a treaty with Japan, the US would have gained little advantage, and threats of a rapid increase in imports from Japan must have prevented it.

To conclude, interdependence in investment was much less in the Pacific economy than in the Atlantic, though interdependence in trade was already deep. Perhaps asymmetry in the Pacific was one of the causes that prevented Japan from entering the America-centred free trade sphere. The Pacific economies still had less political importance than Atlantic economies.

Concluding remarks

Braudel pointed out that 'In most cases unfavorable economic conditions finally tolled the knell of the old center, which was already in a threatened position, and confirmed the emergence of the new one' (Braudel (1977) p. 86). His proposition may be true of the 1930s, a period which corresponds with its 'unfavorable economic conditions' mentioned earlier. The Depression brought to an end the Atlantic economy's role as a single 'centre' of the world, and prepared for the rise of the Pacific economy as a new centre. Pacific trade and its patterns of settlements were previously dependent upon the 'core' in the world system, but in the 1930s it became relatively independent and came to have a dynamism of its own.

Whether there were continuities or discontinuities between the pre-war and post-war periods remains unsolved. Which was more important after WWII, intra-Asian trade or Pacific trade? Petri (1993) emphasises that post-war reconstruction and economic growth in Asian countries resulted not in a revival of the pre-war Japan-centred 'Great East Asia Co-prosperity Sphere,' but in rapid growth of the 'Pacific economic sphere'. The 'gravity coefficients'[10] related to Pacific trade continued to rise over three decades in the post-war period, but the coefficients inside East Asia drastically decreased and never recovered to the pre-war level. Frankel (1993) also argues that Pacific trade played a more important role in the growth of Asian exports. According to him, trade linkages among APEC countries tended to be stronger (statistically more significant) than those among East Asian countries only or among EAEC countries only, analysed with multiple regression using the gravity coefficients as dependent variables.

To sum up these conclusions, post-war Asian development depended not upon the growth of intra-Asian trade, but rather upon the growth of Pacific trade. The United States was abundant in natural resources and capital, but scarce in labour, while East Asia in particular was abundant in labour, even compared with Western Europe. The modern theory of international trade tells us that such contrasting factor endowments must have promoted expansion of Pacific trade (Hongyi (1998)). Which will be more important in the future, growth of intra-Asian trade at the expense of the Pacific trade, or continuous growth of Pacific trade?

The historical origin of Pacific trade also remains an unsolved issue, but East Asian industrialisation was based upon an export-oriented strategy for each country, and the American economy as the most important customer for East Asia's manufacturers helped East Asia develop rapidly. The first to adopt this strategy was Japan, which, already in the nineteenth century, had exported silk and other labour-intensive articles to the other side of the Pacific. From the late nineteenth century, the Japanese economy expanded exports in two directions: to Asia and to America, as Saito (1991) suggests. The Japanese economy adapted itself to the expansion of the US economy, linking the Pacific trade with the intra-Asian trade, and gained economic benefits from both sources. It remains to be discussed elsewhere what historical meaning the emergence of the Pacific economy had, and the relationship between Asia and the other Pacific countries.

Notes

1 Multilateral settlements were explained by the League of Nations as follows:

> If a country A is entitled to a net payment from country B on account of an export surplus or services performed and cannot be paid through a corresponding influx of gold from B, that country has to acquire the currency required for settlement through a surplus, as a rule in merchandise trade, with a third country, C. Country C, in its turn, has to compensate for its import surplus from B with an export surplus to D, and so it continues until the circle is closed by an export surplus from the last of the countries involved A.
>
> (League of Nations (1942) pp. 73–4)

2 The pioneering work that deals with intra-Asian settlements is Mukai (1975), though his stance is different from ours.
3 See Yomoda (2003) about the details of estimating methods.
4 This article refers to China to a lesser extent, because China's data was hard to compare as a result of the separation of Manchuria from China and the Sino-Japanese war, and also because Chinese changes in international settlements were treated as less significant. See Latham (1981) and Yomoda (2003) for details.

5 Multilateral (or triangular) trade means 'balances in trade with individual countries not reflected in the aggregate balance – that is, balances with opposite sign, offsetting each other' and it is 'calculated as the difference between the total of import or export balances (ignoring their sign) in trade with individual and' total import or export balance (quoted from League of Nations (1933) p. 62). The 'multilateral trade dependency ratio' here is a ratio of the 'multilateral trade' value to the total trade value. See also Shirakizawa (1999).

6 Yasuba (1996) is an interesting and controversial paper insisting that it was in the 1930s that Japan came to recognise their country was suffering from a shortage of natural resources. This paper also emphasised the drastic changes in Japan's trade structure during the decade.

7 The colonial governments attempted to increase Southeast Asia's receipts from the United States and their payments to the colonial authorities (League of Nations (1939) p. 40).

8 The Bank of Taiwan and the Yokohama Specie Bank, Japanese major semi-government banks, contributed to some extent in promoting intra-Asian settlements even in the early 1930s (Yoshihara (1986)).

9 The results of a series of 'probit' analyses are partly indicated as below:

Constant	EX/IM	Log (EX + IM)	INV ratio	INV value	Latin	Log likelihood
−0.7880	−0.00663**	0.2538**	0.01928***			−28.862
(−1.5600)	(−2.5017)	(2.0008)	(2.6718)			($R^2 = 0.2888$)
−0.3904	−0.00425**	0.2538*		0.0000267		−32.781
(−0.8621)	(−2.0069)	(1.9901)		(0.0637)		($R^2 = 0.1930$)
−0.9711	−0.00661**	0.2847**	0.01669**		0.4712	−28.264
(−1.7624)	(−2.4648)	(2.1029)	(2.1579)		(1.0899)	($R^2 = 0.3007$)

Notes
EX/IM: export–import ratio of the US; INV ratio: ratio of investment from the US; INV value: investment values; LATIN: Latin American Dummy (Latin American countries = 1, the other = 0). *T*-values are in parenthesis. $N = 58$. * = significant at the 0.10 level; ** = significant at the 0.05 level; *** = significant at the 0.01 level.

10 It is a measure of trade intensity and shows the strength of trade links between two regions. The coefficient is an index showing trade growth or contraction compared with the world trade in general. The coefficient from country X to Country Y, for example, is calculated by dividing the ratio of export value from X to Y to the total export of X, by the ratio of Y's total import to total world trade. Petri (1993) termed the ratio as 'double relative measure' and Matsumoto (1996) termed it as 'trade intensity'.

References

English articles

Banerji, A.K. (1963) *India's Balance of Payments*, Bombay: Asia Publishing House.

Beasley, W.G. (1987) *Japanese Imperialism 1894–1945*, Oxford: Clarendon Press.

Boomgaard, P. and Brown, I. (eds) (2000) *Weathering the Storm: The Economies of Southeast Asia in the 1930s Depression*, Leiden: KITEV Press.

Braudel, F. (1977) *Afterthoughts on Material Civilization and Capitalism*, Baltimore: Johns Hopkins University Press.

"British-American Trade Agreement" in *Economist*, November 26, 1938.

Brown, I. (ed.) (1989) *The Economies of Africa and Asia in the Inter-War Depression*, London: Routledge.

Brown, R.A. (1994) *Capital and Entrepreneurship in South-East Asia*, New York: St. Martin's Press.

Carr, E.H. (1956) *The Twenty Years' Crisis 1919–1939*, 2nd ed., London: Macmillan (first edition published in 1946).

Department of State, USA (1935) *Foreign Relations of the United States, 1935*, Vol. III, Washington: Government Printing Office.

Department of State, USA (1936) *Foreign Relations of the United States, 1936*, Vol. IV, Washington: Government Printing Office.

Dietrich, E. (1940) *The Far Eastern Trade of the United States*, New York: Institute of Pacific Relations.

Drabble, J.H. (1991) *Malayan Rubber: The Interwar Years*, Houndmills, Basingstoke, Hampshire: Macmillan.

Flynn, D.O., Frost, L. and Latham, A.J.H. (eds) (1999) *Pacific Centuries: Pacific and Pacific Rim History since the Sixteenth Century*, London, New York: Routledge.

Frankel, J.A. (1993) 'Is Japan Creating a Yen Bloc in East Asia and the Pacific?', in Frankel, J. A. and Kahler, M. (eds) *Regionalism and Rivalry: Japan and the United States in Pacific Asia*, Chicago, IL: University of Chicago Press.

Hillman, J. (1988) 'Malaya and the International Tin Cartel', *Modern Asian Studies*, Vol. 22, No. 2.

Hongyi, H.L. (1998) 'Factor Endowments, Trade Direction, and Growth Performances of the Americas and East Asia in the Nineteenth and Twentieth Centuries', http://wconwpa.wustl.edu/ prints/dev/papers/9710/9710004.abs

Jones, E., Frost, L. and White, C. (eds) (1993) *Coming Full Circle: An Economic History of the Pacific Rim*, Boulder, CO: Westview Press.

Kahn, A.E. (1946) *Great Britain in the World Economy*, New York: Columbia University Press.

Latham, A.J.H. (1978) *The International Economy and the Undeveloped World 1865–1914*, London: Croom Helm.

Latham, A.J.H. (1981) *The Depression and the Developing World 1914–1939*, London: Croom Helm.

League of Nations (1933) *Review of World Trade, 1932*, Geneva.

League of Nations (1939) *Review of World Trade, 1938*, Geneva.

League of Nations (1942) *Network of World Trade*, Geneva.

Lewis, C. (1938) *America's Stake in International Investment*, Washington, DC: Brooking Institution.

Miller, S.M., Latham, A.J.H. and Flynn, D.O. (eds) (1998) *Studies in the Economic History of the Pacific*, New York: Routledge.

Peek, G.N. (1935) *Letters to the President on Foreign Trade and International Investment Position of the U.S.* (in E-3-1-1-2-1 in the Diplomatic Record Office of the Ministry of Foreign Affairs of Japan).

Petri, P.A. (1993) 'The East Asian Trading Blocs: An Analytical History', in Frankel, J.A. and Kahler, M. (eds), *Regionalism and Revalry: Japan and the United States in Pacific Asia*, Chicago, IL: University of Chicago Press.

Saul, S.B. (1960) *Studies in British Overseas Trade 1870–1914*, Liverpool: Liverpool University Press.

Sayre, F.B. (1936) *America Must Act*, Boston, MA: World Peace Foundation.

Simmons, C. (1987) 'The Great Depression and Indian Industry: Changing Interpretations and Changing Perceptions', *Modern Asian Studies*, Vol. 21, No. 3.

Sugihara, K. (1986) 'Patterns of Asia's Integration into the World Economy, 1880–1913', in Fischer, W., McInnes, R.M. and Schneider, J. (eds), *The Emergence of a World Economy 1500–1914*, Part 2, Wiesbaden.

Tasca, H.J. (1938) *Reciprocal Trade Policy of the United States*, Philadephia, PA: University of Pennsylvania Press.

Woodruff, W. (1982) *The Impact of Western Man: A Study of Europe's Role in the World Economy, 1750–1960*, Washington, DC: University Press of America.

Yasuba, Y. (1996) 'Did Japan Ever Suffer from a Shortage of Natural Resources Before World War II?', *Journal of Economic History*, Vol. 56, No. 3.

Japanese articles

Akita, H. and Kagotani, N. (eds) (2001) *1930-nendai no Ajia Kokusai Keizai Chitsujo* (International Order of Asia in the 1930s), Hiroshima: Keisuisha.

Inoue, T. (1994) *KiKi no naka no Kyocho Gaiko* (Cooperative Diplomacy in the Crisis), Tokyo: Yamakawa-Shuppansha.

Kagotani, N. (2000) *Ajia Kokusai Tsusho Chitsujo to Kindai Nihon* (International Commercial Order in Asia and Modern Japan), Nagoya: Nagoya daigaku shuppankai.

Kano, K. (1995) 'Kokusai boeki kara mita 20 seiki tonan ajia shokuminchi keizai', (The 20th-Century Southeast Asian Colonial Economy Seen from the Perspective of International Trade), *Rekishi Hyoron*, No. 539.

Kato, Y. (1993) *Mosaku suru 1930-nendai* (The 1930s of Japan's group), Tokyo: Yamakawa shuppansha.

Matsumoto, T. (1996) 'Senzenki nihon no Boeki to Soshikikan Kankei' (Trade Structure in Pre-war Japan and the World Trade), in Matsumoto (ed.) *Senzenki Nihon no Boeki to Soshikikan Kankei* (Trade and Inter-organisational Relations in Pre-war Japan), Shin-Hyoron.

Mukai, H. (1979) 'Ajia no boeki kozo to kokusai shushi' (Trade Structures and Balances of Payments in Asia), in Ono, K. and Yoshinobu, S. (eds) *Ryotaisenkanki no Ajia to Nihon* (Asia and Japan in the Interwar Period), Tokyo: Ohtsuki shoten.

Nawa, T. (1937) *Nihon Bosekigyo to Gemmen Mondai Kenkyu* (Studies of Japanese Spinning Industry and Raw Cotton Problems), Osaka: Daido Shoin.

Saito, O. (1991) 'Ajia no umi to Ajia ni se o muketa hatten shiko' (Asian Sea and Japan's Orientation to Develop with Her Back to Asia), in Hamashita, T. and Kawakatsu, H. (eds) *Ajia Koekiken to Nihon Kogyoka* (Asian Trading Sphere and Japanese Industrialisation), Tokyo: Fujiwara shoten.

Shirakizawa, A. (1999) *Daikyokoki Nihon no Tsusho Mondai* (The Commerce Problems of Japan in the Great Depression), Tokyo: Ochanomizu shobo.

Takamitsu, Y. (1996) '1930-nendai: Antei eno Mosaku ni okeru Amerika gaiko' (American diplomacy in search for Stability: 1934–37) *Hitotsubashi Ronso*, Vol. 116, No. 1.

Ueyama, K. (1994) 'Tsusho masatsu ni okeru tairitsu to dakyo (Conflicts and Compromises in Trade Frictions), in Ueyama, K. and Sakata, Y. (eds), *Tairitsu to Dakyo* (Conflicts and Compromises), Daiichi Hoki.

Yomoda, M. (2003) 'Takakuteki boeki kessaimo no henshitsu to Ajia keizai' (Changes in Multilateral Trade Settlement Network and Asian Economy) in Kawakatsu, H. (ed.) *Ajia Taiheiyo Keizaiken-shi* (History of Asia-Pacific Economic Sphere), Tokyo: Fujiwara shoten.

Yoshihara, T. (1986) 'Senkanki nihon no tai "nampo" boeki kinyu no kozo' (The Structure of Trade Finance with Southeast Asia in the Interwar Japan), in Shimizu, H. (ed.) *Ryotaisenkanki Nihon-Tonan Ajia Kankei no Shoso* (Some Aspects of Relations between Japan and Southeast Asia in the Interwar Period), Tokyo: Ajia Keizai Kenkyujo.

12 Inter-Asian competition for the British market in cotton textiles

The political economy of Anglo-Asian cartels, *c.*1932–60

David Clayton

Entrepreneurs and firms compete. They respond to price signals and innovate to generate profits. But they also alter price signals to generate income (in the form of 'rent'), without using resources more productively. Non-commercial strategies often require collusion and can take the form of cartel agreements to restrict output and control prices. Cartels not only undermine welfare and efficiency but can also reduce the social costs of re-allocating resources and are commonly employed by entrepreneurs and firms during cyclical down turns. Historically, they have been easier to implement, cheaper to run and longer lasting where production has been concentrated in fewer hands, and where demand has been stable. Consequently, they have not been common in the cotton textiles trade, a cyclical one, undertaken by many small units of production and distribution, operating from many different locations. As scholars have shown, national cartels have also been more prevalent than international ones (Barbetzat (1990); Wurm (1993)).

This chapter builds on recent work to show how the British cotton textile industry negotiated agreements with the industries of India, Pakistan and Hong Kong to restrict imports into the United Kingdom (Aggarwal (1985); Singleton (1991)). The industry expended a significant amount of resources on these 'rent-seeking' strategies. From the summer of 1956 until the autumn of 1959, it conducted a series of unilateral talks in Asia. The final agreements put limits on imports of cotton piece goods (finished and unfinished) and set ceilings on imports of 'made-up' goods. They were scheduled to last three years, but throughout the 1960s and 1970s, further rounds of negotiations renewed and revised the agreements. These 'voluntary export restraint' (VER) agreements were tools to manage the transfer of comparative advantage from West to East. For British governments, they were a good substitute for other forms of protection – tariffs or quotas. Politicians encouraged industrialists to negotiate them and used the coercive powers of the state to secure agreements. By studying the implementation of Anglo-Asian VERs, we can understand how the British state and business interests responded to Asian industrialisation.

Imperialism and protectionism

On average and over the long term, freer trading conditions generate higher levels of economic growth and equity. In the short term, however, individual countries can benefit from protection, as the policy insulates economies from exogenous shocks and aids 'supply-side' changes. Historically protectionism has been common because states and rent-seeking coalitions want to reap these short-term gains (Williamson and O'Rourke (1999)). From a political perspective, free trade is more likely when either a strong hegemonic economic power or strong coalitions of powers resist 'rent-seeking' behaviour and act as 'buyers and lenders of last resort'. In the nineteenth century, the British Empire, took on these institutional roles, and post-1945, the world moved to freer trade guided by powerful institutions, particularly The General Agreement on Tariffs and Trade (GATT), which was backed by US administrations. Nevertheless, for many parts of the developing world there was an alternative narrative, as many western markets were restricted to low-cost producers from the Third World.

Protectionism in textiles and clothing was particularly damaging to low-income countries, hampering export-orientated industrialisation. A variety of shields were employed across the developed world to protect these industries: in Western Europe, quotas, in America and the United Kingdom, VER agreements (Singleton (1997), pp. 165–86). (Given the price differential between low-cost producers in the developing world, tariffs were of little use.) Quotas and VER agreements distorted the operation of the market and ossified existing patterns of trade. Moreover, as protectionism was a tool of western foreign policy, it also had a very uneven impact. Many countries were not members of the GATT so could be easily discriminated against, while quotas and VERs were often not subject to 'Most Favoured Nation' criteria. During the 1960s and 1970s, the rules of the GATT were amended to codify and extend such non-price discrimination. Some studies have suggested that for geo-strategic reasons, western governments positively discriminated in favour of non-communist states such as Taiwan, South Korea, Singapore, Hong Kong and Japan (Chiu (1995)).

Britain's pattern of trade discrimination against developing countries was shaped by its imperial policy. In the twentieth century, the British Empire adopted discriminatory commercial policies. In 1932 at the Ottawa Conference, Commonwealth countries codified and extended a system, which provided preference for British goods; this was based on the *quid pro quo* of exemption from the 10 per cent general *ad valorem* duty imposed by the British Import Duties Act (1932) (Drummond (1974); Meredith (1975)). This new protectionist British Empire created 'soft markets' for British industrialists, which may have undermined British competitiveness, but there is little hard evidence to support the case (Macdougall and Hutt (1964)). Cain and Hopkins even suggest that imperial policy promoted financial rather than industrial interests (Cain and Hopkins (1993)).

Attempts by Lancashire industrialists to use the empire to stifle Asian competition in cotton textiles have a long history, dating back to when British 'gun boat' diplomacy opened up markets. In the twentieth century, such political strategies again came to the fore (Clarke (1972); Marrison (1996)). By the inter-war period, the industry was heavily dependent on contracting demand in overseas markets, especially in low-income ones in the Commonwealth and colonies, a structural problem compounded by a severe cyclical downturn. British entrepreneurs may also have been less efficient than competitors due to long-standing supply-side constraints acting on firms (Lazonick (1983)). The 1932 Import Duties Act provided protection in domestic and colonial markets, but the tariffs were not high enough to protect the industry from producers based in Japan and China (including Hong Kong), which were beginning to sell to low-income consumers in Asia and Africa.

From 1932, British producers of light industrial products continued to expend resources lobbying for further protectionism. They were led by the cotton textile industry, which employed large numbers of people in Lancashire and had a strong bargaining position because National and Conservative governments held numerous parliamentary seats in Lancashire, many with narrow majorities. To have a better chance of holding on to power, these governments knew they needed to meet the demands of cotton textile industrialists. There were, however, strong counter arguments. Further protection against low-cost producers in developing countries had international repercussions, hurt consumers at home and in the colonies and would not necessarily encourage the industry to undertake supply-side reforms, perceived to be necessary if the industry was to survive long term without state subsidies; it might also set a 'bad' precedent for other industries faced by competition from low-cost producers overseas. Moreover, until the later 1950s, the main demand-side problem faced by the industry was the decline of exports, much more difficult for the government to arrest.

Rose has suggested that the British cotton textile industry did not gain as much protection as its counterpart in the United States, because, with 'power' lying with the executive (rather than with parliament), British governments were less responsive to the demands of industrialists, whose ability to 'rent-seek' was hampered by its reliance on networks as a mode of organisation (Rose (1997), (2000)). Certainly, as indicated later, British governments were much more likely to grant concessions to the cotton textile industry before elections (hence 1955 and 1958–59), and even at such times ministers had to overcome strong resistance from bureaucrats. But the archival evidence shows that the industry had the direct ear of ministers, including the Prime Minister and Chancellor as well as the President of the Board of Trade. Another factor need to be considered, as the structure of international politics explains why the government protected the industry from Japanese and Chinese competition but not from exports from India, Pakistan and Hong Kong, an imperial gap in Britain's protective shield.

In the early 1930s, the British government persuaded the British cotton textile industry to try and negotiate a cartel arrangement with Japanese producers. The government was reluctant to overtly protect British and colonial markets against Japanese exports, fearing it might damage Anglo-Japanese relations and undermine the welfare of colonial subjects. These Anglo-Japanese negotiations came to nothing and in 1934, the government instructed the colonies to introduce quotas on Japanese textile piece goods, based on average exports between 1927 and 1931, a period when Japan had not fully penetrated colonial markets. Thereafter, however, colonial consumers bought from domestic suppliers or from other low-cost colonial exporters – particularly those in Hong Kong – rather than from British producers (Miners (2002)). These controls did not even have a severe impact on the Japanese industry, as most of Japan's trade was with non-colonial markets in Asia (Sugihara (1986), (1990), (1998)).

In the post-war period, the British cotton textile industry continued to work in tandem with the government to restrain Japanese competition (Yokoi (2003)). The government introduced stringent quotas on Japanese imports to the British market and persuaded colonial governments to do the same (as a means of managing sterling balances and to promote British textile exports). In addition, British governments lobbied to delay Japan's entry into the GATT, a body, which at least in theory prevented such discriminatory action against individual countries. When Japan did become a member of the Treaty, Britain (and other powers) ensured that Japan gained a 'Most Favoured Nation' status with conditions attached. The Board of Trade and the Treasury easily circumvented Foreign Office concern about the impact of these policies on Anglo-Japanese and Anglo-American relations. As in the pre-war period, it is doubtful, however, whether this piecemeal protection seriously affected the pattern of world trade in cotton textiles. Japan quickly regained its status as the world's largest exporter, penetrating a large range of markets outside the British Empire; the British industry continued to decline.

In 1958, the government also introduced a stringent quota on imports of Chinese cotton textiles, mainly to strengthen the negotiating hand of delegations from Lancashire, who by then were trying to secure VERs with Indian, Pakistan and Hong Kong industrialists (Clayton (2000)). The international repercussions of this commercial policy were not significant; Sino-British relations were already poor and Communist China was not a member of the GATT. In the 1960s, Britain also imposed quotas on import of cotton textiles from other countries, particularly those from Taiwan and southern Europe. Once quotas were introduced, industrialists argued that precedents had been set, and that, without further unilateral measures, exporters could simply divert goods through other economies: piece-meal protection begat more piece-meal protection.

It was much more difficult, however, for British governments to introduce quotas on exports from India, Pakistan and Hong Kong, parts of the British Empire, or former parts of it. Important issues for imperial policy were at stake. Industrialisation in the British Empire in Asia broke down a long-standing 'Ricardian' division of labour between an industrialised (British) core and a primary producing (imperial) periphery. In the inter-war period, an inter-departmental committee was appointed to report on this new pattern of trade, which was beginning to emerge in the cotton textile, garment and footwear trades (Miners (2002)). The committee found that exports to Dominion markets of light manufactures made by oriental labour were 'evil'. But it ruled out protection as a solution. Instead, in order to alleviate some of the perceived problems of this trade and perhaps more importantly to pacify industrial lobbyists at home, the British government adopted three tactics: it encouraged industries to negotiate voluntary inter-industry agreements to restrict colonial exports; it encouraged colonies to improve labour laws to stop 'unfair competition'; and finally, it imposed tighter bureaucratic controls to ensure that exports from the colonies comprised goods made mainly in the Empire, a regulation to prevent colonies merely re-exporting non-colonial goods to circumvent tariff and quotas protection. The success of these non-price bureaucratic impediments to trade is questionable. Chinese industrialists in Hong Kong could, at least before the 1950s when measures were tightened, easily circumvent controls (Mills (1942), pp. 453–8). This policy remained unchanged until the outbreak of the war, when to manage chronic balance of payments problems, import quotas were introduced on a wide range of imports from the colonies. When these restrictions were removed at the end of the 1940s, as part of a wider post-war strategy of liberalising British external trade, the pre-war pattern of Britain–Asian empire trade re-emerged (Milward and Brennan (1996)).

From the late 1940s, British industrialists once again lobbied for changes to British policy. The British cotton textile industry needed to protect demand because, after an initial post-war export boom, the industry became increasingly reliant on domestic demand and on consumers in a limited number of Commonwealth markets in Australia and Africa. In all these markets, industrialists in Lancashire faced severe competition from low-cost Asian producers. From the mid-1950s onwards, it became increasingly evident to politicians, bureaucrats and industrialists that only high barriers to trade would ensure that a sizeable proportion of the industry survived. The Board of Trade estimated that low-cost imports had gained 10 per cent of the home market in 1956, rising rapidly to 18 per cent in 1957.[1] Most of these imports came from the Asian Commonwealth. Rose estimates that from the mid- to late-1950s 60–80 per cent of British imports of cotton textiles came from India, Pakistan and Hong Kong, and that by the end of the decade they met nearly 25 per cent of domestic consumption (Rose (2000), pp. 255–9).

Within Whitehall departments, officials were highly sceptical about the economics of protection. Despite government subsidies available in the late 1940s, the industry had not rationalised, hence there were doubts within the Treasury and Board of Trade whether the industry would reduce costs if afforded protection. Higher levels of protection for cotton textiles would also have increased demands from other light industrial manufacturers for state support. Protection was debated frequently at a Cabinet level, and some marked conflicts emerged. In 1955, the President of the Board of Trade, Peter Thorneycroft, ruled out further protection, but argued that the Purchase Tax on cotton textiles should be reduced to stimulate demand for cotton textiles. In response, 'Rab' Butler, the Chancellor of the Exchequer, despite long-standing Treasury opposition to protection for cotton textiles, argued that a quota was preferable to altering the Purchase Tax, which would reduce government revenue and stoke inflation.[2] The Treasury lost the battle and soon reverted to a more liberal stance. It found strong allies in the Colonial Office and the Commonwealth Relations Office. During the late 1950s, these bureaucratic divides remained in place: the Board of Trade was in favour of protection (with conditions attached), the Treasury, the Colonial Office and the Commonwealth Relations Office were against. The Prime Minister,

Harold Macmillan, was more sympathetic to industrial (and hence party–political) demands.

As time wore on, the potential political costs of not providing the industry with further protection became too high to bear. During the 1950s, the Cotton Board, a quasi-public industrial board, which had replaced the Manchester Chamber of Commerce as the main collective voice for the industry, lobbied hard for more protection. The Board, hampered by marked sectional divides, adopted cautious, conciliatory tactics. Its ability to influence ministers fluctuated closely with the electoral cycle. Conservative governments, under Anthony Eden and Harold Macmillan were aware that if cotton textile entrepreneurs embarked on a public campaign criticising government policy, marginal seats in Lancashire, and thus perhaps power, would be lost. In 1955, there were nine Conservative seats with majorities of less than 3,000; in 1958, it was estimated that if VER agreements were not secured before the election then the government would lose seats in Preston (two), Darwin, Bolton, Oldham, Bury, Middleton, Clitheroe and perhaps even in Manchester and Cheshire.[3] Lancashire-based politicians (Members of Parliament, Lords and councillors), trade unionists and industrialists all warned the Conservative Party of the risks it was incurring.[4] These were heightened because the opposition Labour Party had, in collaboration with the unions, publicly promised that if elected, it would use quotas to restrict imports from the Asian Commonwealth.

The upshot of these political pressures was a government-sponsored scheme to rationalise the industry, to be introduced from 1959 (Miles (1968); Higgins and Toms (2000)). This provided a strong incentive to extend and reinforce barriers of entry into the British market, especially as industrialists and trade unionists were making it clear to government ministers that they would not collaborate unless the domestic market was fully protected. As chronicled later, these political pressures caused the British government to coerce industrialists within the Asian Commonwealth into 'voluntary' agreements, restricting their exports to Britain.

Why did governments not act earlier? And, why did they not use quotas – a much more immediate and effective shield than VERS – against all Asian exporters? The answers lie in the complex politics of decolonisation.

Conservative governments in the 1950s believed that if they protected British markets from Asian Commonwealth imports, the matrix of agreements, which Britain had negotiated with the Commonwealth to provide mutually beneficial protection from 'foreign' competitors would collapse. By the 1950s, these agreements were, however, less important economically than politically. During the 1950s, the system of Imperial Preference became economically moribund. The GATT precluded Britain from increasing any margin or preference, and thereafter inflation gradually eroded the level of protection. The pattern of world trade was also changing, with demand for industrial exports expanding fastest in high-income 'foreign' markets in Europe and North America. By the mid-1950s, the Board of Trade noted that there was 'now little dynamic life' left in Commonwealth free entry and that 'any significant breach in the system would be likely to touch off a chain reaction leading to its collapse'.[5] Nevertheless, British governments did not want these agreements to end prematurely. The Board of Trade perceived it to be in Britain's economic interests in the short term to 'defer renegotiating the Ottawa agreement as long as possible', given that it yielded 'substantial benefits for our exports', half of which went to Commonwealth markets. More significantly, British diplomats could use the arrangements as bargaining chips to secure concessions when negotiating new trading relations with European nationstates and within the GATT. For political reasons, Britain also had to ensure that entry into European common markets did not jeopardise relations with the Commonwealth and the colonies, as common European barriers to trade might mean Britain discriminated against these economies. Whether inside Europe or out, restrictions imposed by a British government on colonial or Commonwealth imports would seriously weaken Britain's ability to challenge protection by Europeans against low-cost colonial and Commonwealth producers.

Governments were extra cautious because Imperial Preference was perceived to be a highly unstable institution. For example, while it was *legally* possible to introduce quotas (but not tariffs) on Indian textiles without parliamentary approval, a trade governed by the 1939 Anglo-Indian Trade Agreement, *politically* any discrimination would have been against the *spirit* of the agreement.[6] If quotas were imposed, British civil servants predicted that the Indian government would try and re-negotiate the treaty, and Britain, with few concessions to offer Indian exporters, would lose preferences in a market to which Britain exported £100 million in the mid-1950s.[7] Moreover, many Commonwealth members, such as Australia and New Zealand, which allowed British exports preference across the whole range of goods, were by then questioning the value of Imperial Preference; in part because while British preferences were *ad valorem*, many reciprocal preferences were expressed in specific terms and hence were eroded by inflation.[8] The Board of Trade believed Dominion governments would respond to any British trade discrimination against Commonwealth producers by trying to re-negotiate Ottawa agreements.

In July 1956, the Indian and British governments set about encouraging their cotton textile industries to negotiate a VER as a short-term fix to the problem. The British government was reacting to direct pressure from the Federation of British Industries (FBI), which in June 1956 had come out in favour of protecting the cotton textile industry, but without 'disrupting Empire preference'. British industrialists were sharply divided on the issue, with those exporting capital goods to Commonwealth markets willing to accept voluntary restrictions but not government quotas, which might jeopardise Imperial Preference. Sir Graham Hayman, President of the FBI, admitted in private to ministers at the Board of Trade that, although Imperial Preference was a 'wasting asset', it made tactical sense to wait until policy on Europe was 'settled' before reforming imperial economic relations: Imperial Preference was, he argued, 'one of the best cards we had to play in negotiations with Europe.[9] This policy position was re-affirmed two years later at the Commonwealth Economic Conference, at which the 'market disruption' caused by low-cost Asian exports was a key subject for debate. The basic principles of Commonwealth freer trade were up-held, but the conference agreed that when 'exports threaten to disrupt an established industry in the importing country, solution should be sought through consultation between industries concerned'.[10] The conference adopted British government policy: industrialists and not the state would manage 'market disruption'.

Unfortunately, VER negotiations between Indian and British textile industrialists proved extremely problematic. The Indians wanted Hong Kong included in any cartel, which posed a different set of issues for policy makers. The Indian government coerced its industrialists into an agreement, but a quick settlement proved illusive because the colonial government in Hong Kong – supported by the Colonial Office – refused to put pressure on Chinese textile interests. As described later, only when VER negotiations between industrialists from Lancashire and Hong Kong looked like collapsing completely did the British government use its coercive power to secure a deal. This tactical shift caused marked intra-government disagreements and damaged relations between Britain and Hong Kong.

There was no statutory bar on imposing quotas on colonial imports, but the government had informed the colonies that the government had no intention of altering the duty-free status of their exports; it did so first informally and in a piecemeal fashion, and then formally and publicly in 1958, when the Import Duties Act was being debated in Parliament and at the Commonwealth Economic Conference.[11] British civil servants argued that if Britain was to impose quotas on colonial imports, British ministers could no longer object to individual countries – notably Germany, France and the United states – and European powers acting collectively protecting their markets from imports from British colonies. The Colonial Office argued that this was 'an absolutely fundamental point of principle'.[12] A Board of Trade paper noted that protection imposed on colonial exports would 'destroy the whole economic and political relationship between the United Kingdom and the Colonial territories and this would be too high a price to pay for protection'; it would also make it very difficult for Britain to hold on to the waiver in the GATT, allowing Britain to treat a colony as part of the United Kingdom.[13] (The withdrawal of duty free entry would also make it difficult to use import duties for balance of payments reasons, as the colonies would be much more reluctant to collaborate with Britain.) In 1958, a Board of Trade paper confirmed that 'we are particularly concerned not to apply restrictions against Hong Kong', as 'any restrictions will be regarded by the world as colonialism, ie a restriction imposed on Hong Kong taking advantage of the fact that Hong Kong, because of her colonial status has no GATT rights against us'.[14]

These arguments were given weight by some moral, financial and economic factors specific to the Hong Kong case. There was a feeling across Whitehall that, as it had been a western economic embargo on Communist China, which had damaged the entrepôt trade of the colony and made it dependent on industrial exports, there were humanitarian reasons for not further discriminating against the Hong Kong economy.[15] For Treasury officials, these humanitarian issues ultimately manifested themselves as a potential drain on fiscal resources. They were aware that the British government might need 'to meet the budgetary cost of sustaining a million refugees in an idleness which could have social repercussions'.[16] The bargaining position of Hong Kong was given a further boost by a timely cost-benefit analysis of Hong Kong undertaken in 1957, which concluded that overall Britain gained economically and strategically from holding on to the colony.[17] (A weakening of economic ties between Britain and Hong Kong could potentially have strengthened anti-colonial movements, but, as the alternative to British rule was controlled by Communist China, the politics of decolonisation were complex in Hong Kong.)

Inter-industry negotiations: a chronology

Phase one: July 1956 to May 1957

In 1956, Raymond Streat, Chairman of the Cotton Board, suggested that the government approach Nehru, the Indian Prime Minister about a voluntary agreement.[18] Peter Thorneycroft, the President of the Board of Trade, supported the initiative as it would 'not commit the Government' and not have a significant impact on the commercial treaty with India.[19] When Eden put this idea to Nehru, he approved of it and arranged for Indian industrialists to talk to a delegation from Lancashire. By January 1957, an Anglo-India understanding had been reached. For three years (1957–60) imports of all cotton manufactures (piece goods and 'made-ups') would be limited to 140 million square yards (henceforth msy) per year. The deal, however, was subject to a similar agreement being struck with the industries of Pakistan and Hong Kong.[20]

As even voluntary restrictions on colonial trade jeopardised colonial industrialisation, the British government decided (despite strong resistance from the Hong Kong government and the Colonial Office) to encourage talks, but not to coerce colonial industrialists into an agreement.[21] Inter-industry talks in Hong Kong began early in 1957 but soon broke down. An agreement was reached with one of the many trade associations representing textile interests in Hong Kong, but Chinese manufacturers soon pulled out of it, having thought the delegation from Lancashire was offering them a guaranteed (not a maximum) level of imports.[22] As Hong Kong's industrialists had indicated that they might be more sympathetic if Pakistan exports were restricted, in May 1957 Anglo-Pakistan talks started. These quickly ended when the Hong Kong Cotton Spinners' Association publicly announced that it would not accept any voluntary restrictions on Hong Kong exports.[23] According to the Hong Kong government, cotton spinners in the colony had decided that an agreement including made-ups would be impossible to implement because the garment trade comprised a large number of small producers, who were not organised into strong trade associations. The prospects for a deal looked bleak. Pakistan's industrialists said they would not agree to unilateral restrictions, but would accept a common multilateral ceiling for all Commonwealth imports, to allow its nascent industry to expand.

Phase two: May 1957 to March 1958

The government's strategy to 'put the whole burden on Lancashire to persuade [*sic*] the Hong Kong industry to take part in the discussions' had failed, the problem being that: 'no one seems to worry about the possibility of the UK Government, or the industry itself, being able to impose its will on the Hong Kong textile industry'.[24] After talks had stalled, Lancashire industrialists demanded a government statement approving 'voluntary' restrictions on Hong Kong exports. Instead of issuing one, the Cabinet investigated the possibility of a 'peril point' on Hong Kong exports, an idea first suggested by Alexander Grantham, the Governor of Hong Kong, who remained opposed to constraints on colonial industrialisation.[25]

The 'peril point' was a ceiling figure, set by industrialists in India, Pakistan and the United Kingdom (but not Hong Kong) to secure VERs on Anglo-Indian–Pakistan trade and encourage (informally) Hong Kong to curtail the growth of exports.[26] The scheme, however, had many drawbacks and British industrialists, for one, thought the plan unworkable.[27] Given that textile industrialists in Britain and India could not sanction the growth of Hong Kong exports at a high rate, a peril point would soon be exceeded and Anglo-Indian–Pakistan VERs would collapse. Such a course of events would only intensify pressure on the government for quotas on Commonwealth trade.[28] The British government also had the 'greatest difficulty' in setting a viable figure[29]. Even if opposition within the Colonial Office could be circumvented, what figure would the government choose? The Hong Kong government suggested a total ceiling of 121 million square yards (msy) (85 msy for piece goods and 36 msy of cloth equivalent for made-ups); the Board of Trade was thinking in terms of 320 msy of imports in total for India, Pakistan and Hong Kong.[30] In any case, the whole premise was not sound: an informal quota on Hong Kong exports needed to be publicised if it was to restrain Hong Kong exporters, but this was not politically feasible.

The general issue of how to enforce VERs was a vexed one for policy makers. The British industry wanted the government to police them, as self-regulation was perceived to be costly and not watertight: an estimated 30 per cent of merchants would ignore a voluntary scheme, and consequently loyal merchants might not have signed up for one. The Board of Trade was generally in favour of using licences to police VERs, but the Colonial Office and Commonwealth Relations Office were against state involvement. In March 1957, the Cabinet sided with the Board of Trade position, agreeing that the government would eventually monitor agreements. For the first 12 months of any voluntary arrangements, however, the private sector would, for political reasons, police arrangements. At this stage the British and Hong Kong governments were still divided on the issue: the Colonial Secretary was opposed to policing from the United Kingdom; the Hong Kong government refused to licence exports from the colony.[31] (Industrialists in Hong Kong opposed policing from the United Kingdom, as 'quota holders would be able to play off suppliers, one against another, and break down prices to uneconomic levels'.[32]) Eventually, the colonial government was forced to change its position, part of a more systematic effort by the British state to alter prevailing attitudes in Hong Kong during phase three of the negotiations.

In July 1957, David Eccles, the President of the Board of Trade, gained Cabinet approval to press for a resumption of inter-industry talks between Lancashire and Hong Kong.[33] Harold Macmillan, the Prime Minister, was influential. He stated that

> In my view, it does not really much matter how high the quota is so long as some ceiling can be given to the Lancashire textile industry. It is bad enough to have lost the foreign market, it is pretty rough to lose the home market too.[34]

As the UK trade commissioner in Hong Kong continued to report that without diplomatic pressure from the United Kingdom, there was no chance of an Anglo-Hong Kong agreement, Macmillan got the Colonial Secretary to inform the Governor of Hong Kong that a VER was a 'sheet-anchor' to maintain Imperial Preference and hence in the colony's interests.[35] As precursors to a further visit by Cotton Board delegates to Hong Kong, Grantham was instructed to bring together a group of Hong Kong industrialists and to establish the 'essential margin' for Hong Kong exports.[36]

This governmental shift provided some shaky foundations for further talks between Lancashire, India and Pakistan, needed because by then provisional figures agreed by industrialists early in 1957 were out of date. Businessmen in India and Pakistan, however, now aware that Hong Kong's industrialists would hold out for a high quota, were intent on hard bargaining. By late 1957, the position of the Indian industry had also deteriorated; the volume of exports had fallen and an estimated 90 per cent of mills were making losses.[37] Pakistan industrialists, who believed the Indian industry had been 'disingenous' in ruling out tri-partite talks, demanded a quota of 40 msy, a figure way beyond what was acceptable to Lancashire or Indian producers.[38]

Consequently, negotiations to get Asian industrialists to reduce their demands were drawn out, forcing the Board of Trade to throw its weight behind Lancashire.[39] Trade commissioners in Asia collected information for UK industrialists and covertly put pressure on South Asian industrialists, including Nazir A. Sheikh, one of the 'leading businessmen in Lahore', and Kasturbhai Laibhai, the first president of the Indian Cotton Mill owners Association.[40] When Laibhai indicated that only the Indian government could force the industry into an agreement, Macmillan lent a diplomatic hand. He met with the Prime Minister of Pakistan and Indian Minister of Commerce and Industry.[41] He informed the Pakistan government that if there was a voluntary agreement, then the 'government would do their utmost by all means short of compulsion' to 'fix a figure' for Hong Kong exports.[42] The Board of Trade, however, was sceptical whether this intervention would secure agreements. Given the prevailing attitude of Hong Kong's industrialists, it believed politicians and businessmen in the sub-continent had to be told exactly how Britain could coerce Hong Kong into an agreement, and so set about formulating strategies to that end.[43]

Phrase three: March 1958 to December 1958

From mid-1958, Macmillan became more personally involved, resolving differences within Whitehall and meeting with and making speeches to industrialists and politicians in the United Kingdom and overseas.[44] In March, he persuaded Cotton Board leaders, ready to pull out of talks, to keep working for VERs and to refrain from publicly campaigning from protection.[45] By 1958, he had accepted that the industry needed a period of respite during which it could contract and diversify.[46] In October, when renewed negotiations stalled, he spoke at the Cotton Board annual conference, and according to one source stopped Board members pulling out of talks altogether.[47]

The most visible manifestation of the new approach was a visit to Hong Kong in March 1958 by Frank Lee, the permanent under-secretary at the Board of Trade. Lee talked to Chinese industrialists, colonial officials – who were now 'on-side' – and to prominent members of the ex-patriate business community.[48] He informed them that while the present British government would not sanction the use of quotas on Hong Kong, the Labour Party, if elected, would.[49] Lee, however, made a tactical blunder, limiting his discussion to grey cloth, not finished cloth and made-ups, and in the end failed to solicit any ceiling figure: Hong Kong industrialists were demanding a quota on piece goods between 75 and 120 msy; Lancashire wanted 65. Lee encountered serious divisions within the Hong Kong business community: he reported that while the spinners wanted an agreement to stop 'future trouble', the Chinese Manufacturers' Association was opposed to one.[50] He believed that there was a 'limit to which anyone can press these divided and unhappy men into accepting voluntary agreements and I fear we may have reached it': a Chinese industrialist told him that if he had to make a choice between 'murder' and 'suicide' he would opt for 'murder'.[51]

Despite such pessimism, Lee's visit laid the foundations for a further round of inter-industry talks. In May 1958, trilateral talks between Lancashire, India and Pakistan began, and in July, they culminated in another provisional (and conditional) agreement. India agreed to a three year quota of 140 msy; this included made-ups and represented an 8 per cent increase over imports in 1957; Pakistan eventually agreed to a quota of 30 msy;[52] they were less concerned than the Indians about including finished piece goods and made-ups but initially insisted on a high quota, of between 50 and 60 msy.[53] In order to secure a provisional agreement, British and Pakistan governments brokered a deal, whereby the Liverpool Cotton Association agreed to buy more raw cotton from Pakistan as a *quid pro quo* for a lower quota.[54]

Although Lee's visit had generated much 'good will' in Hong Kong business circles, once talks between Lancashire and Hong Kong began in September 1958, differences between the UK and Hong Kong industries over the level and composition of a quota became apparent.[55] Hong Kong's industrialists insisted on a quota, 50 per cent greater than the imports in 1957, a rate of growth unacceptable to any of the other parties; Lancashire industrialists wanted a comprehensive agreement, including finished piece goods and made-ups, but for Hong Kong industrialists, such a deal was unworkable and unrealistic: it prevented Hong Kong entrepreneurs developing a more sophisticated production cycle and set a bad precedent for other overseas markets – especially in the United States, where garment manufacturers were demanding protection from Hong Kong exports.[56] At the time, there was also growing concern in the United Kingdom over the rise of garment imports from Hong Kong. Trade associations representing clothing manufacturers pressurised the government for restrictions, estimating that Hong Kong imports had reached 5 per cent of domestic production. Imports had penetrated deeper in certain sectors such as gloves and mens' shirts and Hong Kong's manufacturers were improving the quality of their goods, and were no longer just competing on price. The real concern was dumping: they believed that if some of the colony's other markets became protected then imports might rise to 15 per cent.[57] As there was no evidence of market 'disruption', the government would not how-ever support their case, especially as this was neither a strategically or politically important sector. Consequently, clothing manufacturers needed the Cotton Board to take up their fight.[58]

A. Lennox-Boyd, Secretary of State for the Colonies, and Robert Black, the Governor, were opposed to a deal including made-ups, or finished cloth. Black argued that if he supported the inclusion of made-ups in any VER his 'usefulness as a Governor would be terminated', as industrialists and 'unofficials' (un-elected representatives of the community sitting on the executive and legislative councils) would lose all confidence in him.[59] 'The Board of Trade was increasingly frus-trated by their attitudes. Lee argued that the Hong Kong government needed 'to abandon a position of "sea-green incorruptibility" in the ivory tower'. By July, he was 'tempted' to propose a temporary quota on Hong Kong imports to force industrialists to the negotiating table.[60] An intervention by Macmillan was needed, and, in July, he instructed the Governor that the Hong Kong industry had to be persuaded 'to negotiate for "made-ups"', as a comprehensive three-year deal would have 'the effect of taking this whole issue out of politics'.[61]

This new hard-line attitude was also evident when inter-industry talks in Hong Kong commenced. Black and John Cowperthwaite, the influential Financial Secretary, tried to persuade Hong Kong's industrialists that a settlement was in the general interest of the colony; when talks stalled, Macmillan reminded them that if there was no VER the Labour Government would in any case introduce quotas, a course making it 'difficult' for the United Kingdom to 'support' Hong Kong in the GATT and 'elsewhere'.[62] Behind the scenes, he informed his Cabinet colleagues that they 'would need to consider in the very near future whether, if agreement proved impossible, they would sacrifice the interests of the British industry to the maintenance of our traditional policy as regards colonial trade'.[63]

British ministers also began to circumvent the colonial administration, persuading prominent London-based members of Hong Kong's ex-patriate business community to campaign for a VER. The Board of Trade had long nurtured contacts with John Keswick (Jardine Matheson) and Arthur Morse (the Hong Kong and Shanghai Banking Corporation). These influential figures subsequently pressed 'their friends' in Hong Kong and advised Lord Rochdale (Chairman of the Cotton Board) to try and win over both Lawrence Kadoorie and George Marden, who had financial inter-ests in 'Chinese' textile enterprises. Marden was perceived to be the 'most powerful single figure "behind the scenes"', but, as he was not "controlled" by any 'London interests' and often 'quite unscrupulous', officials at the Board of Trade were scep-tical whether he would broker a settlement.[64] Macmillan also persuaded C.F. Cobbald, the Governor of the Bank of England, to use his good offices with 'some of the most prominent City people with Hong Kong interests'.[65]

The upshot of these informal links was a request made by J.D. Clague, head of the Hong Kong Textile Negotiating Committee, for a £10–15 million loan, a *quid pro quo*, to be used to restructure the Hong Kong textile sector. Treasury officials thought such a loan would not have the 'desired effect', was 'out of scale' compared to other colonial development loans and would set a bad precedent, and noted that 'the encouragement of new industry in Hong Kong might create new problems of low-cost competition for UK industry'.[66] Evidently, industrialisation had altered an imperial political economy, whereby capital was exported from London on the understanding that British and other empire markets would be kept open to colonial exporters to allow the loans to be paid off. Cobbald (Bank of England) however did offer some informal assistance, promising Morse that 'if an agreement were reached which created difficulties for Hong Kong, His Majesties Government would do all in their power to assist'.[67]

In December 1958, concessions from both sides eventually produced a settlement. The Cotton Board accepted a higher quota – 164 msy of cloth equivalent. Hong Kong agreed that certain made-ups would be restricted, by an informal hidden ceiling. The voluntary agreement was to be policed (for political reasons) by the Hong Kong government, with the Board of Trade providing technical support.[68]

Phase four: January–October 1959

From February until the end of September 1959, there was a further round of negotiations between Lancashire, Indian and Pakistan producers. Due to the hard bargaining by Hong Kong industrialists, the long-standing provisional Indo-British– Pakistan agreements had to be scrapped. Negotiations to secure new ones lasted from February until October, during which time the Cotton Board had to increase an original (improved) offer of 150–175 msy to secure an agreement.[69]

From February until June, the prospects of an agreement looked slim. Despite two rounds of inter-industry talks in London, Indian producers were highly reluctant even to start bargaining, failing to provide either Lancashire delegates or their own politicians with realistic revised figures, as a starting point for negotiations.[70] Lalbhai was intransigent. Despite doubts over whether the Indian industry could even raise output to meet the existing provisional quota (140 msy), he demanded a new quota of 250 msy, based on the same percentage increase granted to Hong Kong. He argued that the deal Lancashire had struck with Hong Kong had 'completely destroyed the basis' of the Anglo-Indian agreement.[71] He made it clear that he would only agree if forced to by the Indian government.[72] Unlike previous rounds of negotiations, the Cotton Board was not provided with detailed information from the Indian government (sent via Board of Trade representatives) on the level of quotas Indian delegates were likely to accept. Consequently, during talks the Cotton Board refused to revise its figures, fearing that if talks broke down, it would merely have set a new base level for subsequent ones.

At home, these delays increased pressure from industrialists in Lancashire to end negotiations, especially given that parliament was by then discussing a package of measures to rationalise the cotton textile industry. Furthermore, during August, it also looked as if even the agreement signed with Hong Kong would collapse, when industrialists in the colony demanded a 'quota holiday' whilst negotiations between India and Lancashire continued; as negotiations in the subcontinent had been so prolonged that imports from Hong Kong had reached their voluntary quotas ceiling and thus orders were increasingly being placed with Indian and Pakistan suppliers. This threat put pressure on industrialists in India and Pakistan to come to an agreement, but it was intervention by the Indian government, which finally secured a settlement. Throughout the negotiations, representatives of the Board of Trade had been in discussion with members of the Indian government and Macmillan had periodically sent messages to Nehru urging a settlement. Once it was clear the Indian government would put pressure on industrialists, the UK government stepped up pressure on the Cotton Board to secure a settlement. Once an Anglo-Indian agreement had been reached, Pakistan industrialists soon agreed to the same proportional increase as granted to India.

Both agreements remained contingent on the continuation of the Anglo-Hong Kong VER, and hence British industrialists soon turned their 'rent-seeking' attentions to re-negotiations in the colony. The British government took an early decision to support them, as it was essential to have VER protection for domestic producers while the state was providing re-equipment grants to the industry.[73] Moreover, as Asian producers were unlikely to agree to further rounds of talks whilst imports increased from new sources, such as Spain, the government began to consider applying new import quotas. As in the mid-1950s, piece-meal protection begat more piece-meal protection.

Inter-industry negotiations: an analysis

Inter-industry negotiations were plagued by co-ordination problems and by conflicts of interest, which, without an early and overt application of state power, were difficult to resolve. Generic problems common to all cartels and some specific historical ones can be discerned.

Only the British industry, whose market share had plummeted, and the Indian industry, whose market share was likely to fall in the future, had incentives to come to an agreement. The cotton textile industry in Pakistan was small and wanted exports to expand; the Hong Kong industry was expanding output at a rapid rate, and was virtually totally dependent on overseas demand, so had to fore-stall protection for as long as possible. Merchants both in the United Kingdom and overseas meanwhile sought to import as many goods as possible before any restrictions were introduced; according to H.A. Angus, the director of the Department of Commerce and Industry in Hong Kong, 'everyone had been making hay when the sun was shining'.[74] Asian producers recognised that this was a key battle, setting precedents for other developed markets. Whilst Hong Kong industrialists were negotiating with delegations from Lancashire, the French government imposed quotas on Hong Kong imports and American garment manufacturers persuaded the American administration to try and secure 'voluntary' restraints on imports from Hong Kong.[75] There was also a further issue in the background: British entry into European free trade blocs. Both the UK and Hong Kong industrialists were aware that European governments were pressing for a rule that goods would only be allowed in duty free if they were at least 50 per cent European made, a proposal which would have made it more difficult for Hong Kong exporters to penetrate British and European markets.

The multilateral form of the agreement caused further difficulties. The British industry had to negotiate bilaterally with each industry in turn; only once, in 1958, did it negotiate simultaneously with delegations from India and Pakistan. Consequently, a frustrating pattern emerged. Two parties would agree a level for future exports, conditional on subsequent agreements with others. But then these parties demanded quotas so high that they jeopardised the initial agreements. The serious time lag between talks, combined with rapid shifts in the scale and direction of trade, made such co-ordination problems worse.

Patterns of industrial organisation in all four locations shaped the way each industry approached the talks. Each delegation represented a range of opinions, which had to be accommodated if a deal was to be effectively implemented (and policed) locally. The Indian industry was based mainly in Bombay and many industrialists were members of the Bombay Mill Owners Association. The Pakistan industry mainly comprised spinning, with very little weaving capacity. The Hong Kong industry, however, was deeply divided along functional and ethnic lines. Most cotton spinners were from Shanghai, ran large, capital-intensive factories and had high sunk costs. Most cotton cloth weavers were Cantonese; and operating a diverse range of large modern and smaller, traditional firms. There were ethnic and economic conflicts between them. Garment makers were highly numerous and usually small scale. Only the spinners had a representative body, which spoke for the whole industry.[76] The 1958 Hong Kong Cotton Textile Negotiating Committee comprised representatives of the Hong Kong Cotton Weavers Manufacturer's Association, the Hong Kong Cotton Weavers' Association, the Hong Kong Cotton Spinners Association, the Chinese Manufacturers' Association and the Hong Kong Exporters Association.

Functional divides within the British industry also made the task of Cotton Board negotiators difficult. Producer groups – spinners and weavers – were in favour of comprehensive agreements, covering made-ups and finished goods. Merchants and finishers, however, who could survive without the same level of protection by processing imported cloth or even buying the finished product, ensured that delegations from Lancashire only negotiated on the basis of retained rather than total imports.[77]

Conclusion

The pattern of British trade discrimination against Asia was shaped by an imperial political economy. In the short term, this gave India, Pakistan and Hong Kong and other parts of the British Empire and Commonwealth, a slight advantage over non-Commonwealth Asian producers of cotton textiles. The British state was not fully insulated from the rent-seeking demands of domestic producers, but international political forces prevented it from acting quickly to protect the British cotton textile industry against all low-cost producers. The resultant negotiations between Asian and Lancashire industrialists to put in place VER arrangements were long drawn out, and governments had to act covertly to implement them.

Acknowledgements

Thanks to participants at seminars at the Universities of York and Glasgow for their comments on preliminary thoughts, some of which were published in 'Free Trade, protection and the British empire in the 1950s: some evidence from a Hong Kong case study', *Discussion Papers in Economics*, 99/10, University of York. Thanks also to John Singleton, Douglas Farnie, Ron Weir and Simon Smith for guidance on sources and orientation.

Notes

1 UK, PRO, BT258/372, 'Brief for the Prime Minister's Commonwealth Tour: Cotton Textiles' (no date or author specified; draft).
2 UK, PRO, Prime Minister Private Office (PREM) 11/2825, letter from 'Rab' Butler to Prime Minister (Eden), 1 March 1955; CAB128/79, 27 April 1955.
3 UK, PRO, PREM11/2825, minute from (Lord) Woolton (Party Chairman) to the Prime Minister (Anthony Eden), 27 January 1955; PREM11/2526, note by Douglas Clover (Chairman of the Conservative Party in the North Western Area) to the Prime Minister (Harold Macmillan), 27 January 1958.
4 For the broad political lobby note, UK, PRO, BT258/373, note of meeting at the Board of Trade, 4 March 1958, with the mayors of Oldham, Todmorden, Bolton, Burnley and Blackburn.
5 UK, PRO, BT/241/294, Board of Trade (henceforth BT) briefing document: 'Commonwealth: Duty Free Entry for Commonwealth Goods: Consideration of Inter-departmental Report', no author specified, 24 May 1956.
6 UK, PRO, BT258/424, minute by M.E. Welch, 17 February 1956; and BT258/377, minute by S.D. Wilks – 'The Legal Position with Regard to Duties on Commonwealth Goods' – 13 August 1958.
7 UK, PRO, PREM11/2825, Brief (prepared 'personally' by the President of the Board of Trade, Peter Thorneycroft) for the Prime Minister (Anthony Eden), for his meeting with the Cotton Board on 24 March 1955; UK, PRO, BT258/373, Imports of Cotton textiles from India, Pakistan and Hong Kong, brief for the Prime Minister's meeting with the Lancashire industry, included in minute by A.E. Percival, 3 March 1958.
8 In order to introduce more flexibility to British external policy, the Commonwealth agreed to a Gentleman's Agreement, which allowed Britain to apply some duties on Commonwealth goods if prior consent was gained. Britain used this to raise the general level of tariffs on imports mainly deriving from non-Commonwealth sources without compromising either the no-new preference rule, or the free entry obligation under Ottawa. Britain also used waivers under Article I.
9 UK, PRO, BT258/424, minute [of meeting between the President of the Board of Trade and Norman Kipping and Graham Hayman, FBI] by F. W. Glaves-Smith, 11 June 1956. For the attitudes of FBI members, note: UK, PRO, BT258/424, letter from C. Henniker Heaton [Director of the Federation of Master Cotton Spinners Association] to K. McGregor [Board of Trade], 18 June 1956; letter from Sir Graham Hayman [Federation of British Industries] to Peter Thorneycroft [President of the Board of Trade], 13 June 1956, FBI memorandum to the Grand Council, June 1956 [secretly disclosed to Board of Trade officials, and enclosed in minute by Glaves-Smith, 11 June]; and minute by K. McGregor, 6 June 1956.
10 UK, PRO, DO35/8481, Report of the Commonwealth Trade and Economic Conference, 1 October 1958.
11 UK, PRO, BT258/377, minute by S.D. Wilks – 'The Legal Position with Regard to Duties on Commonwealth Goods' –13 August 1958.

12 UK, PRO, CO852/1710, Hong Kong textile exports to the UK, brief for the Secretary of State (A. Lennox-Boyd) for discussion with the Prime Minister (Macmillan).

13 UK, PRO, BT/241/294: BT briefing document 'Duty-Free Entry for Commonwealth Goods', July 1955.

14 UK, PRO, BT258/373, Imports of Cotton textile from India, Pakistan and Hong Kong, brief for the Prime Minister's meeting with the Lancashire industry, included in minute by A.E. Percival, 3 March 1958.

15 UK, PRO, PREM11/2530, letter from Robert Black, Governor Hong Kong, to Hilton Poynton, Colonial Office (henceforth CO), 21 June 1958.

16 UK, PRO, PREM11/1038, letter from Butler (Chancellor of the Exchequer) to the Prime Minister (Eden), 17 August 1955.

17 UK, PRO, CO1030/859, The value and cost of the colony of Hong Kong to the United Kingdom, February 1957.

18 UK, PRO, BT258/195, letter from Raymond Streat (Chairman of the Cotton Board) to S.A.F. Dakin, 26 September 1956.

19 UK, PRO, PREM11/2825, note by Thorneycroft to Prime Minister (Eden), 3 July 1956; and Prime Minister to Butler, 4 July 1956.

20 UK, PRO, BT258/370, Calendar of the Clegg Mission.

21 UK, PRO, PREM11/2825, letter from A.L.B. (Butler) to Prime Minister, 17 July 1957.

22 UK, PRO, BT258/195; letters from G.B.W. Harrison (UK Trade Commissioner Hong Kong) to E. Atherton, 11 and 30 January, 5 February, 1957; BT258/195, letter from E.B. David to A.N. Galsworthy (CO), 23 April 1957.

23 UK, PRO, BT258/374, note of conversation with H.A. Angus (Department of Commerce and Industry, Hong Kong) (by Frank Lee), 25 April 1958.

24 UK, PRO, BT258/371, minute for Sir Edgar Cohen by Percival, 18 September 1957.

25 UK, PRO, BT258/371; telegram from the Hong Kong Governor (A. Grantham) to Secretary of State for Colonies (Lennox-Boyd), no. 1442, 9 September 1957; CAB128 (57) 9, 25 July 1957. For a government record of the industries attitude, note UK, PRO, BT258/371, 'Brief for the President's Meeting with Sir Cuthbert Clegg (Cotton Board; Cotton Spinners Manufacturers Association) For 19 September 1957: Cotton Textile Imports.'

26 UK, PRO, PREM11/2825, note from the President of the Board of Trade (David Eccles) to Prime Minister (Macmillan), 13 September 1957; CAB128(60)7, 1 August 1957.

27 UK, PRO, PREM11/2526, minutes of a meeting between the President of the Board of Trade (Eccles) with officials from the Colonial Office, the Commonwealth Relations Office, and a delegation from the Cotton Board Delegates, headed by Lord Rochdale, 20 February 1958.

28 PRO, UK, BT258/371, letter from Eccles (President of the Board of Trade) to Prime Minister (Macmillan), 13 September 1957.

29 UK, PRO, BT258/371, minutes by A.D. Neale, 17 July 1957.

30 UK, PRO, BT258/372, minute by Roberts, 7 November 1957.

31 UK, PRO, BT258/195, minute by Roberts, 22 February 1957.

32 UK, PRO, BT258/379, minutes of talks (between Lancashire and the Hong Kong Textile Negotiating Committee), 23 September 1958; minutes of second meeting, 25 September 1958; telegram from Hong Kong (by Atherton, BT) to Board of Trade, 26 September 1958 (reporting back on third meeting)

33 UK, PRO, CAB129/88/185, Cotton Imports, Memorandum by the President of the Board of Trade, 31 July 1957; BT258/371, letter from Eccles (President of the Board of Trade) to Prime Minister (Macmillan), 13 September 1957; CAB128(68)1, 17 September 1957.

34 UK, PRO, T258/371; personal minute by the Prime Minister (Macmillan), serial no. M. 325/57, sent to the Colonial Secretary (Lennox-Boyd), 13 July 1957.

35 UK, PRO, BT258/371, paraphrase of Cabinet discussion, 23 July 1957; BT258/372, letter from Frederick Erroll, United Kingdom Trade Commissioner, Hong Kong, to K. McGregor, 4 October 1957.
36 UK, PRO, BT258/371; telegrams from the Secretary of State for Colonies (Lennox-Boyd) to Hong Kong, no. 981, 1 October 1957, no. 1037, 11 October 1957 and no. 1062, 18 October 1957; telegram from Hong Kong to Secretary of State for Colonies, no. 877, 14 October 1957; BT258/371, letter from J.S. Sadler (United Kingdom Trade Commissioner, Hong Kong) to K. McGregor, 4 October 1957; minutes of meeting between Grantham, Governor, C.B. Burgess, acting Colonial Secretary, J.J. Cowperthwaite, Financial Secretary, H.A. Angus. Director of Department of Commerce and Industry; and note from John Profumo to Prime Minister, 16 September 1957.
37 UK, PRO, BT258/372, telegram from C.H. Baylis, UK Trade Commissioner, India, 1074/87 [recording meeting with Neville Wadia, Chairman, Cotton Textile and Export Promotion Council]; telegram from UK Trade Commissioner, India, 1 January 1958; and BT258/373, letter from Baylis to Levine, 15 January 1958.
38 UK, PRO, BT258/373, letter from R.M. McIntosh (probably UK Trade Commissioner, Pakistan) to S.H. Levine, 15 Febuary 1958; BT258/372, minute by Roberts (of meeting with Nazir A. Sheikh, President, West Pakistan Textile Industry Federation).
39 UK, PRO, PREM11/2530, notes from L.E.M. Taylor, private secretary to the Minister of State, to N.F. Cairncross, private secretary to the Prime Minister (Macmillan), 8 May, and 9 May 1958; and minute by the minister of state, 12 May 1958; letter from the UK Trade Commissioner, Pakistan (probably, McIntosh) to the Board of Trade, 17 February 1958.
40 UK, PRO, BT258/372, minute by Roberts, 4 November 1957 (on lunch with Naseer A. Sheikh, President of the West Pakistan Textile Industry Federation) and letter from Baylis, UK Trade Commissioner, Bombay, to Levine, 15 January 1958.
41 UK, PRO, BT258/373, letter from Baylis to Levine, 15 January 1958; PREM11/2526, letter from Prime Minister to Desai (Indian Minister for Commerce and Industry), 9 January 1958; minute for meeting between the Prime Minister and the Pakistan Prime Minister, 14 January 1958; minutes of meeting between the Prime Minister and Desai (Minister of Commerce and Industry), 9 January 1958.
42 UK, PRO, BT258/373, record of conversation between the Prime Minister (Macmillan) and Moraji Desai, Ministry of Commerce and Industry 9 January 1958; extract from the record of a meeting between the Prime Ministers of the UK and Pakistan and other Pakistan ministers and officials, held in Karachi, 14 January 1958; minute by A.D. Neale, 17 February 1958 (of a meeting between the Macmillan and Eccles, held at Chequers across a weekend).
43 UK, PRO, BT258/373, minute by Dakin, 4 February 1958 and note for the President of the Board of Trade (Eccles), 7 February 1958.
44 UK, PRO, BT258/374, minute by M.C. Gibbs (of Cabinet meeting), 17 March 1958.
45 UK, PRO, BT258/374, minute by Dakin, note of meeting at No. 10 Downing Street at 11.30 a.m. on Friday 17 March; minute by M.C. Gibbs (of Cabinet discussion of 'imports of cotton textiles', meeting 640/1), 17 March 1958; UK, PRO, BT258/372, letter from the Minister of State (Erroll), Board of Trade, to Prime Minister (Macmillan), 3 January 1958.
46 UK, PRO, CAB128/32 (53) 5, 10 July 1958.
47 UK, PRO, PREM11/2825, minute of Prime Minister's Visit to the Cotton Board Conference, Harrogate, by Lee, Board of Trade; minute by L.H. Robinson, 20 October 1958; BT258/372, letter from the Minister of State (Erroll) to Prime Minister (Macmillan), 3 January 1958; BT258/373, brief for visit of Lord Rochdale, 20 February 1958 and note of a meeting held at the Board of Trade, 20 February 1958; PREM11/2825, minute by Lee, 20 October 1958; PREM11/2526, letter from Rochdale (Cotton Board) to Eccles, President of the Board of Trade, 12 February 1958.

48 UK, PRO, BT258/374, letter from Lee to the President of the Board of Trade (Eccles), 28 March 1958.

49 UK, PRO, PREM11/2526, brief for Lee visit to Hong Kong by Eccles (President of the Board of Trade), 14 March 1958; and UK, PRO, BT258/374, Hong Kong General Chamber of Commerce, 'Exports of Cotton Piece Goods to the UK', note of a meeting with Sir Frank Lee, 25 March 1958.

50 UK, PRO, PREM11/2526, minutes from Eccles to Prime Minister (Macmillan), 3 March 1958; UK, PRO, BT258/374, telegram from Hong Kong (Lee) to the Board of Trade, no. 12, 26 March 1958; minute by R. Hill, 27 March; BT258/374, noted from Eccles (Minister of State) to Prime Minister (Macmillan), 28 March 1958.

51 UK, PRO, BT258/374, telegram from Hong Kong (Lee) to Board of Trade (Roberts), no. 28, 1 April 1958.

52 UK, PRO, BT258/377, (copy of) Cotton Board 310/58, 'An Understanding Reached Between Accredited Representatives of the Cotton Industries of India, Pakistan and the United Kingdom on Retained Imports of Duty Free Manufactures'.

53 UK, PRO, BT258/375, letter from Taylor to Cairncross, 9 May 1958; letter from Baylis (UK Trade Commissioner, India) to Dakin, 28 May 1958.

54 UK, PRO, BT258/375, (copy of a) note by the Secretary of State for Commonwealth Relations, 13 May 1958, including letter from A.J. Bryne to Sayed Wajid Ali Shah, 7 May 1958; and (copy of a) letter from the Commonwealth Relations Office to the Prime Minister (Macmillan) (not dated); (copy of) telegram from UK Trade Commissioner, Pakistan, no. 884, 26 May 1958; minute by Roberts, 27 May 1958.

55 UK, PRO, BT258/375, letter from Douglas Clague (John D. Hutchinson and Co. Ltd) to Lee, 15 April 1958.

56 UK, PRO, BT258/379, minutes of talks (between Lancashire and the Hong Kong Textile Negotiating Committee), 23 September 1958; minutes of second meeting, 25 September 1958; telegram from Hong Kong (by Atherton, BT) to Board of Trade, 26 September 1958 (reporting back on third meeting).

57 UK, PRO, BT258/375, minute by C.M.P. Brown, 29 April 1958 and by Dakin, 30 April 1958; BT258/732, minute by M.V. Muskett, 11 June 1958; note of a meeting with the Shirt Collar Tie Manufacturers Federation, 2 July 1958; minute of Apparel and Fashion Industry Association, 29 July 1958; letter from M.K. Reid (the Wholesale Clothing Manufacturers Federation of Great Britain) to Lee, 30 October 1958.

58 UK, PRO, BT259/732, Imports of Cotton Clothing from Hong Kong, Board of Trade Brief, 6 November 1958.

59 UK, PRO, BT258/377, (copy of) letter from Lennox-Boyd (Colonial Secretary) to Prime Minister (Macmillan), 31 July 1958; PREM11/2530 and BT258/377, telegram from Hong Kong (Govenor Black) to London, 25 July 1958; and telegram from Hong Kong to London, no. 659, 14 August 1958, (reporting comments by the Director of the Commerce and Industry Department Angust); BT258/375, letter from Poynton (CO) to Lee, 28 May 1958.

60 UK, PRO, BT258/377, minute by Lee, 30 July 1958.

61 UK, PRO, CAB129/93. Cotton Imports, note by the Prime Minister; BT258/377, telegram from London (PM) to Hong Kong (Governor), no. 629, 22 July 1958; telegram from London (PM) to Hong Kong (Governor), no. 666, 2 August 1958; PREM11/2530, minute by Lennox-Boyd (Secretary of State of the Colonies) to Prime Minister (Macmillan) 5 June 1958; minute by Lee, 23 June 1958; draft statement to be made to Lord Rochdale; minutes of meeting between the Prime Minister, the President of the Board of Trade with the Cotton Board, 4 July 1958.

62 UK, PRO, BT258/379, telegram from Hong Kong to London (BT), no. 863, 2 October 1958; PREM11/2825, minute by Prime Minister (Macmillan) to Secretary of State for Colonies (Lennox-Boyd), 14 December 1958; CAB128 (86) 6, 18 December 1958.

63 UK, PRO, CAB128 (84) 8, 10 December 1958.

64 UK, PRO, BT258/378, minute by Lee, 1 September 1958; minute by Roberts (of meeting with Prime Minister with Board of Trade officials, 28 August 1958), 29 August 1958; letter from Lee to Rochdale, 5 September 1958 (reporting a lunch meeting with Arthur Morse, Hong Kong and Shanghai Bank, 4 September); PREM11/2825, minute by Frank Lee (of a meeting with John Keswick, Jardine Matheson) Board of Trade, 21 October 1958 and 23 October 1958; note from Frank Lee to the President of the Board of Trade, 21 Febuary 1958, also note UK, PRO, BT258/195; letter by A.E. Percivial to A.N. Galsworthy [CO], 22 October 1956; minutes of a meeting at the Board of Trade, with J.B. Kite and H.J. Collar (both leading members of the China Association, a London-based group representing the interests of those trading in and with China), 5 July 1956.

65 UK, PRO, BT258/378, letter from A.J. Phelps to J.A. Howard-Drake, 13 September 1958; PREM11/2530, minute by A.J. Phelps to Prime Minister (Macmillan) (of meeting with the Governor of the Bank of England), 8 September 1958; letter from the Bank of England to Phelps, 23 September 1958; Phelps minute to the Prime Minister (Macmillan), 25 September 1958.

66 UK, PRO, BT258/379, minute by D. Steel, 25 September 1958 (of telephone conservation with Phelps, at No. 10 Downing Street, relating to a telegram from Michael W. Turner, Chief Manager, Hong Kong and Shanghai Bank and member of the Hong Kong Executive Council); telegram from Hong Kong to London, no. 835, 25 September 1958.

67 UK, PRO, BT258/379, copies of note from Governor of the Bank of England to Arthur Morse, (Hong Kong and Shanghai Bank), and note by C.F.C. (Cobbald), 26 September 1958, enclosed in a letter from Leslie Rowan (Treasury) to Sir Edgar Cohen (BT), 29 September 1958.

68 UK, PRO, CAB129 (58) 245, Cotton Imports from Hong Kong, Memorandum by the President of the Board of Trade, 3 December 1958.

69 UK, PRO, BT258/845 (BT briefing document), A history of the cotton inter-industry discussions: Indian and Pakistan agreement, 1959: short summary (not dated and no author given).

70 UK, PRO, BT258/383, note from Roberts to Phelps, 29 May 1959.

71 UK, PRO, BT258/383, telegram from UK High Commissioner, Delhi, no. 93, 16 January 1959.

72 UK, PRO, BT258/383, copy of letter from Roberts to Lee, 17 Febuary 1959; telegram from UKTC, Delhi, no. 736, 22 May 1959.

73 UK, PRO, BT258/845, IM3, Cotton Textiles – agreement between the Cotton Board and the Indian and Pakistan Industries, 23 June 1961; CAB129/74, Cotton Industry: Draft Statement by President of the Board of Trade, 28 March 1959.

74 UK, PRO, BT258/378, letter from Atherton to D. Kelvin-Stark (CO), 26 August 1958 (reporting a meeting with Forbes, a Manchester converter); BT258/382, letter from E. Atherton to Harris, 20 December 1958.

75 For this problem, note UK, PRO, PREM11/2825, telegram from Hong Kong to the Secretary of State for the Colonies, 1 November 1958.

76 UK, PRO, PREM11/2530, note by Frank Lee, permanent under-secretary of state at the Board of Trade, to N.F. Cairncross, private secretary to the Prime Minister (Macmillan) (no date specified).

77 UK, PRO, BT258/372, minute by Atherton, 2 December 1957: who estimated that 80 per cent of Hong Kong imports were retained and 65 per cent of Indian imports.

Bibliography

Unpublished material

British Board of Trade Records: BT258.
British Cabinet Office Records: CAB128, CAB129.

British Colonial Office: C01030, CO852.
British Dominion Office: DO35.
British Prime Ministers Office Records: PREM11.
British Treasury Records: T236.

Published material

Aggarwal, Vinod K. (1985) *Liberal Protectionism: The International Politics of Organised Textile Trade*, Berkeley, CA: California University Press.
Barbezat, Daniel P. (1990) *International Cooperation and Domestic Cartel Control: The International Steel Cartel, 1926–1938*, Ann Arbor, MI.
Cain, P.J. and Hopkins, A.G. (1993) *British Imperialism: Innovation and Expansion, 1688–1914*, London: Longman.
——(1993) *British Imperialism: Crisis and Deconstruction, 1914–1990*, London: Longman.
Chiu, Stephen W.K. (1995) *East Asia and the World Economy*, London: Sage.
Clarke, E. (1972) 'The End of Laissez Faire and the Politics of Cotton', *The Historical Journal*, xv 3, pp. 493–517.
Clayton, David (2000) 'British Foreign Economic Policy Towards China 1949–60', *Electronic Journal of International History*, http://ihr.sas.ac.uk/publications/ejihart6.html
Drummond, Ian M. (1974) *Imperial Economic Policy, 1917–39: Studies in Expansion and Protection*, London: Allen & Unwin.
Higgins, David and Toms, Steven (2000) 'Public Subsidy and Private Divestment: The Lancashire Cotton Textile Industry, c. 1950–1965', *Business History*, Vol. 42, no. 1, January, pp. 59–84.
Lazonick, W. (1983) 'Industrial Organisation and Technological Change: The Decline of the British Cotton Industry', *Business History Review*, 57, pp. 195–236.
Macdougall, D. and Hutt, R. (1964) 'Imperial Preference: A Quantitative Analysis', *Economic Journal*, 96, pp. 233–57.
Marrison, Andrew (1996) *British Business and Protection 1903–1932*, Oxford: Clarendon Press.
Meredith, David (1975) 'The British Government and Colonial Economic Policy 1919–1939', *Economic History Review*, 28, pp. 484–99.
Miles, Caroline (1968) *Lancashire Textiles: A Case Study of Industrial Change*, Cambridge: Cambridge University Press.
Mills, Lennox A. (1942) *British Rule in Eastern Asia: A Study of Contemporary Government and Economic Development in British Malaya and Hong Kong*, London: Oxford University Press.
Milward, Alan S. and Brennan, George (1996) *Britain's Place in the World: A Historical Enquiry into Import Controls*, London: Routledge.
Miners, Norman (2002) 'Industrial Development in the Colonial Empire and the Imperial Economic Conference at Ottawa, 1932', *The Journal of Imperial and Commonwealth History*, Vol. 30, no. 2, May, pp. 65–66.
Rose, Mary (1997) 'The Politics of Protection: An Institutional Approach to Government Industry Relations in the British and US Cotton Industries, 1945–73', *Business History*, 39, pp. 128–51.
——(2000) *Firms, Networks and Business Values: The British and American Cotton Industries since 1750*, Cambridge: Cambridge University Press.

Schenk, Catherine R. (2001) *Hong Kong as an International Financial Centre: Emergence and Development 1945–65*, London: Routledge.

Singleton, John (1991) *Lancashire on the Scrapheap: The Cotton Industry, 1945–1970*, Oxford: Oxford University Press.

Singleton, John (1997) *The World Textile Industry*, London and New York: Routledge.

Sugihara, K. (1986) 'Patterns of Asia's Integration into the World Economy, 1880–1913', in W. Fischer, R. McInnes and J. Schneider (eds) *The Emergence of a World Economy, 1500–1914*, Wiesbaden: In Kommission bei F. Steiner.

——(1990) 'Japan as an Engine of the Asian International Economy, c. 1880–1936', *Japan Forum*, 2, pp. 127–45.

——(1998) 'Intra-Asian Trade and East Asia's Industrialization, 1919–1939', in G. Austin (ed.) *Industrial Growth in the Third World, c. 1870 – c. 1990: Depressions, Intra-Regional Trade, and Ethnic Networks*, LSE Working Papers in Economic History No. 44/98.

Williamson, Jeffrey and O'Rourke, Kevin (1999) *Globalisation and History: The Evolution of a 19th Century Atlantic Economy*, Cambridge, MA: MIT Press.

Wurm, Clemens (1993) *Business, Politics and International Relations: Steel, Cotton and International Cartels in British Politics, 1924–1939*, Cambridge: Cambridge University Press.

Yokoi, Noriko (2003) *Japan's Postwar Economic Recovery and Anglo-Japanese Relations, 1948–1962*, London: RoutledgeCurzon.

13 An edible oil for the world

Malaysian and Indonesian competition in the palm oil trade, 1945–2000

Susan Martin

Introduction

The story of the palm oil trade since 1945 is a remarkable tale of technical innovation, cut-throat competition and the successful construction of new inter-Asian trading relationships. This chapter will focus on the trade dimension, but it should be clearly understood at the outset that beneath the dramatic and highly visible pattern of the sea change in trading networks lies a groundswell of profound transformation in both end uses and palm oil production methods.

In the nineteenth and early twentieth centuries, palm oil had its place in the British imperial economic order as an industrial commodity, used as a flux in tinplating; as an ingredient in soap and candle making; and only to a very limited extent for edible purposes (Lynn (1997); Martin (1988), p. 28). In West Africa, the first region to develop a palm oil export trade, the oil was a staple ingredient in the local diet, but European visitors regarded it as an exotic curiosity (B.O.W.K. (1925)). By the 1920s it was clear that the oil had a potential food application outside Africa in the margarine and compound lard industries. However these industries, which were in any case better developed in the United States of America than in Europe, required bland, pale oils – and palm oil in its natural state is dark red, strongly flavoured and heavily aromatic (Lim (1967), pp. 130–2; Khera (1976), pp. 228–30; Moll (1987), p. 159).

During the Second World War the quest for vegetable-based alternatives to butter and lard became urgent. The new refining techniques developed then were further improved during the 1950s and 1960s, until by 1970 it was possible to transform palm oil into an 'invisible ingredient', flavourless and colourless. The oil could then be split down into fractions, making it as soft or hard, as liquid or solid, as the Western manufacturer desired. By adding flavours, colours, other blended oils and nutritional supplements, palm oil could be turned into a convincing replica of almost any other oil or fat. From now on it became known primarily as an edible, rather than an industrial commodity and its role in world trade was transformed (Berger and Martin 2000). In the late 1960s palm oil accounted for 6 per cent of world exports of oils and fats; in the late 1990s this share was 38 per cent. Over the same period, total world exports of palm oil rose from 600,000 to 12,000,000 tonnes per annum (Hartley (1988), p. 42; MPOB Statistics (2002), tables 6.5 and 6.9; Corley and Tinker (2003), pp. 7–11).

Table 13.1 World exports of palm oil, 1909–2000 (thousand tonnes per annum)

Year	Malaya (Malaysia)	Netherlands East Indies (Indonesia)	Belgian Congo (Zaire)	Nigeria	World total
1909–13	0	0	2	82	124
1924–28	1	15	19	124	202
1936–40	49	200	67	138	494
1950–54	49	122	137	183	530
1955–59	61	121	160	180	555
1960–64	108	114	138	148	599
1965–69	220	153	124	68	707
1970–74	614	234	86	6	1,367
1975–79	1,332	393	30	8	2,429
1980–84	2,700	335	8	1	3,870
1985–89	4,333	801	0	0	6,280
1990–94	6,136	1,597	0	0	9,158
1995–99	7,519	2,402	0	0	11,579
2000	9,081	4,140	0	0	15,004

Sources: Martin (1988), pp. 148–9; Empire Marketing Board (1932), p. 123; Creutzberg (1975), pp. 97–8; Lim (1967), p. 336; Mielke (1988), Past section 77; Mielke (1999), Palm Oil, p. 45; MPOB (2002), table 6.9.

As shown in Table 13.1 this explosion in world demand and export trade has mainly benefited two Asian exporters – Malaysia and Indonesia – rather than the African producers, notably Nigeria and the Congo (formerly the Belgian Congo, then Zaire) which had dominated the international palm oil trade in the 1940s and 1950s.

In part the Asian success after 1960 reflects a recovery, particularly on the part of Indonesia, from the disruptions of the Second World War, the struggle for independence and the economic experiments which followed. It also reflects the tragic effects of political instability and the over-taxing of cash crop producers in Africa. However, in the case of Malaysia, there is much more to the story. The spectacular growth of Malaysia's palm oil industry since 1960 provides an exceptional case study of economic success in a tropical setting (Martin (2003)). Not content with their original role in growing oil palms and carrying out the primary processing of the oil, Malaysia's producers have set up successful refineries and oleochemical plants, and have linked their search for new techniques firmly to the development of new Asian, as well as Western markets.

In the case of the Malaysian palm oil industry, a successful independent industry has been built on colonial foundations, yet, as will be demonstrated below with the aid of detailed trade statistics, the trade has by no means been confined to the old hub-and-spoke routes of the British Empire. In contrast with Indonesia (formerly the Netherlands East Indies), which until the mid-1990s continued to rely heavily on Europe for its export markets, and to channel its trade through the Dutch port of Rotterdam, Malaysia since the 1960s has developed exports of palm oil to China, India, Pakistan, Egypt and the Gulf States. This success was founded upon the establishment of a local refining industry, guided by market research and exploiting the cultural ties of Malaysia's Indian, Chinese and Islamic populations, in order to develop palm oil products which could readily be used to meet the needs of Asian consumers. Japanese and Western businesses also helped Malaysians to develop new products tailored to their own home markets, demonstrating the continuing interest of foreign investors in a country which has consistently welcomed good guests.

Ironically, given the leading role played by American suppliers, customers and investors in the development of the world economy during the era of globalisation, American technology, finance and markets have played little part in the palm oil story since the Second World War. The war stimulated the development in America of processing methods designed to turn soya bean oil too, into an 'invisible ingredient' (Lim (1967), pp. 130–2; Wilson (1968), pp. 6–12, 67–71). Once these processing methods had been perfected in the 1950s, and as the production of soya beans to provide animal feed took off in the United States of America in the early 1960s, the American market for palm oil virtually disappeared. The 1970s brought a limited revival of American imports, especially of Malaysian processed rather than Indonesian crude palm oil, but by the mid-1980s this growth had levelled off (Mielke (1999), Past section 77). Having won the battle in their home market, the American producers of soyabean oil then began searching for export opportunities in Asia. They mounted a vigorous propaganda campaign to convince consumers, at home and abroad, that their oil was healthier than palm oil and other 'tropical greases' which, they alleged, caused heart disease (Gurunathan (1995)). The final part of this chapter will examine Malaysian responses to this smear campaign, and show how it influenced the process of innovation in the 1990s.

The world trade in palm oil, 1909–45

The trading networks of the early twentieth century were radically different from those which have underpinned Malaysia's market success since 1970. As shown in Table 13.2, on the eve of the First World War the United Kingdom and the Netherlands were acting as central importing 'hubs' from which supplies flowed out in the form of re-exports to most other buyers, including America. The main exception to this rule was France, which was able to obtain supplies directly from its own African Empire. The statistical limitations of contemporary sources make it hard to determine how much palm oil was actually consumed within each of the two 'hub' countries, but the picture becomes clearer in the 1920s, when America, Germany and Italy began importing most of their palm oil directly from producing countries, and a series of one-to-one trading relationships developed. Many trade routes went towards each colonial metropole from its own dependencies: Malaya and British West Africa, including Nigeria, serving the United Kingdom; French West and Central Africa supplying France; the Belgian Congo, Belgium; and the Netherlands East Indies, Holland. There was a limited amount of re-export trade within Europe, which evened out the balance of supply and

Table 13.2 Net imports of palm oil into the principal importing countries, 1909–30 (thousand tonnes per annum)

Countries	1909–13 (Average)	1924–28 (Average)	1929	1930
United States of America	28	64	119	130
United Kingdom ⎱	about 60	59	57	48
Netherlands ⎰	jointly	13	9	9
Germany	12	15	20	29
Italy	8	18	16	22
France	15	17	8	11
World total	124	202	246	277

Source: Empire Marketing Board (1932), p. 127.

demand in each metropolitan country (Empire Marketing Board (1932) pp. 125–6).

Until 1930, the main uses of palm oil in the West were for soap production and tin plating. In the late 1920s palm oil began to be used in America as an ingredient in the margarine industry, but imports for this purpose remained relatively small, at 560 tonnes per annum in 1929–30 (Empire Marketing Board (1932), pp. 128–9). During the 1930s the American margarine industry developed further, and buyers displayed a strong preference for palm oil from Sumatra, the principal source region in the Netherlands East Indies. Malayan supplies went mainly to the United Kingdom, India and Canada, where they were used to a limited extent for edible purposes, and to a much greater extent for the established industrial uses. In 1936 British buyers accounted for 46 per cent of Malayan palm oil exports, with a further 34 per cent being taken by Canada and 10 per cent by India (Lim (1967), p. 137).

Although Malayan and Sumatran supplies went to different buyers, they used similar methods of bulk shipment. Crude palm oil is semi-solid at ambient temperatures in the tropics, and completely solid in temperate climates, and the new tanks, which had been pioneered by William Lever in his Congo operations, contained steam pipe coils for heating it. This greatly eased the task of pumping the oil in and out when the steamers were in port. In order to take advantage of this new technology, many small producers joined forces, and it was but a short step for them to make co-operative selling arrangements as well, typically organised in Liverpool and the other metropolitan European trading centres. The commercial pressures of the 1930s hastened this process, which culminated in 1936 in the formation of an International Palm Oil Pool, linking both Malayan and Sumatran suppliers. The Pool organised all sales and shared the profits among producers in proportion to the volume of oil supplied. It lasted until 1940, and many producers felt that it enabled them to make the most of the improved world trading conditions of the time. The more adventurous firms like Malaya's United Plantations Ltd, however, who wanted to develop new products to serve the growing Indian and emerging Middle Eastern markets, quickly found themselves coming into conflict with the Pool's metropolitan controllers (Martin (2003), ch. 2).

During the Second World War, the Japanese occupation of Malaya and Sumatra in 1941–42, followed swiftly by the disruption of Pacific shipping lanes by American and allied forces from mid-1942, effectively ended the export trade in palm oil from both countries. Many oil palm estates in Malaya were left untended, or underplanted with food crops like cassava. In Sumatra, many palms were cut down. Palm oil processing plants fell into disrepair, facing their original owners with a Herculean task of reconstruction when they returned in 1945–46. Meanwhile, in Nigeria as elsewhere in British West Africa, smallholder palm oil producers fell into the grip of the new West African Produce Control Board. This organisation, established in 1942 after the fall of Malaya to Japan, effectively worked to channel supplies to the British Ministry of Food, while paying producers substantially less than their palm oil was worth on the free market. In 1949 it was succeeded by the Nigeria Oil Palm Produce Marketing Board, which maintained the same pricing policy. Ultimately the policy helped to convince smallholders that their best options were to sell palm oil on the local food market, or to exit from the industry altogether, thus paving the way for the collapse of Nigerian palm oil exports after the 1950s (Beasley (1987), chs 14–15; Moll (1987), p. 112; Martin (1988), ch. 10 (2003), ch. 3; Tate (1996), ch. 35; Kratoska (1998), chs 6–9; Tomaru (2000), ch. 2).

Innovation and growth in Malaysia, 1945–70

In the immediate aftermath of the Second World War, palm oil producers in the Belgian Congo and Nigeria seemed to hold a decisive advantage over their Southeast Asian rivals in the competition for world markets. As shown in Table 13.1, by the early 1950s production in Malaya had only just recovered to pre-war levels, and in Indonesia the process of reconstruction was by no means complete. Nigerian exports, meanwhile, had held steady during the war, and throughout the 1950s officials were eagerly encouraging farmers to expand further. Experts were on hand to urge smallholders to improve the quality of their palm oil, and to buy palm oil hand presses or set up small-scale mills, in order to compete more effectively with plantation-based producers elsewhere. Even after Nigerian independence in 1960 and up to the outbreak of the Nigerian Civil War in 1967, local officials continued to take this line, with the support of the British Ministry of Overseas Development. They remained in blissful ignorance of the impact that low prices were having on farmers' underlying commitment to the industry (Martin (1988), ch.10; Tropical Products Institute (1965)).

In the Belgian Congo, by contrast, the export-oriented palm oil industry had long been plantation-based, as it was in South-east Asia. Major technical advances had been made through government-sponsored agronomic research at the Institut National pour l'Etude Agronomique du Congo Belge, at Yangambi, culminating in the 1941 publication of reliable breeding methods for the Tenera hybrid variety of oil palm. The Tenera palm had an exceptionally oil-rich, pulpy fruit, offering a 40 percent increase in plantation yields of palm oil per hectare. At last, it offered plantation producers the prospect of competing with their smallholder rivals not only on quality, but also on cost. Unilever's subsidiary Huileries du Congo Belge quickly set to work planting up their estates with the new materials. They then found that conventional pre-war hydraulic presses failed to cope with the pulpy Tenera fruit, and their engineers set to work, in collaboration with official scientists based at Mongana, designing a revolutionary screw-type model. Palm oil exports from the Congo rose throughout the 1950s, threatening Nigeria's position as world market leader (Fieldhouse (1978), pp. 529–31; Hartley (1988), pp. 202–10; Martin (2003), chs 5 and 7).

The triumph of Southeast Asian producers since 1960 would have been hard to predict from the vantage point of 1950, and indeed it owes as much to unpredictable political developments as to underlying economic strengths and weaknesses. The 'Congo crisis' of 1960 and the prolonged period of instability which followed, combined with a period of nationalisation in the Zaire of the mid-1970s, effectively deterred Unilever from further investment in that country (Fieldhouse (1978), pp. 541–5). The company re-focused its resources on Malaysia, which had become independent under a tolerant liberal regime in 1957, and which had effectively resolved its own internal problems with the ending of the Emergency, a long-standing struggle against jungle-based guerillas, in July 1960 (Clutterbuck (1984), ch. 9; Harper (1999), ch. 3). Communal tensions between the Chinese, Indian and Malay citizens of Malaysia remained, and came to a head once more in the riots of 13 May 1969, but these difficulties pale into insignificance by comparison with the endemic armed struggles in Zaire (known once again as the Congo since 1997).

Unilever's choice of Malaysia rather than Indonesia was no accident. The Netherlands East Indies, like the Belgian Congo, had experienced a conflict-ridden and problematic transition to independence. The defeat of the Dutch in 1949 had been followed by the expropriation of Dutch property, including palm oil plantations, in 1957–58; the nationalisation of other foreign enterprises followed (Hill (2000), p. 2; Moll (1987), p. 112; Booth (1998)). The expansion of the palm oil industry, which had remained essentially estate-based, stopped. Output did not recover to pre-war levels until the end of the 1960s, by which time the pattern of sales had shifted, as in the case of Nigeria, towards the growing market for food in local towns (Moll (1987), p. 115; Booth (1988), p. 211).

From the late 1950s until the late 1960s, Malaysia thus became the focal point for the process of innovation within the palm oil industry. Experiments in breeding the Tenera palm had begun locally as early as 1947, and proceeded rapidly through a remarkable process of collaboration between Agricultural Department scientists and a wide range of private firms. The spirit of co-operation within the industry at national level was further encouraged by the Incorporated Society of Planters, which regularly published research findings in its journal, *The Planter*, and began holding conferences in the late 1960s. Since 1979 many further conferences have been held by the Palm Oil Research Institute of

Malaysia (PORIM; Malaysian Palm Oil Board, or MPOB, since 2000), whose scientists are responsible both to the Malaysian Ministry of Primary Industries and to the private sector, which directly funds their work (Hartley (1988), pp. 192–202, 270–2; Martin (2003), ch. 5).

The spirit of co-operation within the Malayan palm oil industry of the late 1940s was useful not only in furthering the process of innovation, but also in countering the efforts of the British Ministry of Food to reduce producer prices. In contrast to the Nigerian smallholders, who were dispersed and powerless in the face of Marketing Board price decisions, the Malayan industry was highly organised. A small number of substantial producers had re-united into a Palm Oil Committee as early as December 1945. They negotiated a series of contracts with the Ministry of Food, which bought their entire output of palm oil from July 1946 to December 1952, at prices which rose steadily from a base level of £46 per tonne ex-estate in 1946, as compared with £12–13 per tonne ex-estate in the late 1930s. At one firm, Bernam Oil Palms Ltd, these prices allowed for gross profit margins averaging 73 per cent between 1946 and 1949, as compared with 57 per cent during the post-depression years of 1936–39 (Martin (2003), ch. 3).

After 1952 prices continued to rise, just as producers began to realise that the Tenera palm could dramatically reduce their costs. Meanwhile, the development of synthetic rubber was eroding the market for natural rubber, which until then had been the country's main agricultural export. While smallholders, who were relatively low-cost producers, remained loyal to rubber, the European-owned plantation companies gradually switched over to oil palms (Khera (1976), pp. 183; Moll (1987), pp. 140–62; Tate (1996), pp. chs 39–40). The economies of scale and quality gains provided by mill-based processing meant that, within the palm oil industry unlike the rubber industry, estate producers could maintain a competitive edge. From the early 1960s the Malaysian government was also encouraging the development of oil palm smallholder production through the Federal Land Development Authority (FELDA) and through local schemes run by the various Malaysian States. A remarkable feature of this development, by contrast with the Nigerian pattern, was that it was focused on large groups of people, rather than allowing for the dispersal of individual smallholders into independent household units. Effectively the group smallholdings were run like plantations, in which the smallholders worked very much like estate employees, under a centralised management. Only the systems of ownership and reward were different (Graham and Floering (1984); Malek and Barlow (1988)).

The development of Malaysia's palm oil industry after 1960 proceeded at breakneck speed, and in 1966 Malaysia became the world's leading exporter, overtaking Indonesia for the first time with an export volume of 181,000 tonnes for the year, as compared to Indonesia's 177,000 tonnes. At the same time, as shown in Table 13.1, world exports of palm oil were growing fast. Between 1960–64 and 1970–74 total world exports grew by 130 per cent, and in the decade which followed, the corresponding rise was 180 per cent. In the wake of this massive increase in supply, it is all the more remarkable that the nominal European (c.i.f.) prices for palm oil actually rose, from an average of US$220 per tonne in

1960–64, to US$360 per tonne in 1970–74 and US$570 per tonne in 1980–84. In real terms, that is when deflated by the industrial countries' wholesale price index, the prices paid for Malaysian palm oil in Europe rose from a base level of 100 per cent in 1960–64 to 118 per cent in 1970–74. The petroleum oil price shocks of the mid-1970s upset this trend for palm oil, as for so many other commodities within the world economy. In 1980–84 the real prices paid for palm oil in Europe averaged 77 per cent of the early 1960s level, and for 1990–94 the corresponding figure is 42 per cent (IMF (1987), pp. 110–13, 180–1; IMF (1996), pp. 108–11, 162–3; Mielke (1998), Past section 120–1).

At first glance these price trends are dismaying, but they should be set against the background of the 15-fold increase in the world supply of palm oil which occurred between 1960–64 and 1990–94. Malaysian producers were able to maintain profitability in the face of falling real prices, through innovations like the screw press and the Tenera palm, which dramatically cut the cost of production. Meanwhile, as will be shown in the following section, they searched successfully for new techniques of further processing and new Asian market openings. Through innovative product-market development they created new edible uses and effectively expanded the world market for palm oil, cushioning the impact upon prices of their collective decision to expand supply.

Malaysian success in devoloping Asian markets, 1960–2000

Three key innovations were essential to the growth of world demand for Malaysian palm oil after 1960. Firstly, new refining techniques developed in Europe and America in the 1960s allowed palm oil to be processed into the bland, pale, odourless 'invisible ingredient' which industrial food manufacturers required. Secondly, the power of the palm oil selling Pool was broken, allowing sales to be made directly by Malaysian producers to Asian buyers. Finally, refineries were successfully established within Malaysia, allowing locally based entrepreneurs to experiment with fresh palm oil products designed to meet Asian, rather than American or European, food manufacturers' and consumers' needs.

The European catering and convenience food industries which had emerged to serve the barrack and factory canteens of the Second World War continued to grow apace after the war ended, for the work of reconstruction absorbed many people's time (Leeming (1991), pp. 154–69; Davis (1978), chs 3 and 10). Scientists continued searching for new processing methods to adapt a wide range of raw materials to the fresh needs of industrial food production. Palm oil benefited from this trend, with the invention and improvement of techniques to bleach, deodorise and purify the oil, and ultimately to split it down into olein, stearin and various mid-fractions with strikingly different physical and chemical properties. Unilever's strong manufacturing and marketing presence in the industrial West, combined with its long-standing commitment to research into palm oil milling techniques in the Congo, placed the firm in an ideal position to take the lead in this process. Another early entrant was Harrisons & Crosfield, an Agency House or trading company, which had close links both with Malayan oil palm planters and with British manufacturers (Wilson (1968), chs 1–2; Pugh (1990), ch. 7; Jones (2000), ch. 10).

By the late 1960s both Unilever and Harrisons had developed new milling techniques and quality testing methods to support the launch of new brands of crude palm oil, labelled 'Special Prime Bleach' and 'Lotox' respectively (TPI (1965), pp. 85–95, 96–104; Martin (2003), ch. 7). However, such brands were clearly aimed at the needs of Western refiners serving the tastes of Western consumers, and some Malaysian producers were already aware that this was an extremely narrow market on which to rest all their hopes of future demand growth. Western consumers were already affluent and well fed, and Western populations were growing relatively slowly by comparison with those in the developing world, where the consumption per capita of edible oils and fats could also be expected to rise as prosperity increased. Unilever had already set up a small palm oil refinery in Malaysia, producing soap, margarine, vanaspati (a soft, spreadable substitute for butter-based ghee) and cooking oil for the local market (Khera (1978)). The further development of a local refining industry would, however, have been extremely difficult if the export trade in palm oil and its products had continued to be under the tight control of a London-based committee. United Plantations and Bernam Oil Palms, two firms of Scandinavian origin which had been early entrants to the palm oil industry, now saw their opportunity to play a key role in its development.

Malaya's palm oil pooling arrangements had earlier come under threat in 1952, when the Ministry of Food ended its monopsony buying practices and when the producer-owned co-operative Malayan Palm Oil Bulking Company faced the expiry of its 20-year lease on the large bulk oil installation in Singapore harbour. The Guthrie Agency House Group, which was one of the three biggest palm oil exporters in Malaya, took over the Singapore installation. United Plantations and Bernam Oil Palms, two closely allied firms which merged to become United Plantations Ltd in 1966, set up their own custom-built installation in Penang, while the third major palm oil exporter, Socfin, established an independent facility in Port Swettenham. Guthries, however, was reluctant to abandon the practice of co-ordinating sales at the European end, and persuaded United Plantations and Bernam Oil Palms to join a fresh Pooling Agreement in November 1952. In 1954 Socfin agreed to join the Pool, and a formal agreement was made, covering not only the three Shipping Agents, but also all firms shipping palm oil through their three bulking installations. Each of the three founder Shipping Agents had the right to dissolve the Pool, and also had representatives on its Joint Selling Committee (JSC) based in London. All palm oil sales had to be authorised by the JSC, which kept a record of the terms of each contract. Guthries, as Secretaries of the Pool, would calculate the average price received at the end of each quarter, and arrange for cheques to be passed between member companies to cancel out the variations in prices paid. Members were free to make their own arrangements for fulfilling their contracts, but Guthries were keen to organise sales to countries like India through their own channels, taking a commission on each sale (Khera (1976), ch. 8; Martin (2003), ch. 8).

During the 1960s United Plantations became increasingly frustrated with this arrangement. When attempting to develop a fledgling business supplying air-bleached palm oil in drums to buyers in the Indian soap industry, they found themselves compelled to sell and buy back their own red palm oil from the Pool, before being allowed to use it as a raw material. Like the directors of Unilever, they were convinced that there was a vast potential market in Asia, and were beginning to understand that the establishment of local refineries was essential to unlock this potential. A few other Asian countries, like Japan, already had local processing plants capable of handling palm oil, but most did not. Indian buyers, in particular, expressed a strong preference for buying palm oil which had already been refined to the point at which it had similar characteristics to the other oils which were already processed locally (Bek-Nielsen (1992), p. 96).

United Plantations' interest in palm oil refining gathered strength in 1968, when the Malaysian government passed the Investment Incentives Act encouraging export-oriented industrialisation (Lim (1973), pp. 254–68; Fong (1986), pp. 26–36). After sending senior engineers on fact-finding missions to Europe and India, and concluding agreements to co-operate with the Indian Tata Oil Mills Company and the Belgian fractionation equipment manufacturer Florent Tirtiaux, the company Chairman Olof Grut and Chief Engineer Borge Bek-Nielsen announced the incorporation of Unitata Sendirian Berhad, a specialised refinery operation, on 27 May 1971. On 1 October 1971 they served notice of United Plantations' intention to dissolve the Malaysian Palm Oil Pool (Khera (1976), p. 281; Martin (2003), ch. 8).

When the Pool was dissolved on 1 January 1972, several other Malaysian palm oil producers including FELDA seized the opportunity to relocate the centre of sales negotiations from London to Kuala Lumpur. A new organisation, the West Malaysian Palm Oil Producers' Association, was set up to organise the new selling arrangements, but FELDA reserved the right to make direct sales to any foreign government or official buying agency, and the monolithic character of the late colonial marketing system was never to return. In 1980 the incorporation of the Kuala Lumpur Commodity Exchange paved the way for a new era of fully competitive trading (Khera (1976), pp. 280–4; Moll (1987), pp. 155–62).

Guthries and other Agency Houses remained highly reluctant to enter the business of palm oil refining within Malaysia, believing that quality deterioration on the long journey to Europe would make the refined product no more valuable than crude red palm oil. However, Bek-Nielsen's vision proved more attractive to Asian entrepreneurs, especially Japanese and local Chinese investors who set up specialised large-scale refineries based at the ports. By 1980, virtually all the palm oil exported from Malaysia was in processed rather than crude form (Thoburn (1977), p. 165; Moll (1987), pp. 141–2; Lindblad (1998), pp. 116–18). As will be shown in Tables 13.3–13.5, the pattern of trade now became strikingly different from the late colonial model, in which supplies of Malayan palm oil had flowed largely through Singapore as a staging-post en route to Europe, bypassing all other Asian destinations except India, Iraq and, to a very limited extent, Japan.

Table 13.3 Exports of palm oil from Malaya (Malaysia) via Singapore, 1936–2000 (thousand tonnes per annum)

Year	Total Malayan (Malaysian) palm oil exports	Malayan exports of palm oil via Singapore	Singapore's trade as a percentage of the Malayan total
1936–40	49	30	62
1950–54	49	30	62
1955–59	61	27	44
1960–64	108	34	31
1965–69	220	74	34
1970	375	133	36
1975	1,160	156	13
1980	2,280	654	29
1985	3,240	968	30
1990	5,850	779	13
1995	6,120	414	7
2000	9,080	336	4

Sources: As Table 13.1 and Khera (1976); Huff (1994), pp. 372–385; Mielke (1987), W. Malaysia 182; Mielke (1991); Malaysia 275–6; Mielke (1995); Malaysia 49; Mielke (1998), Malaysia 51; Moll (1987), p. 159; MPOB (2002), table 4.14.

Table 13.3 illustrates the decline in Singapore's role as a staple port for Malayan palm oil, which began with the establishment of fresh bulking installations at Penang and Port Swettenham in the mid-1950s. From the late 1960s, Singapore's own government encouraged the process of growth away from the old colonial identity of a 'staple port', firstly through export-oriented industrialisation, and then in the late 1970s through the development of international services (Huff (1994), pp. 31–42). In the early 1980s there was a brief revival of Malaysia's palm oil re-export trade through Singapore, but in contrast to the pattern of the late1940s, this was founded on the growth of inter-Asian rather than transcontinental trade. Singapore was no longer merely a staging-post en route to the United Kingdom (Khera (1976), p. 265; Moll (1987), p. 159).

The figures given in Tables 13.4 and 13.5, showing the ultimate destinations of Malaysian exports, have been adjusted to remove the confusing effect of these changes in Singapore's role. For each year, the exports from Malaysia to Singapore have been re-allocated among the other importing countries according to their respective shares of Malaysia's direct export trade. This method has produced a fair approximation of the total quantity of Malaysian palm oil imported to each country. In the case of Indonesia, which is covered in Tables 13.6 and 13.7, the same method was used for the years 1987–91, in which 7 per cent of processed palm oil exports passed through Singapore. In later years for processed palm oil, and in all years for crude palm oil, the procedure was unnecessary, because Indonesia's trade via Singapore in these cases was negligible.

Having adjusted for the Singapore effect, it can be seen from Table 13.4 how greatly Malaysian trading patterns for palm oil shifted during the 1970s,

Table 13.4 Leading destinations of Malaysian palm oil exports, 1936–80 (thousand tonnes per annum)

Country	1936	1956	1961	1970	1975	1980
United Kingdom	14	31	35	160	190	160
West Germany				20	30	60
Netherlands				20	190	230
Soviet Union					60	80
United States of America				30	350	170
Canada	10	11	18	19	30	20
Iraq			15	70	80	40
India	3	17	19	0	30	580
Pakistan					10	120
Japan	2	0	0	0	70	140
Other	1	1	9	63	120	680
World total	30	60	96	375	1,160	2,280

Sources: Lim (1967), p. 137; Mielke (1994), Past section 81; Khera (1976), pp. 263–5; Moll (1987), p. 159.

following the dissolution of the London-based selling Pool. Rotterdam in the Netherlands joined the well-established British ports of London, Liverpool and Hull as a significant hub for the European trade. Pakistan, the Soviet Union and other new markets began to accept palm oil, and there was a short-lived import boom in North America.

After 1980 it becomes possible to study the import trends for Malaysian palm oil in more detail, thanks to the industry 'Bible', *Oil World Annual*, produced by the Mielke family in Hamburg and their dedicated team of researchers who travel the world collecting statistics. The *Oil World* figures are minutely detailed, and have been processed into a much simpler form to produce Tables 13.5–13.7. Table 13.5 shows how effectively Malaysia had developed a wide range of customers by the 1980s, and how the process of diversification has continued ever since. PORIM has assisted the trend through its Palm Oil Familiarisation Programmes and its Technical Advisory Service, whose officers began travelling worldwide in 1979. One reason for Malaysia's eagerness to diversify its export markets may be glimpsed in Table 13.4. Between 1965 and 1977 the Indian market was barred by protectionism, while the Iraqi market declined rapidly after 1975, recovering in the 1980s only to decline again after 1990. As shown in Table 13.5, this changeability was typical of Asian markets. They offered rapid growth, but this was founded on shifting sands.

The revival of Indonesian competition, 1980–2000

Malaysia's success in developing a local palm oil refining industry serving Asian markets did not remain unchallenged for long. By the end of the 1980s two main challenges had emerged, which will be discussed in the two remaining sections of

Table 13.5 Leading destinations of Malaysia's processed palm oil exports, 1982–2001 (thousand tonnes per annum)

Country	1982–86	1987–91	1992–96	1997–2001
United Kingdom	90	125	110	70
West Germany/Germany	45	60	60	130
Netherlands	175	210	290	720
Italy	30	40	70	120
Soviet Union/Eastern Europe	260	220	20	90
United States of America	200	180	180	200
Canada	20	15	5	5
Egypt	25	230	385	440
Iraq	110	135	10	0
Jordan	60	100	160	145
Saudi Arabia	95	120	150	160
Turkey	70	160	190	160
United Arab Emirates	5	10	60	150
Nigeria	65	10	40	40
South Africa	0	0	80	150
Australia	50	70	95	100
India	780	645	470	1,880
Pakistan	415	755	1,135	1,120
Bangladesh	30	150	80	115
Burma/Myanmar	10	55	190	160
Vietnam	0	0	30	120
South Korea	120	200	200	210
People's Republic of China	30	540	1,030	1,100
Hong Kong	10	15	120	170
Japan	210	290	360	410
Other	305	695	1,000	985
World Total	3,210	5,030	6,520	8,950

Sources: Mielke (1987), W. Malaysia 182; Mielke (1991), Malaysia 275–6; Mielke (1995), Malaysia 49, Mielke (1998), Malaysia 51, Mielke (2002), Malaysia 57.

this chapter. Firstly, Indonesian exports began to grow again; and secondly, American producers of soyabean oil, palm oil's main competitor in world trade, began to wage a propaganda campaign to win consumer hearts and minds.

In the late 1970s and early 1980s Malaysia's government followed the example set by Indonesia and Zaire in earlier years, and initiated a partial nationalisation of the plantations sector. The tactics they used were relatively mild: parastatal corporations like Permodalan Nasional Berhad (Pernas, the National Equity Fund) were set up to invest on behalf of the Bumiputeras (Malays, or 'sons of the soil'). The parastatals bought shares in the Agency Houses at normal stock market prices, and while some transactions, as in the case of Sime Darby and Guthries, were carried out as hostile 'dawn raids', several others were conducted amicably. United Plantations, for example, conducted an agreed sale of shares to FIMA (Food Industries of Malaysia), whose Chairman Tan Sri Haji Basir bin

Table 13.6 Leading destinations of Indonesia's crude palm oil exports, 1987–2001 (thousand tonnes per annum)

Country	1987–91	1992–96	1997–2001
United Kingdom	90	65	5
West Germany/Germany	60	90	80
Netherlands	330	420	480
Italy	60	100	40
Spain	10	50	50
Soviet Union/Eastern Europe	15	15	5
United States of America	5	10	5
Canada	5	5	0
Mexico	0	0	10
Egypt	0	20	5
Jordan	5	5	0
Turkey	5	20	0
Kenya	75	80	50
Australia	10	5	0
India	55	20	330
Pakistan	0	40	0
Bangladesh	0	5	10
Malaysia	50	120	80
Vietnam	0	0	10
People's Republic of China	35	80	130
Japan	10	10	0
Other	40	60	65
World total	860	1,220	1,355

Sources: Mielke (1991), Indonesia 251; Mielke (1995), Indonesia 24; Mielke (1998), Indonesia 25; Mielke (2002), Indonesia pp. 27–8.

Ismail has served for many years as Chairman of PORIM and then MPOB. Both sides gained a great deal from the new partnership (Lindblad (1998), chs 6 and 7; Jones (2000), ch. 11; Martin (2003), ch. 9).

After the takeovers, some British parent companies such as Harrisons & Crosfield, which in any case had historic ties with Indonesia, decided to direct new capital flows towards that country rather than towards Malaysia, even though Malaysia began welcoming foreign investors again for carefully selected new plantation projects in October 1986 (Lindblad (1998), p. 117; Pugh (1990), pp. 265–72). More recently the Malaysian-owned Kumpulan Guthrie Sendirian Berhad has acquired the 200,000 hectare Minamas estates, adding to its already substantial investment in Indonesia's palm oil industry (Ng (2002)).

Malaysian investment not only helped to fund the rehabilitation and expansion of Indonesia's palm oil plantation sector, but also eased the flow of new ideas and technology across the Strait of Malacca to Medan, in Sumatra, which was the focal point of the Indonesian revival (Moll (1987), pp. 110–15; Hill (2000), pp. 139–140). At the same time, Indonesia was developing its own equivalent of FELDA, the Nucleus Estate Scheme or Perkebunan Inti Rakyat (PIR). Introduced in 1981, PIR had developed 90,000 hectares of oil palm land by the end of 1985.

Table 13.7 Leading destinations of Indonesia's processed palm oil exports, 1987–2001 (thousand tonnes per annum)

Country	1987–91	1992–96	1997–2001
United Kingdom	10	5	15
West Germany/Germany	5	20	60
Netherlands	25	70	180
Italy	5	10	20
Spain	5	20	70
Soviet Union/Eastern Europe	30	20	30
United States of America	15	30	10
Egypt	0	10	45
Sudan	10	0	25
Yemen	0	10	30
Turkey	0	10	65
Kenya	0	30	20
Tanzania	0	0	50
Nigeria	0	0	25
South Africa	0	0	50
India	40	110	660
Pakistan	0	10	30
Bangladesh	5	10	60
Sri Lanka	0	0	10
Burma/Myanmar	0	10	40
Malaysia	5	5	60
People's Republic of China	15	85	380
Hong Kong	0	10	30
Japan	0	5	5
Other	40	80	150
World total	210	560	2,120

Sources: Mielke (1991), Indonesia 251; Mielke (1995), Indonesia 24; Mielke (1998), Indonesia 25; Mielke (2002), Indonesia pp. 28–9.

Both PIR and the estate sector produced palm oil for local use as well as for export. When suitably refined, palm olein (the liquid fraction of the oil) made a highly acceptable substitute for coconut oil in local food uses (Taniputra *et al.* (1987)).

The marketing of palm oil in Indonesia has been highly regulated by the government throughout the post-war period, initially by direct control through the Joint Marketing office, and more recently by variations in export tax levels. A high priority has consistently been given to ensure a sufficiently high supply of crude palm oil to local refineries catering for domestic food requirements (Moll (1987), p. 115; Anon (1999)). Yet exports of palm oil from Indonesia have grown rapidly since the mid-1980s, as shown in Table 13.1. Tables 13.6 and 13.7 illustrate the shift in trading patterns, towards processed rather than crude oil exports, and towards Asian rather than European markets, which took place in the 1990s. Indonesia may be seen to be following Malaysian trends in the palm oil export trade, as in the social organisation and technology of production, with a time lag of approximately 15 years.

Malaysian producers, and the researchers of the MPOB, have naturally been following these developments with interest and a degree of concern, since Malaysia's land and labour costs are widely acknowledged to be higher than Indonesia's (Hill (2000), p. 140; Ramli (2000)). Nevertheless, the high degree of Malaysian involvement in the Indonesian industry, combined with the long history of successful collaboration between both sets of producers in marketing, research and development, means that this concern is unlikely to become hostility. Instead, from the late 1980s onwards, producers from both nations have found themselves united in facing a common threat: the American soyabean producers' propaganda campaign.

American competition and the war of oils

Soyabean oil and palm oil had competed directly against each other in the edible-oil markets of the world since the 1960s, when processing methods had been developed to turn each one into an 'invisible ingredient'. As Malaysian palm oil exports grew in the 1980s, so too did American production of soyabean oil. The United States produced an annual average of 2.2 million tonnes of soyabean oil in the period 1960–64; this had risen to 3.7 million tonnes by 1970–74 and 5.2 million tonnes by 1980–84, on the eve of the American soyabean producers' anti-palm-oil offensive. Over the same period, exports of American soyabean oil grew far less rapidly, from half a million tonnes per annum in 1960–64 to 0.9 million tonnes per annum in 1980–84 (Mielke (1988), Past sections 25–6).

In the mid-1980s, American soyabean producers were confident that they had won the competitive battle against palm oil on their home ground. As shown in Tables 13.4–13.7, American imports of palm oil from the two leading world exporters Malaysia and Indonesia had already fallen well below their mid-1970s peak by 1980, and remained around the level of 200,000 tonnes per annum throughout the 1980s and 1990s. However, American exporters of soyabean oil looked with envy on Malaysia's spectacular success in South Asian markets in the early 1980s. They knew that in these markets, palm oil's natural physical characteristics gave it a strong advantage over soyabean oil. Soya oil, which requires costly hydrogenation in order to achieve the semi-solid consistency desired by South Asian consumers of vanaspati, is also less stable than palm oil at the high temperatures used in frying applications (Hui (1996), pp. 323–39, 527–37). American soyabean producers therefore looked for another source of competitive advantage, and by 1986 they had found it in the shape of growing health concerns over the links between heart disease and saturated fats.

In 1986 the American Soybean Association (ASA) decided to launch an intensive media campaign designed to brand palm oil as a saturated fat, or in the words of their full-page press advertisements, an unhealthy tropical grease. They were well aware of the emotive impact of health issues, especially in the affluent, over-fed West but also in the highly educated circles of South Asia's governing elites. Their campaign was devious in the extreme, focusing on the chemical characteristics of unfractionated palm and palm kernel oils. Palm kernel oil, which is derived from the central nut rather than the pulpy outside layer of the oil palm fruit, has radically different characteristics from palm oil, but it is extremely difficult to persuade the lay public that the two names, which sound so similar, refer to two such different commodities. The ASA took advantage of this linguistic confusion to associate palm oil in the popular imagination with the highly saturated palm kernel and coconut oils. The Association also campaigned vigorously in asking the American Food and Drug Administration (FDA) to impose compulsory warning labels on all products containing any one of these three, in the ASA's terminology, 'tropical oils' (Gurunathan (1995), chs 1 and 7).

Can the palm oil industry be the only successful Third World growth sector to have suffered from such an attempt to use legitimate health or environmental concerns as a new form of trade barrier? One suspects not, but it may be an exceptionally easy case to prove, for the Malaysians were incensed by the ASA's campaign, and the industry was prosperous enough to be able to raise the funds, and sufficiently well organised to use them effectively, in defeating the immediate labelling threat. As soon as the ASA campaign was launched in 1986, the Malaysian government and the plantation companies united in their response. They commissioned a number of respected nutritional scientists to examine the full range of nutritional properties of both palm and soya oils. In the 15 years since then, these scientists have gradually established that the specific kind of fatty acids contained in palm oil have a benign effect on blood cholesterol. Furthermore, once soya oil has been hydrogenated to make it semi-solid, it contains a distinctive group of fatty acids, trans isomers, which are absent from the naturally semi-solid palm oil. Trans isomers have a damaging effect on blood cholesterol and may have further undesirable effects on health (Hui (1996), pp. 34, 211, 355–63, 575–81; FAO (1997), p. 5).

Although the details of this case were not known in 1986, the Malaysians felt they had a strong case for opposing the underhand tactics used by the ASA to confuse palm oil with palm kernel oil in the public imagination. Dato' Seri Dr Lim Keng Yaik, the newly appointed Minister for Primary Industries, quickly put together a team including PORIM's Professor Tan Sri Augustine Ong, the experienced food scientist Kurt Berger and a palm oil engineer renowned for his enthusiasm for quality, United Plantations' Dato' (later Tan Sri) B. Bek-Nielsen. They toured America giving conference presentations and fielding queries about palm oil, and confronting their ASA critics at every opportunity. However, their opponents were not easily discouraged, even when the scientific results began to be published and were well received within the professional community of nutritionists in 1987–88. Eventually it took a further intervention by the governments of Indonesia and the Philippines, who petitioned America's Reagan administration in support of Malaysia's position, to persuade the FDA to reject the ASA's case for labelling (Gurunathan (1995), chs 3–8; Sodhy (1991), pp. 446–55).

Malaysian palm oil producers were not satisfied with this victory alone, rightly as subsequent events have shown. The American soyabean producers' smear campaign against 'tropical greases' had captured popular imagination, and the basic confusion between the characteristics of palm and palm kernel oils continues to be evident in newspaper and magazine features and popular books on nutrition. The MPOB and the Malaysian Palm Oil Promotion Council (MPOPC) continue to combat this confusion and to publicise the positive scientific findings on palm oil. For example, regular features on nutrition, complete with full references to research publications in scientific journals, appear in the MPOB magazine *Palm Oil Developments*, which circulates widely among firms and research organisations in Asia, as well as Africa, America and Europe. Nevertheless, it is an uphill struggle.

A final response to the ASA campaign, and one which has achieved some success in Western markets, has been the redesigning of the product itself. Experiments began with a new hybrid oil palm, the Oleifera Guineensis, which aimed to blend the high yields of the standard African and South-east Asian *Elaeis guineensis* genus with the high iodine value, and high unsaturated fat content of the much rarer South American *Elaeis oleifera* genus. Dr N. Rajanaidu of PORIM led the way in the collection of new planting materials to support this programme, together with Tan Yap Pau of United Plantations, who was working with the veteran agronomist Charles Hartley (Rajanaidu (1986); Martin (2003), ch. 10). United Plantations was the first private-sector enterprise to plant the new hybrid palm on a commercial scale, and by 1989 was able to produce significant quantities of vitamin-rich palm oil with a low saturated fat content. By subjecting the oil to a rigorous process of double fractionation in Tirtiaux's innovative membrane presses, the firm's Unitata refinery was then able to produce a super-olein brand named 'Nutrolein', from which the saturated fat element had been almost completely eliminated.

Like the separate brands of 'red palm oil' launched by a number of other firms in the 1990s, notably the J.C. Chang group's 'Carotino' and the 'Red Palm Superolein' of Golden Hope Plantations (formerly owned by Harrisons & Crosfield), United Plantations' 'Nutrolein' is deodorised and purified, but not bleached (Kokken (1990); Anon (2000)). It retains the original rich colour of the crude palm oil eaten for centuries in west Africa, while being free of the impurities and saturated fats which inevitably remain after the smallholders' manual processing. Red palm oil can now be valued for its rich content of vitamins A and E, and of antioxidants which can be valuable not only in combating heart disease, but also in reducing vulnerability to cancer (Hui (1996), pp. 339, 362–3). Currently it represents but a tiny fraction of Malaysia's palm oil trade, with exports averaging 1,000 tonnes per annum over the period 1999–2001. Yet in the long run this product, which has so many echoes of the industry's distant past, may prove to be the key to its future.

Bibliography

Anon (1999) 'Indonesia: Export Tax for Crude Palm Oil Slashed to 10%', *Oils & Fats International*, August, p. 5.

Anon (2000) 'Well-Oiled', *Malaysian Business* magazine, 16 September.

B.O.W.K. (1925) 'Palm Oil "Chop": A Delectable Alternative to Curry', *The Planter*, V, 8, p. 219.

Beasley, W.G. (1987) *Japanese Imperialism, 1894–1945*, Oxford: Clarendon Press.

Bek-Nielsen, B. (1992) 'Techno-Economic Status of the Malaysian Palm Oil Industry', in K. Ragupathy (ed.), *Facing 2020: The Challenges to the Plantation Industry*, Kuala Lumpur: Institute of Strategic and International Studies.

Berger, K.G. and Martin, S.M. (2000) 'Palm Oil', in K.F. Kiple and K.C. Ornelas (eds), *The Cambridge World History of Food*, Vol. 1, Cambridge: Cambridge University Press.

Booth, A. (1988) *Agricultural Development in Indonesia*, Sydney: Allen and Unwin.

Booth A. (1998) *The Indonesian Economy in the Nineteenth and Twentieth Centuries*, London: Macmillan.

Clutterbuck, R. (1984) *Conflict and Violence in Singapore and Malaysia, 1945–1983*, Singapore: Graham Brash.

Corley, R.H.V. and Tinker, P.B. (2003) *The Oil Palm*, Oxford: Blackwell Science.

Creutzberg, P. (ed.) (1975) *Changing Economy in Indonesia*, Vol. 1, *Indonesia's Export Crops, 1816–1940*, Amsterdam: Royal Tropical Institute.

Davis, B. (1978) *Food Commodities*, London: Heinemann.

Empire Marketing Board (1932) Nos 54 and 61, *Survey of Oilseeds and Vegetable Oils*, Vol. 1, *Oil Palm Products*, London: Empire Marketing Board.

FAO (1997) *Food and Nutrition Papers*, 57, *Fats and Oils in Human Nutrition*, Rome: Food and Agriculture Organization of the United Nations.

Fieldhouse, D.K. (1978) *Unilever Overseas: The Anatomy of a Multinational, 1895–1965*, London: Croom Helm.

Fong, C.O. (1986) *Technological Leap: Malaysian Industry in Transition*, Singapore: Oxford University Press.

Graham, E. with Floering, I. (1984) *The Modern Plantation in the Third World*, London: Croom Helm.

Gurunathan, K. (1995) *The War of Oils*, Penang, Malaysia: Principal Quest.

Harper, T.N. (1999) *The End of Empire and the Making of Malaya*, Cambridge: Cambridge University Press.

Hartley, C.W.S. (1988) *The Oil Palm (Elaeis Guineensis Jacq.)*, London: Longman.

Hill, H. (2000) *The Indonesian Economy*, Cambridge: Cambridge University Press.

Huff, W.G. (1994) *The Economic Growth of Singapore: Trade and Development in the Twentieth Century*, Cambridge: Cambridge University Press.

Hui, Y.H. (ed.) (1996) *Bailey's Industrial Oil and Fat Products*, 5th edn, Vol. 2, *Edible Oil and Fat Products: Oils and Oil Seeds*, New York: Wiley.

IMF (1987) *International Financial Statistics Yearbook*, Washington: International Monetary Fund.

IMF (1996) *International Financial Statistics Yearbook*, Washington: International Monetary Fund.

Jones, G. (2000) *Merchants to Multinationals: British Trading Companies in the Nineteenth and Twentieth Centuries*, Oxford: Oxford University Press.

Khera, H.S. (1976) *The Oil Palm Industry of Malaya: An Economic Study*, Kuala Lumpur: Penerbit Universiti Malaya.

Khera, H.S. (1978) 'Production and Consumption Pattern of Oil Palm Products in Malaysia' in *Market Development of Palm Oil Products: Seminar Proceedings, 27 March–1 April 1978*, Geneva: United Nations, International Trade Centre UNCTAD/GATT.

Kokken, M.J. (1990) 'Super Oleins from Palm Oil Fractionation', *PORIM Bulletin* 20, May, pp. 13–20.

Kratoska, P.H. (1998) *The Japanese Occupation of Malaya 1941–1945: A Social and Economic History*, London: Hurst.

Leeming, M. (1991) *From Manna to Microwave*, London: BBC Publications.

Lim, C.-Y. (1967) *Economic Development of Modern Malaya*, Kuala Lumpur: Oxford University Press.

Lim, D. (1973) *Economic Growth and Development in West Malaysia, 1947–1970*, London: Oxford University Press.

Lindblad, J.T. (1998) *Foreign Investment in South-East Asia in the Twentieth Century*, London: Macmillan.

Lynn, M. (1997) *Commerce and Economic Change in West Africa: The Palm Oil Trade in the Nineteenth Century*, Cambridge: Cambridge University Press.

Malek bin Mansoor and Barlow, C. (1988) 'The Production Structure of the Malaysian Oil Palm Industry with Special Reference to the Smallholder Subsector', *PORIM Occasional Paper* No. 24.

Martin, S.M. (1988) *Palm Oil and Protest: An Economic History of the Ngwa Region, South-Eastern Nigeria, 1800–1980*, Cambridge: Cambridge University Press.

——(2003) *The UP Saga*, Copenhagen: Nordic Institute of Asian Studies Press.

Mielke, S. (ed.) (1987) *Oil World Annual*, Hamburg: ISTA Mielke.

Mielke, S. and Mielke, T. (eds) (1988) *Oil World 1958–2007*, Hamburg: ISTA Mielke.

Mielke, T. (ed.) (1989, 1991, 1994, 1995, 1998 and 2002) *Oil World Annual*, Hamburg: ISTA Mielke.

Mielke, T. (ed.) (1999) *Oil World 2020: Supply, Demand and Prices from 1976 through 2020*, Hamburg: ISTA Mielke.

Moll, H.A.J. (1987) *The Economics of the Oil Palm*, Wageningen, Netherlands: Centre for Agricultural Publishing and Documentation (PUDOC).

MPOB (Malaysian Palm Oil Board) (2002) *Malaysian Palm Oil Statistics 2001*, Kuala Lumpur: MPOB.

Ng, P.S.C. (2002) 'Guthrie Defends Decision to Stake Future in Indonesia', *The Star* Newspaper, Kuala Lumpur, 2 July.

Pugh, P. (ed.) Nickalls, G. (1990) *Great Enterprise: A History of Harrisons & Crosfield*, London: Harrisons & Crosfield.

Rajanaidu, N. (1986) 'Elaeis Oleifera Collection in Central and South America', in *Proceedings of International Workshop on Oil Palm Germplasm and Utilisation, 26–27 March 1985*, Kuala Lumpur: PORIM and International Society of Oil Palm Breeders, pp. 84–94.

Ramli, A. (2000) 'Forecast of Malaysian and Indonesian Palm Oil Production', *MPOB Oil Palm Bulletin* 40, May, pp. 23–4.

Sodhy, P. (1991) *The US–Malaysian Nexus: Themes in Superpower – Small State Relations*, Kuala Lumpur: ISIS.

Taniputra, B., Labis, A.U., Pamin, K. and Suheimi Syukur (1987) 'Progress of Oil Palm Industry in Indonesia in the Last Fifteen Years (1971–1985)', in Abdul Halim bin

Hassan, Chew Poh Soon, B.J. Wood and E. Pushparajah (eds), *Proceedings of the 1987 International Oil Palm/Palm Oil Conferences*, I: *Agriculture*, Kuala Lumpur: PORIM and ISP, pp. 27–35.

Tate, D.J.M. (1996) *The RGA History of the Plantation Industry in the Malay Peninsula*, Kuala Lumpur: Oxford University Press.

Thoburn, J.T. (1977) *Primary Commodity Exports and Economic Development: Theory, Evidence and a Study of Malaysia*, London: Wiley.

Tomaru, J. (2000) *The Postwar Rapprochement of Malaya and Japan, 1945–61: The Roles of Britain and Japan in South-East Asia*, London: Macmillan.

Tropical Products Institute (1965) *The Oil Palm: Papers Presented at the London Conference, 3–6 May 1965*, London: Ministry of Overseas Development.

Wilson, C. (1968) *Unilever 1945–65*, London: Cassell.

Index

Note: Page numbers in italic refer to figures and tables.

Printed in the United States
by Baker & Taylor Publisher Services